Diversity,
Social Justice, and
Inclusive Excellence

Diversity,
Social Justice, and
Inclusive Excellence

Transdisciplinary and Global Perspectives

Edited by

Seth N. Asumah

and

Mechthild Nagel

Published by State University of New York Press, Albany

For information, contact State University of New York Press, Albany, NY
www.sunypress.edu

Production by Ryan Morris
Marketing by Anne M. Valentine

Library of Congress Cataloging-in-Publication Data

Diversity, social justice, and inclusive excellence : transdisciplinary and
    global perspectives / edited by Seth N. Asumah and Mechthild Nagel.
        pages cm
    Includes bibliographical references and index.
    ISBN 978-1-4384-5163-3 (hardcover : alk. paper)
    1. Cultural pluralism.   2. Social justice.   3. Racism.   4. Blacks—Race
identity—United States.   5. People with mental disabilities—Government
policy—United States.   6. Oppression (Psychology)   7. Sex role.
I. Asumah, Seth Nii, 1954– editor of compilation.

    HM1271.D5843 2014
    305.800973—dc23   2013025547

10 9 8 7 6 5 4 3 2 1

To
Lorraine Y. Brathwaite—S.N.A.

To
Philip Otieno—M.N.

To
All those who have sacrificed their lives for social justice
and those who are engaged in the struggle
to eradicate oppression and injustice

Contents

List of Illustrations

Tables

Figures

Preface

Diversity has become a hallmark of twenty-first century academia in the United States. No institution wishes to be left behind in discursive formations about difference and the impact of identity politics. Clearly, experiences based on culture, race, ethnicity, sex, gender, class, religion, citizenship, age, and developed abilities continue to shape all aspects of human conditions, and the "life of the mind" has to take notice. Diversity discourse also takes into account how to make sense of intercultural and global interactions. The sociopolitical dynamics of the categories above are fluid and continue to change with the transformation of group political consciousness, the authority of the state in distributing justice, and the effects of globalization on both agents of power and target groups of those who have suffered historical and current marginalization, exploitation, and powerlessness. Yet, no one category of the components of diversity listed above has monopoly over oppression in order to claim the benefits of social injustice or disavows of global paralysis due to cultural imperialism and violence. Micro- and macrocultures of injustice and the new forms of the politics of exclusion resulting in the denial of justice, equity, and inclusive excellence for students of color, underrepresented policy beneficiaries, many historically and newly marginalized groups, people with disabilities, women, homosexuals, Muslims, immigrants, and the working poor, not just in the United States of America, but around the globe have called for a kaleidoscopic approach and transdisciplinary perspectives in examining global diversity, social justice, and inclusive excellence. Inclusive Excellence (IE), supported by the Association of American Colleges and Universities (AAC&U) has come to mean that diversity is a key component of a comprehensive strategy for achieving institutional excellence. Diversity is essential for reaching and ensuring academic excellence for all students attending college, and deliberate actions must be taken to educate all students to succeed in a diverse society and arm them with complex intercultural accoutrements for success in the twenty-first century (AAC&U, 2002).

Does the election of Barack Obama to the Office of the Presidency mean we have reached the postracial era in the United States, or does his preference for selecting Black instead of mixed race on the census complicate the dynamics of identity politics and the politics of difference? What does this election mean to the discourse regarding White privilege in our classrooms and around the globe? Does the Liberian presidency of Ellen Johnson Sirleaf, the first woman to be president in Africa, indicate that male hegemony has surrendered to the forces of feminism or Africana womanism, and has the glass ceiling been finally shattered? Does the Chinese presence in Africa or the United States' recent killing of Osama Bin Laden in Pakistan speak to new forms of cultural imperialism and Islamophobia? How do we interpret the new immigration waves around the world and the effects of globalization on age, learned ability, race, gender, social class, and their interconnectedness with systemic injustice?

With respect to the interlocutors of diversity, the questions above can only be answered properly if educators and students of diversity and social justice become culturally competent and know how race, ethnicity, gender, class, religion, citizenship, learned ability, sexual orientation, and their intersectionalities are psycho-socially and culturally constructed, systemic and global. The categories of diversity shape our experiences in the classroom, communities, United States and the world over. To be responsible, culturally competent citizens, who reside in productive nation states, whose interaction with other people in the world is inevitable, we have no choice but to work to eradicate oppression and the injustices associated with "othering" before they become an anathema of our humanity.

This edited volume assembles several essays that focus on the components of diversity, social justice, and inclusive excellence, not just within the United States, but in other parts of the world. The categories will include but are not limited to culture, race, class, gender, learned ability, religion, sexual orientation, and immigration and their intersectionalities. A critical aspect of this book is the idea that diversity categories have overlapping and interconnected elements that operate not in isolation but are concomitant with sociopolitical structures and global dynamics. There is a plethora of works on diversity and social justice, but too often, the topic is approached with a rather narrow focus on race, gender, and class. Even in such cases, the anthologies and textbooks are limited to the United States, as if the rest of world has nothing to do with diversity. Absent the global perspectives in many books on diversity, most students in the United

States are not exposed to the conditions of life and social justice systems that are different from the prevailing ones in this country, even though the global matrices of domination constitute the larger segment of the world's human experience.

Furthermore, this volume maintains an impetus that is trans-disciplinary and multiperspectival, which sets the book apart from other works that are sociologically or psychologically based. We hope to present an anthology which is not just a collection of readings but to develop a corpus and superstructure built on an analytical foundation of systemic oppression, racial frame, intersectionality, and global perspectives on diversity. Indubitably, this approach is sharpened by the work of seasoned scholars, well-vested in their field of study and lived experiences.

Scholars of diversity and multiculturalism often approach topics of analyzing the victim status of historically oppressed groups from a sociological standpoint vis-à-vis their relationships with hegemonic powers and matrices of domination within nation states. By contrast, our project has an intercultural, not simply multicultural dimension; it will transcend those artificial boundaries to query how global systems and matrices of domination are interconnected and how, paradoxically, they enrich discursive consciousness.

Some of the earlier works that examine most of the diversity categories in terms of matrices of domination, oppression and identity politics include Marion Iris Young's classic volume on *Justice and the Politics of Difference* (1990). Yet, the work is based strictly on feminist theory and political theory that interrogate the philosophical reduction of social justice to only distributive terms. Young purports that good society is based on cultural differences in the policy arena. Even though, her book is rich in theoretical analysis, it is restricted to the United States, and only the Epilogue is designed to address the issues of international social justice, which is not embedded throughout the work.

Diversity, Multiculturalism and Social Justice by Seth N. Asumah and Ibipo Johnston-Anumonwo (2002) moves away from strictly feminist and political theory framework and adds international dimension to diversity studies; however, the work is based on Young's classic essay, "The Five Faces of Oppression," with case studies from Africa and the United States. That book's disciplinary foundation is political science and geography. Furthermore, Asumah and Johnston-Anumonwo's book is out of print, though Binghamton University Press (Global Publications) has arranged with State University of New York Press to reprint copies based on demand. Yet, the disciplinary thrust of the Asumah and Anumonwo book is narrow. This book, as mentioned earlier, will utilize transdisciplinary and multidisciplinary tools to give readers broader perspectives on diversity. It will also give readers the idea that as the world becomes even more interconnected, the work on diversity and social justice is becoming more complex and multidisciplinary. Newly oppressed groups and historically oppressed ones are redefining their spaces, places, and angles of participation in the sociopolitical process, and we have to find new approaches from binary assessments to kaleidoscopic ones, and this volume is designed to achieve that aim.

Adams, Bell and Griffin's book on *Teaching for Diversity and Social Justice* (Routledge, 1997) is an integrated approach for teachers and students of diversity and social justice education to facilitate discourse on oppression, racism, sexism, classism, heterosexism, anti-Semitism, and ableism. This volume is more focused on pedagogical approaches, and it is limited on global dimensions. Inderpal Grewal and Caren Kaplan (McGraw Hill, 2006), *Introduction to Women's Studies: Gender in a Transnational World*, takes a global and historical approach in investigating race, class, and gender and their relations to women's issues in specific locations. Even though this anthology takes a transnational approach, its intellectual and disciplinary focus is rooted in women's studies. *Readings for Diversity and Social Justice: An Anthology on Racism, Anti-Semitism, Sexism, Heterosexism, Ableism, and Classism* by Maurianne Adams, Warren J. Blumenfeld et al. (2010) centers on oppression and social justice issues with over 40 chapters. Yet, this fine text has little in the way of global perspectives. Andersen and Hill Collins's anthology, *Race, Class, and Gender* (Wadsworth, 2010, 2013), is an excellent book that centers on the intersectionality of race, class, and gender and the matrices of domination. Nevertheless, this interdisciplinary reader dwells on analyses that are strictly sociological. The book's diversity scope is limited to race, class, and gender, with no reference to other categories of analysis or global forces of diversity, and it may be too lengthy (66 chapters) for instructors looking to assign chapters to students to get their money's worth for the semester.

Another element of uniqueness for this anthology is the chapter on animal rights. Animal rights a growing concern among diversity educators, yet it is an overlooked field of study, since diversity and multicultural education focuses on human beings, not nonhuman animals. Animal rights advocates speak of a prevailing speciesism, and our anthology seeks a small but important corrective to this obvious lack of attention. Furthermore, given that several authors focus on a discussion with Iris M. Young's classic "The Five Faces of Oppression" essay, we thought it would be opportune to include Gruen's article.

Her article demonstrates well to what extent nonhuman animals are also affected by oppression, whether it is exploitation, marginalization, violence, cultural imperialism, or powerlessness.

This volume's strength lies in our ability to bring diversity and social justice to the global stage, present a corpus of diversity through transdisciplinary perspective, and offer unique insights of diversity and social justice from the United States and other parts of the world.

Design of the Anthology and Pedagogical Provision

The major goal in designing this anthology is to produce a book that could be used as a scholarly guide for undergraduate and graduate students and others who are interested in the issues on diversity and social justice. We want students and interlocutors of diversity around the world to know how their lives and the lives of the groups they do not belong to are shaped by the hegemony of the nation state, global forces, matrices of domination, race, class, gender, religion, learned ability, sexual orientation, and immigration. We begin with a preface that lays out the conceptual framework of the volume and end with concluding chapters by authors from around the world that are designed to address the theme that diversity is ubiquitous and it is here to stay, so the work in social justice will be an unfinished and evolving business from generation to generation.

The first section of the volume contains a theoretical framework for doing diversity in the twenty-first century, since the American polity and globalization are rapidly changing how nation states interact. Yet, the faces of oppression continue to interrogate the forces of social justice, so Iris Young's chapter on "Five Faces of Oppression" will serve as a springboard for other discussions in the volume. Since diversity issues involve difficult discourse and discursive consciousness, Elizabeth Davis-Russell and Gale Young's essay on "The Vicissitudes of Cultural Competence: Dealing with Difficult Classroom Dialogue" guides our thinking and teaching of diversity categories and the difficulty associated with multicultural communication in and outside the classroom is included in the first section of this anthology.

The second section of the anthology embodies essays on race, gender, sexual orientation, learned ability/disability, and immigration/citizenship issues in the United States. The authors, titles, and brief synopsis of the chapters for the second section of the volume are as follows: in "Teaching Feminist Pedagogy on Race and Gender: Beyond the Additive Approach?" Mechthild Nagel questions whether the analysis of distinct forms of oppression has been rendered obsolete by calls for an intersectional analysis on race, class, and gender. She argues that both practices ought to coexist depending on the epistemic reality. Nagel's second essay, "Beyond the Pale: Reflections on the Vulnerability of Black Life in the United States," reflects on the meaning of the trope "beyond the pale" in order to draw attention to White supremacy, the discourse of normalcy, and deviance in the era of mass incarceration of Black people in the United States. Ibipo Johnston-Anumonwo's essay, "Women's Work Trips and Multifaceted Oppression," reveals the power and versatility of Iris Marion Young's classic article "The Five Faces of Oppression," as it lends itself to an application of analyzing access to transportation to work by women of color in urban and suburban geographies. In "Racial Identity and Policy Making: Redefining Whiteness," Seth N. Asumah argues that once Whites recognize their identity and White privilege as an unearned asset, they can capitalize on "Whiteness"—not as a weapon of oppression, but as a positive tool in improving race relations and public policy. The diversity categories of race and gender are presented in the cyber world by examining the threat perceptions of cyberstalking in various cases and studies in the chapter, "Examining Cyberstalking Through the Prism of Race and Gender" by Tosha A. Asumah and Debra F. Glaser. The authors conclude in their essay that significant findings support their study showing that there are gender differences in terms of perception of threat, in regards to cyberstalking characteristics. Christopher Latimer, "Framing the Same-Sex Marriage Issue as Equity," introduces the reader to the literature on public opinion and examines same-sex marriage from different perspectives. He provides the theoretical background on framing and its persuasive effects and implications for this discussion on same-sex marriage. He scrutinizes framing strategies of the courts in relation to gay and lesbian civil rights and same-sex marriage, concluding the chapter with the implications of framing for attitudes concerning same-sex marriage. Elizabeth Purcell notes that Iris Marion Young's oppression model actually needs to be augmented in her chapter "Oppression's Three New Faces: Rethinking Iris Young's 'Five Faces of Oppression' for Disability Theory." She includes stigma, questioned personhood, and societal incapacity as additional "faces."

The issues concerning the rights for people with disabilities continue in this section of the book with Nancy J. Hirschmann, who develops a typology of invisible disabilities, depending on social context, social categories, or discriminatory attitudes in her essay, "Gender and the Politics of Invisible Disability." In Diane C. Gooding and William T. L. Cox's chapter, "Stigmatized, Marginalized, and Ill: The Oppression of People With Serious Mental Illness," the authors demonstrate through concrete examples how and why people with serious mental illness are exposed to and suffer all the five faces of oppression and the ways that stigma is an oppressive force causing and perpetuating societal inequities for SMI people. Seth N. Asumah and M. Todd Bradley, in "Rethinking United States' Immigration Policy, Diversity and the Politics of Exclusion" interrogate United States' immigration policy and conclude that uniculturalists are blind-sighted by their ideological position in assessing the realities of the immigration debate in multicultural America. Lori Gruen anchors the second section of this anthology with her essay, "The Faces of Animal Oppression." She uses Iris Marion Young's framework of oppression and thus moves beyond the anthropocentric discourse that is predominant in diversity textbooks. She shows effectively how nonhuman animals also face marginalization, powerlessness, and violence among other faces of oppression.

The third section of the volume is composed of essays on global diversity and social justice issues in selected area of the world. Gowri Parameswaran's "The Tale of Two Worlds: Unpacking the Power of the Global North Over the Global South" applies Peggy McIntosh's seminal article on the white knapsack of privilege to a discussion of distribution of uneven resources and privileges enjoyed by societies in the Global North vis-à-vis peoples living in the Global South. Susan C. Dewey and Cema Bolabola's chapter, "Feeding the City and Financing the Family: Women Market Traders in Suva Fiji," gives a nuanced look at employment opportunities for poor women in Fiji and the resilience they draw on in spite of adverse economic conditions. Issues on China's new hegemonic role in the world and the effects of that country's neocultural imperialist model in the process of development in Africa are analyzed by Seth N. Asumah, in the essay, "China in Africa: Dislocating Cultures, Reexamining the Role of the Nation State and the China Model in the Process of Development." In "Political Struggle of Rural Migrant Hostesses for First-Class Citizenship in Postsocialist China," Tiantian Zheng highlights the contradictions of rural migrant women's identities, depicted as second-class citizens, and yet as bar hostesses, they clamor for upper-class status and thus use their agency to rewrite the narrative of sexist stereotypes. The people with disability discussions in the second section of the anthology find a home in the third section by analyzing disability on the global stage. Janet Duncan, in "Understanding Disability Rights in a Global Context" contests that "constituting the largest minority in the world, cutting across all ethnic, cultural, economic and social ties," the numerical preponderance of people with disability should translate into more policy programs for "public education, health, and inclusive community living," but unfortunately, the world has not reached that stage yet and the global picture for a disability rights agenda remains bleak. Seth N. Asumah's, "Islam, Rentier States, and Democracy in the Middle East and Africa" examines one of the world's most prominent monotheistic religions and its adherents' struggle with rentier politics and democracy. Asumah completes the essays for the anthology by bringing the intersectionality of culture, race, class, governance, and power to the global context in his chapter, "African Relational Democracy: Reframing Diversity, Economic Development, and Society-Centered Governance for the Twenty-First Century."

Audience

This volume is designed with undergraduate as well as advanced and graduate students of the works on diversity, multiculturalism and social justice in mind. The anthology will also be attractive and appeal to elementary and secondary school teachers, scholars, non-scholars, and activists in transnational diversity and social justice studies. The transdisciplinary nature of the volume will appeal to students and scholars in anthropology, ethnic studies, education, philosophy, social and cultural geography, political science, psychology, sociology, social work, health, gender studies, race studies, cultural studies, international relations, and global studies. The book will represent voices of both superordinate and subordinate cultures, the historically oppressed, and Western and non-Western distinguished scholars.

Acknowledgments

One cannot complete an anthology without the endeavors of contributing authors and many people behind the scene. We have been
assisted by many colleagues in our work on this project. It would
have been impossible to produce this book without the support of
our families, colleagues at the State University of New York College
at Cortland, and friends. Over the years our students, faculty, and
staff who have participated in our Summer Institute for Infusing
Diversity into the Curriculum and our statewide diversity project
involving SUNY Oneonta and SUNY New Paltz have contributed
significantly in shaping our ideas about diversity, social justice, and
inclusive excellence. The challenging questions of the participants
of the Diversity Institute and insightful responses in our meetings
have enhanced our ability to teach courses in the areas of diversity
and social justice.

We extend our appreciation for the support given by our institution, SUNY Cortland, for this project. Our unlimited gratitude goes
to Erik Bitterbaum, president, SUNY Cortland, for his generosity
and continuing support for our research and intellectual endeavors.
We extend our sincere thanks to R. Bruce Mattingly, dean, School
of Arts and Sciences; Amy Henderson-Harr, Research and Sponsored
Programs; and Robert Spitzer, Chair, Department of Political Science
for their irreplaceable support and advice. We also thank Pamela
Schroeder for proofreading and formatting the final manuscript. To
Deborah Dintino, we could not have done it without your invaluable assistance during the entire process of putting the manuscript
together. Our special appreciation goes to Michael Rinella and Ryan
Morris, SUNY Press, for their assistance, guidance, and expertise in
the production of the anthology. We would also like to extend our
gratitude to Rafael Chaiken, SUNY Press, for his crucial role in working on the manuscript and his collegiality throughout the process. To
the reviewers, who provided valuable comments during the process,

thus helping us to sharpen our thoughts, thank you very much. For those who we have forgotten to extend our appreciation to in this process, we humbly apologize. This anthology represents the product of challenging and collaborative efforts of coauthorship and coeditorship, and ultimately, we assume full responsibility for its contents.

Seth N. Asumah and Mechthild Nagel
State University of New York Cortland

PART I

Doing Diversity for Cultural Competence, Social Justice, and Inclusive Excellence

CHAPTER ONE

Five Faces of Oppression*

IRIS MARION YOUNG

Someone who does not see a pane of glass does not know that he does not see it. Someone who, being placed differently does see it, does not know the other does not see it. When our will finds expression outside ourselves in actions performed by others we do not waste our time and our power of attention in examining whether they have consented to this. This is true for all of us. Our attention, given entirely to the success of the undertaking, is not claimed by them as long as they are docile. . . . Rape is a terrible caricature of love from which consent is absent. After rape, oppression is the second horror of human existence. It is a terrible caricature of obedience.

—Simone Weil

I have proposed an enabling conception of justice. Justice should refer not only to distribution, but also to the institutional conditions necessary for the development and exercise of individual capacities and collective communication and cooperation. Under this conception of justice, injustice refers primarily to two forms of disabling constraints, oppression and domination. While these constraints include distributive patterns, they also involve matters that cannot easily be assimilated to the logic of distribution: decision-making procedures, division of labor, and culture. Many people in the United States would not choose the term *oppression* to name injustice in our society. For contemporary emancipatory social movements, on the other hand—socialists, radical feminists, American Indian activists, Black activists, gay and lesbian activists—oppression is a central category of political discourse. Entering the political discourse in which oppression is a central category involves adopting a general mode of analyzing and evaluating social structures and practices that is incommensurate with the language of liberal individualism that dominates political discourse in the United States. A major political project for those of us who identify with at least one of these movements must thus be to persuade people that the discourse of oppression makes sense of much of our social experience. We are ill prepared for this task, however, because we have no clear account of the meaning of oppression. While we find the term used often in the diverse philosophical and theoretical literature spawned by radical social movements in the United States, we find little direct discussion of the meaning of the concept as used by these movements.

In this chapter, I offer some explication of the concept of oppression as I understand its use by new social movements in the United States since the 1960s. My starting point is reflection on the conditions of the groups said by these movements to be oppressed: among others women, Blacks, Chicanos, Puerto Ricans and other Spanish-speaking Americans, American Indians, Jews, lesbians, gay men, Arabs, Asians, old people, working-class people, and the physically and mentally disabled. I aim to systematize the meaning of the concept of oppression as used by these diverse political movements, and to provide normative argument to clarify the wrongs the term names.

Obviously the above-named groups are not oppressed to the same extent or in the same ways. In the most general sense, all oppressed people suffer some inhibition of their ability to develop and exercise their capacities and express their needs, thoughts, and feelings. In that abstract sense all oppressed people face a common condition. Beyond that, in any more specific sense, it is not possible to define a single set of criteria that describe the condition of oppression of the above groups. Consequently, attempts by theorists and activists to discover a common description or the essential causes of the oppression of all these groups have frequently led to fruitless disputes about whose oppression is more fundamental or more grave. The contexts in which members of these groups use the term *oppression* to describe the injustices of their situation suggest that oppression names, in fact, a family of concepts and conditions, which I divide into five categories: exploitation, marginalization, powerlessness, cultural imperialism, and violence.

In this chapter I explicate each of these forms of oppression. Each may entail or cause distributive injustices, but all involve issues of justice beyond distribution. In accordance with ordinary political usage, I suggest that oppression is a condition of groups. Thus before explicating the meaning of oppression, we must examine the concept of a social group.

Oppression as a Structural Concept

One reason that many people would not use the term *oppression* to describe injustice in our society is that they do not understand the term in the same way as do new social movements. In its traditional usage, *oppression* means the exercise of tyranny by a ruling group. Thus many Americans would agree with radicals in applying the term oppression to the situation of Black South Africans under apartheid. Oppression also traditionally carries a strong connotation of conquest and colonial domination. The Hebrews were oppressed in Egypt, and many uses of the term *oppression* in the West invoke this paradigm.

Dominant political discourse may use the term *oppression* to describe societies other than our own, usually Communist or purportedly Communist societies. Within this anti-Communist rhetoric both tyrannical and colonialist implications of the term appear. For the anti-Communist, Communism denotes precisely the exercise of brutal tyranny over a whole people by a few rulers and the will to conquer the world, bringing hitherto independent peoples under that tyranny. In dominant political discourse it is not legitimate to use the term *oppression* to describe our society, because oppression is the evil perpetrated by the Others.

New left social movements of the 1960s and 1970s, however, shifted the meaning of the concept of oppression. In its new usage oppression designates the disadvantage and injustice some people suffer not because a tyrannical power coerces them, but because of the everyday practices of a well-intentioned liberal society. In this new left usage, the tyranny of a ruling group over another as in South Africa, must certainly be called oppressive. But oppression also refers to systemic constraints on groups that are not necessarily the result of the intentions of a tyrant. Oppression in this sense is structural, rather than the result of a few people's choices or policies. Its causes are embedded in unquestioned norms, habits, and symbols, in the assumptions underlying institutional rules and the collective consequences of following those rules. It names, as Marilyn Frye puts it, "an enclosing structure of forces and barriers which tends to the immobilization and reduction of a group or category of people" (Frye, 1983a, p. 11). In this extended structural sense oppression refers to the vast and deep injustices some groups suffer as a consequence of often unconscious assumptions and reactions of well-meaning people in ordinary interactions, media and cultural stereotypes, and structural features of bureaucratic hierarchies and market mechanisms— in short the normal processes of everyday life. We cannot eliminate this structural oppression by getting rid of the rulers or making some new laws, because oppressions are systematically reproduced in major economic, political, and cultural institutions.

The systemic character of oppression implies that an oppressed group need not have a correlate oppressing group. While structural oppression involves relations among groups, these relations do not always fit the paradigm of conscious and intentional oppression of one group by another. Foucault (1977) suggests that to understand the meaning and operation of power in modern society we must look beyond the model of power as "sovereignty," a dyadic relation of ruler and subject, and instead analyze the exercise of power as the effect of often liberal and "humane" practices of education, bureaucratic administration, production, and distribution of consumer goods, medicine, and so on. The conscious actions of many individuals daily contribute to maintaining and reproducing oppression, but those people are usually simply doing their jobs or living their lives, and do not understand themselves as agents of oppression.

I do not mean to suggest that within a system of oppression individual persons do not intentionally harm others in oppressed groups. The raped woman, the beaten Black youth, the locked-out worker, the gay man harassed on the street are victims of intentional actions by identifiable agents. I also do not mean to deny that specific groups are beneficiaries of the oppression of other groups, and thus have an interest in their continued oppression. Indeed, for every oppressed group there is a group that is *privileged* in relation to that group.

The concept of oppression has been current among radicals since the 1960s, partly in reaction to Marxist attempts to reduce the injustices of racism and sexism, for example, to the effects of class domination or bourgeois ideology. Racism, sexism, ageism, homophobia, some social movements asserted, are distinct forms of oppression with their own dynamics apart from the dynamics of class, even though they may interact with class oppression. From often heated discussions among socialists, feminists, and antiracism activists in the last ten years, a consensus is emerging that many different groups must be said to be oppressed in our society, and that no single form of oppression can be assigned causal or moral primacy (see Gottlieb, 1987). The same discussion has also led to the recognition that group differences cut across individual lives in a multiplicity of ways that can entail privilege and oppression for the same person in different respects. Only a plural explication of the concept of oppression can adequately capture these insights.

Accordingly, I offer below an explication of five faces of oppression as a useful set of categories and distinctions that I believe is comprehensive, in the sense that it covers all the groups said by new left social movements to be oppressed and all the ways they are oppressed. I derive the five faces of oppression from reflection on the condition of these groups. Because different factors, or combinations of factors, constitute the oppression of different groups, making their oppression irreducible, I believe it is not possible to give one essential definition of oppression. The five categories articulated in this chapter, however, are adequate to describe the oppression of any group, as well as its similarities with and differences from the oppression of other groups. But first we must ask what a group is.

The Concept of a Social Group

Oppression refers to structural phenomena that immobilize or diminish a group. But what is a group? Our ordinary discourse differentiates people according to social groups such as women and men, age groups, racial and ethnic groups, religious groups, and so on. Social groups of this sort are not simply collections of people, for they are more fundamentally intertwined with the identities of the people described as belonging to them. They are a specific kind of collectivity, with specific consequences for how people understand one another and themselves. Yet neither social theory nor philosophy has a clear and developed concept of the social group (see Turner et al., 1987).

A social group is a collective of persons differentiated from at least one other group by cultural forms, practices, or way of life. Members of a group have a specific affinity with one another because of their similar experience or way of life, which prompts them to associate with one another more than with those not identified with the group, or in a different way. Groups are an expression of social relations; a group exists only in relation to at least one other group. Group identification arises, that is, in the encounter and interaction between social collectivities that experience some differences in their way of life and forms of association, even if they also regard themselves as belonging to the same society.

As long as they associated solely among themselves, for example, an American Indian group thought of themselves only as "the people." The encounter with other American Indians created an awareness of difference: the others were named as a group and the first group

came to see themselves as a group. But social groups do not arise
only from an encounter between different societies. Social processes
also differentiate groups within a single society. The sexual division
of labor, for example, has created social groups of women and men in
all known societies. Members of each gender have a certain affinity
with others in their group because of what they do or experience, and
differentiate themselves from the other gender, even when members
of each gender consider that they have much in common with members of the other, and consider that they belong to the same society.

Political philosophy typically has no place for a specific concept
of the social group. When philosophers and political theorists discuss
groups they tend to conceive them either on the model of aggregates
or on the model of associations, both of which are methodologically
individualist concepts. To arrive at a specific concept of the social
group it is thus useful to contrast social groups with both aggregates and associations. An aggregate is any classification of persons
according to some attribute. Persons can be aggregated according to
any to number of attributes—eye color, the make of car they drive,
the street they live on. Some people interpret the groups that have
emotional and social salience in our society as aggregates, as arbitrary classifications of persons according to such attributes as skin
color, genitals, or age. George Sher, for example, treats social groups
as aggregates, and uses the arbitrariness of aggregate classification
as a reason not to give special attention to groups. "There are really
as many groups as there are combinations of people and if we are
going to ascribe claims to equal treatment to racial, sexual, and other
groups with high visibility, it will be mere favoritism not to ascribe
similar claims to these other groups as well" (Sher, 1987a, p. 256).

But "highly visible" social groups such as Blacks or women
are different from aggregates, or mere "combinations of people" (see
French, 1975; Friedman and May, 1985; May, 1987, chap. 1). A social
group is defined not primarily by a set of shared attributes, but by a
sense of identity. What defines Black Americans as a social group is
not primarily their skin color; some persons whose skin color is fairly
light, for example, identify themselves as Black. Though sometimes
objective attributes are a necessary condition for classifying oneself
or others as belonging to a certain social group, it is identification
with a certain social status, the common history that social status
produces, and self-identification that define the group as a group.

Social groups are not entities that exist apart from individuals
but neither are they merely arbitrary classifications of individuals
according to attributes that are external to or accidental to their
identities. Admitting the reality of social groups does not commit one

to reifying collectivities, as some might argue. Group meanings partially constitute people's identities in terms of cultural forms, social situation, and history that group members know as theirs because these meanings have been either forced on them or forged by them or both (cf. Fiss, 1976). Groups are real not as substances, but as forms of social relations (cf. May, 1987, pp. 22–23).

Moral theorists and political philosophers tend to elide social groups more often with associations than with aggregates (e.g., French, 1975; May, 1987, chap. 1). By an association I mean a formally organized institution, such as a club, corporation, political party, church, college, or union. Unlike the aggregate model of groups, the association model recognizes that groups are defined by specific practices and forms of association. Nevertheless it shares a problem with the aggregate model. The aggregate model conceives the individual as prior to the collective because it reduces the social group to a mere set of attributes attached to individuals. The association model also implicitly conceives the individual as ontologically prior to the collective, as making up, or constituting groups.

A contract model of social relations is appropriate for conceiving associations, but not groups. Individuals constitute associations; they come to together as already formed persons and set them up, establishing rules, positions, and offices. The relationship of persons to associations is usually voluntary, and even when it is not, the person has nevertheless usually entered the association. The person is prior to the association also in that the person's identity and sense of self are usually regarded as prior to and relatively independent of association membership. Groups, on the other hand, constitute individuals. A person's particular sense of history, affinity, and separateness, even the person's mode of reasoning, evaluating, and expressing feeling, are constituted partly by her or his group affinities. This neither means that persons have no individual styles, nor are unable to transcend or reject a group identity. Nor does it preclude persons from having many aspects that are independent of these group identities.

The social ontology underlying many contemporary theories of justice is methodologically individualist or atomist. It presumes that the individual is ontologically prior to the social. This individualistic social ontology usually goes together with a normative conception of the self as independent. The authentic self is autonomous, unified, free, and self-made, standing apart from history and affiliations, choosing its life plan entirely for itself.

One of the main contributions of poststructuralist philosophy has been to expose as illusory this metaphysics of a unified self-making subjectivity, which posits the subject as an autonomous origin or an underlying substance to which attributes of gender, nationality, family role, intellectual disposition, and so on might attach. Conceiving the subject in this fashion implies conceiving consciousness as outside of and prior to language and the context of social interaction, which the subject enters. Several currents of recent philosophy challenge this deeply held Cartesian assumption. Lacanian psychoanalysis, for example, stood by the social and philosophical theory influenced by Cartesian assumptions, which conceived the self as an achievement of linguistic positioning that is always contextualized in concrete relations with other persons, with mixed identities (Coward and Ellis, 1977). The self is a product of social processes, not their origin.

From a rather different perspective, Habermas indicates that a theory of communicative action also must challenge the "philosophy of consciousness," which locates intentional egos as the ontological origins of social relations. A theory of communicative action conceives individual identity not as an origin but as a product of linguistic and practical interaction (Habermas, 1987, pp. 3–10). As Stephen Epstein describes it, identity is "a socialized sense of individuality, an internal organization of self-perception concerning one's relationship to social categories that also incorporates views of the self perceived to be held by others. Identity is constituted relationally, through involvement with—and incorporation of—significant others and integration into communities" (Epstein, 1987, p. 29). Group categorization and norms are major constituents of individual identity (see Turner et al., 1987).

A person joins an association, and even if membership in it fundamentally affects one's life, one does not take that membership to define one's very identity, in the way, for example, being Navaho might. Group affinity, on the other hand, has the character of what Martin Heidegger (1962) calls "thrownness": *one finds oneself as* a member of a group, which one experiences as always already having been. For our identities are defined in relation to how others identify us, and they do so in terms of groups that are always already associated with specific attributes, stereotypes, and norms.

From the thrownness of group affinity it does not follow that one cannot leave groups and enter new ones. Many women become lesbians after first identifying as heterosexual. Anyone who lives long enough becomes old. These cases exemplify thrownness precisely because such changes in group affinity are experienced as transformations in one's identity. Nor does it follow from the thrownness of group affinity that one cannot define the meaning of group identity for oneself; those who identify with a group can redefine the meaning and norms of groups' identity. Indeed, oppressed groups have sought to confront their oppression by engaging in just such redefinition.

The present point is only that one first finds group identity as given, and then takes it up in a certain way. While groups may come into being, they are never founded.

Groups, I have said, exist only in relation to other groups. A group may be identified by outsiders without those so identified having any specific consciousness of themselves as at group. Sometimes a group comes to exist only because one group excludes and labels a category of persons, and those labeled come to understand themselves as group members only slowly, on the basis of their shared oppression. In Vichy France, for example, Jews who had been so assimilated that they had no specifically Jewish identity were marked as Jews by others and given a specific social status by them. These people "discovered" themselves as Jews and then formed a group identity and affinity with one another (see Sartre, 1948). A person's group identities may be for the most part only a background or horizon to his or her life, becoming salient only in specific interactive contexts.

Assuming an aggregate model of groups, some people think that social groups are invidious fictions, essentializing arbitrary attributes. From this point of view, problems of prejudice, stereotyping, discrimination, and exclusion exist because some people mistakenly believe that group identification makes a difference to the capacities, temperament, or virtues of group members. This individualist conception of persons and their relation to one another tends to identify oppression with group identification. Oppression, in this view, is something that happens to people when they are classified in groups. Because others identify them as a group, they are excluded and despised. Eliminating oppression thus requires eliminating groups. People should be treated as individuals, not as members of groups, and allowed to form their lives freely without stereotypes or group norms.

This author takes issue with that position. While I agree that individuals should be free to pursue life plans in their own way, it is foolish to deny the reality of groups. Despite the modern myth of a decline of parochial attachments and ascribed identities, in modern society group differentiation remains endemic. As both markets and social administration increase the web of social interdependency on a world scale, and as more people encounter one another as strangers in cities and states, people retain and renew ethnic, locale, age, sex, and occupational group identifications, and form new ones in the processes of encounter (cf. Ross, 1980, p. 19; Rothschild, 1981, p. 130). Even when they belong to oppressed groups, people's group identifications are often important to them, and they often feel a special affinity for others in, their group. I believe that group differentiation is both an inevitable and a desirable aspect of modern social processes. Social justice requires not the melting away of differences, but institutions that promote reproduction of and respect for group differences without oppression. Though some groups have come to be formed out of oppression, and relations of privilege and oppression structure the interactions between many groups, group differentiation is not in itself oppressive. Not all groups are oppressed. In the United States, Roman Catholics are a specific social group, with distinct practices and affinities with one another, but they are no longer an oppressed group. Whether a group is oppressed depends on whether it is subject to one or more of the five conditions I shall discuss below.

The view that groups are fictions does carry an important antideterminist or antiessentialist intuition. Oppression has often been perpetrated by a conceptualization of group difference in terms of unalterable essential natures that determine what group members deserve or are capable of, and that exclude groups so entirely from one another that they have no similarities or overlapping attributes. To assert that it is possible to have social group difference without oppression, it is necessary to conceptualize groups in a much more relational and fluid fashion.

Although social processes of affinity and differentiation produce groups, they do not give groups a substantive essence. There is no common nature that members of a group share. As aspects of a process, moreover, groups are fluid; they come into being and may fade away. Homosexual practices have existed in many societies and historical periods, for example. Gay men or lesbians have been identified as specific groups and so identified themselves, however, only in the twentieth century (see Ferguson, 1989, chap. 9; Altaian, 1981).

Arising from social relations and processes, finally, group differences usually cut across one another. Especially in a large, complex, and highly differentiated society, social groups are not themselves homogeneous, but mirror in their own differentiations many of the other groups in the wider society. In American society today, for example, Blacks are not a simple, unified group with a common life. Like other racial and ethnic groups, they are differentiated by age, gender, class, sexuality, region, and nationality, any of which in a given context may become a salient group identity.

This view of group differentiation as multiple, cross-cutting, fluid, and shifting implies another critique of the model of the autonomous, unified self. In complex, highly differentiated societies like our own, all persons have multiple group identifications. The culture, perspective, and relations of privilege and oppression of these various groups, moreover, may not cohere. Thus, individual persons, as constituted partly by their group affinities and relations, cannot be unified; they are heterogeneous and not necessarily coherent.

The Faces of Oppression

Exploitation

The central function of Marx's theory of exploitation is to explain how class structure can exist in the absence of legally and normatively sanctioned class distinctions. In precapitalist societies domination is overt and accomplished through directly political means. In both slave society and feudal society the right to appropriate the product of the labor of others partly defines class privilege, and these societies legitimate class distinctions with ideologies of natural superiority and inferiority.

Capitalist society, on the other hand, removes traditional juridically enforced class distinctions and promotes a belief in the legal freedom of persons. Workers freely contract with employers and receive a wage; no formal mechanisms of law or custom force them to work for that employer or any employer. Thus, the mystery of capitalism arises: When everyone is formally free, how can there be class domination? Why do class distinctions persist between the wealthy, who own the means of production, and the mass of people, who work for them? The theory of exploitation answers this question. Profit, the basis of capitalist power and wealth, is a mystery if we assume that in the market goods exchange at their values. The labor theory of value dispels this mystery. Every commodity's value is a function of the labor time necessary for its production. Labor power is the one commodity that in the process of being consumed produces new value. Profit comes from the difference between the value of the labor performed and the value of the capacity to labor which the capitalist purchases. Profit is possible only because the owner of capital appropriates any realized surplus value.

In recent years, Marxist scholars have engaged in considerable controversy about the viability of the labor theory of value this account of exploitation relies on (see Wolff, 1984, chap. 4). John Roemer (1982), for example, developed a theory of exploitation that claims to preserve the theoretical and practical purposes of Marx's theory, but without assuming a distinction between values and prices and without being restricted to a concept of abstract, homogeneous labor. My purpose here is not to engage in technical economic disputes, but to indicate the place of a concept of exploitation in a conception of oppression.

Marx's theory of exploitation lacks an explicitly normative meaning, even though the judgment that workers are exploited clearly has normative as well as descriptive power in that theory (Buchanan, 1982, chap. 3). C. B. Macpherson (1973, chap. 3) reconstructs this theory of exploitation in a more explicitly normative form. The injustice of capitalist society consists in the fact that some people exercise their capacities under the control, according to the purposes, and for the benefit of other people. Through private ownership of the means of production, and through markets that allocate labor and the ability to buy goods, capitalism systematically transfers the powers of some persons to others, thereby augmenting the power of the latter. In this process of the transfer of powers, according to Macpherson, the capitalist class acquires and maintains an ability to extract benefits from workers. Not only are powers transferred from workers to capitalists, but also the powers of workers diminish by more than the amount of the transfer, because workers suffer material deprivation and a loss of control, and hence are deprived of important elements of self-respect. Justice, then, requires eliminating the institutional forms that enable and enforce this process of transference and replacing them with institutional forms that enable all to develop and use their capacities in a way that does not inhibit, but rather can enhance, similar development and use in others.

The central insight expressed in the concept of exploitation, then, is that this oppression occurs through a steady process of the transfer of the results of the labor of one social group to benefit another. The injustice of class division does not consist only in the distributive fact that some people have great wealth while most people have little (cf. Buchanan, 1982, pp. 44–49; Holmstrom, 1977). Exploitation enacts a structural relation between social groups. Social rules about what work is, who does what for whom, how work is compensated, and the social process by which the results of work are appropriated operate to enact relations of power and inequality. These relations are produced and reproduced through a systematic process in which the energies of the have-nots are continuously expended to maintain and augment the power, status, and wealth of the haves.

Many writers have cogently argued that the Marxist concept of exploitation is too narrow to encompass all forms of domination and oppression (Giddens, 1981, p. 242; Britain and Maynard, 1984, p. 93; Murphy, 1985; Bowles and Gintis, 1986, pp. 20–240). In particular, the Marxist concept of class leaves important phenomena of sexual and racial oppression are unexplained. Does this mean that sexual and racial oppression are nonexploitative, and that we should reserve wholly distinct categories for these oppressions? Or can the concept of exploitation be broadened to include other ways in which the labor and energy expenditure of one group benefits another, and reproduces a relation of domination between them?

Feminists have had little difficulty showing that women's oppression consists partly in a systematic and unreciprocated transfer of powers from women to men. Women's oppression consists not merely in an inequality of status, power, and wealth resulting from men's excluding them from privileged activities. The freedom, power, status and self-realization of men is possible precisely because women work for them. Gender exploitation has two aspects, transfer of the fruits of material labor to men and transfer of nurturing and sexual energies to men. Christine Delphy (1984), for example, describes marriage as a class relation in which women's labor benefits men without comparable remuneration. She makes it clear that the exploitation consists not in the sort of work that women do in the home, for this might include various kinds of tasks, but in the fact that they perform tasks for someone on whom they are dependent. Thus, for example, in most systems of agricultural production in the world, men take to market the goods women have produced, and more often than not men receive the status and often the entire income from this labor.

With the concept of sex-affective production, Ann Ferguson (1979; 1984; 1989, chap. 4) identifies another form of the transference of women's energies to men. Women provide men and children with emotional care and provide men with sexual satisfaction, and as a group receive relatively little of either from men (cf. Brittan and Maynard, pp. 142–148). The gender socialization of women makes us tend to be more attentive to interactive dynamics than men, and makes women good at providing empathy and support for people's feelings and at smoothing over interactive tensions. Both men and women look to women as nurturers of their personal lives, and women frequently complain that when they look to men for emotional support they do not receive it (Easton, 1978). The norms of heterosexuality, moreover, are oriented around male pleasure, and consequently many women receive little satisfaction from their sexual interaction with men (Gottlieb, 1984).

Most feminist theories of gender exploitation have concentrated on the institutional structure of the patriarchal family. Recently, however, feminists have begun to explore relations of gender exploitation enacted in the contemporary workplace and through the state. Carol Brown argues that as men have removed themselves from

responsibility for children, many women have become dependent on
the state for subsistence as they continue to bear nearly total responsibility for child rearing (Brown, 1981; cf. Boris and Bardaglio, 1983:
A. Ferguson, 1984). This creates a new system of the exploitation
of women's domestic labor mediated by state institutions, which she
calls public patriarchy.

In twentieth-century capitalist economics the workplaces that
women have been entering in increasing numbers serve as another
important site of gender exploitation. David Alexander (1987) argues
that typically feminine jobs involve gender-based tasks requiring
sexual labor, nurturing, caring for others' bodies, or smoothing over
workplace tensions. In these ways women's energies are expended
in jobs that enhance the status of, please, or comfort others, usually
men; and these gender-based labors of waitresses, clerical workers,
nurses, and other caretakers often go unnoticed and undercompen-
sated.

To summarize, women are exploited in the Marxist sense to the
degree that they are wage workers. Some have argued that women's
domestic labor also represents a form of capitalist class exploitation
insofar as it is labor covered by the wages a family receives. As a
group, however, women undergo specific forms of gender exploitation
in which their energies and power are expended, often unnoticed
and unacknowledged, usually to benefit men by releasing them for
more important and creative work, enhancing their status or the
environment around them, or providing them with sexual or emotional service.

Race is a structure of oppression at least as basic as class or
gender. Are there, then, racially specific forms of exploitation? There
is no doubt that racialized groups in the United States, especially
Blacks and Latinos, are oppressed through capitalist superexploitation resulting from a segmented labor market that tends to reserve
skilled, high-paying, unionized jobs for Whites. There is wide disagreement about whether such superexploitation benefits Whites as
a group or only benefits the capitalist class (see Reich, 1981), and I
do not intend to enter into that dispute here.

However, one answers the question about capitalist superexploitation of racialized groups, is it possible to conceptualize a form of
exploitation that is racially specific on analogy with the gender-specific forms just discussed? I suggest that the category of *menial* labor
might supply a means for such conceptualization. In its derivation
"menial" designates the labor of servants. Wherever there is racism,
there is the assumption, more or less enforced, that members of the
oppressed racial groups are or ought to be servants of those, or some

of those, in the privileged group. In most White racist societies this means that many White people have dark or yellow-skinned domestic servants, and in the United States today there remains significant racial structuring of private household service. But in the United States today much service labor has gone public; anyone who goes to a good hotel or a good restaurant can have servants. Servants often attended the daily—and nightly—activities of business executives, government officials, and other high-status professionals. In our society there remains strong cultural pressure to fill servant jobs—bellhop, porter, chambermaid, busboy, and so on—with Black and Latino workers. These jobs entail a transfer of energies whereby the servers enhance the status of the served.

Menial labor usually refers not only to service, however, but also to any servile, unskilled, low-paying work lacking in autonomy, in which a person is subject to taking orders from many people. Menial work tends to be auxiliary work, instrumental to the work of others, where those others receive primary recognition for doing the job. Laborers on a construction site, for example, are at the beck and call of welders, electricians, carpenters, and other skilled workers, who receive recognition for the job done. In the United States, explicit racial discrimination once reserved menial work for Blacks, Chicanos, American Indians, and Chinese, and menial work still tends to be linked to Black and Latino workers (Symanski, 1985). I offer this category of menial labor as a form of racially specific exploitation, as a provisional category in need of exploration.

The injustice of exploitation is most frequently understood on a distributive model. For example, though he does not offer an explicit definition of the concept, by "exploitation" Bruce Ackerman seems to mean a seriously unequal distribution of wealth, income, and other resources that is group based and structurally persistent (Ackerman, 1980, chap. 8). John Roemer's definition of exploitation is narrower and more rigorous: "An agent is exploited when the amount of labor embodied in any bundle of goods he could receive, in a feasible distribution of society's net product, is less than the labor he expended" (Roemer, 1982, p. 122). This definition too turns the conceptual focus from institutional relations and processes to distributive outcomes.

Jeffrey Reiman argues that such a distributive understanding of exploitation reduces the injustice of class processes to a function of the inequality of the productive assets classes own. This misses, according to Reiman, the relationship of force between capitalists and workers, the fact that the unequal exchange in question occurs within coercive structures that give workers few options (Reiman, 1987; cf. Buchanan, 1982, p. 49; Holmstrom, 1977). The injustice of exploitation consists in social processes that bring about a transfer of energies from one group to another to produce unequal distributions, and in the way in which social institutions enable a few to accumulate while they constrain many more. The injustices of exploitation cannot be eliminated by redistribution of goods, for as long as institutionalized practices and structural relations remain unaltered, the process of transfer will re-create an unequal distribution of benefits. Bringing about justice where there is exploitation requires reorganization of institutions and practices of decision making, alteration of the division of labor, and similar measures of institutional, structural, and cultural change.

Marginalization

Increasingly in the United States, racial oppression occurs in the form of marginalization rather than exploitation. Marginals are people the system of labor cannot or will not use. Not only in Third World capitalist countries, but also in most Western capitalist societies, there is a growing underclass of people permanently confined to lives of social marginality, most of whom are racially marked—Blacks or Indians in Latin America, and Blacks, East Indians, Eastern Europeans, or North Africans in Europe.

Marginalization is by no means the fate only of racially marked groups, however. In the United States a shamefully large proportion of the population is marginal; old people and increasingly people who are not very old but get laid off from their jobs and cannot find new work; young people, especially Black or Latino, who cannot find first or second jobs; many single mothers and their children; other people involuntarily unemployed; many mentally and physically disabled people; Americans Indians, especially those on reservations.

Marginalization is perhaps the most dangerous form of oppression. A whole category of people is expelled from useful participation in social life and thus potentially subjected to severe material deprivation and even extermination. The material deprivation marginalization often causes is certainly unjust, especially in a society where others have plenty. Contemporary advanced capitalist societies have in principle acknowledged the injustices of material deprivation caused by marginalization, and have taken some steps to address it by providing welfare payments and services. The continuance of this welfare state is by no means assured, and in most welfare state societies, especially the United States, welfare redistributions do not eliminate large-scale suffering and deprivation. Material deprivation, which can be addressed by redistributive social policies, is not, however, the extent of the harm caused by marginalization. Two categories of injustice beyond distribution are associated with marginality in advanced capitalist societies. First, the provision of welfare itself produces new injustice by depriving those dependent on it of rights and freedoms that others have. Second, even when material deprivation is somewhat mitigated by the welfare state, marginalization is unjust because it blocks the opportunity to exercise capacities in socially defined and recognized ways. I shall explicate each of these in turn.

Liberalism has traditionally asserted the right of all rational autonomous agents to equal citizenship. Early bourgeois liberalism explicitly excluded from citizenship all those whose reason was questionable or not fully developed, and all those not independent (Pateman, 1988, chap. 3; cf. Bowles and Gintis, 1986, chap. 2). Thus, poor people, women, the mad and the feebleminded, and children were explicitly excluded from citizenship, and many of these were housed in institutions modeled on the modern prison: poorhouses, insane asylums, schools.

Today the exclusion of dependent persons from equal citizenship rights is only barely hidden beneath the surface. Because they depend on bureaucratic institutions for support or services, the old, the poor, and the mentally and physically disabled are subject to patronizing, punitive, demeaning, and arbitrary treatment by the policies and people associated with welfare bureaucracies. Being a dependent in our society implies being legitimately subject to the often arbitrary and invasive authority of social service providers and other public and private administrators, who enforce rules with which the marginal must comply, and otherwise exercise power over the conditions of their lives. In meeting needs of the marginalized, often with the aid of social scientific disciplines, welfare agencies also construct the needs themselves. Medical and social service professionals know what is good for those they serve, and the marginals and dependents themselves do not have the right to claim to know what is good for them (Fraser, 1987a; K. Ferguson, 1984, chap. 4). Dependency in our society thus implies, as it has in all liberal societies, a sufficient warrant to suspend basic rights to privacy, respect, and individual choice.

Although dependency produces conditions of injustice in our society, dependency in itself need not be oppressive. One cannot imagine a society in which some people would not need to be dependent on others at least some of the time: children, sick people, women recovering from childbirth, old people who have become frail, depressed or otherwise emotionally needy persons, have the moral right to depend on others for subsistence and support.

An important contribution of feminist moral theory has been to question the deeply held assumption that moral agency and full citizenship require that a person be autonomous and independent. Feminists have exposed this assumption as inappropriately individualistic and derived from a specifically male experience of social relations, which values competition and solitary achievement (see Gilligan, 1982; Friedman, 1985). Female experience of social relations, arising both from women's typical domestic care responsibilities and from the kinds of paid work that many women do, tends to recognize dependence as a basic human condition (cf. Hartsock, 1983, chap. 10). Whereas on the autonomy model a just society would as much as possible give people the opportunity to be independent, the feminist model envisions justice as according respect and participation in decision making to those who are dependent as well as to those who are independent (Held, 1987b). Dependency should not be a reason to be deprived of choice and respect, and much of the oppression many marginals experience would be lessened if a less individualistic model of rights prevailed.

Marginalization does not cease to be oppressive when one has shelter and food. Many old people, for example, have sufficient means to live comfortably but remain oppressed in their marginal status. Even if marginals were provided a comfortable material life within institutions that respected their freedom and dignity, injustices of marginality would remain in the form of uselessness, boredom, and lack of self-respect. Most of our society's productive and recognized activities take place in contexts of organized social cooperation, and social structures and processes that close persons out of participation in such social cooperation are unjust. Thus while marginalization definitely entails serious issues of distributive justice, it also involves the deprivation of cultural, practical, and institutionalized conditions for exercising capacities in a context of recognition and interaction.

The fact of marginalization raises basic structural issues of justice, in particular concerning the appropriateness of a connection between participation in productive activities of social cooperation, on the one hand, and access to the means of consumption, on the other. As marginalization is increasing, with no signs of abatement, some social policy analysts have introduced the idea of a "social wage" as a guaranteed socially provided income not tied to the wage system. Restructuring of productive activity to address a right of participation, however, implies organizing some socially productive activity outside of the wage system (see Offe, 1985, pp. 95–100), through public works or self-employed collectives.

Powerlessness

As I have indicated, the Marxist idea of class is important because it helps reveal the structure of exploitation: that some people have their power and wealth because they profit from the labors of others. For this reason I reject the claim some make that a traditional class exploitation model fails to capture the structure of contemporary society. It remains the case that the labor of most people in the society augments the power of relatively few. Despite their differences from nonprofessional workers, most professional workers are still not members of the capitalist class. Professional labor either involves exploitative transfers to capitalists or supplies important conditions for such transfers. Professional workers are in an ambiguous class position, it is true, because they also benefit from the exploitation of nonprofessional workers.

While it is false to claim that a division between capitalist and working classes no longer describes our society, it is also false to say that class relations have remained unaltered since the nineteenth century. An adequate conception of oppression cannot ignore the experience of social division reflected in the colloquial distinction between the "middle class" and the "working class," a division structured by the social division of labor between professionals and nonprofessionals. Professionals are privileged in relation to nonprofessionals, by virtue of their position in the division of labor and the status it carries. Nonprofessionals suffer a form of oppression in addition to exploitation, which I call powerlessness.

In the United States, as in other advanced capitalist countries, most workplaces are not organized democratically, direct participation in public policy decisions is rare, and policy implementation is, for the most part, hierarchical, imposing rules on bureaucrats and citizens. Thus, most people in these societies do not regularly participate in making decisions that affect the conditions of their lives and actions, and in this sense, most people lack significant power. At the same time, domination in modern society is enacted through the widely dispersed powers of many agents mediating the decisions of others. To that extent many people have some power in relation to others, even though they lack the power to decide policies or results. The powerless are those who lack authority or power even in this mediated sense, those over whom power is exercised without their exercising it; the powerless are situated so that they must take orders and rarely have the right to give them. Powerlessness also designates a position in the division of labor and the concomitant social position that allows persons little opportunity to develop and exercise skills. The powerless have little or no work autonomy, exercise little creativity or judgment in their work, have no technical expertise or authority, express themselves awkwardly, especially in public or bureaucratic settings, and do not command respect. Powerlessness names the oppressive situations Sennett and Cobb (1972) describe in their famous study of working-class men.

This powerless status is perhaps best described negatively: the powerless lack the authority, status, and sense of self that professionals tend to have. The status privilege of professionals has three aspects, the lack of which produces oppression for nonprofessionals. First, acquiring and practicing a profession has an expansive, progressive character. Being professional usually requires a college education and the acquisition of a specialized knowledge that entails working with symbols and concepts. Professionals experience progress first in acquiring the expertise, and then in the course of professional advancement and rise in status. The life of the nonprofessional by comparison is powerless in the sense that it lacks this orientation toward the progressive development of capacities and avenues for recognition.

Second, while many professionals have supervisors and cannot directly influence many decisions or the action of many people, most nevertheless have considerable day-to-day work autonomy. Professionals usually have some authority over others, moreover either over workers they supervise, or over auxiliaries, or over clients. Nonprofessionals, on the other hand, lack autonomy, and in both their working and their consumer-client lives often stand under the authority of professionals. Though based on a division of labor between "mental" and "manual" work, the distinction between "middle class" and "working class" designates a division not only in working life, but also in nearly all aspects of social life. Professionals and nonprofessionals belong to different cultures in the United States. The two groups tend to live in segregated neighborhoods or even different towns, a process itself mediated by planners, zoning officials, and real estate people. The groups tend to have different tastes in food, decor, clothes, music, and vacations, and often different health and educational needs. Members of each group socialize for the most part with others in the same status group. While there is some intergroup mobility between generations, for the most part the children of professionals become professionals and the children of nonprofessionals do not.

Thus, third, the privileges of the professional extend beyond the workplace to a whole way of life. I call this way of life "respectability." To treat people with respect is to be prepared to listen to

what they have to say or to do what they request because they have
some authority, expertise, or influence. The norms of respectability
in our society are associated specifically with professional culture.
Professional dress, speech, tastes, and demeanor, all connote respectability. Generally professionals expect and receive respect from others. In restaurants, banks, hotels, real estate offices, and many other
such public places, as well as in the media, professionals typically
receive more respectful treatment than nonprofessionals. For this
reason nonprofessionals seeking a loan or a job, or to buy a house
or a car, will often try to look "professional" and "respectable" in
those settings.

The privilege of this professional respectability appears starkly
in the dynamics of racism and sexism. In daily interchange women
and men of color must prove their respectability. At first they are
often not treated by strangers with respectful distance or deference.
Once people discover that this woman or that Puerto Rican man is
a college teacher or a business executive, however, they often behave
more respectfully toward her or him. Working-class White men, on
the other hand, are often treated with respect until their working-
class status is revealed.

I have discussed several injustices associated with powerlessness: inhibition in the development of one's capacities, lack of decision
making power in one's working life, and exposure to disrespectful
treatment because of the status one occupies. These injustices have
distributional consequences but are more fundamentally matters of
the division of labor. The oppression of powerlessness brings into
question the division of labor basic to all industrial societies: the
social division between those who plan and those who execute.

Cultural Imperialism

Exploitation, marginalization, and powerlessness all refer to relations
of power and oppression that occur by virtue of the social division
of labor—who works for whom, who does not work, and how the
content of work defines one institutional position relative to others.
These three categories refer to structural and institutional relations
that delimit people's material lives, including but not restricted to
the resources they have access to and the concrete opportunities they
have or do not have to develop and exercise their capacities. These
kinds of oppression are a matter of concrete power in relation to
others—of who benefits from whom, and who is dispensable.

Recent theorists of movements of group liberation, notably feminist and Black liberation theorists, have also given prominence to

a rather different form of oppression, which following Lugones and
Spelman (1983) I shall call cultural imperialism. To experience cultural imperialism means to experience how the dominant meanings
of a society render the particular perspective of one's own group
invisible at the same time as they stereotype one's group and mark
it out as the Other.

Cultural imperialism involves the universalization of a dominant group's experience and culture, and its establishment as the
norm. Some groups have exclusive or primary access to what Nancy
Fraser (1987b) calls the means of interpretation and communication in a society. As a consequence, the dominant cultural products
of the society, that is, those most widely disseminated, express the
experience, values, goals, and achievements of these groups. Often
without noticing they do so, the dominant groups project their own
experience as representative of humanity as such. Cultural products
also express the dominant group's perspective on and interpretation
of events and elements in the society, including other groups in the
society, insofar as they attain cultural status at all.

An encounter with other groups, however, can challenge the
dominant group's claim to universality. The dominant group reinforces its position by bringing the other groups under the measure
of its dominant norms. Consequently, the difference of women from
men, American Indians or Africans from Europeans, Jews from Christians, homosexuals from heterosexuals, workers from professionals
becomes reconstructed largely as deviance and inferiority. Since only
the dominant group's cultural expressions receive wide dissemina-
tion, their cultural expressions become the normal, or the universal,
and thereby the unremarkable. Given the normality of its own cultural expressions and identity, the dominant group constructs the
differences that some groups exhibit as lack and negation. These
groups become marked as Other.

The culturally dominated undergo a paradoxical oppression, in
that they are both marked out by stereotypes and at the same time,
rendered invisible. As remarkable, deviant beings, the culturally
imperialized are stamped with an essence. The stereotypes confine
them to a nature that is often attached in some way to their bodies,
and thus cannot easily be denied. These stereotypes so permeate
the society that they are not noticed as contestable. Just as everyone knows that the earth goes around the sun, so everyone knows
that gay people are promiscuous, that Indians are alcoholics, and
that women are good with children. White males, on the other hand,
insofar as they escape group marking, can be individuals.

Those living under cultural imperialism find themselves defined from the outside, positioned, placed, by a network of dominant meanings they experience as arising from elsewhere, from those with whom they do not identify and who do not identify with them. Consequently, the dominant culture's stereotyped and inferiorized images of the group must be internalized by group members at least to the extent that they are forced to react to behavior of others influenced by those images. This creates for the culturally oppressed the experience that W. E. B. Du Bois called "double consciousness"—"this sense of always looking at one's self through the eyes of others, of measuring one's soul by the tape of a world that looks on in amused contempt and pity" (Du Bois, 1969 [1903], p. 45). Double consciousness arises when the oppressed subject refuses to coincide with these devalued, objectified, stereotyped visions of him- or herself. While the subjects desire recognition as human, capable of activity, full of hope and possibility, they receive from the dominant culture only the judgment that they are different, marked, or inferior.

The group defined by the dominant culture as deviant, as a stereotyped Other, *is* culturally different from the dominant group, because the status of Otherness creates specific experiences not shared by the dominant group, and because culturally oppressed groups also are often socially segregated and occupy specific positions in the social division of labor. Members of such groups express their specific group experiences and interpretations of the world to one another, developing and perpetuating their own culture. Double consciousness, then, occurs because one finds one's being defined by two cultures: a dominant and a subordinate culture. Because they can affirm and recognize one another as sharing similar experiences and perspectives on social life, people in culturally imperialized groups can often maintain a sense of positive subjectivity.

Cultural imperialism involves the paradox of experiencing oneself as invisible at the same time that one is marked out as different. The invisibility comes about when dominant groups fail to recognize the perspective embodied in their cultural expressions as a perspective. These dominant cultural expressions often simply have little place for the experience of other groups, at most only mentioning or referring to them in stereotyped or marginalized ways. This, then, is the injustice of cultural imperialism: that the oppressed group's own experience and interpretation of social life finds little expression that touches the dominant culture, while that same culture imposes on the oppressed group its experience and interpretation of social life.

Violence

Finally, many groups suffer the oppression of systematic violence. Members of some groups live with the knowledge that they must fear random, unprovoked attacks on their persons or property that have no motive but to damage, humiliate, or destroy the person. In American society women, Blacks, Asians, Arabs, gay men, and lesbians live under such threats of violence, and in at least some regions Jews, Puerto Ricans, Chicanos, and other Spanish-speaking Americans must fear such violence as well. Physical violence against these groups is shockingly frequent. Rape Crisis Center networks estimate that more than one third of all American women experience an attempted or successful sexual assault in their lifetimes. Manning Marable (1984, pp. 238–241) catalogs a large number of incidents of racist violence and terror against Blacks in the United States between 1980 and 1982. He cites dozens of incidents of the severe beating, killing, or rape of Blacks by police officers on duty, in which the police involved were acquitted of any wrongdoing. In 1981, moreover, there were at least 500 documented cases of random White teenage violence against Blacks. Violence against gay men and lesbians is not only common, but has been increasing in the last five years. While the frequency of physical attacks on members of these and other racially or sexually marked groups is very disturbing, I also include in this category less severe incidents of harassment, intimidation, or ridicule simply for the purpose of degrading, humiliating, or stigmatizing group members.

Given the frequency of such violence in our society, why are theories of justice usually silent about it? I think the reason is that theorists do not typically take such incidents of violence and harassment as matters of social injustice. No moral theorist would deny that such acts are very wrong. But unless all immoralities are injustices, they might wonder, why should such acts be interpreted as symptoms of social injustice? Acts of violence or petty harassment are committed by particular individuals, often extremists, deviants, or the mentally unsound. How then can they be said to involve the sorts of institutional issues I have said are properly the subject of justice?

What makes violence a face of oppression is less the particular acts themselves, though these are often utterly horrible, than the social context surrounding them, which makes them possible and even acceptable. What makes violence a phenomenon of social injustice, and not merely an individual moral wrong, is its systemic character, its existence as a social practice. Violence is systemic because it is directed at members of a group simply because they are members of that group. Any woman, for example, has a reason to fear rape. Regardless of what a Black man has done to escape the oppressions of marginality or powerlessness, he lives knowing he is subject to attack or harassment. The oppression of violence consists not only in direct victimization, but in the daily knowledge shared by all members of oppressed groups that they are *liable* to violation, solely on account of their group identity. Just living under such a threat of attack on oneself or family or friends deprives the oppressed of freedom and dignity, and needlessly expends their energy.

Violence is a social practice. It is a social given that everyone knows happens and will happen again. It is always at the horizon of social imagination, even for those who do not perpetrate it. According to the prevailing social logic, some circumstances make such violence more "called for" than in others. The idea of rape will occur to many men who pick up a hitchhiking woman; the idea of hounding or teasing a gay man on their dorm floor will occur to many straight male college students. Often several persons inflict the violence together, especially in all-male groupings. Sometimes violators set out looking for people to beat up, rape, or taunt. This rule-bound, social, and often premeditated character makes violence against groups a social practice.

Group violence approaches legitimacy, moreover, in the sense that it is tolerated. Often third parties find it unsurprising because it happens frequently and lies as a constant possibility at the horizon of social imagination. Even when they are caught, those who perpetrate acts of group-directed violence or harassment often receive light or no punishment. To that extent society renders their acts acceptable.

An important aspect of random, systemic violence is its irrationality. Xenophobic violence differs from the violence of states or ruling-class repression. Repressive violence has a rational, albeit evil, motive: rulers use it as a coercive tool to maintain their power. Many accounts of racist, sexist, or homophobic violence attempt to explain its motivation as a desire to maintain group privilege or domination. I do not doubt that fear of violence often functions to keep oppressed groups subordinate, but I do not think xenophobic violence is rationally motivated in the way that, for example, violence against strikers is.

On the contrary, the violation of rape, beating, killing, and harassment of women, people of color, gays, and other marked groups is motivated by fear or hatred of those groups. Sometimes the motive may be a simple will to power, to victimize those marked as vulnerable by the very social fact that they are subject to violence. If so, this motive is secondary in the sense that it depends on a social practice of group violence. Violence-causing fear or hatred of the other at least partly involves insecurities on the part of the violators: its irrationality suggests that unconscious processes are at work. I think such unconscious fears account at least partly for the oppression I have here called violence. It may also partly account for cultural imperialism

Cultural imperialism, moreover, itself intersects with violence. The culturally imperialized may reject the dominant meanings and attempt to assert their own subjectivity, or the fact of their cultural difference may put the lie to the dominant culture's implicit claim to universality. The dissonance generated by such a challenge to the hegemonic cultural meanings can also be a source of irrational violence. Violence is a form of injustice that a distributive under-standing of justice seems ill equipped to capture. This may be why contemporary discussions of justice rarely mention it. I have argued that group-directed violence is institutionalized and systemic. To the degree that institutions and social practices encourage, tolerate, or enable the perpetration of violence against members of specific groups, those institutions and practices are unjust and should be reformed. Such reform may require the redistribution of resources or positions but in large part can come only through a change in cultural images, stereotypes, and the mundane reproduction of relations of dominance and aversion in the gestures of everyday life.

Applying the Criteria

Social theories that construct oppression as a unified phenomenon usually either leave out groups that even the theorists think are oppressed, or leave out important ways in which groups are oppressed. Black liberation theorists and feminist theorists have argued persua-sively, for example, that Marxism's reduction of all oppressions to class oppression leaves out much about the specific oppression of Blacks and women. By pluralizing the category of oppression in the way it was explained in this chapter, social theory can avoid the exclusive and oversimplifying effects of such reductionism.

I have avoided pluralizing the category in the way some others have done, by constructing an account of separate systems of oppres-sion for each oppressed group: racism, sexism, classism, heterosex-ism, ageism, and so on. There is a double problem with considering each group's oppression a unified and distinct structure or system. On the one hand, this way of conceiving oppression fails to accom-modate the similarities and overlaps in the oppressions of different groups. On the other hand, it falsely represents the situation of all group members as the same.

I have arrived at the five faces of oppression—exploitation, marginalization, powerlessness, cultural imperialism, and violence—as the best way to avoid such exclusions and reductions. They function as criteria for determining whether individuals and groups are oppressed, rather than as a full theory of oppression. I believe that these criteria are objective. They provide a means of refuting some people's belief that their group is oppressed when it is not, as well as a means of persuading others that a group is oppressed when they doubt it. Each criterion can be operationalized; each can be applied through the assessment of observable behavior, status relationships, distributions, texts, and other cultural artifacts. I have no illusions that such assessments can be value-neutral. But these criteria can nevertheless serve as means of evaluating claims that a group is oppressed, or adjudicating disputes about whether or how a group is oppressed.

The presence of any of these five conditions is sufficient for calling a group oppressed. But different group oppressions exhibit different combinations of these forms, as do different individuals in these groups. Nearly all, if not all, groups said by contemporary social movements to be oppressed suffer cultural imperialism. The other oppressions they experience vary. Working-class people are exploited and powerless, for example, but if employed and White do not experience marginalization and violence. Gay men, on the other hand, are not exploited or powerless, but they experience severe cultural imperialism and violence. Similarly, Jews and Arabs as groups are victims of cultural imperialism and violence, though many members of these groups also suffer exploitation or powerlessness. Old people are oppressed by marginalization and cultural imperialism, and this is true of physically and mentally disabled people. As a group women are subject to gender-based exploitation, powerlessness, cultural imperialism, and violence. Racism in the United States condemns many Blacks and Latinos to marginalization, and puts many more at risk, even though many members of these groups escape that condition: members of these groups often suffer all five forms of oppression.

Applying these five criteria to the situation of groups makes it possible to compare oppressions without reducing them to a common essence or claiming that one is more fundamental than another. One can compare the ways in which a particular form of oppression appears in different groups. For example, while the operations of cultural imperialism are often experienced in similar fashion by different groups, there are also important differences. One can compare the combinations of oppression groups experience, or the intensity of those oppressions. Thus, with these criteria one can plausibly claim that one group is more oppressed than another without reducing all oppressions to a single scale.

Why are particular groups oppressed in the way they are? Are there any causal connections among the five forms of oppression? Causal or explanatory questions such as these are beyond the scope of this discussion. While I think general social theory has a place, causal explanation must always be particular and historical. Thus, an explanatory account of why a particular group is oppressed in the ways that it is must trace the history and current structure of particular social relations. Such concrete historical and structural explanations will often show causal connections among, the different forms of oppression experienced by a group. The cultural imperialism in which White men make stereotypical assumptions about and refuse to recognize the values of Blacks or women, for example, contributes to the marginalization and powerlessness many Blacks and women suffer. But cultural imperialism does not always have these effects.

Note

*This chapter appeared in Iris Marion Young, *Justice and the Politics of Difference* (1990). Reprinted with permission from Princeton University Press, Princeton, NJ.

References

Ackerman, B. (1980). *Social justice and the liberal state*. New Haven: Yale University Press.

Alexander, D. (1987). Gendered job traits and women's occupations. Ph.D.dissertation, Economics, University of Massachusetts.

Boris, E., & Bardaglio, P. (1983). The transformation of patriarchy: The historic role of the state. In I. Diamond (Ed.), *Families, politics and public policy*. New York: Longman.

Bowles, S., & Cintis, H. (1982). Crisis of liberal democratic capitalism: The case of the United States. *Politics and Society, 11*, 1–94.

Bowles, S., & Cintis, H. (1986). *Democracy and capitalism*. New York: Basic.

Brittan, A., & Maynard, M. (1984). *Sexism, racism and oppression*. Oxford: Blackwell.

Buchanan, A. (1982). *Marx and justice*. Totowa, NJ: Rowman and Allanheld.

Buchanan, A. (1989). Assessing the communitarian critique of liberalism. *Ethics, 99* (July), 852–182.

Coward, R., & Ellis, J. (1977). *Language and materialism*. London: Routledge and Kegan Paul.

Delphy, C. (1984). *Close to home: A materialist analysis of women's oppression*. Amherst: University of Massachusetts Press.

Du Bois, W. E. B. (1969) [1903]. *The souls of Black folk*. New York: New American Library.

Easton, B. (1978). Feminism and the contemporary family. *Socialist Review, 39* (May/June), 11–36.

Epstein, S. (1987). Gay politics, ethnic identity: The limits of social constructionism. *Socialist Review, 17* (May–August), 9–54.

Ferguson, A. (1984). On conceiving motherhood and sexuality: A feminist materialist approach. In J. Trebilcot (Ed.), *Mothering: Essays in feminist theory*. Totowa, NJ: Rowman and Allanheld.

Ferguson, A. (1989). *Blood at the root*. London: Pandora.

Ferguson, K. (1984). *The feminist case against bureaucracy*. Philadelphia: Temple University Press.

Foucault, M. (1970). *The order of things*. New York: Random House.

Fraser, N. (1987a). Women, welfare, and the politics of need interpretation. *Hypatia: A Journal of Feminist Philosophy, 2* (Winter), 103–122.

Fraser, N. (1987b). Social movements vs. disciplinary bureaucracies: The discourse of social needs. CHS Occasional Paper No. 8. Center for Humanistic Studies, University of Minnesota.

French, P. (1975). Types of collectivities and blame. *The Personalist, 56* (Spring), 160–69.

Friedman, M. (1985). Care and context in moral reasoning. In C. Harding (Ed.), *Moral dilemmas: Philosophical and psychological issues in the development of moral reasoning*. Chicago: Precedent.

Friedman, T., & Williams, E. B. (1982). Current use of tests for employment. In A. Wigdor & W. Garner (Eds.), *Ability testing: Uses, consequences, and controversies, Part II*. Washington, DC: National Academy Press.

Frye, M. (1983a). Oppression. In *The politics of reality*. Trumansburg, NY: Crossing.

Frye, M. (1983b). On being White: Toward a feminist understanding of race supremacy. In *The politics of reality*. Trumansburg, NY: Crossing.

Frye, M. (1977). *Discipline and punish*. New York: Pantheon.

Frye, M. (1980). *Power/Knowledge*. New York: Pantheon.

Frye, M. (1987). Beyond caring: The de-moralization of gender. In M. Hanen & K. Nielsen (Eds.), *Science, morality and feminist theory*. Calgary: University of Calgary Press.

Frye, M. (1989). Impracticality of impartiality. *Journal of Philosophy, 86* (November), 645–656.

Frye, M., & May, L. (1985). "Harming women as a group." *Social Theory and Practice, 11* (Summer): 297–234.

Frye, M. (1981). *A contemporary critique of historical materialism*. Berkeley and Los Angeles: University of California Press.

Frye, M. (1984). *The constitution of society*. Berkeley and Los Angeles: University of California Press.

Giddens, A. (1976). *Central problems of social theory.* Berkeley: University of California Press.

Gottlieb, R. (1984). The political economy of sexuality. *Review of Radical Political Economy, 16* (Spring): 143–165.

Gottlieb, R. (1987). *History and subjectivity.* Philadelphia: Temple University Press.

Habermas, J. (1973). *Theory and practice.* Boston: Beacon.

Heidegger, M. (1982). *Being and time.* New York: Harper and Row.

Holmstrom, N. (1977). Exploitation. *Canadian Journal of Philosophy, 7* (June), 353–369.

Lugones, M. C., & Spelman, E. V. (1983). Have we got a theory for you! Feminist theory, cultural imperialism and the demand for "the woman's voice." *Women's Studies International Forum, 6,* 573–581.

Macpherson, C. B. (1962). *The political theory of possessive individualism.* Oxford: Oxford University Press.

Macpherson, C. B. (1973). *Democratic theory: Essays in retrieval.* Oxford: Oxford University Press.

Marable, M. (1984). *Race, reform and rebellion: The second reconstruction in Black America, 1945–82.* Jackson: University Press of Mississippi.

May, L. (1987). *The morality of groups: Collective responsibility, group-based harm, and corporate rights.* Notre Dame, IN: Notre Dame University Press.

Murphy, R. (1985). Exploitation or exclusion? *Sociology 19* (May), 225–243.

Reich, M. (1981). *Racial inequality.* Princeton: Princeton University Press.

Reiman, J. (1987). Exploitation, force, and the moral assessment of capitalism: Thoughts on Roemer and Cohen. *Philosophy and Public Affairs, 16* (Winter), 3–41.

Roemer, J. (1982). *A general theory of exploitation and class.* Cambridge: Harvard University Press.

Ross, J. (1980). Introduction. In J. Ross & A. Baker Cottrell (Eds.), *The Mobilization of collective identity.* Lanham, MD: University Press of America.

Rothschild, J. (1981). *Ethnopolitics.* New York: Columbia University Press.

Sartre, J. P. (1948). *Anti-Semite and Jew.* New York: Schocken.

Sennett, R., (1974). *The fall of public man.* New York: Random House.

Sennett, R., & Cobb, J. (1972). *The hidden injuries of class.* New York: Vintage.

Sher, G. (1987a). "Groups and the Constitution." In G. Ezorsky (Ed.), *Moral rights in the workplace.* Albany: State University of New York Press.

Sher, G. (1987b). Predicting performance. In E. F. Paul, F. D. Miller, J. Paul, & J. Ahrens (Eds.), *Equal opportunity.* Oxford: Blackwell.

Turner, J. C, Hogg, M. A, Oakes, P. V., Rucher, S. D., & Wethrell, M. S. (1987). *Rediscovering the social group: A self-categorization theory.* Oxford: Blackwell.

Wolff, R. P. (1968). *The poverty of liberalism.* Boston: Beacon.

Wolff, R. P. (1977). *Understanding Rawls.* Princeton: Princeton University Press.

Wolff, R. P. (1984). *Understanding Marx.* Princeton: Princeton University Press.

CHAPTER TWO

The Vicissitudes of Cultural Competence

Dealing With Difficult Classroom Dialogue*

GALE YOUNG AND ELIZABETH DAVIS-RUSSELL

As we have entered the twenty-first century, our discussions in higher education seem to have expanded from a focus on cultural sensitivity to cultural competence. How culturally competent is the faculty member who is confronted with a class of culturally diverse students, or a clinician who enters into a psychotherapy relationship with a culturally different client? In this chapter, we shall provide a definition of cultural competence that includes not only individuals, but systems as well. We will then discuss the components of cultural competence and what is necessary to become culturally competent. We will present a discussion of difficult dialogues, a consequence of movement toward cultural competence, and conclude with some recommendations on how to deal with difficult dialogues in the classroom.

Competence denotes the ability to perform; therefore, the definition of cultural competence that seems most congruent with our perspective is one that is inclusive of attitudes, behaviors, and policies (Cross, Bazron, Dennis, & Isaacs, 1989). This definition specifies that these three must be congruent. On the individual level, the individual must possess a set of congruent attitudes and behaviors that enables him to work effectively in cross-cultural situations. Yet institutions can possess cultural competence, for they can have policies that enable the institution to function effectively in cross-cultural situations.

There are several elements of cultural competence (Cross et al., 1989). One of these is valuing diversity. The individual or institution has moved beyond the levels of tolerance, acceptance, and respect, to a level of affirmation, solidarity, and critique (Nieto, 1992).

Another element of cultural competence is the capacity of the individual or institution to engage in cultural self-assessment (Cross et al., 1989). In that self-assessment, the individual engages in an examination of her feelings, attitudes, and perceptions toward her own social groups and other racial, ethnic, cultural, gender, and sexual orientation group. At the California School of Professional Psychology (CSPP), this has occurred in the intercultural labs for students, and in faculty and staff retreats for faculty and staff, respectively. On the institutional level, the Multicultural Education, Research, and Training Institute (MERIT Institute) conducts an audit that assesses the institution's commitment to cultural diversity. The audit is inclusive of the institution's policies and practices.

Culturally competent individuals and institutions have a consciousness of the dynamics inherent when cultures interact (Cross et al., 1989). They are not only aware of the "dynamics of difference," but also of the dynamics of misinterpretation and misjudgment. These can lead to difficult dialogues, and as we see later in this chapter, the potential for explosive encounters. Culturally competent individuals and institutions are knowledgeable about different communication styles. They understand that one brings culturally prescribed patterns of communication, etiquette, and problem solving to interpersonal interactions, and are aware of the fact that violation of the norms of one another can have serious consequences.

Individuals and institutions possess institutionalized cultural knowledge and also possess developed adaptations to diversity (Cross et al., 1989). On the institutional level, the latter means moving from rhetoric to establishing policies and practices that convey that diversity is an integral part of the institution. It is a natural part of doing business. On the individual level, it means listening with an open heart, and noticing others' feelings and thoughts, as well as one's own. It means responding without judgment and arrogance. It also means allowing oneself to feel and be present in the jagged racial divide, to feel so intensely the differences that divide and simultaneously the commonalties that bind.

Cultural competence is not a luxury. It is a necessity for faculty and clinicians alike. As faculty working to educate and train students from many different cultural backgrounds, imagine this scenario: your class is discussing the day's reading assignments on how families have viewed children differently over the centuries. A European American White student, drawing from her own experience working in a social service agency with people of color, says, "It seemed like those people didn't really care about their children." Several African American students in the class take offense and demand, "What do you mean by 'those people'?" The student who made the comment is puzzled and feels put on the spot. The students who are offended by her comment are not going to be put off; they want to deal directly with her for what they perceive as her racism. Everyone else in the room is waiting to see what happens. Welcome to difficult dialogue!

The possibility that a difficult dialogue will occur is heightened whenever course materials reflect a multicultural perspective, when students are racially or culturally diverse or when the instructor's ethnicity, gender, and sexual orientation are different from the students. This chapter will consider ways to transform these kinds of emotionally charged classroom encounters into opportunities for meaningful dialogues about race, culture, gender, class, and sexual identity. It will explore the dynamics that can make such discussions difficult and present a model of effective strategies for engaging students in cognitive and emotional inquiry and open-minded discussion about multicultural issues.

What Is a Difficult Dialogue?

Difficult dialogues, obviously, can occur about any subject, in any situation and between individuals of the same race, culture, gender, and sexual orientation. Many of the dynamics explained in this chapter pertain to the larger scope of difficult dialogues. However, this chapter focuses on the dynamics and patterns that emerge when those difficult dialogues are about and across race, culture, sexual orientation, and gender lines.

Difficult classroom dialogues occur when differences in perspectives are made public, and are challenged or judged to be offensive, often with intense emotions aroused among participants and observers. Such dialogues immediately spotlight the race, gender, culture, and sexual orientation of the participants. The normal classroom conversation stops, and verbal exchanges are no longer student-to-student or faculty-to-student, but White-to-Black, male-to-female, gay-to-heterosexual, and so on. Whether or not a person would normally attach much meaning to these identities, the interaction calls attention to them, and students and faculty alike can find themselves experiencing a strong personal reaction. Confronted with a different cultural perspective, students may experience a variety of responses, from anger at having been "lied to" in the past to disbelief or dismissal of the new information. Instructors may feel threatened by the sudden awareness that some of their students know more about certain subjects than they do, and that their ignorance or biased perspective may become all too apparent to the class.

Difficult dialogues can take different forms. The normal classroom conversation can explode into an intense exchange, which may be characterized by friendly intellectual debate, or veer toward strongly worded disagreement, angry confrontation, or personal attack. From mild to mean, these exchanges have the potential for serious polarization, during which the educational process comes to a standstill. In the worst-case scenario, all attempts at dialogue fail, and verbal (or even physical) violence occurs; some students storm out of the room and go so far as to withdraw from the course. Students descend on the department chair or dean to file a complaint, and the campus paper covers the "incident" and calls you in for an interview. When the class meets again, tension fills the air like fumes that any spark could ignite.

Difficult dialogues can also brew in silence. Ironically one signal that a difficult dialogue is simmering is the absence of visible emotion. Students are quiet, dutiful, and respectful but apparently uninterested in discussion. Feelings are heating up, but there is a lid of polite and deadening silence over them. In this situation, little or nothing is communicated among the students. They leave the class muttering, "Man, am I glad this class is over, I hate these PC classes," or "I'm not about to say anything and have everyone jump all over me." Day after day, the instructor finds the same silent resistance. It's a long semester, and the teaching evaluations are a disaster.

However, difficult dialogues can also become exciting educational opportunities. In the best-case scenario, a difficult dialogue occurs and the students and instructor move beyond the discomfort, the fear of confrontation, and the tendency to be judgmental. Students demonstrate a willingness to ask questions. The students become energized and curious, taking conversational risks, and inquiring about what others know and feel. The tension in the situation is not only recognized, but it is used as a lightning rod for cognitive inquiry and insight.

An example of this happened in a class of ours, in which the students were discussing stereotypes as learned behavior. A Latino student said, "I don't like this about myself, but when I see a White man driving a Lexus, I say to myself, 'There goes a CEO, a lawyer, a successful person.' But when I see a Black man in a Lexus, I say, 'There goes a drug dealer.' I learned all this from the media."

An African American young woman replied, "I say 'Go Man,' and I say to you [the Latino student] 'You're wrong and you should know better.'" She then burst into tears and ran out of the room. An older African American woman followed her, signaling to me that she would comfort her. The bell rang, and class was over. A spontaneous difficult dialogue had presented itself.

Before class convened two days later, we prepare a structure for continuing the discussion that included the students engaging in *mindful listening to self* (which we will discuss in greater detail later in the chapter), followed by a period for reflective writing. Then, each student was invited to share one question or feeling they experienced during or after the encounter. The tension and pain that they felt were thus brought out into the open, and the lesson that stereotypes are learned, alive in each of us, and a cause of suffering was more real than any lecture could ever have made it.

Why Are Dialogues About Gender, Race, and Culture So Difficult?

When in a diverse group, people often avoid discussions of race, class, gender, and sexual identity for fear of creating discomfort, embarrassment, or hostility. The avoidance, in the guise of politeness, can take such forms as making light of the topic, shifting topics, or simply ignoring anything said that happens to relate to the topic. This *code of silence* is a reflection of a societal denial that cultural factors matter, and that things such as sexism, racism, and White privilege exists. In the classroom, it can prevent students from gaining experience in difficult dialogues. Because many faculty lack knowledge and awareness beyond their own cultural experience, they feel awkward and timid about discussing—let alone facilitating—student discussions about race, gender, sexual identity, and class issues. In order to avoid feeling that awkwardness or making others uncomfortable, they perpetuate the code of silence.

Race Relations in the United States: Intensely Visceral and Cerebral

Too many people refer to interracial interactions as walking on eggshells, or walking through a minefield. The racial divide is wide with sharp and jagged edges. Many European Americans feel guilty for the legacy of oppression or defensive over their position of historical privilege. They do not feel race privileged. Even when they acknowledge their White privilege, they do not know what to do about it.

Most European Americans believe dearly in the sacred principle of equality and to be called a racist means they are being accused of violating that principle. Being called a racist, for most European Americans, packs the same punch as being called a child molester. For both Whites and people of color, race relations trigger the deeper issues of both identity (Who am I?) and worth (Am I good enough?). Many, if not most, people of color must navigate daily the effects of stereotypes. From subtle to obvious, members of other cultural groups question their worth, judge them to be less qualified, tokens, or a commodity. Many people of color believe they must be twice as good to be perceived as half as much. They get tired of the extra burden of having to navigate the daily tides of racial projections. So, it is understandable why it just seems safer to avoid the topic.

Moreover, because of the inextricable emotional dimension of race relations, most faculty view difficult dialogues as violating academic protocol. The Western academic tradition has typically held emotions to be irrational and not appropriate to the intellectual pursuits of academia. Faculty are trained to emphasize cognitive processes in the classroom, and to treat emotions as private and personal.

Finally, for both students and faculty, difficult dialogues heighten an awareness of personal vulnerability. From a psychological perspective, people craft their identity from the stories they have been told (by family, peers, religious leaders, and society) about what it means to be of a certain race, culture, gender, or sexual identity. Usually, they don't question these identities until others challenge them, which can happen when feeling attacked or spotlighted. Yet, in a classroom with diverse students or a multicultural curriculum, these identity factors (race, culture, gender, class, and sexual identity) can become a point of reference for how students perceive and relate to one another and to the instructor. When instructors deny or ignore the importance of these aspects of identity, they communicate a message to students that the students' feelings in these areas don't belong in the classroom and that perhaps their experiences and knowledge about their ethnicity are not worthy of academic attention. These types of interpretations can contribute to students questioning their overall worth and acceptability to the academic world. And, yet, to acknowledge and discuss them may take instructors outside their academic training and leave them feeling vulnerable.

During difficult dialogues, instructors may feel vulnerable because they don't know when to be the expert and when to let go, when to refer to their own identity and when to refer to the cognitive content. The faculty we work with speak of their lack of intercultural competence. They are embarrassed by how little they really know about the different cultures in the United States. They are often horrified when they realize how few, if any, actual friends they have from a different race or culture, and how few, if any books, movies, plays, and so on, they've read or seen by and about members from a different culture. Faculty report that even when they have friendly intercultural relationships with colleagues, the topic of race or culture rarely arises. As faculty, we are trained to be the experts, to be in charge of a subject matter. Most of us are not experts in race and culture issues. We are out of our element, and when confronted with a lack of knowledge and very different experience we may begin to question our identity and place. No wonder instructors want to defend against this vulnerability by attempting to avoid or contain difficult dialogues. Yet, paradoxically, instructors' awareness and acceptance of their own vulnerability can increase their empathy for their students' vulnerability.

How Can Difficult Dialogues Have Successful Outcomes?

One indication that a difficult dialogue is successful is when students come to integrate cognitive knowledge with emotional responses. Despite the feelings that may be aroused, they become curious about what they don't know or understand, and curious about the feelings as well. As part of this integration, they come to see themselves and their classmates as both emotional and intellectual beings. As they strive to get to know, communicate with, and understand one another, they gain respect for themselves and for their classmates.

Another indication of success is when students begin talking to each other about issues they would normally find threatening. They demonstrate the courage and willingness to ask questions, listen carefully to the responses, and speak honestly about their own perspective. We regularly do a fishbowl exercise after students read McIntosh's (1988) classic essay on White privilege. When White students discuss the essay among themselves, there are two dominant themes: (1) they are truly surprised that not everyone shares the same privileges (for example, not being followed in a store, being able to assume you can buy a house, rent an apartment anywhere you can afford, and so on); and (2) they get defensive and try to pick the essay apart. When the students of color discuss the essay, there are three dominate themes: (1) genuine disbelief and mistrust that Whites don't know they have White privilege; (2) anger about White privilege; and (3) appreciation for McIntosh laying it out so clearly.

In the end, we put the students together and ask them to re-enact the fishbowl conversations using role-play. After the role-play, the difficult dialogue begins. This difficult dialogue is successful when students begin asking questions that reveal their own vulnerability and true curiosity. Examples of questions and statements that may contribute to a genuine dialogue include: What do you see when you look in the mirror, a woman or a White woman? How do you instruct your children on how to handle racial name-calling? Help us understand what it feels like to be White. How is your life at school different from your life at home? How do you handle always wondering if someone is being friendly to you in a store so they can help you or guard you? Taking a risk might also take the form of self-disclosure, such as a story about how the person was oblivious to White privilege or wrongly assumed they were being stereotyped.

A further indication of successful dialogue is when students and instructors begin seeing their vulnerability as a strength. They become aware of the desire to be understood and to understand other human beings across race, culture, and gender lines: this urge to speak genuinely and to understand others becomes stronger than the urge to protect their own perspectives. Paradoxically, successful difficult dialogues often occur when individuals become aware of their defensiveness and have the courage to acknowledge it in the dialogue (for example, "Wow, I'm feeling so defensive right now. I wonder why?"). Instructors can encourage this practice by giving examples from their own experiences that disclose their own defensiveness and stereotyping.

Dealing With Difficult Dialogue:
A Model for Multicultural Inquiry

The following model for facilitating difficult dialogues is grounded in our over 20 years of teaching race-related courses at a racially diverse campus, incorporating ideas from ongoing discussions with many colleagues. It contains four elements:

1. Creating a climate for inquiry

2. Focusing on cognitive inquiry

3. Focusing on emotional inquiry

4. Developing skills for mindful listening

Creating a Climate for Inquiry

In order to prepare students for a difficult dialogue, it is important to create a climate for inquiry within the classroom. This means encouraging students to develop an enthusiasm for seeking, exploring, and loving the questions more than the answers. The following questions can help introduce them to this idea of inquiry:

- What is the goal of inquiry—to find answers or questions or both?

- How are self-reflection and speculation involved?

- What kind of questions do you ask when you are truly interested in inquiry?

- What is involved in an attitude of inquiry?

We offer a perspective from Chodron (1991), who regards the willingness to inquire as "not caring whether the object of our inquisitiveness is bitter or sweet" (p. 3). Rather, genuine inquiry involves the courage to question what we think we already know to be true. Or, put another way, inquiry is finding the questions to our answers. We ask students to consider what it might mean *to not* have a vested interest in whether they liked or didn't like the answer. Would that be possible? What might be the benefits and drawbacks of this attitude?

One way to demonstrate how to transform *answer-driven* statements into *inquiry-driven* questions is for the instructor to put a topic on the board, such as "Therapy and the Single Mother," and then ask the students to generate statements that reflect what they think they know to be true. Students will generally say things like most single mothers are African Americans, or, most are on welfare. After several statements are on the board, the instructor then can ask the students for their sources. Students rarely quote a source; rather, they just assume it's true from the media or have heard it someplace. Even when a more accurate answer is given (for example, most single mothers are White), the instructor does not give away the "right answer." At this point, she continues to encourage the students to inquire more specifically into what they truly know and don't know about the topic and particular clients. They can also be asked to consider what they know about different perspectives on the topic. Are there different sources of knowledge that reflect different views on how, for example, men and women, various cultural groups, gays and heterosexuals, and different socioeconomic classes understand this issue? Finally, the instructor can ask students, if they didn't have to worry about "being right, or smart," what questions would they have about the topic?

Focusing on Cognitive Inquiry

Cognitive inquiry in this model means going beyond learning about the theories and research findings that make up a discipline, to investigate the underlying contexts and assumptions that shape its knowledge base. As all of the chapters in this book have pointed out, psychology has not generally taken sociocultural factors into account, in that its theories and research applications have been developed mainly by and about Euro-American males. It is useful to invite students to consider such things as the origin of the concept of Whiteness and color that continues to be maintained as a social construct within the United States, and the development and significance of ethnic identity within a color-conscious society. Depending on the course, instructors can guide students toward an understanding of differences in values, attitudes, beliefs, and communication norms among ethnic, national, racial, and gender groups, and an understanding of the effects of economic scarcity or abundance on human development and behavior.

Although most instructors are not experts in the cultural, historical, socioeconomic, and social identity dimensions for each controversial issue, they can model and stimulate inquiry by telling students what they themselves don't know and the questions they want to explore. The goal is to cultivate students' curiosity for discovering knowledge. It would be useful, for example, if during a difficult dialogue on "Therapy and the Single Mother," students would want to explore such questions as: What is the ethnic breakdown of single mothers? Where do single mothers live? What is the breakdown by states and cities? What is the educational achievement level for mothers, fathers, and the children? What support (financial, housing, child care, and so on) do grandparents and other extended family play in the life of single parents? What community support is available to single mothers and their children? How does a mother's race, culture, and socioeconomic background influence the responses to the above questions? How do society's values on marriage affect its policies on single mothers? How does the stress of being a single mother affect her mental health?

Asking such questions involves courage, the courage to reveal what one doesn't know. It takes courage and self-awareness to resist getting caught up in an opinion war or a code of silence. This means noticing feelings—of inadequacy, fear, anger, or guilt—that may come up, and knowing how to consider them in ways that enhance rather than undermine cognitive inquiry.

Focusing Emotional Inquiry

Many people believe that knowledge automatically translates into competent and appropriate attitudes and behavior. Yet, information about other cultural and racial groups can actually increase hostility. Racist and culturally based prejudices can exist along with substantive knowledge to the contrary. The issues of race, culture, and gender are decidedly personal and emotional, and if instructors don't take the emotional dimension into account in the classroom, they may not achieve their cognitive goals. Goleman (1995) has made a very persuasive case that emotional intelligence is in fact interdependent with and as important as cognitive intelligence. If emotional inquiry *is* going to be part of the class, then the topic of feelings should be discussed at the outset. What follows are some basic points we've found helpful when we teach emotional inquiry and some methods for facilitating students' inquiry into their own and other's emotional responses. The foundations for our thinking rely heavily on many of the writings of Welwood, most recently *Toward a Psychology of Awakening* (2000) and Gendlin's *Focusing* (1978).

Feelings are temporal. Feelings come and then they go. We can talk about our feelings in the past or imagine them in the future, but they occur only in the present moment. In that present moment we may feel many emotions simultaneously or in rapid succession: emotions that may be conflicting, intense, and confusing, or gentle and easily understood. If a feeling is particularly strong, it may feel like a permanent state, leading to the conviction that something must be done to attend to or alleviate it.

Feelings are not inferences. It is important to help students learn to distinguish between a feeling, such as discomfort, and inferences about the feeling (such as, you are making me uncomfortable, or I don't want to feel this anymore, so I will do something to stop the feeling). White students who feel remorse or anger about the history and state of racism may begin spinning inferences (for example, that this is a terrible country, that racism is not their fault, that people of color must hate them). What happens is that the feeling becomes translated into a particular inference, which allows them to bypass the actual experience of remorse and anger. If unexamined, this kind of inference can solidify and numb other emotions in the process. Students often need assistance discerning the feeling from the inference.

Feelings are often reactive. Feelings are often responses to past experiences, as well as to current stimuli. An emotional reaction to an outspoken classmate may be shaped more by one's cultural background, earlier family dynamics, or previous life experiences than by the actual content of the classmate's utterance. Students need to learn that because feelings are so affected by one's own personal histories, they cannot be trusted as guides for taking rational action in the present.

Emotions and reactions in response to multicultural material. Sue and Sue (1990) have identified the six most common reactions students experience when working with multicultural curricula. They include:

1. Anger, which is often expressed as, Why Blame Me? How dare you? It's your fault.

2. Sadness and remorse, which often translates into, I am bad. I feel so guilty. I don't know what else to do—I feel so sad.

3. Despair often gets communicated as, I can't do anything to change this, and I feel ashamed of being White. I feel like racism will never end.

4. Fear often comes out as, You can't expect me to give up what I've earned, I am scared. They control everything. Why shouldn't they hate me, I'm White, they will just assume I'm like other whites and therefore they will try to hurt me.

5. Intellectualization is a reaction to not wanting to deal with the feelings and comes out in the form of denying the relevancy of feelings and claiming the primacy of the content issues.

6. Withdrawal is another form of not being ready to discuss the feelings and is most often expressed by lowered eyes, silence, and leaving the room.

Noticing and Acknowledging Feelings. Instructors may find it helpful to provide class time to explain the common reactions and feelings and to ask students to add to the list. But, if the instructor stopped here, the discussion about emotional reactions would remain an intellectual issue, so it is important for faculty to give students an opportunity to practice acknowledging their feelings in the moment before they engage in inquiry. They need practice in learning to listen to feelings. To *notice* one's own or another's feelings is to take that moment and check in: What is going on with me right now? What am I sensing is going on with this person right now? Usually what happens here is a jumble of unidentified physical sensations or confused observations, but when given a few moments, the stimuli will settle into a discernible pattern that can be acknowledged, such as, I feel nervous, scattered, hungry, tired, and so on. It is important to tell students that the feelings will change.

Once students have noticed and labeled their feelings, they can then begin to notice the difference between the feelings themselves and the inferences identified with them. For example, a student reported on this process by saying:

> At first, I noticed feelings of hunger and wariness, and then resentment and guilt set in. I first began to think about what I wanted to eat and when I might be able to get a rest. Then the resentment came in that you were making me think about race when I was working so hard and didn't even have time to eat. Then I felt guilty for being so self-centered and for all the racial injustices in the world and that I really had it easy.

When the student reported on this experience in class, we were able to assist the class in discerning the differences between her feelings (hunger, wariness, anger, and guilt) and her inferences (I will eat, rest, blame the instructor for making me think about these things, blame myself for thinking my hunger is more important than racial injustice, and so on).

As the feelings and inferences are identified, the instructor can ask students to explore the emotional content further. Some questions might be: What more is going on underneath this feeling—for example, anger? What am I angry about, really? Why do I want to blame the instructor? What am I afraid of? Why do I get angry when this issue comes up? Unlike cognitive inquiry, where questions get asked and strategies generated for finding out answers, emotional inquiry encourages the asking and holding of the questions. It involves waiting and listening to the responses.

It is helpful to remind students that they don't need to judge, change, deny, or indulge their feelings. Rather they can continue to acknowledge and inquire, and just notice what emerges. It is essential to provide enough time for students to process the feelings they have acknowledged, as well as to invite students to inquire into the relationship between the cognitive content and their emotions.

Developing Skills for Mindful Listening

Listening, once defined by a radio disc jockey as waiting for your turn to interrupt, is better practiced as the full and mindful attention to understanding one's own or another's message. Listening, when engaged mindfully, is the key to establishing an open and inquisitive environment, and is a prerequisite for all the other teaching and learning methods discussed here. Mindfulness, in the Western tradition (Gudykunst & Kim, 1992; Langer, 1989), is the ability to see and transcend the stereotypes, scripts, categories, and automatic reactions that prevent us from responding effectively and appropriately; the assumption is that an act of will is all that's needed to access this ability. In the Eastern tradition, however, mindfulness is a 2,500-year-old practice for cultivating this ability, which allows us to become more open to information and people we might have perceived as different or threatening (Trungpa, 1988).

Mindful listening is a method that is best applied to both listening to self and listening for other. The assumption is that we can best listen to others when we regularly listen to ourselves. Mindful listening to other involves placing the attention on the other and his or her message. The goal is to understand the message from the other person's perspective, not to agree or disagree, win, lose, or make a judgment. The basic instructions for this method include:

Focusing on the Other Person. By holding attention on what the other person is saying and feeling, the listener tries to understand the other's message from the other's perspective.

Trying to Be Nonjudgmental. The listener attempts to communicate the desire to understand, which is markedly different than expressing agreement or disagreement.

Paraphrasing. The listener tries to clarify his or her level of understanding, by repeating back in his own words what the other person has said.

Engaging in Gentle Inquiry. The listener asks questions that will allow him to put himself in the other person's shoes. Gentle inquiry isn't interrogation.

Noticing. The listener seeks conscious awareness of his own internal dialogue and external behavior, which brings him back to focusing on the other person. In this sense it is a self-correcting step.

Because even the most skilled listeners forget these principles, interrupt, and offer agreement or disagreement, it is useful to remind students of the guidelines, and to allow them practice time during each difficult dialogue. It is also important for students to engage in mindful listening on their own. Once learned, it can become a useful habit.

Putting the Model into Practice

When a difficult dialogue arises—or when the instructor anticipates that it might—the following systematic approach of combining mindful listening to self with mindful listening to other can be very useful:

Sit Comfortably. Ask students to sit respectfully (whatever that means to them) but comfortably, to put down pens, pencils, drinks, and so on. They can close their eyes or look diffusely at the floor.

Noticing. Ask students to notice their feelings—both physical and emotional—and their thoughts. Invite them to be gentle with themselves and notice the feelings and thoughts they are experiencing. They are likely to become lost in their thoughts, so encourage them to focus on the feeling as well. If they notice that they are lost in thoughts, they should return to breathing (allow two to five minutes).

Breathing. Ask students to notice their breathing, which may allow them to become aware of their thoughts and feelings (allow two to five minutes).

Focusing. Ask students to focus their attention on a potentially difficult question that is derived from an idea presented in a reading, lecture, or class discussion. Ask them to focus on the question. A helpful metaphor is to have the students ask themselves the question (posed by the instructor), and then as if their mind were a movie screen, to watch what shows up without getting caught up in it (allow two to five minutes).

Waiting. Remind students to wait and hold the question and to try not to analyze or search their minds. Rather, the purpose of waiting is to clear a space so that many thoughts and feelings can make themselves known to the individual. You can remind the students that if they are making inferences by judging or arguing with themselves or others, or if they have drifted off into a daydream, once they notice that, they should acknowledge what they were thinking and return to their breathing and to the question at stake. If they feel sleepy and distracted, or if intense feelings come up, they are instructed to try to just acknowledge that it is happening and then return to their breathing and the question. Remind them that there is no right answer, no need to fix or change anything. Their only assignment right now is to notice and acknowledge that they are responding to this particular topic (allow two to five minutes).

Emotional Inquiry. At this point, encourage students to engage in gentle inquiry in the same way they would if they were listening to another person. The questions might be: What is going on here? Why am I so angry? Why did I wander off and not want to think about the material? Why did I feel so nervous, tired, and so on? (Allow two to five minutes.)

Cognitive Inquiry. Here again, encourage students to focus their inquiry toward the cognitive knowledge. The questions might be: What do I know? What troubles me about this concept? What more do I need to know in order to understand this idea? (Allow two to five minutes.)

Writing. Ask students to write down what they noticed and to describe their experiences with this mode of inquiry. (Allow two to five minutes.)

Discussion. At this point, the instructor can engage in any number of teaching and learning strategies. For example, students can be placed in pairs or groups to discuss the question posed by the instructor, or the instructor can ask for a word, a sentence, or a question from each person that relates to the students' experience with the question. It is helpful to remind students about the principles to practice mindful listening to other. (Allow ten to thirty minutes.)

Taking the Plunge: An Example

Imagine this scenario: It is early in the course, and you have just barely begun to address the concept of mindful listening. After a brief presentation that touches on a multicultural topic, you ask for questions and comments on the lecture and readings. An African American man who is older than most of the other students consistently responds to your questions; he doesn't really answer them, but instead, uses them to espouse his beliefs and views. His statements invariably begin or end with "the White Man." He says the "White Man" did this, "the White Man" did that, and "the White Man" is responsible for whatever. None of the other students, regardless of ethnicity, want to respond to him or draw his attention for fear of being accused of being "the White Man" or "the White Man's lackey."

What do you do? How might you evoke the spirit of inquiry into this situation? Addressing possible cognitive issues and questions, you might begin by:

- Discussing that "the White Man" is a shorthand way of saying institutional racism.

- Establishing a definition for institutional racism.

- Asking all the students: What does "the White Man" mean to them?

- Asking the students: What questions do they have about the phrase "the White Man"?

- Asking students to identify the kind of information they need to know in order to more fully understand what "the White Man" means.

- Inviting emotional inquiry, you might begin by

- Asking the students to take a moment, and notice and acknowledge what goes on inside of them when they hear "the White Man."

- Asking them to inquire into their feelings, in the manner discussed earlier.

After students have had a chance to notice and inquire into their emotions, you can then make fruitful use of one of the writing, discussing, or sharing options described above. The second author of this chapter closes on a personal note. A while ago, in the Academic Senate, a contentious colleague spoke out about the uselessness of establishing a standing committee for Equity and Diversity. Identifying with my judgments, I immediately quit listening and began my plan of attack. I spoke not in response to him but in response to all the other people I knew who had similar opinions. In an "academically civil" way I matched his arrogance with my own and lost touch with my own feelings. What would have happened if I had just listened with an open heart, noticed his feelings and thoughts, and my own? How might I have responded? I don't know, but it would have been different and less arrogant. In those rare moments when I allow myself to feel and be present in the jagged racial divide, I feel so intensely the differences that divide, and, simultaneously, the commonalties that bind.

Increasingly, I find that in those moments when I befriend my own prejudice, ignorance, and emotional tides, I am awed, humbled, and often quite sad and sometimes full of wrath, but also I am more honest and compassionate with my students and colleagues, no matter what their attitudes or messages. Situations hurt, anger, and disturb more. Sometimes the feelings scare me but they no longer scare me off, or not for long. My students' feelings are no longer unwanted, ignored, or intellectualized away. Their feelings are a welcome addition to the classroom. Education—to be relevant, as W. E. B. Du Bois (1973) reminds us—must grow out of the life experiences of those being educated. So the more we can practice listening to our own experiences and each other's we will see, hear, feel, and understand how different and how similar we are. By bringing the confusions and muddy emotions of race relations into the center of the class, we acknowledge and feel the truth of the racial divide and paradoxically by doing so, we begin to feel more connected to ourselves and to each other.

Note

*This chapter was reprinted with permission from Jossey-Bass, a Wiley Company.

References

Chodron, P. (1991). *The wisdom of no escape and the path of loving-kindness.* Boston & London: Shambhala.

Cross, T. L., Bazron, B. J., Dennis, K. W., & Isaacs, M. R. (March 1989). *A monograph on effective services for minority children who are severely emotionally disturbed* [Monograph]. Washington, DC: National Technical Assistance for Children's Mental Health Center for Child Health and Mental Health, Georgetown University Child Development Center.

Du Bois, W. E. B. (1973). *The education of black people: Ten critiques, 1906–1960.* H. Aptheker (Ed.). New York: Monthly Review Press.

Gendlin, E. T. (1978). *Focusing.* New York: Bantam Books.

Goleman, D. (1995). *Emotional intelligence: Why it can matter more than IQ.* New York: Bantam Books.

Gudykunst, W. B., & Kim, Y. Y. (Eds.). (1992). *Readings on communicating with strangers.* New York: McGraw-Hill.

Langer, E. J. (1989). *Mindfulness.* Reading, MA: Addison-Wesley.

McIntosh, P. (1988). *White privilege: Working paper.* Wellesley College Center for Research on Women, Wellesley, MA.

Nieto, S. (1992). *Affirming diversity: The socialpolitical context of multicultural education.* New York: Longman.

Sue, D. W., Arredondo, P., & McDavis, R. J. (1992). Multicultural organizational development: Implications for the counseling profession. *Journal of Counseling and Development, 70,* pp. 477–486.

Sue, D. W., & Sue D. (1990). *Counseling the culturally different: Theory and practice* (pp. 112–117). New York: John Wiley & Sons.

Trungpa, C. (1988). *Shambhala: The sacred path of the warrior.* Boston: Shambhala.

Welwood, J. (2000). *Toward a psychology of awakening.* Boston: Shambhala.

PART II

Gender, Race, Class, Homosexuality, Disability, Immigration, and Animal Oppression in the United States

CHAPTER THREE

Teaching Feminist Pedagogy on Race and Gender

Beyond the Additive Approach?

MECHTHILD NAGEL

Feminist standpoint theory and critical race theory have popularized an *interlocking systems of oppression* approach that raises serious questions about the durability of feminist and antiracist epistemic practices loyal to an "additive" approach (King, 1988/1995; Spelman, 1988). This chapter addresses a dilemma in feminist philosophy: How do we engage effectively with historical texts that marginalize the subaltern other? I argue that the interlocking approach does make our epistemic practices more robustly truth-seeking; however, it seems to undermine the "ampersand" or additive approach that feminist philosophers have used to ferret out discriminatory evaluations in the "classic" androcentric texts and in the contemporary life-world. My question is whether we can continue to teach and investigate race and gender as if they were isolated facts of life or whether we can appropriate a combination of additive and intersectional analysis, which engender a meaningful practice of solidarity.

In their textbook *Theorizing Feminisms*, editors Elizabeth Hackett and Sally Haslanger (2006) ask the following self-reflective study question: "Does thinking about intersectionality reveal weaknesses in Haslanger's discussion of the social construction of gender, Wendell's discussion of the social construction of disability, or Young's discussion of oppression"? (p. 40). I would like to offer an affirmative answer and at the same time point to the difficulty of articulating a rich account of intersectionality of systems of domination in particular when teaching courses on prejudice and discrimination.

I find it troubling that it remains a major challenge for me to teach the interlocking approach to undergraduates in the U.S. context. Perhaps part of the problem is that our textbooks and methodology are overly loyal to the additive distinctions that Deborah King (1988/1995) and Elizabeth Spelman (1988) have argued against over 20 years ago. We simply lack the models that show a different approach. However, two philosophers, who wished to overcome this divide, are Carole Pateman (1988) and Charles Mills (1997). Their seminal texts on the sexual and racial contract, respectively, provided a singular focus and critique on implicit and explicit gender/race bias in the social contract tradition. By authoring a joint book (2007) on these biases and on global dimensions of the racial-sexual contract, Pateman and Mills provided an important philosophical model for an interlocking analysis. Mills, in particular, validates the perspectives of women of color feminists in his pertinent essay "Intersecting Contracts" (2007), since they had historically, philosophically, and legally no privileged access to the racial-sexual contract, and he endorses Crenshaw's analysis that they had in fact been rendered ontologically invisible or suspect (p. 198). Being written out of history and philosophy strengthened Black women's resolve to "talk back" (bell hooks, 1999) and to lay claims to an intersectional analysis of oppression (p. 191). In her paper "Gender and Race: (What) Are They? (What) Do We Want Them To Be," Sally Haslanger (2000) argues that an analysis of gender and race categories should be guided by four concerns "in the fight against injustice": (1) identify persistent inequalities and explain how they are socially constructed; (2) identify the effects of interlocking oppression, following Crenshaw (1993); (3) understand that disciplines themselves such as philosophy, religion, science, and law "might be 'gendered' and/or 'racialized'"; and (4) take into account the agency of those who are oppressed so that they can be empowered as critical social agents (Haslanger, p. 36). I would go further to add (5) a need to decolonize philosophy, giving voice and listening to those—and assigning their writings in our classes—who have been marginalized and silenced in "the canon." Furthermore, rather than "empowering" oppressed people, I would hold with Foucault that power comes from below, and does not need to seek authorization by those who are in privileged positions.

U.S. feminist theory has moved far by first staking out claims in terms of dual systems theory (gender and class oppression as cofoundational), then tri-systems theory (gender, race, and class) to a more nuanced discussion of intersectionality approach of trying to understand how multiple forms of oppression crisscross and sustain privilege as well as discrimination. Textbooks such as James Sterba's *Social and Political Philosophy* (2003) specifically endorse "feminist and multicultural perspectives," but when looking closely, they discuss classical Western texts almost exclusively under the guise of "women as opposed to people of color," which is the typical guise of White solipsism—Whiteness being located in a privileged epistemic position and in fact being central to theorizing about inequalities (cf. Spelman, 1988, pp. 116–120). Even though the juxtaposition of Hobbes's *Leviathan* with diaries from Las Casas describing Spanish imperialism is imaginative and presents students tools for ideological critique vis-à-vis social contract theory, it is incapable of transcending the "ampersand problem" of "women and . . ." (cf. Spelman, ibid.). Sterba's text then reinscribes the ampersand problem in the following way: there are feminist texts and there are multicultural texts, but it cannot be the case that there are feminist texts that are multicultural and vice versa. Clearly, the dialogue with the Western tradition is still lodged within a White context that simply has too few analytical tools for addressing the ontological positionality of nonbinary identities such as "women of color," mixed race people, gender nonconforming or trans people. Elizabeth Spelman (1988) has shown a way of thoughtfully analyzing classical texts and highlighting the ampersand problem, but it seems that her analysis does not make it into philosophical diversity education and the textbooks of the new millennium. There are exceptions, though. Contrasting her position with Marilyn Frye's additive analysis, Sally Haslanger rightly argues, "there are contexts in which being Black *and male* marks one as a target for certain forms of systematic violence (e.g., by the police). In those contexts, contrary to Frye's suggestion, *being male* is not something that a Black man 'has going *for* him'" (Haslanger, 2000, p. 41). In a way, using Foucault's phrase of the homosexual having become a new species, the same can be said of African American men under the state's surveillance:

> Once Blackness and crime, especially drug crime, became conflated in the public consciousness, the "criminalblack-man," as termed by legal scholar Kathryn Russell (1988), would inevitably become the primary target of law enforcement. Some discrimination would be conscious and deliberate, as many honestly and consciously would believe that Black men deserve extra scrutiny and harsher treatment. Much racial bias, though, would operate unconsciously and automatically—even among law enforcement officials genuinely committed to equal treatment under the law (Alexander, 2010, pp. 104–105).

Similarly, although not as well theorized by White feminist philosophers, one could argue that Black women qua raced group face implicit bias that goes beyond a gender cum race construction of social identity. Many Black women writers reveal that they find themselves raced first in a White supremacist society and specifically, vis-à-vis the Prison Industrial Complex: Black women are dramatically overincarcerated in comparison to White women due to the selective enforcement of the War on Drugs (a ratio of six to one; cf. Barry, 2010). While they may have avoided the negative tag of the "criminalblackwoman," Black women, and in particular Black lesbians, have written about the exclusionary practices they experience in history and feminist politics as if they have been treated to a new species being—namely, being treated to many "controlling images" of stereotypes that are rooted in U.S. chattel slavery (Hill Collins, 1990; Davis, 1981; Hull, Bell Scott, & Smith, 1982; hooks, 1981; Lorde, 1984; Combahee River Collective, 1977/83). The mammy, the jezebel, the welfare queen, and the matriarch are some of the enduring racial-sexual stereotypes targeting African American women (cf. Hill Collins, 1990; Riggs, 1987).

Yet, there are occasions where an additive analysis seems to have salience. Linda, a student of mine in a historically White Midwestern U.S. university, did a thought experiment prior to our discussion of the additive analysis. She visited the student union for leisure time activity and wanted to play foosball with a number of students, all of them passing (at least to her) as White men. They refused her offer to play with them. She walked away trying to sort out reasons for this rude refusal. A little later, she went back to see if anybody else had joined them. Sure enough, she spotted an Asian male student who participated. Linda is from Peru and has darker skin color than most students on campus. When she identified the new play situation, she realized it was because of her (perceived) gender, not because of her (perceived) race that prompted the exclusion. Perhaps I should have followed up her important contribution to our class discussion with a reading of Iris Marion Young's classic text "Throwing Like a Girl" (1990). Her text along with the much anthologized essay "Oppression" by Marilyn Frye (1983) are two of the salient philosophical texts in diversity education that still have great pedagogical value introducing the concept of sexist discrimination in isolation from other categories such as race and class. Of course, Frye's text performs a modicum of intersectionality by addressing gender and sexual expression of girls. Frye's examples reflect feminist critiques of the cult of true womanhood, which is an ideal propped up for the benefit of White middle-class U.S. women, yet, interestingly, I find great resonance with her analysis in the diverse classrooms I have taught in U.S. and German academic institutions that have drawn students from across the globe. So there is something about patriarchal ideology that women of diverse ethnic, racial, religious, class, and sexual orientation can relate to.

"Doing" Intersectionality

Feminist sociologists such as West and Zimmerman (1987) have pioneered the study of "doing gender," which has recently found new exploration in the "doing gender diversity" (Plante and Maurer 2009). Black feminists such as Patricia Hill Collins, bell hooks, and Angela Y. Davis have shown the way of an "undoing" of the additive analysis. Their approach has been described as "intracategorical intersectionality" (McCall, 2005, p. 1773) because they tend to focus on neglected identities and social groups (p. 1774) and acknowledge diversity of experiences within these marginalized groups (p. 1782). McCall differentiates the intracategorical complexity from anticategorical (i.e., postmodern or poststructuralist positions) and intercategorical complexities, the latter using categories in a strategic sense to "document relationships of inequality among social groups" (p. 1773).

In her influential pedagogy text *Teaching to Transgress*, bell hooks (1994) writes about influences that have resonated with her politics of location as well as informed her search for truth:

> [With respect to] the discussion of feminism and sexism, I want to say that I felt myself included in *Pedagogy of the Oppressed*, one of the first Freire books I read, in a way that I never felt myself—in my experience as a rural black person—included in the first feminist books I read, works like *The Feminine Mystique* and *Born Female*. In the United States we do not talk enough about the way that class shapes our perspective on reality. Since so many of the early feminist books really reflected a certain type of white bourgeois sensibility, this work did not touch many black women deeply; not because we did not recognize the common experiences women shared, but because those commonalities were mediated by profound differences in our realities created by the politics of race and class (hooks, 1994, pp. 51–52).

It is the case that an additive approach to race, class, and gender furnishes us with analytic tools of understanding these distinct
categories. However, they don't overdetermine the politics of location.
As hooks's reflection points out, the additive analysis gives us very
little insight on the reading predilection of a young woman's epistemic standpoint. Why could the text of a White Brazilian man (who
admitted to sexist bias in his works) have more intellectual appeal
and contribute to the psychosocial and political formation of a young
Black Southern, rural woman than homegrown texts of White women
such as Betty Friedan and Carole Bird, which led to consciousness-
raising of an entire generation of women and no less, to the second
wave of feminism in the United States? Clearly, it is not enough to
"blame" bell hooks for "false consciousness" when she finds Freirian
liberatory education more life-affirming and resonating with her more
profoundly than White liberal middle-class revaluation of U.S. society in the 1960s and 1970s. I imagine that Afro-German women
who met with Audre Lorde in the late 1980s and were inspired to
write internationally acclaimed books (cf. Oguntoye et al., 2007) on
their politics of location found themselves relating much better to
the Afrocentric feminism of a Caribbean woman than to the radical
feminism of a White German such as Alice Schwarzer. Critical race
theorist Kimberlé Crenshaw (1991) famously critiques the additive
approach in the following way:

> Among the most troubling political consequences of the
> failure of antiracist and feminist discourses to address the
> intersections of race and gender is the fact that, to the
> extent they can forward the interests of "people of color"
> and "women," respectively, one analysis often implicitly
> denies the validity of the other. The failure of feminism
> to interrogate race means that the resistance strategies of
> feminism will often replicate and reinforce the subordination
> of people of color, and the failure of antiracism to inter-
> rogate patriarchy means that antiracism will frequently
> reproduce the subordination of women (p. 1252).

Not surprisingly, if the blind spots of additive theory are such
as Crenshaw diagnoses, it follows that "women of color" drop out of
the analysis altogether as the oft-cited poetic book title *All the Women
Are White, All the Blacks Are Men, But Some of Us Are Brave: Black
Women's Studies* (1982) makes obvious.

Spelman's particularity theory has been critiqued as throwing
the baby out with the bathwater. Performing an ideological suspicion

of any kind of generalizing about women as a group has the effect of dismissing any serious interest in studying what is common to women (Mikkola, 2008). I would argue that rather than overgeneralizing womanhood, we need to draw on approaches that sensitively describe women's realities that do not lead to the ignorant position that Friedan's work in particular suffers from. Standpoint theory, especially as conceived by sociologist Patricia Hill Collins, seems to me a salient response to Mari Mikkola's objection to Spelman's theory. McCall (2005) agrees by suggesting that intracategorical approaches toward intersectionality use categories to make generalized claims while avoiding "homogenizing generalizations" (p. 1783).

Hill Collins outlines the promises and pitfalls of an intersectionality theory in a particular nuanced way. Her approach resonates with Linda Martín Alcoff's theory of positionality, which avoids sweeping generalizations, White solipsism, and at the same time a bucolic retreat into reactionary individualism. As Alcoff puts it, "being a 'woman' is to take up a position within a moving historical context and to be able to choose what we make of this position and how we alter this context. From the perspective of that fairly determinate though fluid and mutable position, women can themselves articulate a set of interests and ground a feminist politics" (1997, p. 150). Alcoff thus argues for a politics of identity, where identities serve as a point of departure but never become reified or static.

Hill Collins (1998), too, wishes to reject liberal individualism arguing that it is crucial to differentiate between individualized and group oriented intersectionality analysis. Frankly, it is easier to treat race, class, gender analysis to an interlocking review comparing individuals such as a White woman and a Black woman rather than "muddying the waters" with a group-based contextual analysis of multiple identities. In fact, much of classroom discussions and student essay writing takes on the familiar individualized narrative and Hill Collins holds that "valorization of individualism to the point where group and structural analyses remain relegated to the background has close ties to American liberalism" (p. 207). However, any gain for collective bargaining rights, civil rights for African Americans, or reproductive rights for women have come out of a collective struggle, rather than won by individual state actors. Students who don't understand the "borning struggle" of the Civil Rights Movement adhere to the logic of race, class, gender becoming "defined as personal attributes of individuals that they should be able to choose or reject. Thus, because it fails to challenge the assumptions of individualism, intersectionality when applied to the individual level can coexist quite nicely with both traditional liberalism and a seemingly apolitical postmodernism" (ibid.). What is particularly troubling to her as academic is that intersectionality leaves many peers a bit smug about claiming a piece of the oppression pie or salad. They will advocate a theory of "equivalent oppression," suggesting that all are somehow oppressed, which obscures power relations and hierarchical deployment of racial, gender-specific, and class-based forms of discrimination (p. 211).

In addition to the individualistic and group-based analysis differentiation, Hill Collins also offers insights on the valuation of the race, class, and gender axis of interpretation. For Black women living in the United States, "racism overshadows sexism and other forms of group-based oppression" whereas White women "have difficulty seeing themselves as already part of Whites as a group" (p. 208). She postulates that comparing women across racial lines is fraught with special difficulties. Race-class categories are inextricably intertwined for Black women, which is echoed by bell hooks in the quote above, in large part thanks to the history and legacy of slavery in the United States and its concomitant legal containment of African Americans (p. 209). Arguably, the passage of the 13th Amendment to the U.S. Constitution, which abolished chattel slavery at the same time that it codified state-sponsored slavery within the prison system (cf. Nagel, 2008; and James, 2005), buttressed the intersecting relationship of race and class. "Race operates as such an overriding feature of African-American experience in the United States that it not only overshadows economic class relations for Blacks but obscures the significance of economic class within the United States in general" (Hill Collins, p. 209).

Drawing on Marxist feminist standpoint theory, she notes that the race-class axis of oppression is best seen in practices of segregation (housing, education, jobs) and surveillance (p. 210)—presumably Hill Collins refers here to the intense criminalization of Blacks, outpacing even apartheid policing in South Africa. Standpoint theory is useful because "group location in hierarchical power relations produces shared challenges for individuals in those groups. These common challenges can foster similar angles of vision leading to a group knowledge or standpoint that in turn can influence the group's political action. Stated differently, group standpoints are situated in unjust power relations, reflect those power relations, and help shape them" (p. 201). Obviously Black women are also concerned about the gender axis of oppression, but it is harder to assess with the solidarity ideal that standpoint theory invokes than the race-class axis, because women do not live apart from male family members but live within racialized communities and as such "women remain disadvantaged in seeing their connections with other similarly situated women" (p. 221).

Since Hill Collins hits an impasse explaining the intersections of race and gender, we may turn to Iris Marion Young's classic essay of "Gender as Seriality: Thinking About Women as a Social Collective" (1994). Young usefully distinguishes between women who qua women are associated as if they were in a series, and those self-actualized, politicized women who are group-based and share goals and objectives. Her series conceptualization echoes Hill Collins's perspective, since it takes account that women are not bonding in a "beloved community" but may in fact have very little in common across race, national borders, sexual orientation, and so on. "Membership in the series does not define one's identity. The series is a blurry, shifting unity, an amorphous collective" (Young 1994, p. 728). Women seem to constitute a series in the way that commuters waiting in line for a bus have a common purpose in getting on the bus, securing a seat, and getting to their destination using a particular means of transport. They leave their passive stance toward the practico-inert realities, that is, the life-world they are thrown into, and become self-conscious group members, when collectively—as a group—they rally for better transport schedules, lower prices, safe location of bus stops, thus pursuing a common goal by petitioning city hall. It is ironic that Young should select a bus commuter example, because it is so clearly marked by racial-class segregated realities; very few White women use the bus system in U.S. cities. Young notes further:

> [A]s a series *woman* is the name of a structural relation to material objects as they have been produced and organized by a prior history. But the series *women* is not as simple and one-dimensional as bus riders or radio listeners. Gender, like class, is a vast, multifaceted, layered, complex, and overlapping set of structures and objects. Women are the individuals who are positioned as feminine by the activities surrounding those structures and objects (ibid.).

Building on Young's women as series conceptualization and on her later work in social responsibility, Ann Ferguson (2010) argues that one way out of identity-based projects is to rally for solidarity networks; presumably, she has in mind Young's group-based model that is self-conscious about its aims and objectives. Ferguson finds that such "solidarity practices are becoming an achieved social base through a developing global network of alternative economic, political, and social practices that oppose neoliberal capitalist globalization and other global injustices" (p. 185). Solidarity gestures and collective action arising out of an emotional or a sex-affective (Ferguson, 1989) concern, and commitment to social justice may give us a way out of the impasse lamented by Hill Collins.

However, teaching U.S. undergraduates about solidarity practices is not without problems. I have found that students' first response often is either a moral or cultural relativism defense ("people should pursue whatever suits their moral compass") or a "death by culture" (cf. Narayan, 1997) moral outrage argument ("women in those cultures need to be rescued by us, i.e. the West"). In the latter move, students adopt the "speaking for others" stance that has been problematized by Linda Martín Alcoff, Chandra Talpade Mohanty, Gayatri Spivak, and others. My worry is that if we engage with their texts that interrogate Eurocentrism, cultural imperialism, and so forth, students then withdraw to the other extreme, namely of moral relativism, rather than engage in a nuanced solidarity approach of "listening to and learning from" those who face the devastating effects of neoliberalism.

Concluding, I would argue that it is not appropriate to discard the additive analysis altogether, but when focusing on an interlocking systems of oppression it is important to keep in mind the interlocking and solidarity perspectives of bell hooks, Hill Collins, Young, Martín Alcoff, and Ferguson, if feminist theory continues to have salience as critical social theory and not drift into an idealized theory of justice as fairness as advocated by John Rawls. Furthermore, taking my cue from the classic Black feminist studies book title (Hull et al., 1982), we need philosophy readers that do not engage in implicit bias by labeling all Indians as male and all women qua mothers as White or Anglo when critiquing Locke's contract theory. Interrogating *Race, Class, Gender, and Sexuality* (Zack et al., 1998) and "adding" an intersectionality section at the end of the textbook perhaps is similar to the prevalence of 1980s readers and syllabi that focused on (White) feminist theory and then "stirred in" texts on subaltern subjects at the end of the book and course. Fair enough, several of the articles in Zack's book reflect an interlocking systems of oppression analysis such as bell hooks's article "Talking Sex," in the section on sexuality; however, I am hopeful that we will find a better way to make intersectionality of race, gender, and other categorizations a *central* concern of our analysis in order to "decolonize philosophy." Let me be clear that I do not want to throw out the baby with the bathwater: helping undergraduate students understand key categories of race, ethnicity, gender, sex, and so on, is important to help them getting a richer sense of the world around them; however, if it is done at the exclusion of understanding how these categories intersect with each other, it may lead to an "oppression Olympics" that Audre Lorde (1984) warned against, that is, that some forms of exclusionary or supremacist categorizations are more oppressive than others. Alternatively, students may argue for a relativist moral stance, namely, that "if all find themselves in an oppressive force field, then all of us (or, none of us) are oppressed," a position, which opens the door to the nonsensical "reverse racism." This phrase is an invention of U.S. right wing discourse that was meant to attack affirmative action policies. Inevitably, discussions around race and gender lead to "difficult dialogues" between students and teachers and enrich our sense of being in the world and contributing to one that is free from hierarchical, exclusionary thinking. A utopian goal, indeed, but one that is worth striving for.

References

Alexander, M. (2010). *The new Jim Crow: Mass incarceration in the age of colorblindness.* New York: The New Press.

Alcoff, M. L. (1997). Cultural feminism versus post-structuralism: The identity crisis in feminist theory. In L. Nicholson (Ed.), *Second wave: A reader in feminist theory,* pp. 330–355. New York: Routledge.

Barry, E. (2010). From plantations to prisons: African American women prisoners in the United States. In B. Brooten (Ed.), *Beyond slavery: Overcoming its religious and sexual legacies,* pp. 75–88. New York: Palgrave Macmillan.

Collins, P. H. (1998). *Fighting words: Black women and the search for justice.* Minneapolis: University of Minnesota Press.

Collins, P. H. (1990). *Black Feminist Thought.* New York: Routledge.

Combahee River Collective. (1977/1983). The Combahee River Collective statement. In B. Smith (Ed.), *Home girls, A Black feminist anthology.* New York: Kitchen Table: Women of Color Press.

Crenshaw, K. (1993). Beyond racism and misogyny: Black feminism and 2 Live Crew. In M. Matsuda, C. Lawrence, R. Delgado, & K. Crenshaw (Eds.), *Words that wound,* pp. 111–132. Boulder, CO: Westview.

Crenshaw, K. (1991). Mapping the margins: Intersectionality, identity politics and violence against women. *Stanford Law Review, 43*(6), 1241–1299.

Davis, A. Y. (1981). *Women, race, and class.* New York: Random House.

Ferguson, A. (2009). Iris Young, Global Responsibility and Solidarity. In A. Ferguson & M. Nagel (Eds.), *Dancing with Iris: The philosophy of Iris Marion Young.* Oxford: Oxford University Press.

Ferguson, A. (1989). *Blood at the root: Motherhood, sexuality and male dominance.* London: Pandora Press.

Frye, M. (1983). *The politics of reality: Essays in feminist theory.* Berkeley, CA: Crossing Press.

hooks, b. (1999). *Talking back: Thinking feminist, thinking black.* Boston: South End Press.

hooks, b. (1994). *Teaching to transgress: Education as the practice of freedom.* New York: Routledge.

hooks, b. (1981). *Ain't I a woman: Black women and feminism.* Boston: South End Press.

Hoppe, E. A., & Nicholls, T. (eds.). (2010). *Fanon and the decolonization of philosophy.* Lanham, MD: Lexington Books.

Hull, G. T., Bell Scott, P., & Smith, B. (Eds.). (1982). *All the women are white, all the Blacks are men, but some of us are brave: Black women's studies.* New York: Feminist Press.

James, J. (2005). Introduction: Democracy and Captivity. In J. James (Ed.), *The new abolitionists: (Neo)slave narratives and contemporary prison writings.* Albany: State University of New York Press.

King, D. (1988/1995). Multiple jeopardy, multiple consciousness: The context of a black feminist ideology. In B. Guy-Sheftall (Ed.), *Words of fire: An anthology of African-American feminist thought.* New York: New Press.

Lorde, A. (1984). *Sister outsider: Essays and speeches.* Berkeley, CA: The Crossing Press.

McCall, L. (2005). The complexity of intersectionality. *Signs: Journal of Women, Culture and Society, 30*(3), 1771–1800.

Mikkola, M. (2008). Feminist perspectives on sex and gender. *Stanford Encyclopedia of Philosophy.* Retrieved from website: http://plato.stanford.edu/entries/feminism-gender/#WomGro

Mills, C. (1997). *The racial contract.* Ithaca, NY: Cornell University Press.

Mills, C. (2007). Intersecting contracts. In C. Pateman & C. Mills (Eds.), *Contract and domination.* Cambridge, UK: Polity, pp. 165–199,

Nagel, M. (2008, March). Prisons as diasporic sites: Liberatory voices from the diaspora of confinement. *Journal of Social Advocacy and Systems Change, 1*, pp. 1–31. Retrieved from http://cortland.edu/ids/sasc/content/prison_nagel.pdf

Narayan, U. (1997). *Dislocating cultures.* New York: Routledge.

Oguntoye, K., Ayim, M., & Schultz. D. (Ed.). (2007). *Farbe bekennen: Afrodeutsche Frauen auf den Spuren ihrer Geschichte.* Berlin: Orlanda Verlag.

Pateman, C. (1988). *The sexual contract.* Palo Alto, CA: Stanford University Press.

Pateman, C., & Mills, C. (2007). *Contract and domination.* Cambridge, UK: Polity.

Plante, R. F., & Maurer, L. M. (2009). *Doing gender diversity: Readings in theory and real-world experience.* Boulder, CO: Westview Press.

Pharr, S. (1988). *Homophobia: A weapon of sexism.* Oakland, CA: Chardon Press.

Riggs, M. (Director). (1987). *Ethnic notions: Black people in white minds.* [Newsreel]. San Francisco, CA: California Newsreel.

Russell, K. (1988). *The color of crime.* New York: New York University Press.

Spelman, E. (1988). *Inessential woman: Problems of exclusion in feminist thought.* Boston: Beacon Press.

Sterba, J. (2002). *Social and political philosophy: Classical Western texts in feminist and multicultural perspectives.* Florence, KY: Wadsworth Publishing.

West, C., & Zimmerman, D. (1987). Doing gender. *Gender & Society, 1*(2), 125–151.

Young, I. M. (1990). *Throwing like a girl and other essays in feminist philosophy and social theory.* Bloomington: Indiana University Press.

Young, I. M. (1994). Gender as seriality: Thinking about women as a social collective, *Signs, 19*(3),713–738.

Zack, N., Shrage, L., & Crispin S. (1998). *Race, class, gender, and sexuality: The big questions.* Hoboken, NJ: Blackwell.

CHAPTER FOUR

Beyond the Pale

Reflections on the Vulnerability of Black Life in the United States

MECHTHILD NAGEL

The trope "beyond the pale" seems mostly identified with ghettoization of Jews in Imperial Russia. However, it originated from seventeenth-century British paled settlements in occupied Ireland to keep the Irish rebels out. It denotes a transgression of decency standards, namely the proper place of living for Christian (Anglo or Russian) citizens. What does this trope mean to a colonized, enslaved people, to subjects—not citizens (cf. Mamdani, 1996)? Interrogating the trope of "beyond the pale," the chapter brings into conversation criminological considerations with philosophical ones by focusing on the constructions of normalcy and deviance within the United States. Examples draw on the enduring presence of White supremacy and its intersections with age, gender, sexual orientation, and gender nonconformity. Of particular interest is an elaboration of the fragility of Black life given the specter of mass incarceration. Finally, abolitionist alternatives to the carceral society are explored.

In utilizing the metaphor of *Beyond the Pale*, I want to highlight the endurance of social control ideologies in particular those in the name of White ethnocentric patriotism. They make it possible that some ethnic groups become national scapegoats, usually following a political crisis or war. Some of the worst excesses of casting the subaltern beyond the pale have been the residential schools imposed on American Indians (cf. Andrea Smith, 2005, and Richie's documentary film *Our Spirits Don't Speak English*, 2008), on African Americans (think slavery, Jim Crow, and mass incarceration), on Chicanos who endured the Catholic Church's repressive mission system, and on Japanese Americans who were interned in concentration camps during World War II (cf. Takaki, 1995). More recently, it has affected Muslim and Arab boys and men who were disappeared in federal and local prisons and jails in the aftermath of September 11, 2001. Many of them were eventually deported, and thousands of families left "voluntarily" to Canada (Barlas, 2004). The world over, others, too, are catapulted beyond the pale who defy social ideologies of heterosexism, ableism, and sexual mores such as sex workers, gay, lesbian, bisexual, transgender, queer, questioning, intersex (GLBTQQI) persons, disability activists, people living with AIDS, persons engaged in interracial relationships undermining the de facto policy of anti-miscegenation. Being conferred a status beyond the pale may result in imprisonment or social/spatial dislocation for the crime of transgressing the social norm.

As I have done elsewhere (2008) with the trope of diaspora, I wish to deploy "beyond the pale" specifically to discuss anti-Black racism in the United States. In order to understand the fragility of Black life in the United States, the notion of "pale" is significant in several ways. First, it is a fitting metaphor for the acute color consciousness in the United States, dating back to chattel slavery; that is, the division of labor in the fields and in the master's house according to one's hue; and even today economic, juridical, and psychological rewards come with joining the "pale" complexion of those deemed "White" or "light-skinned" (e.g., Viglione, Hannon, & DeFina, 2011). Second, the device of the pale is a stake used for fencing. Marking the binaries and borders Kipling's tale "Beyond the Pale" advocates:

A man should, whatever happens, keep to his own caste, race and breed. Let the White go to the White and the Black to the Black. Then, whatever trouble falls is in the ordinary course of things—neither sudden, alien, nor unexpected (1888).

This leads to (third) the expectation of normalcy. Whites live within the pale, a place of decency (White supremacy, settler colonialism and concomitant systems of oppression of heteropatriarchy, and ableism) shrouded in the myth of belonging and attaining merit: "I deserve to live in peace even if it's at the expense of others who will live in permanent insecurity or war." The pale then no longer only signifies an object but a place of "possessive investment in whiteness" (Lipsitz, 1998), which purchases security and tranquillity—a gated community. In the color scheme of things, the pale functions in opposition to Blackness, as imperial writer Kipling bluntly asserts, never shall Black (female) bodies meet romantically with White men. In his short story, Blackness signifies both Indian and "going native." Kipling's Anglo male protagonist finds allure in the Indian girl who is in turn brutally mutilated by her own male family members on discovery of the shameful miscegenation of the races. In the United States, Blackness is usually reserved for descendants of enslaved populations or self-chosen immigrants from Africa and the African Diaspora. Herbert Gans (2005) points out that dark-skinned Indians may get honorific White status, not afforded to U.S. born light-skinned African Americans. As Andrea Smith (2011) has put it, anti-Black racism is an expression of *property relations.* Chattel slavery has left its symbolic—and legal—markers in the sense that those who are clearly living "beyond the pale" in the United States are those who pass as people descending from Africa. It is then not surprising that Black Americans are overpoliced and criminalized as "deviants." "Existence in Black" (cf. Lewis Gordon, 1996) means to be imprisoned rather than to flourish in schools and colleges, to be on death row and "slow death row" (life imprisonment) rather than making decisions on corporate boardrooms, on think tanks, and other pinnacles of White, juridical, capitalist institutions.

Beyond the pale then is my way of referencing a void in the language of oppression. After all, the (abnormal) fear of women, gynophobia, can turn into the hatred of women, misogyny. Homophobia commonly is thought of as the fear and hatred of those who are perceived to fall outside heterosexual normativity (cf. Pharr, 1988). What of Afrophobia and miso-negritude? The attitude of contempt and fear toward Black people is clearly overdetermined by socioeconomic and geographic origin markers—one's "Black" heritage has to be traced to Africa, preferably via the transatlantic slave route. A dark-skinned South Asian may not face the anti-Black racism in the same way that an American of African descent does. Despite an increase in articles and books, the term *negrophobia* has not established itself within the United States (Armour, 1997; Bauerlein, 2002; Head Roc, 2007; and James, 1993). Some have identified racial domination in terms of White supremacy (bell hooks and others), African American exceptionalism (Gans, 2005), or White racial framing (Feagin, 2010). Even though it is important to highlight the ideology of Whiteness that is clearly not captured by the concept of racism, either White supremacy or White racial framing, while accurate in depicting racist structures and meanings, do not evoke the emotional power of *beyond the pale*, namely, of incredulity, moral outrage, horror, fear and contempt of the Other, which all lead to moral judgment, dismissal, and denying a people recognition, respect, humanity, security, and safety.

In *Bowling for Columbine*, Michael Moore (2002) shows a fictitious clip mocking the *COPS* TV show: a White businessman in a suit being stripped and spread-eagled—clearly, the image of an oxymoron. I vividly remember that the cinema audience laughed at this mockery because to them, it wasn't credible; such act of dehumanization is plainly absurd. Contrast this with the daily act of "assuming the position" by Black male youth ("walking while black") when confronted with a roving police officer in Anytown, USA, suspecting them of gang activity (Alexander, 2010). White men cannot be thought of as "property" to be disposed of at the owner's leisure—yes, as workers they are exploited and occasionally killed due to workplace "benign neglect" of safety features, and so on—but they are not brutalized and living beyond the pale in the way the Black subaltern subject has been for centuries. Moore's liberal critique does not escape from the logic of racism either. In her incisive critique, Kyla Schuller (2003) argues that Moore reinscribes rather than mocks White supremacy:

> [W]hen taken with Moore's subsequent pitching of a show entitled "Corporate Cops" that hunts down corporate criminals, Moore himself seems to be acting the role of a cop tracking down pollution. This self-positioning with the state, or even of replacing the state with his own surveillance, reinforces that the Americans who matter to Moore are those who possess and enforce political power. It further constructs the residents of South Central as shadowy, underground figures who serve only to solidify the authority of white liberal hegemony.

This essay then is a modest attempt to put into relief those shadowy, underground figures who transgress the established White supremacist settler order. Are they marooned outlaws who have nothing to lose but their chains?

The Worth of Black Life in the United States

Let me begin with the state of White supremacy during Obama's presidency, focusing on a single case that just surfaced nationally in February 2011. In 2010, Chad Holley, a 15-year-old got attacked by a police car (might this be considered a deadly weapon?), and then surviving the hit, was further brutalized by Houston's police, including being kicked in the head. Tuning in to blogs, whether it is CNN or another mainstream press, which shows the video footage of the young man being treated as a football, one gets the impression that the near act of lynching was provoked by proper moral outrage: the cops did what they have to do to teach a youngster, who was on the run, a lesson. This was not unlike the sentiments we heard when the police chased down Rodney King; that he was almost killed by deadly blows to his head was not noteworthy because he should have just pulled over instead of risking officer's lives chasing him down. Consider the demonic kicking and blackjacking of defenseless journalist Mumia Abu-Jamal, found near a crime scene of slain police officer Daniel Faulkner in 1981. Abu-Jamal (1995) writes as a marooned abolitionist on Pennsylvania's death-row, "confessing" to be thankful to the nameless White undercover cop who kicked him straight into the Black Panther Party when Abu-Jamal was 15 years old. Repression always engenders resistance.

Such is the response to police brutality by a White incredulous audience: unlike Kipling's White man going in drag (as native woman) and being horrified at the level of the "natives" brutality meted out against his lover, no significant moral outrage occurs when U.S. Whites view—and expressly condone—crass terror directed against the un-paled outlawed humans. It is just normal to witness "police misconduct" of Black male and female bodies, before they get thrown into jail, only to be accused of "resisting arrest," or "assaulting an officer" in addition to any other charge real or imagined. It is a variation on a theme, explored in Fanon's *Black Skin, White Masks* (1967). As Lewis Gordon notes "Frantz Fanon had argued, that the West had no coherent notion of what it means to be normal and black. The former was defined as not black, and the latter was defined as normal only through being abnormal" (2011, p. 126). Black people (especially in a country under the enduring legacy of chattel slavery) are naturalized as deviant and therefore, it is perfectly normal to treat Blacks qua suspects "abnormally." Thus, we note the paradoxical finding: Black citizens who attempt to desert the status of living "beyond the pale" by suing for the right of dignity and integrity of personhood deserve no "legal standing." In the time-honored racist tradition of landmark decisions, namely *Dred Scott v. Sanford* (1857) confirming chattel status and *Plessy v. Ferguson* (1896) reiterating it as neochattel status, that is, Jim Crow, Black plaintiffs are painfully reminded of their tenuous citizenship status. A century later, in *City of Los Angeles v. Lyons* (1983), the era of the New Jim Crow, the U.S. Supreme Court denied relief to plaintiff Adolph Lyons, who petitioned for his safety and human rights by challenging the chokehold practice of the Los Angeles Police Department, which traumatized him; instead "Lyons would have to show that he was highly likely to be subject to a chokehold again," a practice which had already killed twelve Black men (Alexander, 2010, p. 126). With tortured logic, the Court qualified the meaning of standing:

> Lyons would have had not only to allege that he would have another encounter with the police but also to make the incredible assertion either (1) that all police officers in Los Angeles always choke any citizen with whom they have an encounter, whether for the purpose of arrest, issuing a citation or for questioning, or (2) that the City ordered or authorized the police to act in such a matter (Alexander, 2010, p. 127).

Justifiable anguish and fear of police encounters are thrown into the theater of the absurd (again, what to an African American is the meaning of living *within the pale?*) by the U.S. Supreme Court's careful argumentation to defend the colorblind status quo ante. It did so again in the *McCleskey* death penalty case, even in the face of vast credible scientific evidence of the embarrassing fact of anti-Black racism. Named after then-law professor David Baldus, his extensive study of over 2000 capital punishment sentences (CP, hereafter) in Georgia concluded the following:

> Defendants who kill whites get CP in 11 percent of cases
> Defendants who kill Blacks get CP in 1 percent of cases
> CP in 22 percent cases of Black defendant, white victim
> CP in 8 percent cases of white defendant and white victim
> CP in 1 percent of cases of Black defendant and Black victim
> CP in 3 percent of cases of white defendant and Black
>   victim (Baldus, Pulaski, & Woodworth, 1990, p. 315).

Black defendants who kill Whites have greatest chance of getting the death penalty (cited in Duncan, n.d.).

Justice Powell, writing for the majority, never explains why *McCleskey's* Eighth Amendment claim based on the statistical evidence failed to "demonstrate 'a constitutionally significant risk of racial bias.' Rather, Justice Powell's rejection of statistical evidence of discrimination in the death-sentencing context bespeaks an unwillingness to destabilize the capital-sentencing process in any fundamental respect, *regardless of such evidence*" (Baldus, et al., 1990, p. 380; emphasis mine).

Abu-Jamal (1995) cites Justice Powell: "'McCleskey's claim, taken to its logical conclusion, throws into serious question the principles that underlie our entire criminal justice system.'" And Abu-Jamal's rejoinder? "How true. *McCleskey* can't be correct, or else the whole system is incorrect" (Abu-Jamal, 1995, pp. 77–78). Thus, the criminal justice system is put on trial—the ruse of fairness, justice, and impartiality is indeed that—a ruse; and this death penalty case shows vividly the criminal injustice machinations of the system. Let's not forget that prisoner McCleskey was put to death. After his retirement from the bench, Justice Powell noted that he erred in the *McCleskey* case (Dow, 2011). It is noteworthy that today, thanks to the Innocence Project, over 100 people have been freed, and 70% of them are wrongfully convicted African Americans; in rape cases which involved White women as victims, 75% of Black men have been found innocent (Smith & Hattery, 2011). Ida B. Wells (Greaves, 1989) and Angela Davis's (1981) analyses of the myth of the Black rapist, in the nineteenth- and twentieth-century, respectively, still holds true today. African Americans are just not as valuable human beings as any other ethnic group in America, and they may be found guilty, before any use of DNA, and so forth, will find them truly innocent of all charges. Even where they are not criminalized, Blacks in America face economic disadvantages and severe discrimination in the workforce. Even during boom times, unemployment in the Black community remains in the double digits.

During the recent recession, the term *toxic asset*, characterizing subprime loans, became common knowledge. Social critic Sasha Abramsky (2010) has suggested that it is not too farfetched to suggest that this term can be used to showcase the ugliness of White supremacy, namely, that some people in the polity are just beyond redemption—they are "toxic persons" and their status condemns the future generation to a similar level of destitution. In the aftermath of the 2008 financial meltdown, they also bore the brunt of housing foreclosures and unemployment. However, because they are Black and poor, their victimhood on account of the violence of racism and poverty will never be acknowledged—or it will be trivialized as we have seen with numerous police acquittals (witness police assaults on King, Louima, and Diallo). Yet the media will always accentuate Black suspects' perpetrator status. Let us recall how O. J. Simpson's mug shot on the cover of *Time* was altered—his hue was darkened. Skin tone matters. Black women perceived to have light skin saw their prison sentence reduced by 12% and their time served by 11%, according to a study involving over 12,000 North Carolinian Black women (Viglione, Hannon, & Robert DeFina, et al., 2011).

Whose Violence?

It's interesting to see how the state's violence morphs effortlessly into "ghetto violence." Here's what Frederic Goodwin said a week after the opening of White police officers trial who participated in the brutal beating of Rodney King:

> If you look, for example, at male monkeys, especially in the wild, roughly half of them survive to adulthood. The other half die by violence. That is the natural way it is for males, to knock each other off and in fact, there are some interesting evolutionary implications of that because the same hyper-aggressive monkeys who kill each other are also hypersexual, so they copulate more to offset the fact that more of them are dying. Now, one could say that if some of the loss of social structure in this society, and particularly within the high impact inner-city areas, has removed some of the civilizing evolutionary things that we have built up and that may be it isn't just the careless use of the word when people call certain areas of certain cities jungles, that we may have gone back to what might be more natural, without all the social controls that we have imposed upon ourselves as a civilization over thousands of years in our evolution (Goodwin, 1992, cited in Feder, 2007, pp. 73–74).

Goodwin's infamous "Violence Initiative" (a curious framing by someone living "within the pale") was thought to be short lived for its brash eugenics and Social Darwinist ideology, after all he was forced to resign as director from one government agency (Alcohol, Drug Abuse, and Mental Health Administration), only to be rewarded with the directorship of National Institute for Mental Health shortly thereafter, encouraged by Senator Orrin Hatch (Feder, 2007, p. 75). And he continued to enforce his message by giving drugs such as Ritalin to misbehaving, unruly children, disproportionately singling out urban kids in his studies under the guise of a zealous missionary rescue: if they receive serotonin-enhancing medicine in their youth for their defective genes, they are unlikely to grow up to become delinquents and criminals. A Binghamton University student shared with me that in 1993, his second-grade class was indeed subject to such "study" in his school in the Bronx: all students were declared ADHD patients and sent home with a standard letter suggesting to their parents that they may administer Ritalin to their children to curb the affects of ADHD. No testing was done on the students whether they in fact showed any medical symptoms. He credits his mother for challenging the school administration and opting out of the "treatment."

I argue that a "color-blind" version of this "Violence Initiative" has become the G. W. Bush era's intensification of "Zero Tolerance Policy" (started in schools in the late 1980s with drug education programs), and Ritalin administered to young bodies has become so pervasive across the United States that it has recently become the subject of mockery (Robinson, 2010). Furthermore, the unspoken theme of the "Violence Initiative" is a continuation of a theme to hound and mock Black women who are cast as uncaring, absentee mothers and matriarchs.

This theme goes back to Senator Daniel Patrick Moynihan's infamous "Report on the Negro Family" (1965), which he penned to President Johnson at the height of the Civil Rights Movement. Moynihan opined: "In essence, the Negro community has been forced into a matriarchal structure which, because it is so out of line with the rest of the American society, seriously retards the progress of the group as a whole, and imposes a crushing burden on the Negro male and, in consequence, on a great many Negro women as well" (1965). In response to such inflammatory rhetoric, Ryan (1976) coined the term *blaming the victim* because some of Moynihan's analysis lent itself to castigating women in particular for the putative moral failures of the Black community (i.e., out of wedlock births, low marriage rates, etc.), rather than systemic oppression. By the 1980s, the image of the welfare queen was indelibly fixed onto the Black family, even though more Whites were means-tested recipients (61%) than Blacks (33%), according to statistics of the 1990s Census Bureau. Feder notes that even though "welfare queen" and "violent youth" appeared in the media, they were rarely linked in an explicit fashion. However, a family that is deemed pathological (i.e., beyond the pale), vis-à-vis the normative patriarchal White family, sprouts "violent predators," and the root cause of these ills lies with Black mothers. Lee Daniel's film *Precious* (2009, based on Sapphire's novel *Push*) could be read as reinforcing the myth of the matriarchal mother who is depicted as grotesque and monstrous. White patriarchal (*All in the Family*) values signify order, tranquillity, and safety.

As Megan Sweeny points out prior to the Civil War "criminal women of all races have been deemed more depraved than criminal men and beyond hope of redemption. Moreover, African American and immigrant women, who could never be restored to the White, middle-class standard of 'true womanhood,' constituted a disproportionately large percentage of women incarcerated" (2010, p. 24). Moynihan's depictions of Black mothers as overbearing matriarchs thus cements the enduring legacy that Blacks in America are out of step with standard family values (i.e., White, patriarchal values) and not redeemable; they ought to be treated with "benign neglect" (cf. Davis, 1981).

Perhaps Goodwin and Moynihan's "initiatives" also bear some responsibility for the euphemistically named Adoption and Safe Families Act (ASFA, 1997), which has hugely impacted incarcerated parents (see Lee, Genty, & Laver, 2005, and below), particularly the Black community. As Feder reports Goodwin was greatly interested in the primatology research of Stephen Suomi (hence the connection of "monkeys" with "urban jungle"), who hypothesized that infant monkeys separated from the biological mothers and raised in "foster care" had "poor early attachment," low levels of serotonin, and thus were prone to violence (Feder, ibid., p. 82). By extension, clearly, delinquent mothers are to blame for young male "superpredators." ASFA then suggests a bucolic retreat from jungle life by insuring that children in foster care get adopted out as soon as possible—even and especially in cases where the parent's "abandonment" is a state-sponsored measure rather than due to a parent's own volition, namely being subjected to imprisonment in distant places or diasporic sites (Nagel, 2008).

Distance matters, in geographical and psychic terms. Children's visitation of their parent in a distant prison across states, ocean (in the case of Hawaii) or counties is thus often made impossible due to material, temporal, or other constraints such as a state agency's denial of visitation requests. The ASFA law is a haunting reminder of the endurance of slavery—that has never gone way—and its devastating effect on families, especially Black and Latino families, who are facing the brunt of the incarceration frenzy (cf. Nagel, 2008). New York's 2010 ASFA reform bill suggests that discretion can be used in parental termination cases. Yet in some jurisdictions, parental termination has actually increased since the passage of the reform act, and after review of a few cases, I come to the conclusion that it can only be ascribed to administrative punitive enforcement and blatant (illegal) disregard of the interests of both children and incarcerated parents. ASFA has facilitated the "sale" of children to more deserving foster parents who are also coerced into adoption. Each successful placement awards the Department of Social Services with cash.

Adoptions are also popular with foster parents, because they will receive child support until the child's 21st birthday. What remains of discretion in an era of "incentives" given over to the foster care cum adoption services-industrial complex that trump parent-child unification? It is important to be suspicious of so-called reform laws and understand their unintended consequences, which might derail the decarceration process. Once the child is adopted, it is virtually impossible for the incarcerated parent to trace the whereabouts of the child, unless the adult child tries to begin the arduous process of reestablishing contact with the biological parent(s).

Arguably, Alexander's description of the era of mass incarceration as "New Jim Crow" could be more aptly named "neoslavery" given a multitude of policies, laws, and policing methods, which are mutually reinforcing each other to keep Black people, and increasingly Latinos, beyond the pale. However, slavery has not been eliminated with the passage of the 13th Amendment, rather this very amendment allowed for the codification of slavery where freed persons (and others) were found duly convicted of a crime. Thus imprisonment gave rise to the idea of a prisoner being a "slave of the state" lacking any constitutional rights (*Ruffin v. Commonwealth*, 1871). If being within the pale constitutes order and safety for the subject, the prison complex clearly signifies the penultimate place of indecency for the outlawed subject. Death row as well as prolonged segregation into a tomblike cell catapults the outlaw into the ultimate abyss, being deprived of the possibility of tainting humanity or ever reclaiming his or her own humanity.

Transgendered Afrophobia

While Audre Lorde implores us not to engage in an "oppression Olympics," it is difficult to ignore the social identities of gender nonconforming people. Transphobia, especially faced by persons of color, again, in particular by Black trans persons, has been noted as contributing to extreme violation of their human rights—in and outside prisons. The vulnerability, especially for trans women, is exacerbated for those who due to the criminalized activities are incarcerated, as shown in the salient film *Cruel and Unusual* (Baus, Hunt, & Williams, 2006). It follows the life of five trans women who are humiliated, and subjected to ridicule and rape in men's prisons; furthermore, one of them who is denied hormonal treatment takes matters into her own hands and survives a self-inflicted penectomy. Furthermore, the film showcases the highly problematic policy of incarcerating trans women in men's prisons, violating the trans person's human rights and sense of gender identity (cf. Grant, Mottet, & Tanis, 2011). Transphobia in schools and homes leads to disproportionate homelessness among trans youth and the acute discrimination continues to follow them into shelters and prisons that assign gender segregation according to birth sex (Ray, 2006). Transphobia is exacerbated by racism, high levels of unemployment, and poverty (Mogul, Ritchie, and Whitlock, 2011). An expansive survey of 6,450 transgender and gender non-conforming participants highlights enormous challenges they face in terms of individual as well as institutional forms of oppression:

> Discrimination was pervasive throughout the entire sample, yet the combination of anti-transgender bias and persistent, structural racism was especially devastating. People of color in general fare worse than white participants across the board, with African American transgender respondents faring far worse than all others in most areas examined (Grant et al., 2011, p. 8).

For example, 60% of Black transgender participants report harassment and assault by the police in comparison to 24% of White respondents (Grant et al., p. 6). Returning to our indicators, above, gender nonconformity contributes to higher criminalization and incarceration rates, and those rates are even higher for those who are socially disconnected (e.g., lack of accepting family members), people of color, and poor—many experience poverty as a direct result of gender transitioning.

The School-to-Prison Pipeline and Its Gendered and Racialized Dimensions

The world over, when it comes to sentencing and incarceration, the focus inevitably is on boys and men. The much-touted horrible statistic of one in three Black men in the United States will find himself behind bars in his lifetime is exasperated with respect to those youth who drop out of school: over 60% of Black young men who don't finish schooling wind up in the criminal justice system (Western & Pettit, 2010). Black women have faced an astronomical rise in incarceration rates since the beginning of the War on Drugs. "In 2006, one in every 279 African American women was behind bars, compared to one in every 1,064 white women" (Barry, 2010, p. 75). Black women's and girls' rate of imprisonment has outpaced that of men and boys, which has led to a massive expansion of state and federal prison construction, unparalleled in the rest of the world (cf. NCCD, 2010). Thus, the United States is in the unenviable position of being the world's foremost prison nation: constituting 5% of the world's population, it incarcerates 25% of the world's prisoners (Webb, 2009). Even more astonishing is the fact that while Black persons making up 13% of the U.S. "free" population, once imprisoned, they constitute the majority of prisoners and death row candidates. Some jurisdictions have even worse rates of criminalization of Black male youth; Madison, Wisconsin, which is in Dane County, has a Black population of 8%, yet 50% of folks arrested a year are Black. A 2009 taskforce "found that at any given time, nearly half of the county's black men between 24 and 29 are in prison, jail or under some form of state supervision. By comparison, about 3 percent of white men in that same age group are under some type of state correctional control" (Hall, 2011).

However, we see in the United States that younger defendants, including girls, are targeted by the criminal justice system. Black girls receive the brunt of the policing attention. Much of the criminalization aspects of youth start with school suspensions especially given the "Zero Tolerance" policies that have accelerated veritable repression across the U.S. school systems.

According to a recent study (Losen and Skiba, 2010), Black girls "were suspended at four times the rate of white girls" in middle schools. The "racial threat hypothesis" has also found renewed attention vis-à-vis school sanctions. A nationwide study of 294 public schools notes an increase of punitive measures such as suspension and expulsion where there is a proportionate increase of Black students in relation to White students. Black students then tend not to receive more benign sanctions such as parent-teacher conferences or guidance counseling (Payne and Welch, 2010). This is echoed in a recent study "Education Interrupted" by New York Civil Liberties Union (2011):

> Students with disabilities are four times more likely to be suspended than students without disabilities. Black students, who comprise 33 percent of the student body, served 53 percent of suspensions over the past 10 years. Black students with disabilities represent more than 50 percent of suspended students with disabilities. Black students also served longer suspensions on average and were more likely to be suspended for subjective misconduct, like profanity and insubordination (NYCLU, 2011, p. 8).

Black girls who talk back are singled out for repressive punishment, and much evidence has surfaced that school suspensions
are correlated to a higher likelihood of school dropouts and spells of
imprisonment.

Queer girls also find themselves at peril of facing sanctions in
schools, even at a higher rate than queer boys. Their consensual sexual practices "more often trigger punishments than equivalent opposite-sex behaviors." Furthermore, "[a]necdotal reports have suggested
that nonheterosexual girls may be particularly overrepresented in the
juvenile-justice system. Scholars have suggested that the overrepre-
sentation of nonheterosexual girls may relate to the historical role
of the juvenile-justice system in policing girls' sexuality, as well as
a heightened juvenile-justice system and media opprobrium directed
at girls with 'aggressive' or 'masculine' gender presentations" (Himmelstein & Brückner, 2010). This study does not highlight the intersection of perceived sexuality and race/ethnicity, yet from Dewey's
studies of Illinois reformatories (2010) we know that Black lesbians
faced harsher punishment than White lesbian prisoners. Historically
and ideologically speaking, girls and women have been sanctioned
for status crimes (prostitution, running away) and within prisons for
"talking back" when such "crimes" have been of little significance for
"free" and incarcerated boys and men. The White middle-class het-
erosexist ideology of the Cult of True Womanhood, invented around
1820s, continues to hold persons perceived to be girls or women to
standards of passivity, domesticity, and Christian virtues which are
enforced in public patriarchal institutional settings (schools, courts,
prisons, workplaces, etc.). Clearly, gender nonconforming persons will
find themselves othered and face marginalization in myriad ways,
unless they find ways to resist the repression.

Beyond Reform: Resisting and Abolitionist Politics

How do we dismantle White supremacy and its multiple ways of reinforcing racism through other systems of oppression? In the "prison
of slavery," as Angela Y. Davis (1998) has put it, Black people experience "natal alienation and social death" (cf. Patterson, 1982), and
according to Noelle Chaddock Paley, they increasingly face "pre-natal
alienation" due to the horrendous conditions of jails and prisons,
inimical to the well-being of pregnant women (2010). The specter of
the 13th Amendment still looms large in its twisted logic of setting
enslaved people free, at the same time deeming them people with
abstract rights but depriving them of such rights once entering the

prison milieu. What gives? To date, the United States is the only country in the world that sanctions indentured servitude and slavery through the exception clause of the 13th Amendment. Abolitionists of prisons have capitalized on this fact, and we ought to be vigilant until the last vestiges of slavery or the New Jim Crow have been dismantled. If we simply focus on reforms, as National Association for the Advancement of Colored People's (NAACP's) report on prisons and the education-to-prison pipeline does (April 2011), it will, at best, ameliorate dangerous conditions in jails, prisons, detention centers, camps, secret sites run in collusion with the CIA worldwide, and so on, but do little to contribute to decarceration. However, it is important that Black civil rights organizations begin to develop a focused vision to roll back the attack on the Black community. Yet, NAACP's report uses the polite term *over incarceration* in its subtitle rather than the more politically charged term of *mass incarceration*.

Women of color have been particularly active in coalitional work with the trans community in critiquing the rapidly increasing rate of criminalization of girls and women of color as well as trans people of color in the U.S. Justice Now, the National Network for Women in Prisons, and Incite! Women of Color Against Violence have been in the forefront of advocacy. The group Incite! joined the antiprison group Critical Resistance in a manifesto that underscores the penal abolition emphasis in working to end state violence and interpersonal conflicts. They critique liberal feminist collusions with the state and show the state actors' contempt for the rule of law vis-à-vis people of color and trans people and/or Two-Spirit people. What tends not to get theorized by these groups is a focus on disability activism, as youth who have disabilities also get stigmatized and targeted for social control, and even labeled as terrorist (Nocella, 2011).

Instead of tinkering with reform measures, we urgently need abolitionist principles, if we want to start believing in the children and assisting them in fulfilling their dreams of a better future. If not, we could be stuck in a vicious cycle, where the Upstate New York (White) child wishes to be a prison guard of Black and Brown people, and the Black male child defers his wish by first going to prison "to put that behind me, so that I then can go to college when I am grown up" (actual conversation with a 6-year-old). That child has already internalized the logic of targeted mass incarceration, namely that prison is both a certain destination and home for so many of his Black male relatives, and he might as well join them in a rite of passage to manhood, while counting his blessings for not having been shot to death before adulthood. "Welcome home, brother" is indeed a common greeting for the nervous, first arrival who walks through the prison gate in upstate, rural prisons; and he will not be surprised to see so many familiar faces from his neighborhood in downstate New York (cf. Elijah, 2007; Nagel, 2008). Nevertheless, the person marked as felon is stigmatized by his community, as Alexander (2010) movingly describes. I would add that Black women have to endure an even greater burden of shame, especially when dealing with loss of parental rights, since they are considered the cultural bearers and pillar of the community (Johnson, 2004). Shame and guilt are debilitating emotions; instead, the formerly incarcerated along with families of incarcerated as well as community organizations, especially religious and educational institutions, have to build a new civil rights movement to counter the despair of living beyond the pale. Much could be learned from the Latino spearheaded immigration movement, which has also seen many of their people go to jail and secret federal detention sites where they languish before being deported to Mexico or other countries in the Global South. Their demand of ending racial profiling and arrests of immigrants without papers has turned into a victory when the Department of Homeland Security announced in August 2011 that immigrants without criminal histories will no longer face the threat of immediate deportation but instead might be eligible for work permits. Even more impressive is the coalition of Latinos and Blacks united for immigration reform in Mississippi that had the effect of killing all 33 anti-immigration bills in the State Senate thanks to the tireless efforts of Black lawmakers (Eaton, 2011). Such large-scale coalitions that combine immigration, civil rights with workers' rights are needed to tackle the behemoth of the criminal justice system. It can begin with simple small-scale acts of protest. In 2003, I interviewed a Malian Department of Justice chief administrator who was shunned along with his children by people in the streets. They told his children that "your father is a thief—he is stealing people," that is, putting them into jail with long prison sentences. He shared that since hearing their protest, he had a change of heart and is more interested in abolitionist practices than ever before.

Moving Beyond "Beyond the Pale"

Wilson (2011) points out that given the devolution of factory jobs and the shift toward suburban service jobs, Black women now have a greater chance of attaining employment than Black men, since "low-skilled black males are perceived as dangerous or threatening" and thus not suitable to be in front-line customer service roles (pp. 18–19).

William Julius Wilson's agenda includes job creation, urban renewal benefiting Black people, better public education, and strengthening unions. This is all well and good, but it is a myopic proposal, especially in light of his own research, namely that Black people, and Black men in particular, are considered a threat in and outside urban America. Judges give out higher bail and harsher sentences to Black defendants than Whites (Abrams, Bertrand, & Mullainathan, 2011), and probation officers tend to deny leniency and diversion programming to Black youth (Leiber & Brubaker, 2011). When young men are accustomed to "assume the position" when they walk their streets and are frisked by police (Parsons-Pollard, 2011), and this continues to be the case while a biracial man resides in the White House, there is little hope that things will shift dramatically, even if there is a concerted economic and educational revitalization plan in place in multiracial or Black cities.

It is time for a reconsideration of an amnesty proposal first raised by the Black Panther Party's Ten Point Program *before* the advent of mass incarceration of Black people. The program tackled comprehensively the police, military, jobs, education, land, and housing. Today, reforms are occasioned in a toned-down piecemeal approach. *Amnesty* and *reparations* are fighting words of the past, which demand legal redress. The more genteel terms used by lawmakers are *racial threat hypothesis, racial impact study,* or *cross-race identification* that make note of the school-to-prison pipeline or life-on-the-installment plan (considering the high rate of recidivism). Politicians have started to look at a witness's often-faulty identification of a suspect in a line-up. For instance, New Jersey's decided to solve the cross-race identification problem by giving a statement to the jury:

> You may consider the fact that an identifying witness is not of the same race as the defendant and whether that fact might have had an impact on the accuracy of the witness' original perception and the subsequent identification. You should consider that in ordinary human experience, people may have greater difficulty in identifying members of a different race (cited in Deters, 2008).

However, as of Summer 2011, we see a backlash in many jurisdictions that wish to curtail racial impact legislation and New Jersey's jury instructions may be repealed as well. To address racial inequalities in death sentences, North Carolina's Racial Justice Act (1998) prohibits exclusion of death qualified, that is, persons who signal their support of capital punishment, African American jurors. As of 2010, the updated law also requires that courts reverse death penalties for litigants who enter a life sentence for any death row defendant who proves that race was a factor in the imposition of the death sentence. They would be resentenced for life imprisonment (ACLU, 2010). What underlies all these reform-minded legal discussions is a civil libertarian concern about anti-Black perceptions. Will it be enough to undo "the New Jim Crow"—a racial caste system? Even though various alternatives to incarceration reforms have occurred, especially vis-à-vis all youth, "DMC [disproportionate minority contact] rates have not decreased and in some jurisdictions they have worsened" (Coleman, 2011, p. 22). New York City is a case in point. Its police force continues to engage in arbitrary harassment of Blacks: "New York City's African American population is approximately 23 percent, but African Americans make up 50.6 percent of persons in stop-and-frisk encounters" (Sentencing Project, 2011).

Interestingly, Mumia Abu-Jamal (2009) notes in his book on jailhouse lawyering that these "street lawyers" who acquire unconventional legal skills while imprisoned are at risk of more harassment, brutalization, and facing contempt from the prison staff than Black prisoners, political prisoners, and others. I postulate that those who are Black and also jailhouse lawyers would bear the brunt of (solitary) punishment—displaced within the ultimate "beyond the pale." Putting Abu-Jamal's analysis in context of "Jim Crow" or, as I prefer, the enduring legacy of slavery sanctioned by the 13th Amendment of the U.S. Constitution, it makes sense that jailhouse lawyers pose a great threat to the establishment; they are the new conductors on the underground railroad who champion the freedom cry—with equal amounts of courage and with greater idealism given the retaliation and the unlikely returns of freedom from oppression faced on the outside; there is no "up North" to go to these days. As Assata Shakur notes in her autobiography, "I don't have the faintest idea of how it feels to be free" (1987, p. 60).

While legal concepts are couched in neutral terms of *race*, putatively addressing concerns of all racial identity groups, I contend that when it comes to police line-ups, police arrests, bail, indictments, witness errors, (death penalty) sentencing, (perceived) felony status, and impetuous teachers, in the United States, the human drama has been played out on the backs of Black, marooned bodies—and I have not been able to comment on redlining, or morbidity, mortality, unemployment, and the enduring intergenerational stress of incarceration. It is time to challenge the pale; just as feminists have declared that women's rights are human rights, it must hold that Blacks' rights are human rights. It follows that Black life deserves to be considered human life—the world over, and especially in the United States.

References

Abrams, D. S., Bertrand, M., & Mullainathan, S. (2011). Do judges vary in their treatment of race? Research Paper, No. 11-07. Institute for Law and Economics, University of Pennsylvania Law School. Retrieved from http://ssrn.com/abstract=1800840

Abu-Jamal, M. (2009). Jailhouse lawyers: Prisoners defending prisoners v. the U.S.A. San Francisco: City Lights Books.

Abu-Jamal, M. (1995). Live from death row. Reading, MA: Addison-Wesley.

Alexander, M. (2010). The new Jim Crow: Mass incarceration in the age of color blindness. New York: The New Press.

Armour, J. (1997). Negrophobia and reasonable racism. New York: New York University Press.

Baldus, D., C. Pulaski, & G. Woodworth. (1990). Equal justice and the death penalty. Boston, MA: Northeastern University Press.

Barlas, A. (2004). A requiem for voicelessness: Pakistanis and Muslims in the US. Wagadu, 1. Retrieved from http://appweb.cortland.edu/ojs/index.php/Wagadu/article/view/379/722

Barr, M. (2007). Some facts and anecdotes of women arrested and imprisoned in the United States. In M. Nagel & S. Asumah (Eds.), Prisons and punishment: Reconsidering global penality. Trenton, NJ: Africa World Press.

Barry, E. (2010). From plantations to prisons: African American women prisoners in the United States. In B. Brooten (Ed.), Beyond slavery: Overcoming its religious and sexual legacies (pp. 75–88). New York: Palgrave Macmillan.

Bauerlein, M. (2002). Negrophobia: A race riot in Atlanta, 1906. Jackson, TN: Encounter Books/Perseus Book Group.

Baus, J., & Hunt, D. (Dir./Prod.). (2006). Cruel and unusual [DVD]. United States: Reid Productions.

Chesney-Lind, M. (1995). Rethinking women's imprisonment: A critical examination of trends in female incarceration. In B. R. Price & N. J. Sokoloff (Eds.), The criminal justice system and women: Offenders, victims, and workers, 2nd ed. (pp. 105–117). New York: McGraw-Hill.

Coleman, A. (2011). Disproportionate minority contact (DMC): A historical and contemporary perspective. In N. Parsons-Pollard (Ed.), Disproportionate minority contact: Current issues and policies (pp. 19–33). Durham, NC: Carolina Academic Press.

Crooms, L., & Gardiner, J. K. 2004. The prison issue. Feminist Studies, 30(2).

Daniels, L. (Director). (2009). Precious [DVD]. United States: Lee Daniels Entertainment.

Davis, A. Y. (1981). *Women, race, and class*. New York: Random House.

Davis, A. Y. (1998). *The Angela Y. Davis reader*. Joy A. James (Ed.). Hoboken, NJ: Blackwell.

Dodge, M. L. (2002). *"Whores and thieves of the worst kind": A study of women, crime, and prisons, 1835–2000*. DeKalb: Northern Illinois University Press.

Duncan, C. (N.d.). Baldus study. Retrieved from http://www.ithaca.edu/faculty/cduncan/265/baldus.doc

Elijah, J. S. (2007). Political prisoners in the U.S.: New perspectives in the new millennium. In M. Nagel & S. Asumah (Eds.), *Prisons and punishment: Reconsidering global penality*. Trenton, NJ: Africa World Press.

Ensler, E. (2010). *I am an emotional creature: The secret life of girls around the world*. New York: Villard.

Fanon, F. (1967). *Black skin, White masks*. New York: Grove Press.

Feagin, J. R. (2010). *Racist America: Roots, current realities, and future reparations*, 2nd ed. New York: Routledge.

Feder, E. (2007). *Family bonds: Genealogies of race and gender*. Oxford: Oxford University Press.

Gans, H. (2005). Race as class. *Contexts, 4*(4), 17–21.

Gordon, L. (2011). Falguni A. Sheth: Towards a political philosophy of race. *Continental Philosophical Review, 44*, 119–130.

Gordon, L. (Ed.). (1996). *Existence in Black*. New York: Routledge.

Greaves, W. (Director). (1989). *Ida B. Wells: A passion for justice* [DVD]. [Newsreel] United States: California Newsreel.

Head Roc. (2007). *Negrophobia!* Retrieved from www.Head-Roc.Com.

Himmelstein, K. E. W., & Brückner, H. (2010). Criminal-justice and school sanctions against nonheterosexual youth: A national longitudinal study. *Pediatrics* (December), 49–57.

James, D. (1993). *Negrophobia: An urban parable*. New York: St. Martin's Press.

Johnson, P. C. (2004). *Inner lives: Voices of African American women in prison*. New York: New York University Press.

Kipling, R. (1888). Beyond the pale. *Tales from the hill*. Retrieved from: http://ghostwolf.dyndns.org/words/authors/K/KiplingRudyard/prose/PlainTales/beyondpale.html.

Lamb, W., & the Women of York Correctional Institution. (2003). *Couldn't keep it to myself*. New York: HarperCollins.

Law, V. (2009). *Resistance behind bars: Struggles of incarcerated women*. Oakland, CA: PM Press.

Leiber, M. J., & Brubaker, S. J. (2010). Does the gender of the intake probation officer contextualize the treatment of Black youth? *Justice Research and Policy, 12*(2), 51–76.

Lipsitz, G. (1998). *The possessive investment in Whiteness: How White people profit from identity politics*. Philadelphia, PA: Temple University Press.

Mamdani, M. (1996). *Citizen and subject: Contemporary Africa and the legacy of late colonialism*. Princeton, NJ: Princeton University Press.

Mogul, J., Ritchie, A., & Whitlock, K. (2011). *Queer (in)justice: The criminalization of LGBT people in the United States.* Boston: Beacon Press.

Moore, M. (Director). (2002). *Bowling for Columbine* [Motion Picture]. United States: United Artists.

Nagel, M. (2008). "Prisons as diasporic sites: Liberatory voices from the diaspora of confinement," *Journal of Social Advocacy and Systems Change*, 1, pp. 1–31. Retrieved from: http://cortland.edu/ids/sasc/content/prison_nagel.pdf.

Nocella, A. (2011). A disability perspective on the terrorization of dissent (doctoral dissertation), Syracuse University.

Paley, N. C. (2010). Comments on "Girls in Prison" panel at Reimagining Girlhood conference, State University of New York at Cortland, October 24.

Parsons-Pollard, N. (2011). *Disproportionate minority contact: Current issues and policies.* Durham, NC: Carolina Academic Press.

Payne, A. A., & Welch. (2010). Racial threat and punitive school discipline. *Social Problems, 75*(1), 25–48.

Pharr, S. (1988). *Homophobia: A weapon of sexism.* Oakland, CA: Chardon Press.

Richie, C. (Director). (2008). *Our spirits don't speak English* [DVD]. Rich-Heape Films. United States.

Robinson, K. (2010). Changing education paradigms. Retrieved from: http://www.youtube.com/watch?v=zDZFcDGpL4U

Ryan, W. (1976). *Blaming the victim* (Rev. Ed.) New York: Vintage Books.

Smith, E., & Hattery, A. J. (2011). Race, wrongful conviction & exoneration, *Journal of African American Studies, 15*, 74–94.

Shakur, Assata. (1987). *Assata: An autobiography.* Chicago: Lawrence Hill Books.

Smith, A. (2005). *Conquest: Sexual violence and American Indian genocide.* Boston: South End Press.

Solinger, R., Johnson, P. C., & Raimon, M. L., Reynolds, T., & Tapia, R. C. (2010). *Interrupted life: Experiences of incarcerated women in the United States.* Berkeley: University of California Press.

Sudbury, J. (2006). *Global lockdown: Race, gender, and the prison-industrial complex.* New York: Routledge.

Sudbury, J. (2010). Marooned abolitionists: Black gender activists in the anti-prison movement in the U.S. and Canada. *Meridians, 9*(1), 1–29.

Sweeney, M. (2010). *Reading is my window: Books and the art of reading in women's prisons.* Chapel Hill: University of North Carolina Press.

Takaki, R. (1995). *A different mirror: A multicultural history of America.* New York: Little, Brown.

Viglione, J., Hannon, L., & DeFina, R. (2011). "The impact of light skin on prison time for Black female offenders." *Social Science Journal, 48,* 250–258.

Ware, V. (1992). *Beyond the Pale: White women, racism and history.* London: Verso.

Western, B., & Pettit, B. (2010). Incarceration and social inequality. *Daedalus*, Summer, 8–19.

News Media and other Organizational Websites

ACLU. (8/10/2010). Can the Racial Justice Act change the practice of picking all-white juries in North Carolina? Retrieved from : http://www. aclu.org/blog/capital-punishment/can-racial-justice-act-change-practice-picking-all-white-juries-north-caroli

Abramsky, S. (10/8/2010). Toxic persons: New research shows precisely how the prison-to-poverty cycle does its damage. *Slate*. Retrieved from: http://www.slate.com/id/2270328/

CA News. (6/16/10). The Adoption and Safe Families Act (ASFA) expanded discretion bill becomes law. Correctional Association. Retrieved from: http://www.correctionalassociation.org/news/ASFA_becomes_law_June10.htm

CNN. (2/7/11). Uproar in Houston after video shows police beating 15-year-old suspect. Retrieved from http://www.cnn.com/2011/CRIME/02/05/texas.police.beating/index.html?hpt=T2

Deters, R. (2008). Cross-Racial identification—Can Whites tell anyone besides themselves apart? (And vice versa). Retrieved from: http://chicagocrimelaw.wordpress.com/2008/09/16/cross-racial-identification-can-whites-tell-anyone-besides-themselves-apart-and-vice-versa/

Dow, D. R. (7/8/11). Death penalty, still racist and arbitrary. *New York Times*. Retrieved from: http://www.nytimes.com/2011/07/09/opinion/09dow.htm l?ref=general&src=me&pagewanted=print

Eaton, S. (8/29–9/5/11). A new kind of Southern strategy. *The Nation*, 18–21.

Grant, J. M., Mottet, L. A., Tanis, J., Harrison, J., Herman, J. L., & Keisling, K. (2011). *Injustice at every turn: A report of the National Transgender Discrimination Survey.*

Hall, D. (7/25/2011). Reasons for racial disparity in Dane County penal system are complex. *Madison.com*. Retrieved from: http://host.madison. com/wsj/news/local/crime_and_courts/article_fea23fac-b625-11e0-b588-001cc4c002e0.html

Lee, A. F., Philip, M. G., & Laver, M. (2005). The Impact of the Adoption and Safe Families Act on children of incarcerated parents. Child Welfare League of America, Washington, DC. Retrieved from: www.fcnetwork. org/Resource%20Center/cop_pubimpact.pdf

Losen, D. J., & Skiba, R. J. (9/13/2010). Suspended education: Urban middle schools in crisis. The Civil Rights Project/Proyecto Derechos Civilos. Retrieved from: http://civilrightsproject.ucla.edu/research/k-12-education/school-discipline/suspended-education-urban-middle-schools-in-crisis

Moynihan, D. P. (1965). The Negro family: The case for national action. Retrieved from: http://www.blackpast.org/?q=primary/moynihan-report-1965

NAACP. (2011). Misplaced priorities: Over incarcerate, under educate. Retrieved from: http://org2.democracyinaction.org/dia/track.jsp?v=2&c= 8eRlSOjgNTpLu7V%2FsMSiIfzGxhkH%2BX0o

National Center for Transgender Equality and National Gay and Lesbian Task Force. "Injustice at every turn: A report of the national transgender discrimination survey." Retrieved 4/22/11 from: www.thetaskforce. org/reports_and_research/ntds

NCCD Center for Girls and Young Women. (2010). A call for gender equity for girls in the juvenile justice system. National Center on Crime and Delinquency. Retrieved from: http://www.justiceforallgirls.org/call.html

New Jersey, State of. (2011). Megan's Law. Retrieved from: http://www.nj.org/ meg.html

NYCLU. (2011). Education interrupted: The growing use of suspensions in New York City's public schools. Retrieved from: www.nyclu.org/files/ publications/Suspension_Report_FINAL_noSpreads.pdf

Pinkerton, J. (2/8/11). Activists and civil rights groups weigh in on arrest beating video. Security tape's airing inflames public reactions. *Houston Chronicle*. Retrieved from: http://www.chron.com/disp/story.mpl/metro-politan/7419120.html

Ray, N. (2006). *Lesbian, gay, bisexual and transgender youth: An epidemic of homelessness*. New York: National Gay and Lesbian Task Force Policy Institute and the National Coalition for the Homeless. Retrieved from: http://www.thetaskforce.org/reports_and_research/homeless_youth

Schuller, K. (2003). The Americans who matter: Michael Moore's White liberal racism in *Bowling for Columbine*. *Post Road Magazine*, 9. Retrieved from: http://www.postroadmag.com/9/criticism/AmericansWho Matter.phtml

The Sentencing Project. (2011, June 22). NYPD Increases Stop-and-Frisk. *Race & Justice News*.

Webb, J. (2009). Why we must fix our prisons. *Parade*. Retrieved from: http:// www.parade.com/news/2009/03/why-we-must-fix-our-prisons.html

Wilson, W. J. (2011). Being poor, Black, and American: The impact of political, economic, and cultural forces. *American Educator, 35*(1), 10–23, 46.

CHAPTER FIVE

Women's Work Trips and Multifaceted Oppression*

IBIPO JOHNSTON-ANUMONWO

Being employed is an essential aspect of meaningful participation in society for most people. Access to jobs for different social groups is thus a relevant topic of inquiry. Since, like men, a majority of employed women work outside the home, an examination of women's commuting is one way to appraise women's access to jobs.

This chapter will give a conceptual and empirical analysis of women's work trips, using analysis of the multiple faces of oppression posited by Iris Young (1990). The premise of the chapter is that this situation of many working women, that they have more difficulty in getting to work, denies equitable access, and therefore can be tied to social structures of oppression.

Based on evidence from empirical research in a variety of U.S. cities, I present an analysis of women's commuting using Iris Young's conceptual framework of different types of oppression that she identifies as marginalization, powerlessness, cultural imperialism, exploitation, and violence. The chapter focuses on problems faced by women working outside the home in the context of pervasive de facto residential segregation. Their socioeconomic, locational, and mobility characteristics are analyzed to understand the nature of the oppression associated with their work trips. For instance, to what extent does the stereotype that connects motherhood with short trips uphold or undermine the claim that cultural imperialism is involved in judging these women's oppression? How might a multifactorial investigation of job type, monetary compensation, and trip length underscore the intricate links between powerlessness and exploitation for working women? What, if any, form of violence do women encounter while commuting?

I synthesize findings to these questions and show that the conceptual framework of Iris Young's (1990) faces of oppression is both versatile and relevant for interpreting racial and gender differences in employment access. Housing-jobs mismatches and transportation constraints that restrict women's access to jobs contribute to their marginalization in the labor market. The sample of findings reveals that many African American women continue to endure relatively long commutes to get to work because of, and in spite of, transportation, locational, and socioeconomic hindrances. I conclude this chapter by discussing the implications of multifaceted oppression in analyses of women's work trips.

Connecting Commuting With
Multiple Faces of Oppression

Do people have jobs? What are some constraints on people's access to jobs? What jobs do people do? Where do they work? How much do they earn? How do they get to their workplace? These are all questions that can be addressed within a framework that examines connections between commuting and multiple faces of oppression. Young cites unemployment as a form of oppression she terms marginalization because jobless people may be confined to lives of social marginality (Young, 1990). Inadequate access to jobs because of the location of one's home can lead to joblessness. Since the length of the separation between the home and the workplace is an indicator of access to employment, a focus on the work trip can reveal expedient job access or lack thereof.

Another form of oppression, powerlessness, refers to social-class injustices wherein the powerless group lacks the authority or opportunity to negotiate favorable conditions; while exploitation, a third face of oppression, occurs when a group does not benefit from their labor while others do. According to Young, powerlessness can be caused by the social division of labor between nonprofessionals and professionals, with the later group represented in positions of power and privilege. And in her conceptualization of exploitation as a face of oppression, Young emphasizes inadequate compensation, financial or otherwise, that benefits one group at the expense of another. Marginalization, powerlessness, and exploitation all refer to inequality within the context of employment. They are the faces of oppression that place attention on the resources to which people have access, the material benefits possible from waged work, and the opportunities to exercise significant control in the employment context. In essence, these faces of oppression are about which group of workers benefits from whom, who is dispensable, and who gets to work to start with. For powerlessness and exploitation, I look at conventional labor market variables, occupation type, and employment earnings, to analyze these two faces of oppression. Regarding work trips, the empirical literature shows that high-status workers are generally in a better position to afford long commutes compared to low-waged workers (Hanson and Pratt, 1995; Ihlanfeldt, 1992; McLafferty and Preston, 1997).

Cultural imperialism, a fourth face of oppression, involves the universalization of a dominant group's experience and culture, and its establishment as the norm. The culturally dominated undergo a paradoxical oppression in that they are both marked out by stereotypes and at the same time rendered invisible (Young, 1990). Young uses the stereotype that women are good with children as an example of group marking. This example shows the dominance of a patriarchal ideology such that motherhood as a pervasive gender role will influence women's commuting behavior. However, the experience of motherhood is not necessarily a universal one for all women if one considers a race-gender nexus. Indeed Collins (1991) emphasizes that African American women have long integrated economic self-reliance with mothering. She states that "in contrast to the cult of true womanhood, in which work is defined as being in opposition to and incompatible with motherhood, work for Black women has been an important and valued dimension of Afrocentric definitions of Black motherhood" (p. 124). Since Black women's mothering attributes do not conform to White cultural standards, and women may differ then in the degree to which their status as mothers influences their commutes, I compare the influence of household responsibility on women's commute between White and Black working mothers. Although empirical evidence on the role of household responsibility on trip length is mixed (Sultana, 2003), a study by Preston and Hamilton (1993) found that Black mothers had longer trip times than White mothers, a finding that suggests that the touted norm of short commutes for working mothers applies more to White women.

Last but not least, Young states that violence is a systemic form of social injustice and she identifies it as a fifth face of oppression. Although my own studies do not include empirical measures of violence, I address the relevance of violence in women's commuting later in my concluding remarks. Finally, any attempt to conceptually or empirically link commuting with the faces of oppression must also recognize the insidious milieu of U.S. residential segregation that Young describes (Young, 2000).

Social Justice, Residential Segregation, and Locational Access to Jobs

If members of any given group of workers encounter difficulty in transportation due to their locational access to work, this constitutes a significant form of inequity because they could be excluded from being full-functioning members of society. Unemployment or other conditions of not having access to useful participation in life are forms of social injustice because the people affected are potentially subjected to severe material deprivation and related marginal status. Jobless people experience marginalization, and inadequate locational access to jobs can lead to joblessness, which in turn can lead to poverty. As an indicator of access to employment, the separation between the home and the workplace is appropriate for analyzing equitable job access. A brief review of the literature on housing patterns and commuting follows.

There has been little change in patterns of racial residential segregation in the United States (Denton, 1994; Massey & Hajnal, 1995). Because of their relative concentration in central cities, the growth of employment in suburbs impacts Black workers' access to jobs, and increasing numbers of African Americans are commuting outward to suburban workplaces (Pisarski, 2006). Since there continue to be residential differences between Whites and Blacks (Jencks & Mayer, 1990; Young, 2000), an important dimension in geographical access to employment is the experience of workers who commute from inner city residences to suburban workplaces (i.e., "reverse commuting"). The combination of constrained access to suburban housing and to suburban employment for African Americans connects the reality of residential immobility with adverse employment outcomes. Some researchers conclude that persistent racial disparities in access to employment still limit the full economic participation of Black workers in U.S. metropolitan areas (e.g., Dickerson, 2007), a situation that is contrary to the ideal of inclusion that Young advocates in a democratic society (Young, 2000).

A variety of reasons underlies the geographies of home and work for African Americans. They range from preference, poverty, and prejudice to a host of discriminatory exclusionary policies. Some of these include avoidance, hostility, and direct attacks from neighbors; or negative selling and steering by landlords and real estate agents; or loan denials by banks. All of these behaviors are examples of Young's faces of oppression in that they represent harmful consequences, disrespectful behaviors, and systematic restrictions or limits on housing choices for people of color. In spite of the 40-year-old Fair Housing Act, a combination of subtle and blatant unfair practices, including White flight, redlining, and/or predatory lending continue to make residential location patterns strongly differentiated along racial lines. Thus, research findings on workplace access can best be understood in cognizance of the structural character of residential segregation in the United States (Darden & Kamel, 2000; Young, 2000).

Meanwhile, there is some debate about whether women's relatively shorter work trips when compared to men's should be interpreted as advantageous or not (Hanson & Pratt, 1995; England, 1993). A parallel debate evaluates the extent to which ethnic minorities in U.S. cities suffer greater job accessibility constraints than do nonminorities. Inquiries about racial disparities in employment accessibility are central to the spatial mismatch hypothesis. First proposed by Kain (1968), the hypothesis contended that, compared to White residents, inner-city ethnic minorities have poorer access to jobs because of their concentration in segregated residential areas that are distant from, and poorly connected to, major suburban centers of employment growth. Poor access leads to high rates of unemployment and, for those persons able to overcome varied barriers and find work, poor access is reflected in long journeys to work (see Holzer, 1991; Kain, 1992; McLafferty & Preston, 1997; and Preston & McLafferty, 1999 for some thorough reviews).

However, the evidence from the literature is ambiguous largely because of key shortcomings in empirical analyses; for example, some studies inadequately control for ethnic and racial differences in the locational and socioeconomic factors known to influence work trips, while others tend to exclude the impact of suburban workplace location. In correcting for these shortcomings, studies that have examined the role of suburban residence versus inner city residence on the labor market outcomes of Blacks and Whites or the degree of racial differences in access to transportation, employment location, residential mobility, and unemployment levels (e.g., Stoll, 1996; Mouw, 2000) generally support the spatial mismatch hypothesis. Even though early research on the effect of the exodus of jobs to suburban locations on the workplace accessibility of inner-city African Americans rarely included female workers, later studies have investigated spatial mismatch concerns and commuting constraints of women (e.g., McLafferty & Preston, 1992, 1997; Sultana, 2003; Thompson, 1997). In the next section, I synthesize results from a set of studies on women's commuting (Johnston-Anumonwo, 1995, 1997, 2000, 2001, 2003, 2004; Johnston-Anumonwo & Sultana, 2006) as the empirical basis for applying the intersections of different faces of oppression recognized by Iris Young.

Empirical Analysis and Findings

Are there significant racial and gender differences in work-trip behavior? Do people of color spend a longer time commuting than Whites? Does unequal access to private automobiles lead to differences in the time spent traveling to work? Is location of the workplace responsible For any difference in work-trip length? Is there any difference in the commute times of workers with similar socioeconomic attributes? The range of factors necessary for answers about work-trip disparities makes a database like the U.S. Census Public Use Micro-Data Samples (PUMS) appropriate because it contains information on individuals' socioeconomic characteristics and their work trips. In 1980, for the first time, the database included information on work-trip length (i.e., minutes spent traveling from home to work as reported by the respondent), so as of the 2000 census, it is possible to conduct some longitudinal analysis over a period of 20 years. The travel mode is the means of transportation that the worker uses to get to work, for example, public transit or private automobile. Residence and workplace location is either central city or noncentral city (i.e., suburban). I use the standard information on race/ethnicity, occupation, presence of children, and employment earnings that are available in census sources. The cities that I examine are Rochester, New York, Kansas City, Detroit, Miami, and Buffalo, and I include only respondents who are 16 years of age and older. In the rest of the chapter, I collate and interpret the empirical findings on ethnic inequalities in commuting as evidence of multiple and overlapping faces of oppression.

Marginalization: Transportation and Locational Access

Findings of three aspects of work trips—travel mode, trip length, and suburban destination show marginalization.

Travel Mode: Women of Color Rely More on Public Transportation

The results for Buffalo and Kansas City in 1980 show a clear and anticipated pattern of Blacks depending on public transportation more than Whites. Also, in 1990, higher percentages of Blacks use public transit in Kansas City and Detroit; as well as in Miami where Latina women depend more on public transportation than do White women (Table 5.1). Since much research attest to the relatively lengthening effect of public transportation (especially bus transportation) on travel times (e.g., McLafferty & Preston, 1992), greater public transit use by people of color is expected to increase their average work-trip time; hence, one should rightly compare the travel times of workers with the same travel mode only.

Work Trip Length: Auto Use Reduces Travel Time

When the work-trip times of private automobile users are examined, the racial difference is small (and is rarely statistically significant). As shown in Table 5.2 (unlike the overall trip length of workers in the full samples), the difference among women auto users is minimal— around 1 minute. Taylor & Ong (1995) found that among workers with automobiles, there is no racial difference in commuting time, and on this basis they suggest the importance of an "automobile mismatch" in the sense that people of color are less likely to have cars and to use private automobiles for their work trips. Next, I summarize differences in travel time among auto users with similar location or socioeconomic profiles.

Suburban Workplace: Black Reverse Commuters Spend a
Longer Time Getting to Work

Focusing on those workers with suburban destinations, the findings show that among *reverse commuters*, Black women spend a longer time than White women.

The difference in 1980 was 6 minutes in Kansas City (Table 5.3). Table 5.3 also displays trends for Buffalo in 1980, 1990, and 2000 where the gap between Black and White reverse commuters has reduced from almost 6 minutes in 1980 to 3 minutes in 2000. The results are consistent with the spatial mismatch hypothesis that inner-city Blacks have long commutes to *suburban* work destinations, and the specific finding for Buffalo is evidence of remaining travel time differences among inner-city women auto users even in 2000. In short, both cross-sectional and longitudinal data show that women of color have relatively less access to both adequate transportation modes and suburban workplaces.

The empirical findings that I have summarized thus far document the restricted workplace access of African American women,

Table 5.1. Women's Use of Public Transportation (percent)

1980 Buffalo		1980 Kansas		1990 Kansas		1990 Detroit		1990 Miami	
White	Black	White	Black	White	Black	White	Black	White	Latino
9.9	33.6	3.5	21.5	1.4	12.7	0.8	10.9	3.2	6.7

Source: From Johnston-Anumonwo (1995, 2000, 2001, 2003).

Table 5.2. Women's Average Work-Trip Time (minutes)

	1990 Kansas		1990 Detroit		1980 Buffalo		1990 Buffalo		2000 Buffalo	
	White	Black	White	Black	White	Black	White	Black	White	Black
Full Sample	20.2	22.6	21.1	23.9	18.1	22.8	17.8	21.2	19.5	23.7
Auto Users	20.3	21.2	21.2	22.3	17.1	18.5	17.5	18.1	19.3	20.4

Source: From Johnston-Anumonwo (1995, 2000, 2001); Johnston-Anumonwo and Sultana (2006).

Table 5.3. Reverse Commutes of Women Auto Users (minutes)

| | 1980 Kansas | | 1990 Detroit | | 1980 Buffalo | | 1990 Buffalo | | 2000 Buffalo | |
	White	Black	White	Black	White	Black	White	Black	White	Black
Auto Users	20.0	26.0	23.5	25.4	20.3	26.1	19.2	23.5	20.7	23.7

Source: From Johnston-Anumonwo (1995, 2000, 2001); Johnston-Anumonwo and Sultana (2006).

observations that can be interpreted as marginalization. Regarding the three socioeconomic factors that I examine, occupation, child status, and income (to verify powerlessness, cultural imperialism, and exploitation, respectively), the common expectations are that low-status, low-wage workers will be less able to afford long commutes. In fact, Black women can be expected to have shorter commutes since their lower earnings or more domestic obligations would disallow long commutes. First I compare differences in women's trip length by occupation, followed by child status and by income.

Powerlessness, Cultural Imperialism, and Commute Length

Powerlessness can be illustrated through differences between non-professionals and professionals, the latter being the privileged social group. One indicator of this face of oppression is occupation status or position at the workplace. I focus on service workers.

Service Workers: African American Women Service Workers Spend a Longer Time Getting to Work

It is only among service workers that the longer commutes of African American women are significant. Whereas there are no differences between Black and White women who are in clerical, sales, and technical occupations, African American women service workers spend more than 4 minutes longer than White service workers (see Table 5.4 for data on Buffalo and Detroit). Also, Black professionals do not have longer travel times—a finding that fits Iris Young's claim that professionals are privileged in relation to nonprofessionals.

Table 5.4. Differences in Women's Trip Time by Occupation (minutes)

	1990 Buffalo		1990 Detroit	
	White	Black	White	Black
Service occupations	14.8	19.6	17.0	21.5
Clerical, sales, and technical occupations	17.3	17.4	21.2	21.8
Professional/managerial occupations	19.6	16.7	23.3	22.7

Note: Auto users only.
Source: From Johnston-Anumonwo (1995, 2000).

These results are similar to those reported for 1980 by McLaf-ferty and Preston (1991) and Johnston-Anumonwo (2000) for service workers in metropolitan New York City and Detroit, respectively. In those studies, African American women spend over 7 minutes and up to 10 minutes longer on average for their home-to-work trip than European American women. Although the time difference has reduced between 1980 and 1990, a significant fraction of working women are still employed in service occupations (Ehrenreich, 2001); thus, if the occupational and locational elements of the restructured metropolitan labor market continue to evolve as they have over the past two decades, such that African American women remain con-centrated in service jobs, and service jobs continue to suburbanize, then compared to European American women or to other groups of workers, African American women (even when they use a car) are the ones most likely to experience the disadvantage of long commutes to relatively low-waged service jobs in suburban locations.

Working Mothers: African American Mothers
Spend a Longer Time Getting to Work

In the study areas where child status was examined, Black mothers spend a longer time than White mothers (available results shown for Rochester and Buffalo in 1980, as well as for Detroit in 1990— see Table 5.5). One would expect no racial difference among women with the same child status. On the contrary, this finding underscores the paradox inherent in cultural imperialism because Black moth-ers' commuting does not conform to an uncontested expectation of convenient short trips among women with children.

Table 5.5. Work Trip Time of Mothers (minutes)

1980 Rochester		1980 Buffalo		1990 Detroit	
White	Black	White	Black	White	Black
15.4	20.6	16.0	19.7	20.8	23.0

Note: Auto users only.
Source: From Johnston-Anumonwo (2000, 2004).

As employed women who combine motherhood with waged employment, the case of these African American mothers with longer travel times than White counterparts exposes the inaccurate universalization of women's motherhood experiences. Further, women on welfare are stereotyped as Black women who are lazy and do not work, but precisely because the analysis is about gainfully employed mothers, this finding also undermines the stereotype of the Black welfare mother, which is a controlling image that is designed to oppress (Young 1990; Collins, 1991). But Young is clear about the overlapping and interlocking character of the multiple faces of oppression. It is in this light that I jointly examine indicators of powerlessness, cultural imperialism, and exploitation in the next section.

Women With Long Commuting Times: Qualitative Contrasts

The 20-minute one-way commute is a standard cutoff mark in national-level summaries of commuting statistics. For instance, Pisarski (2006) differentiates between relatively short commutes (under 20 minutes), and those exceeding 20 minutes, or even much significantly longer commutes that exceed 60 minutes. In the metropolitan areas studied, women with relatively "long" commuting times (over 20 minutes) are generally those with opposite direction commutes. They are White women who live in the suburbs but work in the central city, and Black women who live in the central city but work in suburban locations. To clarify the situation of these women with above average commuting times, I compare characteristics of the two groups of opposite direction commuters and find significant contrasts in occupations, income, and child status. Specifically, the White women with long suburb-to-city commutes are far more likely to be in managerial/professional jobs, and less likely to be mothers; while Black women with city-to-suburb commutes (reverse commuters) are more likely to be in service jobs and earn lower average incomes (Table 5.6). These are crucial qualitative differences. Other than their long average travel time, White suburb-to-city commuters are relatively well-placed by their higher socioeconomic status and fewer dependent children. The findings that Black reverse commuters earn less and appear to have greater child care responsibilities amplifies the interpretation that the long work trips of Black reverse commuters are more constrained than the long trips of Whites with suburb-to-city commutes. Indeed corroborating earlier evidence exists showing that long commutes by Whites who live in suburbs are compensated by higher wages, while

Table 5.6. Differences among Women with Long Commutes

	1990 Buffalo		1990 Detroit	
	White Suburb to City	Black City to Suburb	White Suburb to City	Black City to Suburb
Travel time (minutes)	24.7	23.5	30.6	25.4
Managers/professionals (percent)	39.3	11.8	41.9	16.8
Service workers (percent)	7.8	32.9	7.5	17.4
Mothers (percent)	32,3	43,4	29.3	41.5
Full-time annual income	$22,296	$20,927	$26,967	$21,770

Note: Auto users only.
Source: From Johnston-Anumonwo (1995, 2000).

this is less likely to be the case for inner-city Blacks (Ihlanfeldt & Young, 1994). It is thus appropriate to check whether women's wages correspond with trip length.

Exploitation: Constrained Commutes for African American Women

For exploitation as a face of oppression, Iris Young stresses compensation, including monetary remuneration. I investigate the element of exploitation in commuting by comparing commuting time differences vis-à-vis employment earnings in Buffalo. For the present purpose, a simple typology of four commute types classifies workers on the basis of short versus long commutes, and low versus high incomes. I include only full-time workers (those who worked 35 hours or more a week) in the analysis, in order to remove the effects of reduced income due to part-time employment. Respondents with earnings below $25,000 are considered low-income workers; while trips shorter than 20 minutes in 2000 are considered short trips.

In the typology (Table 5.7), I differentiate "convenient" and "compensatory" commutes from "compromised" and "constrained" commutes, the former pair being commutes to high-wage jobs. Compromised commutes are those in which either the worker forgoes a higher income for a shorter commute or the worker's low income makes a long commute uneconomical.

Compromised commutes differ from constrained commutes that are typified by long commutes to low-wage jobs. Rutherford and Wekerle (1988) present a similar combination (long commutes and low wages) for "disadvantaged commutes." Convenient commutes combine the advantages of short trips and high wages, and are considered the best of the four possibilities (Johnston-Anumonwo, 1997). How do Blacks and Whites differ in their commute times relative to their earnings? To shift the inquiry from a preoccupation with the

Table 5.7. Typology of Commutes

	Short commute (<20 minutes)	Long commute (=> 20 minutes)
High Income (→ $25,000)	Convenient	Compensatory
Low Income (< $25,000)	Compromised	Constrained

plight of inner-city residents, and permit an analysis of middle-class workers, I focus on suburban residents.

Suburban Residents' Commutes:
Racial and Gender Differences in Earnings

Suburban residents generally have higher incomes, hence, a sizable proportion are in the two high-income commute types. However there are some racial differences. A lower proportion of suburban Black women than White women have compensatory commutes, while a higher proportion of Black women have constrained commutes compared to White women. Among men, suburban Black men have fewer compensatory trips and more compromised commutes than do White men. The 2000 data solidly show that (1) more suburban Black women than White women undergo the constraint of long commutes to low-wage jobs, and (2) the long commutes of suburban Black men are less likely to be compensated with high wages compared to suburban White men.

There are also obvious gender differences (Table 5.8). Men are more likely than women to have convenient commutes (i.e., the "best" commute types), and compensatory ones. Women are more likely than men to have compromised commutes and constrained commutes. These findings suggest the following: (1) they support claims of a well-known wage gap associated with the gender-segregated labor force, since they show that the commutes of women are similar in their disproportionate concentration in the two low-income categories; (2) however, they contest common expectations that low status workers who earn low incomes will have shorter commutes since they show that many women, especially Black women, are enduring relatively long commutes to low-income jobs.

Table 5.8. Commute Types of Suburban Residents in Buffalo 2000 (percent)

	Women		Men	
	White	Black	White	Black
Convenient trips	32.9	32.2	45.7	44.4
Compensatory trips	21.3	11.9	30.8	25.2
Compromised trips	32.4	32.2	15.7	20.5
Constrained trips	13.4	23.7	7.9	9.8

Note: Auto users; full-time workers only.
Source: From: Johnston-Anumonwo and Sultana (2006).

In the final section of the chapter, I elaborate on some implications of all these findings for a conceptual understanding of
women's commutes as manifesting intersecting faces of oppression.

A Multifaceted Oppression Analysis of Women's Commuting

From this selection of cross-sectional and longitudinal results, an
inclusive interpretation of women's work trips is possible. Clearly,
women's commutes are not invariably short; and not all African
American women face the constraints of long trips to low-paying
jobs. My interpretation is that long commutes are disconcerting and
therefore oppressive when the job at the end of the work trip is a
low-wage job.

Work trips to suburban destinations (i.e., outside the central
city) impose a disproportionate commuting time burden on inner-city
Black women, a finding that illustrates restricted access and thereby
explicates the face of oppression that Young identifies as marginalization. Documenting the inadequate monetary compensation for the
journey to work effort, establishes exploitation as a face of oppression
especially for Black women—the group with a disproportionate volume of constrained commutes. The particular case of service workers
(representing low-status occupations as distinct from professionals)
with longer work trips than White counterparts demonstrate the
coincidence of powerlessness and exploitation. The counterintuitive
finding of longer work trips for African American mothers exemplifies the paradox of cultural imperialism. The underlying context of
residential segregation in the study areas attest to the important
connection between race and place that Young emphasizes in her discussion on segregation and inclusion (Young, 2000). Last, the various
findings corroborate the earlier conclusions of McLafferty and Preston
(1991) that many African American women experience a very insidious form of spatial mismatch and face significant transportation and
locational barriers in traveling to work. Keeping in mind that most
of the comparisons are restricted to auto users, the findings show
that even when access to an automobile is not a hindrance, many
African American workers still bear a bigger time cost than European
Americans. Although there is greater reliance by African Americans
on public transportation, the slightly longer times spent by Black
workers may be expected to decrease if Black workers continue to
have more access to private automobiles. However, findings of the
multifactorial comparison of women with long commutes suggest that
it is reasonable to speculate that as employment opportunities expand

more in suburban locations and less in central city locations, African American women are still likely to suffer the inconvenience of long commutes to suburban workplaces. Turner (1997) presents evidence of spatial mismatch as well as evidence of the negative treatment of Blacks by suburban police officers and White residents as testimony of the multiple barriers facing African Americans in gaining access to employment opportunities in suburban Detroit.

In Buffalo, the reality of both a spatial mismatch and an automobile mismatch for African American women proved tragically true in the case of an African American woman who was killed while crossing an expressway in suburban Buffalo on her way to the shopping mall where she was employed. In this outrageous 1995 incident, Cynthia Wiggins was killed in Buffalo, New York, when forced to cross a seven-lane highway in order to get from the bus stop to her job in a suburban mall, because the mall barred city buses from driving into its parking lot (although suburban and tourist buses were permitted). This particular case had racist underpinnings because the management of the suburban mall seemed to have pursued explicit policy decisions preventing buses coming from inner-city Buffalo from stopping at the mall. My empirical analysis did not consider indicators of violence as part of women's work trips, but this case can be interpreted as evidence of structural violence, the fifth face of oppression discussed by Young.

If more jobs were available in central cities, there would be less need to reverse commute to reach suburban jobs. Alternatively, if African Americans face less discrimination for suburban housing, the racial disparity in access to suburban jobs may reduce. Yet, even for those who reside in suburban locations of U.S. metropolitan areas, African Americans still experience segregation (e.g., Darden, 1990; Darden & Kamel, 2000). At present, it is wrong to understate the importance of locational access to Black employment outcomes (see, e.g., Martin, 2004). One should stress that like all studies that use commuting data, these results understate the general problem of access to jobs since the empirical analyses exclude the unemployed (or imprisoned), many of whom are unemployed possibly because of location and transportation reasons. However, examining the work trip with the focus on travel time in particular is appropriate. Time is a resource. In some instances, time is money; therefore lost time is lost money. Although the travel time differences may appear small, the cumulative time cost of the two-way work trip over a long period of time could be considerable, and it amounts to time lost from other tasks. Much of the extra time that Black workers in the respective study areas spend longer than Whites is generally 3 minutes or more, which extrapolates into 25 hours a year—equivalent to an ample portion of a work week. Cast in this light, the longer commute times of Black workers can be interpreted as constituting a racial tax burden.

In conclusion, this analysis of work trips complements the empirical literature on commuting with a conceptual interpretation that highlights the overlapping and multiple faces of oppression that Young expounds. Indeed, these findings which extend to the work trips of twenty-first-century employed African American women, counter continuing stereotypes and overgeneralizations that Black women are welfare dependent, and underscore the continuing significance of multiple forms of oppression in the locational and socioeconomic job inaccessibility of U.S. ethnic minorities or immigrant workers.

Note

*This chapter was previously published in *Dancing with Iris* (2009), and it was reprinted with permission from Oxford University Press.

References

Collins, P. H. (1991). *Black feminist thought*. New York: Routledge.

Cooke T. J., & Shumway, J. M. (1991). Developing the spatial mismatch hypothesis: Problems of accessibility to employment for low wage central city labor. *Urban Geography, 12*, 310–323.

Darden, J. T. (1990). Differential access to housing in the suburbs. *Journal of Black Studies, 21*, 15–22.

Darden, J. T., & Kamel, S. (2000). Black residential segregation in the city and suburbs of Detroit: Does socioeconomic status matter? *Journal of Urban Affairs, 22*, 1–13.

Denton, N. A. (1994). Are African Americans still hypersegregated? In R. D. Bullard, J. E. Grigsby III, C., & Lee (Eds.), *Residential apartheid: The American legacy* (pp. 49–81). Los Angeles: Center for Afro-American Studies, University of California.

Dickerson, N. T. (2007). Black employment, segregation, and the social organization of metropolitan labor markets. *Economic Geography, 83*(3), 283–308.

Ehrenreich, B. (2001). *Nickel and dimed: On (not) getting by in America*. New York: Henry Holt and Company.

England, K. (1993). Suburban pink collar ghettos: The spatial entrapment of women? *Annals of the Association of American Geographers, 83*, 225–242.

Hanson, S., & Pratt, G. (1995). *Gender, work, and space*. New York: Routledge.

Holzer, H. J. (1991). The spatial mismatch hypothesis: What has the evidence shown? *Urban Studies, 28*(1), 105–122.

Holzer, H. J. (1992). Intraurban wage gradients: Evidence by race, gender, occupational class, and sector. *Journal of Urban Economics, 32*, 70–91.

Ihlanfeldt, K. R. (1998). The spatial mismatch hypothesis: A review of recent studies and their implications for welfare reform. *Housing Policy Debate, 9*, 849–892.

Ihlanfeldt, K. R., & Young, M. V. (1994). Housing segregation and the wages and commutes of urban Blacks: The case of Atlanta fast-food restaurant workers. *Review of Economics and Statistics, 76*, 425–433.

Jencks, C. S., & Mayer, S. E. (1990). Residential segregation, job proximity, and Black job opportunities. In L. E. Lynn, Jr. & M. G. H. McGeary (Eds.), *Inner-City Poverty in the United States* (pp. 187–222). Washington, DC: National Academy Press.

Johnston-Anumonwo, I. (1995). Racial differences in the commuting behavior of women in Buffalo, NY, 1980–1990. *Urban Geography, 16*, 23–45.

Johnston-Anumonwo, I. (1997). Race, gender, and constrained work trips in Buffalo, New York, 1990. *Professional Geographer, 49*, 306–317.

Johnston-Anumonwo, I. (2000). Commuting constraints of Black women: Evidence from Detroit. *The Great Lakes Geographer, 7*(2), 66–75.

Johnston-Anumonwo, I. (2001). Persistent racial differences in the commutes of Kansas City workers. *Journal of Black Studies, 31*(5), 651–670.

Johnston-Anumonwo, I. (2003). Commuting and locational access to employment in urban America: Ethnic and racial disparities in three cities. In J. Frazier, F. Margai, & E. Tettey-Fio (Eds.), *Race and place: Equity issues in urban America* (pp. 229–251). Cambridge MA: Westview Press.

Johnston-Anumonwo, I. (2004). Getting to work in spite of the odds: Commuting patterns of African Americans in Rochester and Buffalo, New York. *Afro-Americans in New York Life and History, 28*(1), 73–98.

Johnston-Anumonwo, I., & Sultana, S. (2006). Race, location, and access to employment in Buffalo, NY. In J. W. Frazier & E. L. Tettey-Fio, (Eds.), *Race, ethnicity and place in a changing America* (pp. 115–130). Binghamton, NY: Global Academic Publishing, Binghamton University.

Kain, J. F. (1968). Housing segregation, Negro employment, and metropolitan decentralization. *Quarterly Journal of Economics, 82*, 175–197.

Kain, J. F. (1992). The spatial mismatch hypothesis: Three decades later. *Housing Policy Debate, 2*, 371–460.

Martin, R. W. (2004). Can Black workers escape spatial mismatch? Employment shifts, population shifts, and Black unemployment in American cities. *Journal of Urban Economics, 49*, 179–194.

Massey, D. S., & Hajnal, Z. L. (1995). The changing geographic structure of Black-White segregation in the United States. *Social Science Quarterly, 76*(3), 527–542.

McLafferty, S., & Preston, V. (1991). Gender, race and commuting among service sector workers. *Professional Geographer, 43*, 1–15.

McLafferty, S., & Preston, V. (1992). Spatial mismatch and labor market segmentation for African American and Latina women. *Economic Geography, 68,* 406–431.

McLafferty, S., & Preston, V. (1997). Gender, race, and the determinants of commuting New York in 1990. *Urban Geography, 18,* 192–212.

Mouw, T. (2000). Job relocation and the racial gap in unemployment in Detroit and Chicago 1980–1990. *American Sociological Review, 65,* 730–753.

Pisarski, A. (2006). *Commuting in America III: The third national report on commuting patterns and trends.* Washington, DC: Transportation Research Board.

Preston, V., McLafferty, S., & Hamilton, E. (1993). The impact of family status on Black, White, and Hispanic women's commuting. *Urban Geography, 14,* 228–250.

Preston, V., & McLaferty, S. (1999). Spatial mismatch research in the 1990s: Progress and potential. *Papers in Regional Science, 78,* 387–402.

Rutherford, B. M., & Wekerle, G. R. (1988). Captive rider, captive labor: Spatial constraints on women's employment. *Urban Geography, 9,* 116–137.

Stoll, M. A. (1996). Distance or discrimination? The convergence of space and race in understanding metropolitan racial differences in employment. *SAGE Race Relations, 21,* 3–25.

Sultana, S. (2003). Commuting constraints of Black female workers in Atlanta: an examination of the spatial mismatch hypothesis in married-couple, dual-earner households. *Southeastern Geographer, 43*(2), 249–259.

Taylor, B. D., & Ong, P. M. (1995). Spatial mismatch or automobile mismatch? An examination of race, residence and commuting in US metropolitan areas. *Urban Studies, 32,* 1453–1473.

Thompson, M. A. (1997). The impact of spatial mismatch on female labor force participation. *Economic Development Quarterly, 11,* 138–145.

Turner, S. C. (1997). Barriers to a better break: Employer discrimination and spatial mismatch in metropolitan Detroit. *Journal of Urban Affairs, 19,* 123–141.

Young, I. M. (1990). Five faces of oppression. In I. M. Young, *Justice and the politics of difference* (Chap. 2). Princeton, NJ: Princeton University Press.

Young, I. M. (2000). Residential segregation and regional democracy. In I. M. Young, *Inclusion and Democracy,* pp. 196–235.

Zax, J. F., & Kain, J. F. (1996). Moving to the suburbs: Do relocating companies leave their Black employees behind? *Journal of Labor Economics, 14*(3), 472–504.

CHAPTER SIX

Racial Identity and Policy Making

Redefining Whiteness *

SETH N. ASUMAH

Racial identity presented itself as a matter of trammels and impediments, as "tightening bonds about my feet." As I looked out into my racial world, the whole thing verged on tragedy. My "way was cloudy" and the approach to its high goals by no means straight and clear. I saw the race problem was not as I conceived, a matter of clear, fair competition, for which I was ready and eager. It was rather a matter of segregation, of hindrance and inhibition.

—W. E. B. Du Bois (1914)

In the American polity, race has an agency in almost every policy-making process. Race matters in a heterogeneous, patriarchal society such as the United States of America. Race has been used as an instrument for acquiring different forms of results, whether positive or negative. Race will continue to secure a permanent domain in both our individual and institutional patterns of interaction. Consequently, denial of racial identities and race as an irrepressible agency in the policy-making process could only lead to grave public policy paralysis or policy myopia, with implications not only for subordinate races, but also for the superordinate ones.

The discourse over race and racial identities, implicitly or explicitly, runs through every public policy agenda, whether it is on the national or local levels. Racism in America did not end with the Supreme Court ruling in *Brown vs. the Board of Education of Topeka*

(1954). And sixty years after *Brown*, a re-examination of the United States' national ethos today would indicate that Americans have made progress in some aspects of race relations, but metaracism, a White-dominated policy machinery that supports and sustains White privilege at the expense of people of color, still prevails. Racism and White supremacy didn't end with civil rights legislations in 1964 either. Racism is definitely ubiquitous and has permeated the fabric of the American polity, although many people feel uncomfortable talking about it. The brutal murder of a Black man in Jasper, Texas, in June 1998, in which the perpetrators of the crime tied and dragged the victim on the ground with their truck until his body was dismembered, could not be termed an aberration. Nor are the numerous cases of racial profiling of Blacks, Latinos, and Arab Americans by mostly White police officers and immigration officers. Nonetheless, in the Jasper case, the citizens of that town and many people across the United States, Blacks and Whites alike, voiced their protestation against that act of brutality.

Yet, it is not the "Jasper-styled" racism that destroys America the most, it is metaracism, the form of racism that is very prevalent in the marketplace, socioeconomic, and political institutions of power (Asumah & Anumonwo, 2002). Iris Young (1990) asserts, "almost all traces of a commitment to race superiority have been removed, and only the grinding processes of a White-dominated economy and technology account for the continued misery of many people of color" (p. 59). What is even more devastating is an attitude of complacent optimism by some Americans that we have reached racial equality, and racism is not an issue in the 21st century.

New York Times columnist, Anthony Lewis (1998), for instance, inculpated Stephen and Abigail Thernstrom of Harvard University and the Manhattan Institute in New York, respectively, of believing that "America's race problem has been substantially solved" (p. 14). Though the Thernstroms (1997) claimed that was not their position, they still write, "that the Black condition, White attitudes and race relations have all improved dramatically" (p. 10). Yes, there has been progress, but the intensity and scope of racism in the United States, compared with other heterogeneous, multiracial nation-states merit an ongoing dialogue on race. Ethnicity and racial heterogeneity in the United States place an irrepressible demand on policy making and the body politic, which, in turn, makes racial identity a centripetal force in most political activities.

In this essay, my primary argument is that in heterogeneous, multiracial societies, such as the United States of America, where public policy-makers at all levels are predominantly White, the dominant group's acknowledgment of their Whiteness as power and group-phenomenologically sustained variables, could enhance race relations and facilitate the policy-making process. By consciously accepting race as an agency in every political activity, Whites in America could use their privilege positively in race relations and in the policy-making sphere. Many White policy-makers, in particular, who often struggle with the feeling of guilt when a dialogue on race and racism emerge, will be more empowered to tackle racial problems if they develop a positive White racial identity. When Whites become comfortable in discussing racism and White identity, considering their Whiteness as both privilege and power statuses, they can be more effective in dealing with the American racial divide. Whites have both the economic and political resources to tackle America's racial problems, and a positive, White, group identity is a first step toward racial harmony. Redefining Whiteness involves dissecting White privilege: "The concrete benefits of access to resources and social rewards and the power to shape the norms and values of society which Whites receive, consciously or unconsciously: by virtue of their skin color in a racist society" (Wijeyesinghe, Griffin, & Love, 1997).

In the discourse over racism and White privilege, if Whites mostly see themselves as oppressors or the "bad guys," then the most logical thing for many of them to do is to either avoid such topics or deny the fact that they have the power and resources to do something about racism. Since very few people would like to be associated with the term *oppression*, and since, historically, Whites have utilized oppressive power in America for years, what approach can one take to convince White policy-makers that they have power, as a group, to positively restructure racial dynamics and race relations in the policy-making sphere? This essay is intended to explore the implications of positive White identity development in the policy-making sphere. I will use Janet Helms's 1990 conceptual framework for analyzing White racial identity development as a model for sustaining racial group power in policy making. But, first, a brief discussion of race and racism will serve as a sounding board for redefining Whiteness.

Race and Racism Revisited

The literature on race and racism is impressive. Many Americans could write books about race and racism with little trouble because of our personal experiences with these concepts. The concept and texts of race and racism are already grounded in our cognitive structures and elicit racial groups' moral character. Americans have been put into racial categories for convenience since recorded history. Nevertheless, these categories of race have taken on forms of their own, shaping our precepts, norms, cultures, policy, and patterns of political interactions. So, in the American polity, race matters. Race plays a centripetal role in our polity. If the implications of race on public policy remain unquestioned, the results could be overpowering and debilitating racial problems for the totality of the populace.

To negate the adverse effects of race, one must understand the meaning of it as a social concept. Omi and Winant (1994) define race as a "concept which signifies and symbolizes socioeconomic and political conflicts and interests by referring to different types of human bodies" (p. 63). Though the human bodies referred to in this definition implore characteristics of humans associated with biological phenotypes, these organisms maintain sociohistorical and political properties as a result of their selection in any society. For instance, in American history, under the Supreme Court ruling of *Dred Scott v. Sanford* (1857), Blacks were only considered as pieces of property, not quite human. The status of Blacks in the American polity has been defined by the society, and now Blacks are accepted as "somewhat coequal" of Whites. If the definition and selection of race depend on a political process, then race itself is an "unstable" concept, constantly changing with the political process and it is concomitant with groups' competition to sustain their interests or resolve conflicts. Issues concerning racial categories, for the above mention reason, will continue to be sociopolitical.

The origins of America's rejection of other peoples (races) could be traced from European racial reasoning, which Cornel West (1994) describes as "a division of deceptive consensual racial position based on the history of domination and subjugation of one race over another . . ." (p. 8). When Carolus Linnaeus (1735), the Swedish botanist and European father of taxonomy, wrote his essay titled "Systema Naturae," he created a racial position for Whites in his hierarchy of human classification, with the White race at the apogee of that pyramid and Blacks at the bottom (pp. 5–60). Count Arthur De Gobineau (1854), the French diplomat and scholar, maintained a similar sociopolitical position on the concept of race when he published his work, "Essay on the Inequality of Race." He was providing a synopsis and amplifying the ideas of the then Euro-American perception on race (pp. 2–15).

Reginald Horsman (1995) correctly recapitulates:

In the first half of the nineteenth century many in the United States were anxious to justify the enslavement of the blacks and the expulsion and possible extermination of the Indian. The American intellectual community did not merely absorb European ideas; it also fed European racial appetites with scientific theories stemming from the supposed knowledge and observation of blacks and Indians (p. 3).

Yet, the science Horsman talks about was nothing more than pseudoscience to justify White hegemonic thinking and attitude. Dewey (1940) writes about Thomas Jefferson, one of the authors of the declaration of American independence from Great Britain who asserted, "In memory they are equal to whites, in reason much inferior . . . I advance therefore . . . that the blacks, whether originally a different race, or made distinct by time and circumstances, are inferior to the whites" (p. 52).

Such pseudoscientific characterization of race even by an American president was easily transformed into socioeconomic and political privilege for Whites. Racial formations are therefore not natural. They are constructed by societies to affirm racial positions for public policy agendas. Race is currently understood as a sociohistorical and political concept.

Many of us tend to confuse the concept of race with that of ethnicity. The English word *ethnic* is derived from the Greek *ethnikos*, the adjectival form of *ethnos*, meaning "a nation." Later, the meaning of ethnos evolved to become paradigmatic for conceptualizing groups of different humans in the 1920s and 1930s (Asumah & Anumonwo, 1999, p. 11). Ethnicity emerged as a conceptual challenge to the prevailing biological approach to race that made people of the Black race inferior. Ethnicity has been used as a tool for ethno-nationalism and ethnic cleansing in recent times. Ironically, in America, many Whites refuse to associate themselves with the term *ethnicity*. For some obscure reason, Whites on most college campuses do not associate with the term *ethnic group*. Whenever one hears the term *ethnic students*, it is easy to associate it with Blacks, Latinos, Native Americans, or some groups other than White. This is a White ethnic identity crisis. What then is ethnicity?

Ethnicity is an affiliation or classification of a self-conscious group of people who share similar racial, kinship, cultural, and linguistic values (Barndt, 1991, p. 5). Ethnicity is a sociocultural phenomenon. Ethnic stratifications occur in multiethnic societies where a hierarchical arrangement of ethnic groups could emerge as one group establishes itself as a superordinate group, with power to shape the nature of ethic relation. Within both Black and White races there are different ethnic groups.

Ethnic cleansing is an old practice and has gained currency in recent times. Racism, the ability and power to enforce one's own prejudice or a group's, has had and continues to have a grave impact on all races, although Blacks and other subordinate races have suffered much more of the effects of racism. Simply put, "racism is prejudice plus power"; "Racism structures society so that the prejudices of one racial group are taught, perpetuated, and enforced to the benefit of the dominant group" (Barndt, 1991, p. 20). David Wellman (1977) succinctly characterizes racism as "a system of advantage based on race" (p. 4). In America, the system of advantage is controlled and maintained by Whites.

Racism and all other "isms" operate on a common premise. Most "isms," including racism, have a control group that exercises power and privilege, and a target group that is dominated, subjugated, and marginalized in resource and power distributions. Racism does not only rest on individual action and ignorance. Institutional powers make racism viable. From Main Street to Wall Street, Whites control the institutional structures of power. From the village council to the national government, the same group has the marginal propensity to make most policies in America. Given these premises, and by making reference to racism as group prejudice plus institutional power, Whites in America control and maintain the dominant structures of power to impose their will on other groups and therefore benefit from racism. Certainly, not all Whites are racists, but every White person implicitly or explicitly participates and benefits from the system that racism fosters. Furthermore, White supremacy harbors the most toxic forms of racism, such as the Rodney King beating or the Jasper, Texas, killing of Mr. Byrd.

Peggy McIntosh (1988) informs her readers about the historical "White Privilege" that White America has over the rest of the general populace. McIntosh is particularly clear about this "unearned" privilege for Whites in America (p. 2). With these privilege and power, Whites are in a better position to solve America's racial problems by developing a positive White identity. This is not a crusade to push undue responsibility on White Americans and their image development. However, it is a truism that White Americans constantly fail to acknowledge their race as a group phenomenon, and that Whites, as a group, maintain an "unearned privilege" to tackle America's racial problems. Once Whites have developed a unified, positive group identity, they can effectively shape public policy regarding racial issues.

Searching for White Racial Identity

The process and state of defining for oneself and acknowledging the personal significance, responsibility, and social meaning of belonging to a particular group is referred to as racial identity development (Helms, 1990, p. 6). Although racial and ethnic identities are used interchangeably, and sometimes synonymously, they are different terms. As one can deduce from the earlier discussion in this essay about race and ethnicity, racial identity and ethnic identity have clear distinctions. For instance, an Italian American or a Jewish American may identify him- or herself with a particular ethnic group, but may not consider him- or herself in racial terms as White. Similarly, one may acknowledge the personal linkage to a racial group, Black in this case, but would not associate with the ethnicity of African American or Afro-Cuban. Nonetheless, racial and ethnic identities at times intersect.

At this juncture, one may pose a pressing and mind-boggling question: If racial categorization by Europeans was to serve a racist interest, then why must racial identity produce a positive effective on public policy? The response to the question lies in our approach to essentially planned sociopolitical constructs that give meaning to issues at a particular time in history. Racial identities prevail in many subordinate groups and if superordinate groups relegate their group responsibility as, perhaps, an individual, less important issues, then racial problems will not be effectively tackled. We must therefore discuss racial identity from a different perspective, with a shift in a paradigm, to effectively confront our racial problems in America.

Hence, Beverly Tatum (1997) succinctly proclaims that, "The concept of identity is a complex one, shaped by individual characteristics, family dynamics, historical factors, and social and political contexts" (p. 18). The aggregate variables of individuals in a given entity become a group's identity. Tatum continues:

> Dominant groups, by definition set the parameters within which the subordinates operate. The dominant group holds the power and authority in the society relative to the subordinates and determines how that power and authority may be acceptably used. Whether it is reflected in determining who gets the best jobs, whose history will be taught in school, or whose relationships will be validated by society, the dominant group has the greatest influences in determining the structure of the society (p. 22).

Tatum's assertion supports the premise of the primary argument of this chapter. If the superordinate group has the most power and resources in shaping the dynamics of group interaction and policies, then by not denying the fact that, as a group, it has the privilege of positively restructuring racial relationships; it can consciously produce public policy agendas with the subordinate group's interest in mind. The superordinate group in this aspect is a surrogate of political power and should use it positively to restructure race relations.

The basic difference between White and Black racial identity development is that Blacks learn and understand "Blackness" very earlier on in life, while Whites resist any association with "Whiteness," especially when they are cognizant of the fact that there is a correlation between "Whiteness" and privilege. This situation occurs because Blacks are socialized to be "Black" first, before anything else. Whites, on the other hand, are not socialized to be sociocentric; they are more egocentric in the process of their development. Tatum (1997) correctly notes in her work on racial identity that:

> Like many White people, this young woman had never really considered her own racial and ethnic group membership. For her, Whiteness was simply the unexamined norm. Because they represent the societal norm, Whites can easily reach adulthood without thinking much about their racial group (p. 95).

Putting a normative value on whiteness for the rest of the society constrains subordinate groups in a condition of cultural imperialism. Here, the dominant group reinforces its position by bringing the other groups under the measure of its dominant norm (Young, 1990, p. 59). For this matter, White policy-makers who fail to pay attention to their whiteness characterize their actions as only "normal," and "they are just doing their job."

Seldom do many Whites stop to consider the benefits they accrue in belonging to their race. Nor does it surprise them that they possess such privilege. It is important to emphasize, however, that people who are not blind do not take time out to rave over their vision as a gift, for which they should be grateful. Certainly, having white skin does not grant one the immunity from failure or misfortune. Yet, Whites who fall to the bottom of the socioeconomic pile still have "white privilege" because of the color of their skin. Why is this privilege so important in making public policy? To what extent can public policy be more equitable if Whites positively acknowledge their privilege as a group phenomenon? These questions will be tackled in the following sections.

White Identity and the Policy-Making Process

Human societies overall, including the American polity in particular, are complex. The social sciences have the Herculean task of making this complexity somewhat manageable. Public policy, besides examining what people do and why they develop series of steps to attain certain goals, is also concerned with the best thing to do and whether the best results could be attained through a given idea, approach, or technique. There is a plethora of literature addressing public policy techniques, but almost none has taken account of the racial and ethnic identities of policy makers in multiracial entities, and how that affects the process of policy making and a particular policy package.

One cannot comprehend the essence of group identity in the policy-making apparatus until he or she recognizes the importance of benefits, representation, and the dynamics of alliance in the process of policy making. Legislators are directly involved in the policy process. Implicitly or explicitly, all branches of government—legislature, executive, and the judiciary—have actions that result in some public policy. Representation in these branches is regarded by political scientists as descriptive, symbolic, or substantive. Though Pitkin (1972) utilized these terms in association with the legislature, they are applicable to the other branches of government (p. 5).

Descriptive representation is the degree to which institutions have the same demographic composition as those whom they represent. Symbolic representation is concerned with the extent to which a particular aspect of the general populace has confidence or trust in an institution charged with policy making. Finally, substantive representation is that in which public policy agenda and the laws propounded by policy makers reflect the preferences of the general populace (Pitkin, pp. 5–6). With reference to symbolic representation, Blacks, as well as Whites, have relatively low levels of confidence and trust in the bureaucracy and Congress. Only 14% of the American public said they had great confidence in government. Sixty-seven percent of Blacks have low confidence and trust governments in America (Tatum, 1997). I think these statistics are even worse because of higher levels of secrecy in government associated with the post–September 11, 2001 events. In essence, both Whites and Blacks have distrust for policy makers, but it is much more so for Blacks, because Whites, who spearhead the policy process, refuse to acknowledge their whiteness and privileged positions in the entire process.

The numerical preponderance of White policy-makers at all levels of the American society cannot be overemphasized. In the 105th Congress (1997–1999), for instance, Whites comprise 86% in the House of Representatives and 96% in the Senate. Blacks make up 9% in the House of Representatives and 1% in the Senate (*Congressional Quarterly*, 1998). Latinos, Asian Americans, and Native Americans constitute the remaining membership. Historically, the United States Congress has not been descriptively representative of Blacks in America. Of more than 11,000 persons who have served in that institution, only 102 have been Black (*Congressional Quarterly*, 1998). Overall, the American Congress is not a representative body, so far as subordinate races are concerned. Concomitant with White group identity denial, the policy-making process becomes even more elusive if and when the dominant group fails to incorporate identity politics of acknowledging its power dimension and the presence of race.

The United States Supreme Court has always been actively involved in judicial policy-making through the decisions of the Court. The Court is not only a legal institution; it is a political one, because it arrives at decisions on controversial questions of national policy. Chief Justice Roger B. Taney's infamous opinion in *Dred Scott v. Sanford* (1857) affected the lives of Africans in America until the 1940s. He impugned:

> The question is simply this: can a Negro, whose ancestors were imported into this country, and sold as slaves, become a member of the political community formed and brought into existence by the constitution of the United States, and as such become entitled to all the rights, and privileges, and immunities, guaranteed by that instrument to be citizens . . . We think they are not, and they are not included, were not intended to be included, under the word "citizen" in the Constitution, and can therefore claim none of the rights and privileges which that instrument provides for and secures to a citizen of the United States. On the contrary, they were at that time considered as a subordinate and inferior class of beings, who had been subjugated by the dominant race, and whether emancipated or not, yet remained subject to their authority, and had no rights or privileges (Hall, Wiecek, & Finkelman, 1991, p. 208).

Historically, the Supreme Court has, at times, been a racist institution, refusing to support the universal freedom for Blacks. This is not 1857, yet in 2004, the Court maintained justice with similar racist ideas. Chief Justice Rehnquist wrote this in a memorandum, "I realize it is an unpopular and unhumanitarian position, for which I have been excoriated by 'liberal' colleagues, but I think *Plessy v. Ferguson* was right and should be affirmed" (Kluger, 1977, p. 606). In addition, the Court is quite notorious in refusing to hire Black law clerks.

Chief Justice Rehnquist had 99% White clerks, Scalia, 100% Whites; Souter, 94% Whites; and O'Connor, 91% Whites. From 1972 to 1998, only 1.8% of the law clerks were Black, 1% was Latino, and 4.5% were Asian American (*USA Today*, 1998 p. 4A). In the 2002–2003 term, only 15% of all the law clerks were people of color (Strauss, 2002). The Court's clerkship in the 2013–2014 term consists of three new minorities, Fred Smith, Jr., who is working for Associate Justice Sonia Sotomayor; Elizabeth Wilkins, serving Associate Justice Elena Kagan; and Michael Gerrais, who is a biracial law clerk and will begin his term in 2014 (Young, 2013). All these examples lead to the primary argument of this essay, which holds that White policymakers indulge in actions that involve racial identity politics without accepting the preeminence of their privilege and Whiteness. Once the positions of privilege and group identity are acknowledged and acted on, reason will prevail in the policy-making sphere, and racist policies will be reduced, if not eliminated.

In Weberian characterization, bureaucracy is a rule of official-dom, which maintains forms of power based on knowledge, rationality, and hierarchical structures (Weber, 1969, pp. 3–57). However, even though, the primary function of bureaucracy is to execute the law and implement policy, it also serves quasi-legislative and quasi-judicial functions by administrative rule-making and adjudicating conflicts that arise under those rules in administrative courts and claims of agency beneficiaries. Indubitably, many more Blacks work in the federal bureaucracy. The Civil Rights Acts of 1957, 1960, and 1964 and Title VII of that act which created the Equal Employment Opportunity Commission (EEOC), have all helped to ensure nondiscrimination in federal employment and private companies holding federal contracts (Walton and Smith, 2000, p. 240). Yet, the overall evaluation of the bureaucracy is that it has not been consistently useful in Black America's quest for universal freedom. Occasionally, the bureaucracy has been hostile to the African American quest (p. 241). The fact remains that most of the policy-makers in the higher echelons of the federal, state, and local establishments are predominantly Whites, who refuse to acknowledge any group identity and privilege.

In the racial structural functional model for policy-making below, all stages of the process are controlled primarily by White actors who have no consideration for affinity groups; only affiliation groups, such as political parties, are taken seriously. Policy-makers in this model deal with the abstractions of policy agenda transformed into concrete goals without consideration for race as an indicator privilege, power or powerlessness. Most of these policy-makers and implemented who are White believe they are only "doing their jobs and race should not be a factor." But as we all know, in America, race matters.

Redefining Positive White Identity in the Policy Sphere

Racial identity development theory, according to Janet Helms (1990), is concerned with the socio-psycho-cultural implication of racial group membership, which includes belief systems that evolve in reactions to different perceptions racial groups maintain (pp. 3–25). Since in America racial group membership is emphasized, it is assumed that all groups, including White policy-makers will form a racial identity at a certain time. However, Whites have not come to terms with their whiteness. Helms (1990) asserts:

> Concurrently, the person must become aware of her or his whiteness, learn to accept whiteness as an important part of herself or himself, and to internalize a realistically positive view of what it means to be White (p. 55).

Helms's model can be bifurcated through, first, rejection of racism by Whites, and second, defining a positive White identity. That identity, theoretically, would result in White policy-makers making nonracist policy and seeing themselves as allies to subordinate groups in the entire policy process. While several White allies have resisted the role of oppressor, many of them, unfortunately, are political activists or educators who are not directly involved in the policy process.

Helms's model consists of six stages: Contact, Disintegration, Reintegration, Pseudo-Independent, Immersion/Emersion, and Autonomy (p. 58). At the Contact stage, White policy-makers pay very little attention to their racial group membership. White policy-makers believe that it is "normal" for them to have White privilege. These individuals in this group seldom describe themselves as White.

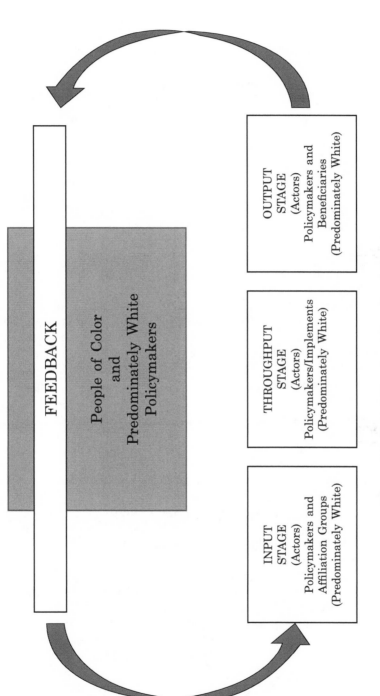

Figure 6.1. Racial Structural Functional Model

This is a universal humanist perspective. White policy-makers here always claim they are "just normal and doing their jobs," even if they engage in racist undertakings. White police officers engaged in racial profiling are one of the prime examples at this stage, claiming for example, that racial profiling is an indispensable tool for police work.

The Disintegration stage forces White policy-makers to begin to see how much their lives, and the lives of subordinate groups, have been affected by racist policies. Uncomfortable with this insight, they tend to deny the validity of information about racism, submerged in a state of cognitive dissonance and denial. White policy-makers at this stage make the case that racism ended in the 1960s, or, they withdraw from discussing it at all. If policy-makers deny the premise of a racial problem at the input stage, there is every possibility that the policy will be devoid of any racial considerations, therefore failing to achieve the policy goal. For instance, it is common for White policy-makers to make the argument that there is no need to write new laws about hate crimes against Blacks or arson of Black churches because there are already laws against crimes in general. What these policy-makers fail to acknowledge is the racial element to these crimes. The third stage, Reintegration, finds White policy-makers blaming the failure of the Black community on Blacks themselves, or the victims. White policy-makers, at this juncture, instruct Blacks to change their attitude and behavior in order to benefit from public policy. As Wellman (1977) correctly notes, such perception allows White individuals to relieve themselves of any guilt or responsibility for advocating social change. The "blame game" contributes to policy myopia: shortsightedness in policy making because of the misperceptions of policy makers in examining problems carefully. They rather blame the problems on policy beneficiaries instead of going to the root cause of the problem—racism.

Acknowledging racism, and understanding it, facilitates the reduction of "blaming the victim" by White policy-makers at the Pseudo-Independent stage. This is the stage at which the development of a positive White identity begins. White policy-makers can easily recognize their hegemonic power in the policy process. and begin to form policy allies with Black policy-makers and beneficiaries. Bell (1997) characterizes hegemonic power as one in which "a dominant group can project a particular way of seeing social reality so successfully that its view is accepted as common sense, as part of the natural order even by those who are disempowered by it"—people of color (p. 11). Here, White policy-makers will transcend the limits of thinking about racism as just an individual issue. They comprehend the sophistication of institutional racism in the American society and refrain from blaming subordinate groups for their own oppression.

The next stage for White racial identity is the Immersion/Emersion stage. Here, White policy-makers make efforts to create a positive White identity. Policy-makers re-examine their own whiteness and finds answers for their privilege. At this point, the feeling of guilt and shame are replaced with a newfound feeling of excitement and pride in whiteness. Policy-makers will become advocates for those who are oppressed because of their race. They can easily unlearn the racism that they learned at an earlier age. With this kind of a mind-set, White policy-makers will not remove themselves anymore from identity politics. They develop better techniques for using White privilege positively.

The final stage, Autonomy, is concomitant with newfound Whiteness. Policy-makers from the superordinate race interact with subordinate groups for positive policy goals. The positive aspect of this autonomy is an equitable policy package for the general populace. This is a stage of group self-consciousness and self-actualization. White policy-makers become more open-minded and are receptive to new information regarding racial dynamics. White policy-makers at this juncture become advocates for antiracist policy goals, but as Helms (1990) cautions, even at this point of self-actualization in race relations, White policy-makers must continue to work toward consciousness-raising for other Whites for stronger alliances, just as Blacks continue to work for the achievement of a new Blackness. Whites could become more excited about their Whiteness when they begin to think and behave as a group that has the human experience to engage the United States honestly and act more morally in the policy arena. The conceptualization of Whiteness as an aspect of White privilege would become a phenomenologically sustained variable which, at best, could enhance race relations and facilitate the process of race relations and policy-making. Unlearning racism would involve both normative and transformative approaches. The normative approach as presented in the chapter includes Helms's model of White identity development. The transformative approach would include institutional reforms and legislations that would probe any policy-making efforts that take hierarchical arrangements of the races in any setting in consideration. We will reach a point of celebrating Whiteness (not White supremacy) when Whites take proactive actions as allies to people of color and respond to making moral judgments about what they do with their success based on

White privilege. The "new Blackness" is defined by Black culture and race that are equipped with the power and ability to transcend posttraumatic slave syndromes, the dynamics of Black exceptionalism, and cross-over experiences.

Conclusion

No nation state is as fertile a laboratory for studying the dynamics of race and race relations as the United States. Nevertheless, owing to the sensitive nature surrounding the discourse on race, its centripetal force in the policy arena has been diluted or avoided by White policy-makers for the sake of convenience and maybe not knowing what to do. The irony of this avoidance or cognitive dissonance is a resultant of even more racial tension and racial policy paralysis. Since Whites maintain the hegemonic power in the policy sphere, hold socioeconomic and political power, and racism is not only an individual but also institutional action or inaction, it is meaningful to examine White privilege and the policy-making sphere through identity politics and positive White racial identity development. The goal in this approach is to redefine Whiteness from a more positive perspective (not from hierarchical racial formation) so that White policy-makers can use their privilege and power position to enhance the process of policy-making for a better race relation. This is not to say that advocating the supereminence of White racial identity is a panacea for America's racial problems: it is one of the many approaches we can use in attaining concrete racial policy goals.

The hallmark of redefining Whiteness positively, though, is the sense of liberation from self-denial and an acknowledgment that whiteness is part of every White person's being in any multiracial and multiethnic polity where Whites are the superordinate group. Again, in a multiethnic and multiracial entity such as the United States, solutions to racial problems must be multiperspectival. In this sense I offer this approach of reexamining Whiteness not from a victimizer's point of view, but as allies to eradicate racism. We must continue to dialogue, because silence over the race question will only magnify the racial divide. As James Baldwin once eloquently said, "Not everything that is faced can be changed. But nothing can be changed until it is faced." In developing positive White racial identity, race will sustain an agency in the policy-making process and change will be possible. We must continue to keep hope alive for a racism-free American public policy.

Note

*Another version of this chapter was previously published in 2004 in the *Western Journal of Black Studies, 28*(4). It was reprinted with permission from the *Western Journal of Black Studies*.

References

Asumah, S. N., & Johnston-Anumonwo, I. (2002). *Diversity, multiculturalism and social justice.* Binghamton, NY: Global Publications.

Asumah, S. N., & Johnston-Anumonwo, I. (1999). *Issues in multiculturalism: Cross-national perspectives,* 2nd ed. New York: Whittier Publications.

Bell, L. A. (1997). Theoretical foundation of social justice education. In M. Adams, L. A. Bell, & P. Griffin (Eds.), *Teaching for diversity and social justice: A sourcebook.* New York: Routledge.

Barndt, J. (1991). *Dismantling racism in America: The continuing challenge to white America.* Minneapolis, MN: Augsburg.

Congressional Quarterly (1998). Biographical directory of the American Congress, 1974–1996. Washington, DC: Fortress Publishers.

De Gobineau, A. (1854). Essay on the inequality of the human races, translated by Adrian Collins (1915). New York: Putman's Sons.

Dewey, J. (1940). *The living thoughts of Thomas Jefferson.* New York: Longman.

Du Bois, W. E. B. (1914, July 14). Does race antipathy serve any good purpose? *Boston Globe.*

Hall, K., Wiecek, W., & Finkelman, P. (Ed.). (1991). Dred Scott v. Sanford 60 U.S. 393, 1857. In *American legal history: Cases and materials.* New York: Oxford University Press.

Helms, J. (1990). *Black and white identity: Theory, research and practice.* Westport, CT: Greenwood Press.

Horsmann, R. (1995). *Race and manifest destiny: The origins of American racial Anglo-Saxonism.* Cambridge, MA: Harvard University Press.

Kluger, R. (1977). *Simple justice: The history of Brown v. Board of Education.* New York: Vintage Books.

Lewis, A. (1998, August 13). The case of Lani Guinier. *New York Review of Books,* p. 14.

Linnaeus, C. (1735). Systema naturae. Amsterdam, Holland: Niewkoop O. B. De Graaf.

McIntosh, P. (1988). White privilege, male privilege, working papers, 189, p. 2.

Omi, M., & Winant, H. (1994). *Racial formation in the United States from the 1960s to the 1990s.* New York: Routledge.

Pitkin, H. (1977). *The concept of representation.* Berkeley: University of California Press.

Strauss, D. (2003). Behind the bench: The guide to judicial clerkship. Barbri
    Group. Chicago: Gilbert Law Publishing.
Tatum, B. (1997). *Why are all the black kids sitting together in the cafeteria?*
    New York: Basic Books. Thernstrom, S., & Thernstrom, A. (1997).
    America in black and white. New York: Touchstone Books.
Walton, H., & Smith, R. C. (2000). *American politics and the African American
    quest for universal freedom.* New York: Longman.
Longman, Weber, M. (1969). *Essays in sociology.* New York: Oxford University
    Press.
West, C. (1994). *Race matters.* New York: Vintage Books.
Wijeyesinghe, C, Griffin, P., & Love, B. (1997). Racism in curriculum design.
    In M. Adams, W. Blumenfeld, C. Castaneda, H. Hackman, M. Peters,
    & X. Zuniga (Eds.), *Readings for diversity and social justice. 3rd ed.*
    New York: Routledge.
Young, M. I. (1990). *Justice and the politics of difference.* Princeton, NJ:
    Princeton University Press.
Young, Y. (2013). SCOTUS law clerk hires and the art of determining one's
    racial identity. Retrieved on October 12, 2013: www.onbeingablack-
    lawyer.com

CHAPTER SEVEN

Examining Cyberstalking Through the Prism of Race and Gender

TOSHA A. ASUMAH AND DEBRA F. GLASER

Introduction: Rethinking Stalking

Having gained coinage since the sixteenth century in the world of poachers, the twenty-first century reference to stalking has been popularized by the media for people who are obsessed with the other and engage in an uninvited intrusion in the other's life. Just as poachers pursued their game illegally, stalkers do the same to their victims, but this time the game is human. The literature on stalking is impressive, yet the research on why people stalk in reference to race and gender is limited. This study examined whether there is a correlation between gender, as well as race, and a perceived threat in regard to characteristics of cyberstalkers. Past research has shown that what people perceive to be threatening varies based on gender and race. With the advances in technology, cyberstalking, has become a growing issue, yet there is no standard law across the United States to combat the problem. This study was conducted to help determine whether the difference in perception of threat could further hinder the development of creating a standard law for the crime. It was found that there was a difference between genders and what is perceived to be threatening, but no difference in terms of race.

Meloy (2007) described stalking as being behaviorally expressed pathological attachment, which can be both insecure and preoccupied. Although researchers have gathered information regarding the characteristics of the stalker, aspects of the phenomenon still require investigation. One third of stalking cases involve physical violence, so stalking should not be considered insignificant (Meloy, 2007). Meloy

(2007) has suggested that stalking has been linked to behaviors during an intimate relationship, such as domestic violence, jealousy, and domination of the partner.

Roberts and Dziegielewski (2006) reviewed 60 cases of stalking from prosecutor's files in two New Jersey counties. They found that in most cases, the stalkers were male and the primary victims were female. Of the stalkers, 67% were noncommitted (single or divorced) males. Of the victims, 73% were noncommitted. Eighty percent of the cases involved current or previous relationships. In 23% of the cases, the perpetrator used a weapon, resulting in serious injury to the victim. In total, 54 cases involved domestic violence, and six were *erotomanic*. The term *erotomanic* describes a delusion that the victim is in love with the perpetrator. These studies highlight the connection between stalking habits and romantic relationships.

Spitzberg (2002) conducted a meta-analysis to examine the research on stalking and stalking phenomena. A literature search was conducted using psychological and legal search engines, and entering derivatives of the term *stalking*. Spitzberg (2002) included 103 studies, with 68,615 participants. Based on results from across the studies, Spitzberg (2002) found that 23.3% of women and 10.5% of men reported experiencing stalking. Forty-nine percent of stalking involved a previous romantic relationship. Prior acquaintances were involved in 22.5% of the cases, and in 18% of the cases, the victim and the perpetrator were strangers.

It is important to recognize that stalking is an international issue. In 2001, Sheridan, Davies, and Boon conducted a study in Britain and Northern Ireland. Sheridan et al. surveyed 95 self-identified victims of stalking who contacted a London-based charity concerned with the promotion of personal safety. Overall 92% of the participants were female, 7% were male, and a couple was considered as one participant (1%). Participants reported that 87% of their stalkers were male, 7% of stalkers were female; and 5% of participants had multiple stalkers. In terms of participants' relationship with their perpetrators, 48% stated that the stalker was an ex-partner, 12% had no prior relationship with the stalker, and 37% stated that they were a former acquaintance. Participants reported that in 91% of the cases the stalker watched the victim, in 82% of the cases victims reported being followed, and in 77% of cases victims reported that the perpetrator tried to obtain information about the victim. Of the participants, 72% reported that these behaviors worsened over time; 53% of victims reported being threatened with physical assault; 32% reported actually being assaulted, 25% reported being victims of attempted murder; and 3% of victims reported being sexually assaulted. Only 21% of participants reported that stalking had ceased at the time of the study. This study exemplifies the notion that stalking habits may be similar in various countries. Similar to studies from the United States (see Roberts and Dziegielewski, 2006; Spitzberg, 2002), a higher percentage of participants reported being stalked by an ex-partner compared to a stranger. Furthermore, in the United States, Britain, and Northern Ireland, women made up a larger percentage of victims than men (Roberts and Dziegielewski, 2006; Spitzberg, 2002).

Spitzberg and Hoobler (2002) suggested that stalking is not just an isolated incident, but a course of conduct in which the stalker invades a person's relative right to personal privacy. Stalking requires evidence of threat or fear, and this threat or fear does not merely have to be perceived by the victim, but could also be perceived by a third party (Spitzberg & Hoobler, 2002). Southworth, Finn, Dawson, Fraser, and Tucker (2007), highlighted the different types of technological devices that stalkers often use, including: caller ID, cell phones, GPS, and spyware.

Stalking is an international problem that presents nearly the same way worldwide. It is an obsessive, unrequited attachment to another person that can lead to a spectrum of behaviors, ranging from invasion of privacy to assault (Meloy, 2007). Researchers have found that overall, in most cases of stalking the stalker-victim dyad was once a romantic couple. Only a small percentage of stalkers are strangers to their victim. Research has shown that most stalkers are White males who were either single or divorced at the time of stalking (Roberts and Dziegielewski, 2006). As technology improves, stalkers are now using other means to reach their victims (Spitzberg & Hoobler, 2002; Southworth, Finn, Dawson, Fraser, & Tucker, 2007). Cyberstalking is becoming more of an issue because it is providing stalkers with myriad ways not only to remain connected to their victims, but also to gain access to private information, and in worst case scenarios, harm victims (Southworth et al., 2007).

Cyberstalking: The Undesirable Baggage of Technology and the Social Media

Cyberstalking is defined as stalking or harassing another person with the use of the Internet, e-mail, or other electronic communication devices (Moriarty & Freiberger, 2008). Examples of cyberstalking include: repeatedly sending e-mails or instant messages, sending viruses, using others' e-mail addresses to establish online subscriptions, stealing online identities to post false information about a victim, and using cell phones and GPS to track the movements of the victim. Moriarty and Freiberger (2008) conducted a study to determine the motivation of the offender, gender of victims and offenders, the relationship between the two parties, and the stalker's behavior. They collected data from reported cyberstalking in the newspaper. From examining two different newspapers and collecting data from 1999 through 2006, researchers found 61 cases of cyberstalking. Approximately half of the cases found involved threatening, harassing or obscene e-mails, about one-third involved live-chat harassment, and about one-fourth involved threatening, harassing, or obscene calls to a cell phone. Most of the cases involved what the research titled *domestic violence issues*. The researchers used the term *domestic violence* to mean that the perpetrator felt a need to try to control, or reinstate control over the victim. Most offenders in this study were male, and most victims had no prior relationship with the perpetrator. Aside from the use of technology, this study demonstrated another difference between stalking and cyberstalking: in cyberstalking the offender tends to be a stranger, as opposed to a previous partner. This is a significant difference, signifying that there may be substantial character difference in those who choose to cyberstalk and those who stalk offline.

Pittaro (2007) stated that most cyberstalking behaviors are premeditated and repetitious. Cyberstalkers can be aggressive in their behaviors, but only border on being illegal under the current statutory laws in most states (Pittaro, 2007). Cyberstalking is fueled by rage, power, control, and anger that may have been precipitated by a victim's action or inaction (Pittaro, 2007). Cyberstalkers are typically White-collar criminals, in the middle to upper class (Pittaro, 2007). They are typically White males, with stable employment and firmly established ties to the community (Pittaro, 2007). Many have a prior criminal record, history of substance abuse, and/or a personality disorder. For the cyberstalker, e-mail is the main means of harassment (Pittaro, 2007). California has the most cyberstalking cases of any state.

McFarlane and Bocij (2003) conducted a study using a modified Stalking Incident Checklist in an attempt to determine a concrete typology of cyberstalking. Researchers found 13 cases of both online and offline stalking. Results yielded 11 cases of people experiencing threats, and of those 11 cases, four had made threats to third parties as well. The data indicated that there was a higher percentage of the stalker and victim being in a professional position, as opposed to student or in a lower-skilled position. Most of those who had experienced stalking had only met via the Internet. Last, there were more males stalking females (75%), than females stalking males. The recognition of these traits is important to research because with this information, more of a typology can be created to predict who might participate in cyberstalking.

Sheridan and Grant (2007) conducted a study in which they surveyed 1,261 victims of stalking and cyberstalking about their experiences. An Internet-based version of the survey was placed on antistalking forums and circulated throughout charities, surveying those in North America, the United Kingdom, and Australia. Researchers created four groups of *stalking types* based on the answers to the questionnaire. The stalking types were: participants who were stalked purely online; those who had a *crossover stalker* (starting online then moving offline); those who had a *proximal stalker* with online usage, meaning the stalker was predominately offline, but used the Internet at times; and the last group were those who were stalked purely offline. A total of 47.5% of participants were stalked using the Internet. Of that sample, only 7.2% were considered victims of cyberstalking. For this group, the stalking originated online, remained online for a minimum of 4 weeks, and most of the victims met the stalker online (73.7%). Sheridan and Grant (2007) compared the groups and found that threats were more often associated with purely offline stalking. In comparison to the other groups, individuals who cyberstalked were more often strangers and acquaintances to the victims as opposed to previous intimate partners. Thus it appears that cyberstalkers are unique because they tend to form attachments with individuals who they did not know prior to online contact. Research must examine this sense of attachment, and how it is developed for the cyberstalker.

McGarth and Casey (2002) outlined the ways in which the Internet allows predators to gain access to victims, as well as the way it perpetuates predator characteristics. McGarth and Casey (2002) stated that chat rooms allow people to disclose more personal information than they would normally. The lack of face-to-face contact and the level of anonymity can lead individuals to lose normal social inhibitions and constraints (McGarth & Casey, 2002). By reducing feelings such as embarrassment and apprehension, the Internet can lead individuals to engage in acts that they might not normally consider. McGarth and Casey (2002) postulated that the reduction of sensory information facilitates fantasy. Without body language, facial expression, or tone of voice, a person can project his or her needs onto an individual, fulfilling his or her fantasies. An increased sense of safety could allow one to move from being merely a voyeur to *cyber fondling, cyber exposing,* or contacting the victim. The Internet gives predators a lot of access to information about victims. Predators can monitor their victim's movements online by sending *Trojan Horses* to the victim's computer, therefore having full access to information (McGarth & Casey, 2002). A Trojan Horse is software that appears to be providing a harmless function for the user, but allows another person access to the computer. The use of this information can also allow the predator to create a bond with victim, to gain trust, and possibly later control of personal accounts.

Research supports the notion that cyberstalking is a new category of offense that requires more research. The literature has shown that cyberstalkers present differently than offline stalkers. The most significant difference between stalkers and cyberstalkers is the choice of the victim. Cyberstalkers typically choose strangers for victims (Moriarty & Freiberger, 2008). This is very dangerous in an era in which the Internet can allow these predators to have access to multiple victims. Nevertheless, the way and manner in which people perceive threat or apparent threat and fear are different based on a number of variables, including gender, race, and location. This complexity illustrates the need for deeper study in the area of cyberstalking in order to be able to identify individuals who engage in predatory behavior, who are a threat to society in ways, that up until now, were unavailable.

Threat Perception

Researchers have often investigated the way that people perceive threat; the way people perceive risk, and what things are found to provoke fear. Although there are mixed findings, most researchers have found that there is a difference in perception between genders. Ferraro (1996) conducted the Fear of Crime survey. Ferraro (1996) conducted the survey by utilizing the random digit dialing procedure in the 33 largest metropolitan areas in the United States, and 117 additional smaller metropolitan areas, or countries chosen on a *probability proportionate to size basis*. There were 1,001 respondents who took part in the study, with 55% of respondents being women. Respondents were asked about their fear on a continuum, starting with being approached by a beggar on the street, to more serious types of victimization, including murder (Ferraro, 1996). The results state that women were more fearful in all 10 of the offenses listed: being approached by a beggar, being cheated or conned out of money, having someone break into their homes while they are away, having

someone break into their homes while they are there, being raped
or sexually assaulted, being murdered, being attacked by someone
with a weapon, having your car stolen, being robbed or mugged on
the street, and having property damaged by vandals (Ferraro, 1996).
Differences between genders were greater for rape, burglary, and
robbery. The most dramatic difference was the difference in fear of
sexual assault (Ferraro, 1996). Men were more likely to perceive
risk at being approached by a beggar or being cheated out of money
(Ferraro, 1996). Fear of rape was stronger than the perceived risk
of rape, for both men and women (Ferraro, 1996).

Ferraro (1996) was one of the first to support the possibility
that there is a gender difference in perception of fear and risk. More
recent studies have also supported this hypothesis. Reid and Konrad (2004) surveyed a random sample of adults in New Orleans.
Two hundred and sixty-nine individuals participated in the survey
(Reid & Konrad, 2004). Individuals answered questions in reference
to their fear of burglary, property crime, sexual assault, and robbery
(Reid & Konrad, 2004). Respondents also answered questions about
their perceived risk of victimization. Women reported a higher level
of fear of sexual assault, as well as robbery (Reid & Konrad, 2004).
For both genders, those that had experienced a recent crime had
higher levels of fear overall. This study supports the research of the
past that supports a gender difference in perception. Aside from more
frequent crimes, others have extended the research to investigate
other types of fearful events.

Nellis (2009) surveyed 527 people by telephone, in the metropolitan areas of New York City and the District of Colombia. The
questions focused on worry and perceived risk of terrorism, actions
taken in response to government-issued alerts about terrorism risk,
exposure to the news in general, exposure to terrorism-related news,
and additional questions about related topics (Nellis, 2009). The participants were 56% women and 43% men. Respondents were asked to
answer on a 10-point scale, ranging from no fear to great fear, about
the worry of becoming a victim of a terrorist attack (Nellis, 2009).
Respondents were asked to think about the time period following the
changes in the United States Terror Advisory System before answering questions on the survey.

The study found that women expressed higher levels of worry
than men. Women were also significantly more likely to seek information (Nellis, 2009). Women were significantly more likely to report
avoidance behaviors, and watched significantly more news (Nellis,
2009). Last, women reported higher levels of perceived risk (Nellis,
2009).

Youn and Hall (2008) surveyed 395 public high school students in a city in the Midwest. The participants were 56% female, with ages ranging from 14 to 18 years old. Researchers assessed susceptibility, severity, and privacy in relation to Internet usage. Youn and Hall (2008) found that there were significant gender differences in privacy risk perception, level of concern, and protection behaviors. Girls' perception of susceptibility to unsolicited e-mails was rated as higher than boys. Perception of privacy risks was more serious for girls than boys; also girls were more concerned with the lack of privacy with the *emarketers*' information practices (Youn & Hall, 2008). Boys were more apt to read unsolicited e-mails, register for websites, and send negative messages to companies that sent spam (Youn & Hall, 2008). This study illustrates that, with the change in technology, both genders may respond to Internet practices and concerns in different ways, finding some practices more risky than others. Research appears to support the difference in gender perception for risk and fear of crime, and the misuse of personal information on the Internet (Ferraro, 1996; Reid & Konrad, 2004; Youn & Hall, 2008).

In addition to the differences in the way that males and females perceive threat, research has also shown that races vary in the way that they conceptualize what is fearful. Pain (2001) conducted a meta-analysis examining the research on gender, race, age, and fear in the city. In research about women's fear in urban California White women's perceptions of vulnerability partially included the perceived threat of rape from men of color. Women of color included race in the construction of their fear, but aside from fears of sexual assault, they also feared racist harassment and violence (Pain, 2001). The research further indicated that the different parts of someone's identity worked in different ways to influence one's fear of crime (Pain, 2001). Women of color tend to report higher levels of fear of rape, and overall, people of color have a higher fear of crime than Whites (Pain, 2001).

In a study conducted by Satterfield, Mertz, and Slovic (2004), further investigation of these differences occurred. A national telephone survey was again conducted to examine perceived risks, worldviews, trust, environmental values, discrimination, vulnerability, and justice. The survey included 19 different sources of risk. Participants were asked to rate the risks on a scale from *almost no risk* to *high risk* (Satterfield et al., 2004). From September 27, 1997 to February 3, 1998 information was collected from individuals in the United States, over the age of 18. Of the people interviewed, 1,192 participants were used, with 672 of the participants being White, 180 Hispanic, 217 African American, 101 Asian, and 22 American Indian and multiracial (Satterfield et al., 2004). At times the racial information was collapsed into White and non-White.

The researchers found that White males uniformly had lower risk ratings when compared to non-Whites and White females (Satterfield et al., 2004). This was the finding for 18 of the 19 risks investigated. The only item where there was a variation to this finding was motor vehicles. For the item of motor vehicles, male ratings were similar on this item regardless of race. Non-White females' ratings were higher than White males on all 19 items. Non-White females differed significantly from White females on 11 items, and non-White males on 10 items (Satterfield et al., 2004). African American and Hispanic females had higher ratings than African American and Hispanic males on 13 of the 19 items. This study further supports the hypothesis that gender and race influence the perception of risk and threat, with White males perceiving the least amount of risk.

Houts and Kassab (1997) conducted a study looking at that fear of crime. In a Midwest city, in 31 of that city's crime reporting areas, the researchers collected information via telephone survey, during the months of March and April in 1993. The 518 participants used consisted of 76.2% Whites, 13.8% African Americans, and 7.7% other. The findings indicated that non-Whites had a higher fear of crime than Whites. Also, African Americans reported greater fear than other minorities (Houts & Kassab, 1997).

Although there is not a lot of information with regard to race and stalking, some research has indicated that there are possible differences in racial perceptions of what is indicative of stalking. In a meta-analysis conducted by Melton (2000), American Indian and Alaskan native women were significantly more likely to report stalking victimization than all other racial and ethnic backgrounds. There was not information to indicate why this is the case, but one variable that could be considered is threat perception.

Phillips, Quirk, Rosenfeld, and O'Connor (2004) completed a study using undergraduate and graduate students from a public college that specializes in training the students in criminal justice and related fields. The students were given one of six vignettes describing interaction between a man and woman (Tom and Mary) who met at a party. Three scenarios were created describing potential stalking behavior, based on New York stalking laws (Phillips et al., 2004). For the three scenarios, one did not meet the standards for the stalking laws, another met the stalking law in the fourth degree, and the final scenario met the stalking law in the third degree. The gender of the perpetrator and victim were changed for two versions of each scenario. Ethnicity was significantly correlated to whether the participant believed the perpetrator would harm the victim, as well as, whether the perpetrator was mentally ill (Phillips et al., 2004). More specifically, Whites were more likely than African Americans to express concern that the perpetrator might harm the target, but they were less likely to consider the behavior indicative of mental illness when compared to Asians or others (Phillips et al., 2004). Although there is not an abundance of research on the correlation between race and perception of stalking, there appears to be variance between races about what defines stalking behavior, as well as whether the behavior is threatening.

Research has indicated that different races perceive threat and risk differently, and that this perceptual difference could possibly impact perceptions of stalking. More research needs to be conducted in the area of threat perception related to stalking and cyberstalking. This research should explore whether race and cultural background impacts threat perception in relation to stalking and cyberstalking characteristics.

Rationale for This Study

In the area of cyberstalking, research has yet to delve into the general perception of whether cyberstalking poses a legitimate threat to society. Answering the question of whether the public believes cyberstalking poses a threat could help to determine whether a standard law should be created to combat issues of cyberstalking. According to the literature, women and men differ in their perceptions of threat. There are also differences in the perception of threat when comparing races. Such differences could further hinder the progression of the creation of a standard law. The present study is designed to answer the questions of whether the general population perceives cyberstalking as a threat, whether there is a difference in perception of threat in relation to cyberstalking based on gender, and last, whether races differ in their perception of threat in relation to cyberstalking. With this information, lawmakers could have more insight into the needs of the people. If the findings of the present study illustrate that there is a general perception of threat in regards to cyberstalking, legislation could combat the threat by creating a federal law for cyberstalking. Also, if races perceive cyberstalking characteristics differently, it would help to understand whether culture is impacting threat and threat perception. This complexity involving gender, race, and culture illustrates the need for deeper study in the area of cyberstalking in order to be able to identify individuals who engage in predatory behavior, and who are a threat to society so that lawmakers can begin to legislate in an area that up until now, there have been very few laws available.

Law and Legislating Cyberstalking

Stalking has not been easily defined in the legal arena, which makes it difficult to prosecute (Sheridan & Davies, 2001). In the United States, some states have begun creating laws to combat stalking; California was the first to create such a law (Sheridan & Davies, 2001). This law was the reaction to the murder of actress Rebecca Schaeffer. In 1989, Robert Bardo shot the actress at her home in Los Angeles. Bardo was mentally ill and obsessed with Schaeffer (Dunn, 2008, Chapter 14). After writing many letters to Schaeffer, and multiple ineffective attempts to meet her, Bardo hired a private detective to obtain her home address, where he killed her (Dunn, 2008, Chapter 14). After this horrible incident, California Penal Code 646.9 was created (Dunn, 2008, Chapter 14). California Penal Code 646.9 became effective as of January 1, 1991 (Youn & Hall, 2008).

Bardo was not the first to access the home of an actress with the intention of harm. In 1982, Arthur Jackson became attracted to actress Theresa Saldana. After recognizing they could never be together, Jackson traveled from Scotland to Los Angeles to kill Saldana. Jackson hired a private detective when he arrived in Los Angeles. The detective obtained Saldana's home address from the Department of Motor Vehicles (Youn & Hall, 2008). Jackson stabbed Saldana 10 times, but was stopped by the intervention of someone nearby.

With both of these high profile cases of stalking ending in grave events, in addition to the creation of the California Penal Code 646.9, the Threat Management Unit of the Los Angeles Police Department was established to handle threatening behavior in Los Angeles, CA (Dunn, 2008, Chapter 14). Major revisions to the penal code were made in 1994. These revisions enhanced the ability of law enforcement and prosecutors to intervene and protect the victim (Youn & Hall, 2008). The revisions state that "any person who willfully, maliciously, and repeatedly follows or harasses another person, and who makes a credible threat with the intent to place that person in reasonable fear for his/her safety, or the safety of his/her immediate family" may be charged with stalking (Youn & Hall, 2008).

In California, three criteria must be met to convict someone of stalking: first, the person must willfully, maliciously, and repeatedly follow or harass another person (on two or more occasions). Second, the person following or harassing must make a credible threat. Last, the person who makes the threat must do so with the specific intent to place the person in reasonable fear for his or her safety, or the safety of the immediate family of such persons (Youn & Hall, 2008).

By 1992, 30 states enacted similar stalking or harassment laws (Youn & Hall, 2008). All states and the District of Colombia had created stalking statutes by 2005 (Youn & Hall, 2008). President Clinton signed the Interstate Stalking Punishment and Prevention Act (Title 18 USC Section 2261) on September 23, 1996 (Youn & Hall, 2008). This act made it a crime to cross state lines to injure or harass a person (Youn & Hall, 2008). According to this act, the victim must be in reasonable fear of death, or serious bodily injury to oneself or an immediate family member. Also, a restraining order that has been issued in one state can be enforceable in another state (Youn & Hall, 2008).

The Current State of Stalking Law

The United States is not the only country creating laws to combat the crime of stalking. In England and Wales there has been the introduction of the Protection from Harassment Act. This Act was instated to cover a broad variety of actions that could be perceived as harassment. It was also instated to be preemptive, therefore combating the issue before it progressed to physical or severe psychological harm (Sheridan & Davies, 2001). Without a solid definition of stalking, people fear that the government will criminalize everyday behavior (Sheridan & Davies, 2001). For Americans there must be a *fear of bodily harm* for the incident to be considered stalking, and for the English and those from Wales, there is only a need to experience two acts of harassment (Sheridan & Davies, 2001). Overall, the lack of a consistent definition is keeping cases of stalking and harassment from being properly prosecuted internationally (Sheridan & Davies, 2001).

One-half million people are stalked each year in the United States (Goodno, 2007). In 1999, 20% of stalking cases in Los Angeles involved cyberstalking, and 60% in New York involved cyberstalking (Goodno, 2007). Most of the stalking cases involved ordinary people (noncelebrities) (Goodno, 2007). As the law is written, the *credible threat standard* that is stated in the definition of stalking is difficult to apply to cyberstalking (Goodno, 2007). With this standard, the question arises that, if the perpetrator resides cross-country, will it have to be proven that the person truly posed a threat at a distance? Postings about a person, but not necessarily received by the person, allow for the question of whether the threat could still pose harm if it is technically not directly communicated. Inciting third parties to assist in harm also creates a legal question. The legal question would be, if the perpetrator is not technically doing the harm, but getting others to act on his or her behalf, who should be prosecuted? When the *reasonable person standard* has been utilized in statutes, it has been successful in prosecuting cyberstalking, because it focuses on the fear that is intentionally being instilled in victims (Goodno, 2007). Instead of using a credible threat standard, the reasonable person standard takes away the need for close proximity, or the need to prove the perpetrator would carry out the threat (Goodno, 2007). Although state and federal statutes are being created, at this time there is not a single statute that encompasses the many issues of cyberstalking.

Laws against stalking vary from state to state, but the same three components are included in each law. The first component is that the behavior is repeated, with a minimum contact requirement. The next component is that the offender must intend or be expected to know that conduct would cause mental or physical harm. The last component is that the victim experiences physical or emotional harm, or fears for his or her safety (Roberts, 2008).

Technology has provided an efficient and more effective means to commit crimes, making it difficult to prosecute offenders (Basu & Jones, 2007). In terms of prevalence and incidence, it is difficult to assess how often cyberstalking occurs, because some may not see the harm in it, or even know that they are being stalked (Basu & Jones, 2007). Furthermore, law enforcement typically does not have the means or the technology to deal with cyberstalking when it is reported (Basu & Jones, 2007).

Although some states have added online communications to their stalking laws, many have not (Ellison & Akdeniz, 1998). Jurisdiction poses a problem for prosecution. Since the Internet can be accessed worldwide, determining who has the jurisdiction to prosecute the offender, if the perpetrator resides in a different state or country than the victim, leaves law enforcement at a loss (Ellison & Akdeniz, 1998). Tracing the perpetrator also becomes difficult when using the Internet because the web can be accessed essentially anywhere (Ellison & Akdeniz, 1998). Any attempts to control anonymity have been ruled unconstitutional (Ellison & Akdeniz, 1998). Researchers have found that people are also unaware of the information that they are sending out when using the Internet; that any time one visits a site the information is logged and stored, and therefore could potentially be used for harassment (Ellison & Akdeniz, 1998). At this time there is no standard law to prosecute cyberstalkers (Ellison & Akdeniz, 1998). There remains the question of whether the general population considers cyberstalking to be a legitimate threat, and if so, whether this can help to create a standard law for prosecution. In the following sections, I discuss the empirical research I conducted at Alliant International University and California State Polytechnic University at Pomona, on Cyberstalking.

Cyberstalking Through the Prism of Race and Gender: The Hypothesis

The first hypothesis for this study is that there will be a difference between genders on perception of threat in cases of cyberstalking. In comparison to males, females will be more apt to perceive characteristics of cyberstalking as threatening. The second hypothesis is that there will be a difference between races on perception of threat in cases of cyberstalking. More specifically, each minority group will perceive characteristics of cyberstalking as more threatening than Whites, therefore, rating characteristics of cyberstalking as more threatening than Whites.

Participants for the Study and Research Design

Participants included 83 students, faculty, and staff from Alliant International University, as well as, Psychology undergraduate students from California State Polytechnic University at Pomona, who were able to read English. This study used a Factorial ANOVA design to determine whether males and females, as well as African Americans, Whites, Latinos, and other racial groups differ in the perception of threat in instances of cyberstalking. This was chosen because the study examined one specific continuous outcome (level of perception of threat), with two different categorical predictor variables (gender and race). The independent variables were gender and race, and the dependent variable was perception of threat. Participants were asked to rate how afraid they are of specific online behaviors taking place by indicating their feelings on a five-point Likert scale (1 = Slightly afraid, 5 = Very afraid). Although this scale ranged from slightly afraid to very afraid, with 3 being neutral, only endorsements of a 4 or a 5 were included in the tabulation for determining perception of threat. Levels 0, 1, and 2 were not included because these endorsements essentially state that the person does not perceive the item to be threatening. Once the tabulation of 4s and 5s was calculated for each person, the total was used to determine whether perception of threat varies based on gender and race.

Research Materials and Data Analysis

Participants were recruited from two sources. At Alliant International University, an e-mail was sent via the systemwide e-mail service at Alliant International University. The e-mail contained a link to a secure website operated by Qualtrics. Some of the indices of the survey were based on the survey used by Spitzberg and Hoobler (2002). In addition to the survey, the participant was asked to answer demographic questions regarding gender, age, race, and time spent online, on social networking sites, and in chat rooms. In the case of California State Polytechnic University Pomona, only psychology undergraduate students were utilized. Those who chose to participate for .5 units extra class credit were able to access the survey through the SONA system.

There were 83 participants who volunteered for the study. Of the 83 participants, 11 submitted only partial data; therefore, the Statistical Package for Social Sciences (SPSS), version 19.0, was used to account for the missing data in all analyses. There were 58 female participants and 23 males. For the racial subgroups, there were 4 African Americans, 24 Whites, 22 Latinos, 23 Asians, and 8 Multiracial (mixed race) participants. Race and gender are seen as the independent variables, and *overall perception of threat* was the dependent variable used for the ANOVA. All of the ratings for the items on the survey that pertained to perception of threat were collected. This information for each participant was put into SPSS. Adding the ratings of 4s and 5s for each of the items, for each participant, and recording the number as the holistic value indicating the level of perceived threat created an overall perception of threat item. This number was then used to determine the extent of that individual's perception of threat toward the given items. This rating was used to conduct the ANOVA.

Examining the first hypothesis, whether there will be a difference between genders in the perception of threat in the case of cyberstalking; the analysis indicated that there was a main effect. Females tended to perceive the items as more threatening than the male participants. The mean score for overall perceived threat for women was 22.54, and for men it was 14.49. Although there were a smaller number of participants than desired, a main effect was still detected, F (1, 72) = 16.09, p < .001. When examining the second hypothesis, whether there will be a difference among races in the perception of threat in the case of cyberstalking, the analysis indicated that there was not a main effect. When examining whether there is a significant interaction among gender, race, and threat perception again, there was no significance found. In summation, after running the ANOVA, a significant factor was gender. Both race and the interaction between gender and race were not significant. The interaction among gender, race and threat perception was also insignificant.

Implications for the Study

The main effect that was observed was that of gender and threat perception. Females had a tendency to have higher ratings for overall perception of threat when compared to the males. The mean rating for females was 22.54 and the mean rating for males was 14.49. This illustrates that on average, female scores were nearly eight points higher than males. This supports the first hypothesis that there would be a difference between genders in perception of threat in the case of cyberstalking. Research, such as the study conducted by Ferraro (1996), has indicated that females tend to have higher ratings of threat perception when compared to their male counterparts. In the Ferraro (1996) study, women rated all of the given items significantly higher than the males. The most significant difference was the fear of sexual assault. The Reid and Konrad (2004) study yielded similar results, with sexual assault being one of the prime fears endorsed. The current study continues to support previous findings, as women on average tended to have higher mean ratings of overall perceived threat. Also, when looking at the variable of sexual assault, cyberstalking has similar intrusive characteristics to those that are connected to sexual assault. This might also speak to why the results of the current study did not vary from the previous studies. With characteristics being similar in nature, they might also evoke similar perceptions of threat. Moreover, in the study by Nellis (2009), women were more likely to express feelings of worry. If women tend to exhibit more worry about the issues presented, they might also express more perceived threat, hence, the finding that women endorse more perceived threat. To incorporate Internet use, the Youn and Hall (2008) study implied that even at a young age, females tend to have more apprehension toward possible victimization, and increased perception of threat. They were more aware of privacy risks and believed themselves to be more susceptible to unsolicited e-mails. With this same sense of perception applied to the current study, females would be more apt to endorse higher levels of perceived threat. The gender norms that society has created may help to perpetuate this belief that women tend to be more susceptible to unwanted advances. Gender norms might also help to reinforce the lack of concern men have toward stalking and stalking characteristics. These norms may have helped to shape the results that were yielded.

Although research indicates that there is a difference in perception of threat among races, this analysis did not support these findings. As discussed, in the meta-analysis conducted by Pain (2001), it was found that women of color feared crime more than their White counterparts. Satterfield et al. (2004) also conducted a study that yielded the same results; White men were the least fearful when compared to people of color and women. With each of these studies yielding similar results, it would be assumed that the current study would also be consistent with previous research, but this was not the case. There was no main effect found when considering race and overall perception of threat ratings. There were mild, but insignificant differences in the mean ratings given. African Americans had the highest mean rating of 20.50, Latinos were second with 19.93, Whites were third with 19.85, Asians fourth with 18.38, and Multiracial had the lowest mean rating of 16.91. It can be seen that the ratings were only slightly different, with the largest interval being between African Americans and Multiracial individuals, with a six-point difference. A power analysis indicated that the amount of participants included would need to be dramatically increased in order to find a main effect. With the given number from the power analysis being 24,660, it speaks to the possibility that race is not a strong determinant of threat perception in the case of cyberstalking. Although it is an important variable in other forms of threat perception, from these results it appears that cyberstalking is not influenced by a person's race. When speculating as to the reasons why this might be true, it would be important to consider the possibility of anonymity. McGarth and Casey (2002) spoke about the level of anonymity created by online interactions. Although gender might be readily offered to connect with the other person, race might be concealed to some degree, which might create more of a sense of comfort. This sense of comfort could decrease fear, perception of threat, or both connected to racially motivated crimes. Pain (2001) also emphasized the fact that women of color constructed their fears around the racial component, and feared racial harassment or violence in addition to rape. Again, without a visual aide, it would be difficult to determine one's race, thus reducing the perception of threat. Also, when examining those that have reported offline stalking, in the Melton (2000) study, American Indian and Alaskan native women were significantly more likely to report stalking victimization than other races, so perhaps other races have not dealt with the elements of offline stalking as frequently, and therefore, cannot fully fathom the threats of online stalking due to lack of exposure. Again, in the study by Phillips et al. (2004), Whites were more likely to express concern for a victim in terms of stalking than the African-American participants. This indicates that Whites might have a higher perception of threat in terms of general stalking, and this might transfer to online stalking as well.

Moreover, when examining the interaction among overall threat perception, race, and gender, there was no significance found. Latinas had the highest mean rating among the women, and African American females had the lowest mean rating, with only a four-point difference in the range. White males had the highest mean rating among the males, with a mean rating of 17.7, and Multiracial males had the lowest, with a mean rating of 11. Since this data was insignificant, the results were most likely due to chance. The African American male interaction was not observed, and therefore not included. Research has indicated that White males typically have the lowest observed perception of threat, but this analysis does not support those findings, or any findings that emphasize an interaction among gender, race, and threat perception. As has already been discussed, there was no main effect observed between race and overall threat perception. This may have impacted the results for the triad of gender, race, and overall threat perception. If there was no main effect between overall threat perception and race, then adding the variable of gender would most likely not create an effect. Although research has shown this multiple variant interaction in the past (Burnham & Lomax, 2009; Houts & Kassab, 1997; Satterfield et al., 2004), it appears that with the lack of the first interaction being supported (race and overall threat perception), then the other interaction was also not supported.

In summary, although there was a main effect found between gender and overall threat perception, this study has various limitations that should be considered.

Limitations to Cyberstalking Research

The first limitation that needs to be considered is the number of participants that were included in the study. The power analysis conducted before the study was completed suggested that at least

158 participants should be utilized to find the desired power of .80. The current study included 83 participants. As evidenced by the main effect found, this reduced number of participants had no impact on the strength of the interaction between gender and overall perception of threat. Although *this* interaction was unaffected, this reduced number of participants may have impacted the other results. The results for the interaction between race and overall perception of threat, as well as the triangulation of the three variables, could have been impacted by the limited number of participants. The post hoc power analysis for the triangulation was very weak, being .43. The given effect size for race yielded that the study would have required the use of 24,660 participants to show an effect, if it were present. Even with this information, the fact that the desired amount of participants was not obtained should still be considered.

Furthermore, although there were enough participants to observe a main effect for gender, the distribution between males and females was not equal. There was a skewed distribution, toward female participants. Field (2009) indicates that the ANOVA is a fairly robust analysis, but when there are violations to normality, there is a possibility that it may not be as robust. Having unequal sample sizes should have little effect on error rate and power, but *can* affect the accuracy and power of F in unpredictable ways. This effect can create a bias in the values (Field, 2009). This skewedness has the potential to have a powerful impact on the results of the analysis, shifting it one way or the other.

There were no African American males included in the study. This is most likely due to the fact that the participants were gathered from a private psychology graduate school, as well as those studying psychology at an undergraduate school. Females are now dominating the field of psychology, thus, there is a lack of representation of males holistically, and moreover, African American males. Therefore, when examining the triangulation, this element could not be accounted for because of the lack of representation. There is no way to determine how African American males view the characteristics of cyberstalking, so there is an element missing from the study that could be beneficial to new research.

Another limitation of the study is missing data. Some participants did not complete the survey. Some questions were left unanswered, requiring the use of the software to correct for this occurrence. Even with the computer's correction, this could have negatively impacted the validity of the results due to uncertainty. Last, the population utilized should also be considered. The survey was distributed to university staff, faculty, and students and may not be able to be generalized to the population at large. All of these limitations will impact the ability to replicate the study and validate the findings.

Although there are limitations to this study, the results indicated that gender can impact the overall threat perception in terms of cyberstalking, and this is an important finding. It adds to the previous research that has exemplified gender difference and threat perception. This data can help to inform future research as others delve deeper into the area of cyberstalking. With that understanding it might be best to look at the areas in which the study can be altered to help future research.

Furthering Our Research on Cyberstalking Through the Prism of Race and Gender

Although the current study helped to reinforce the findings on gender and threat perception, there is a need to continue to examine race and threat perception. Since there were limitations to the present study, it would be imperative to conduct the study once again, making sure to have a more equal distribution in terms of race to include African American males. With a variety of participants, perhaps a main effect would be observed, because there would be enough participants to yield ample power. This would help to determine whether the applied speculations are true concerning race, or whether the results are just due to lack of participants and power.

With the current study having gender skewedness, future studies could balance the number of participants in terms of gender. Once again, having this balance would help to verify that the findings are valid. In addition to this, a comparison of what particular items, if any, were significantly endorsed by either gender would add to research. This would help to indicate what exactly creates perceived threat for each gender.

In addition to this, it might be interesting to examine the reasons why people are using the social networking sites, as well as how stringent one is in terms of privacy settings. By gathering this information it could be compared to given answers to determine if there is a pattern in terms of perceived threat. If one has more stringent privacy settings, he or she may not perceive threat from the networking site. Also, if one is only connecting with already known individuals, threat perception might decrease as well.

It might also be a sound idea to investigate age. To compare the way that age impacts perception of threat in terms of cyberstalking might yield interesting results. As children are now maturing with the ability to have full access to the Internet from birth, this could decrease apprehension. Once people are more accustomed to something, it has the possibility of reducing the feelings of perceived threat. It would be interesting to compare different age groups, races, and genders to determine whether there is a significant difference.

Moreover, since race was not a strong determinant of threat perception, the intersection between race and gender was not fully explored. This provides an opportunity for future researchers to explore this avenue, if replication of the study yields results of race being significant.

Last, since this study was merely investigating threat perception in terms of cyberstalking in the United States, it would be beneficial to expound on this study to incorporate other countries, including those in the third world.

Overall, the current study yielded the significant finding that there are gender differences in terms of perception of threat, in regards to cyberstalking characteristics. Although this is a start for advancing the research toward cyberstalking, there are still a considerable number of possibilities to help improve our knowledge in terms of race, gender, and perception of threat toward cyberstalking.

References

Basu, S., & Jones, R. (2007). Regulating cyberstalking. *Journal of Information, Law, and Technology*. Retrieved from: http://www2.warwick.ac.uk/fac/soc/law/elj/jilt/2007_2/basu_jones/basu_jones.pdf

Cohen, J. (1988). Statistical power analysis for the behavioral sciences, 2nd ed. Hillsday, NJ: Lawrence Erlbaum.

Dunn, J. (2008). Operations of the LAPD operations unit. In J. R. Meloy, L. Sheridan, & J. Hoffman (Eds.), *Stalking, threatening, and attacking public figures* (pp. 325–341). New York: Oxford University Press.

Ellison, L., & Akdeniz, Y. (1998). Cyber-stalking: The regulation of harassment on the Internet. *Criminal Law Review, December Special Edition: Crime, Criminal Justice and the Internet*, 29–48.

Faul, F., Erdfelder, E., Lang, A.-G., & Buchner, A. (2007). G*Power 3: A flexible statistical power analysis program for the social, behavioral, and biomedical sciences. *Behavior Research Methods, 39*, 175–191.

Ferraro, K. F. (1996). Women's fear of victimization: Shadow of sexual assault? *Social Forces, 75*(2), 667–690.

Field, A. (2009). *Discovering statistics using SPSS*, 3rd ed. London: SAGE Publications.

Goodno, N. H. (2007). Cyberstalking, a new crime evaluating the effectiveness of current state and federal laws. *Missouri Law Review, 72*, 66–102.

Houts, S., & Kassab, C. (1997). Rotter's social learning theory, and fear of crime: Differences in race and ethnicity. *Social Science Quarterly, 78*(1), 122–136.

McFarlane, L., & Bocij, P. (2003). An exploration of predatory behavior in cyberspace: Towards a typology of cyberstalkers. *First Monday, 8*(9). Retrieved from: http://pear.accc.uic.edu/htbin/cgiwrap/bin/ojs/index.php/fm/article/view/1076/996.

McGarth, M. G., & Casey, E. (2002). Forensic psychiatry and the internet: Practical perspectives on sexual predators and obsessional harassers in cyberspace. *Journal of the American Academy of Psychiatry and Law Online, 30*(1), 81–94.

Meloy, J. R. (2007). Stalking: The state of the science. *Criminal Behaviour and Mental Health, 17*(1), 1–7.

Melton, H. C. (2000). Stalking: A review of the literature and direction for the future. *Criminal Justice Review, 25*(2), 246–262.

Moriarty, L., & Freiberger, K. (2008). Cyberstalking: Utilizing newspaper accounts to establish victimization patterns. *Victims and Offenders, 3*, 131–141.

Nellis, A. M. (2009). Gender differences in fear of terrorism. *Journal of Contemporary Criminal Justice, 25*(3), 322–340.

Pain, R. (2001). Gender, race, age, and fear in the city. *Urban Studies, 38* (5–6), 899–913.

Phillips, L., Quirk, R., Rosenfeld, B., & O'Connor, M. (2004). Is it stalking? Perceptions of stalking among college undergraduates. *Criminal Justice and Behavior, 31*(1), 73–96.

Pittaro, M. L. (2007). Cyber Stalking: An analysis of online harassment and intimidation. *International Journal of Cyber Criminology, 1*(2), 180–197.

Reid, L. W., & Konrad, M. (2004). The gender gap in fear: Assessing the interactive effects of gender and perceived risk on fear of crime. *Sociological Spectrum, 24* (1), 399–425.

Roberts, A. R., & Dziegielewski, S. F. (2006). Changing stalking patterns and prosecutional decisions: Bridging the present to the future. *Victims and Offenders, 1*(1), 47–60.

Roberts, L. (2008). Jurisdictional and definitional concerns with computer-mediated interpersonal crimes: An analysis on cyberstalking. *International Journal of Cyber Criminology, 2*(1), 271–285.

Satterfield, T. A., Mertz, C. K., & Slovic, P. (2004). Discrimination, vulnerability, and justice in the face of risk. *Risk Analysis, 24* (1), 115–129.

Sheridan, L., & Davies, G. M. (2001). Stalking: The elusive crime. *Legal and Criminal Psychology, 6*(2), 133–147.

Sheridan, L., Davies, G., & Boon, J. (2001). The course of and nature of stalking: A victim perspective. *The Howard Journal of Criminal Justice, 40*(3), 215–234.

Sheridan, L. P., & Grant, T. (2007). Is cyberstalking different? *Psychology, Crime, & Law, 13*(6), 627–640.

Spitzberg, B. H. (2002). The tactical topography of stalking victimization and management. *Trauma, Violence and Abuse, 3*(4), 261–288.

Spitzberg, B. H., & Hoobler, G. (2002). Cyberstalking and the technologies of interpersonal terrorism. *New Media & Society, 4*(1), 71–92.

Southworth, C., Finn, J., Dawson, S., Fraser, C., & Tucker, S. (2007). Intimate partner violence, technology, and stalking. *Violence Against Women, 13*(8), 842–856.

Youn, S., & Hall, K. (2008). Gender and online privacy among teens: Risk perception, privacy concerns, and protection behaviors. *Cyber Psychology and Behavior, 11*(6), 763–765. Retrieved from: http://www.stalkingalert. com/

CHAPTER EIGHT

Framing the Same-Sex Marriage Issue as Equity

CHRISTOPHER P. LATIMER

Similar to other movements supporting the human rights and dignity of marginalized groups, the struggle for gay and lesbian equality in the United States has confronted and endured incredible opposition. Each side of the debate over gay and lesbian civil rights operates inside its own collection of strongly held values, interests, and beliefs. These arguments focus on the equality rights of gay and lesbian couples versus those who believe that morally their religious beliefs dictate that homosexuality is wrong and should not be protected by the state. Even with this fervent and persistent opposition, the scale and pace in the shift toward positive attitudes regarding same-sex marriage over the past 12 years is rather astonishing. What helps to explain this rapid shift in opinion formation for this highly charged issue? The opinion shift in the United States is partly due to a Supreme Court case, *Lawrence v. Texas*, 539 U.S. 558 (2003), concerning decriminalization of homosexuality and a series of nationally prominent state court decisions legalizing same-sex marriage such as *Goodridge v. Dept. of Public Health*, 798 N.E.2d 941 (Mass. 2003). The impact of the language used by the courts in these cases to legitimize the struggles of gays and lesbians to achieve equality should not be dismissed. The court decisions *framed* the issue of gay and lesbian intimacy and same-sex marriage as one of pure equality. Any complete explanation of public opinion change about same-sex marriage must include the framing of this issue by the courts. The push back by opponents of same-sex marriage to frame the issue as one of "morality" has not been as influential as evidenced by the shifts in public opinion. The framing of gay and lesbian civil rights by the courts with particular focus on same-sex marriage in the United States is the basis of this chapter.

Maine, Maryland, and Washington legalized same-sex marriage by popular vote on November 6, 2012. This is the first time that such referenda were passed with the support of a majority of registered voters. Additionally, voters in Minnesota rejected a constitutional amendment that would have defined marriage only as a union between a man and a woman. There are seventeen other states that currently allow same-sex marriage such as Connecticut, Massachusetts, New York, Iowa, Vermont, and the District of Columbia. What is particularly interesting about both the Washington and Maryland examples is that the legislature reversed itself, moving from a statutory exclusion of same-sex marriage to a statutory approval of same-sex marriage. Maine is also an interesting example because a previous same-sex marriage referendum was narrowly defeated by voters in 2009 (Mistler, 2012). The New Jersey Legislature also passed a bill legalizing same-sex marriage in 2012, but the bill was vetoed by Governor Chris Christie who called for the issue to be placed on the ballot by the legislature for a vote by the citizens (Zemike, 2012). The issue of gay and lesbian civil rights is also being discussed on the federal level as demonstrated by the repeal of the "Don't Ask Don't Tell" policy in December 2010 (Wilgoren, 2010). This struggle back and forth on the state level and the repeal of a discriminatory regulation on the federal level not only demonstrates the volatility of this issue but also the fairly significant changes in attitudes about same-sex marriage in a short period of time.

The inconsistency on the federal and state levels may be addressed directly by the United States Supreme Court during the 2013 term. The Court has agreed to hear arguments concerning two cases challenging federal and state laws that define marriage to include only unions of a man and a woman. One case involves the constitutionality of California's ballot Proposition 8 where voters banned same-sex marriage, thereby overturning the California Supreme Court's ruling that same-sex couples have a constitutional right to marry. The justices could rule on narrower grounds that would only apply to same-sex marriages in California, or there is a slight possibility that they might determine whether the Federal Constitution guarantees same-sex marriage rights on a national scale. The second case involves a challenge to the Federal Defense of Marriage Act (DOMA), which also defines marriage as solely between a man and a woman and prevents same-sex married couples from receiving federal benefits. These cases will be decided by June 2012, and will most likely have a tremendous impact on the framing of same-sex marriage in the United States.

It is not just the importance of equality that compels those in favor of same-sex marriage (Badgett, 2006; Cherlin, 2004). The significant economic ramifications have also been cited as a motivational factor for marriage equality. Not having access to the economic benefits that are available to opposite sex married couples is another form of oppression experienced by gays and lesbians that undermines their dignity as human beings (Young, 1990). According to the federal government's Government Accountability Office (GAO), more than 1,138 rights and protections are conferred to United States citizens upon marriage by the federal government; areas affected include Social Security benefits, veterans' benefits, health insurance, Medicaid, hospital visitation, estate taxes, retirement savings, pensions, family leave, and immigration law (Government Accountability Office, 2004). Badgett (2003) found that the resulting difference in Social Security income for gay and lesbian couples compared to opposite-sex married couples is $5,588 each year. Research indicates that the additional economic and financial security of marriage can lead to greater mental and physical health (Brown, 2000; Stack & Eshleman, 1998). States that grant full marriage rights to same-sex couples are not extended those benefits on the federal level due to DOMA. The extension of rights in all areas of both the federal and state laws would be significant to gays and lesbians and their families.

The primary focus of this chapter is to discuss the framing strategies of the *Lawrence* and *Goodridge* opinions. Any comprehensive approach must place special weight on how both supporters and opponents *frame* the issue of same-sex marriage and how that impacts societal attitudes. These attitudes help to provide a basis for the oppression and marginalization suffered by gay and lesbian families and the lack of legal protections that are afforded similarly situated heterosexual married couples. The chapter is organized in the following way. First, the current literature on public opinion and same-sex marriage is examined. Second, the theoretical background on framing and its persuasive effects is provided and their implications for this discussion on same-sex marriage. Next, the framing strategies of the courts in relation to gay and lesbian civil rights and same-sex marriage are scrutinized. Finally, the chapter concludes with a discussion of the implications of framing for attitudes concerning same-sex marriage.

The legalization of same-sex marriage was never discussed at any great length until the Supreme Court of Hawaii held in *Baehr v. Lewin*, 852 P.2d 44 (Haw. 1993) that denying same-sex couples the right to marry may have been in violation of that state's constitutional prohibition on sex discrimination. The citizens of Hawaii quickly responded by passing a constitutional amendment granting the state legislature the power to restrict marriage to heterosexual couples, which resulted in a law banning same-sex marriage. The *Baehr* case also propelled the issue of same-sex marriage onto the national stage and opposition was so intense and immediate that Congress passed the DOMA within months (Cahill, 2004; Lewis, 2011). The House Judiciary Committee justified DOMA by referring to "a collective moral judgment about human sexuality" that "entails both moral disapproval of homosexuality, and a moral conviction that heterosexuality better comports with traditional (especially Judeo-Christian) morality."

This type of religiously based antigay and antilesbian rhetoric has long been used to promote direct government discrimination as well as state ballot initiatives banning gay and lesbian civil rights throughout the United States. While codifying the heterosexual definition of marriage for federal purposes, DOMA also asserted the right of individual states to refuse recognition of same-sex marriages granted in other states. As of 2012, 29 state constitutional amendments and 32 state laws that either ban same-sex marriage directly or define a marriage as being limited to one man and one woman (ProCon.org, 2012). Twenty-three states have both a constitutional amendment and a law that explains the overall numbers being above 50. This initial backlash in the 1990s seems to have receded after 2004, in part because of the *Lawrence* and *Goodridge* decisions.

Over the course of the early twenty-first century, in a series of highly visible and controversial decisions concerning gay and lesbian civil rights and same-sex marriage, federal and state courts presented the citizens of the United States with a then-novel interpretation of these issues that was to frame them as one based on equality. In *Lawrence v. Texas*, 539 U.S. 558 (2003), the Supreme Court in a landmark decision struck down the sodomy law in Texas, and as a result also nullified sodomy laws in the 13 other states where they remained in existence, thereby making same-sex sexual intimacy legal in every state and territory in the nation. The decision also overturned the Supreme Court's previous 1986 ruling, *Bowers v. Hardwick*, which included very harsh and morally infused language. This case precedent was used by many courts against gay and lesbians, most visibly in the context of employment and housing discrimination, custody battles, and immigration. State boards also relied on sodomy laws to deny licenses to gays and lesbians pursuing careers that required certification, such as attorneys, doctors, and teachers. The level of discrimination that was perpetrated against gays and lesbians due to sodomy laws is impossible to determine. In overruling *Bowers*, the

Lawrence decision had tremendous implications for the civil rights of gays and lesbians and their families.

When the Massachusetts's high court ordered the state to issue marriage licenses to same-sex couples approximately five months after the *Lawrence* decision in 2003, President Bush argued for an amendment to the United States Constitution to prohibit same-sex marriages. Even though the initial backlash was connected to a highly contentious presidential election in 2004, which led to 11 states successfully banning same-sex marriage through ballot initiatives, the war for equality was not lost. While commentators and scholars hastily read the defeat of same-sex marriage by voters in each of these states as a definitive statement on public attitudes, trends in public opinion suggest that the public's overall attitude toward same-sex relationships is not entirely clear. The controversy over same-sex marriage continues to be one of the major battlegrounds in the "culture wars" that significantly divide America (Fiorina, 2005). As mentioned throughout this anthology, however, oppression of marginalized and powerless groups is not limited to the United States but is a global phenomenon that needs to be addressed and understood to help our students become culturally competent. The framing of gay and lesbian civil rights by the courts with particular emphasis on same-sex marriage in the United States is the focus of this chapter.

Same-sex marriage is one of the most divisive societal issues facing our nation today, having broad cultural, historical, legal, and religious implications (Lee, 2010; Moats, 2004). It continues to generate a rigorous debate between advocates and opponents. This discussion has affected every level of government within the United States and around the world. While lively debate is an important aspect of the democratic political structure, the abnormally strong intensity and individual fanaticism associated with same-sex marriage more than surpasses the usual energetic arguments of other noteworthy public policy issues. The debate about same-sex marriage is shrouded in unfettered emotion with extreme supporters on both sides ready to spend massive amounts of time, energy, and money to persuade and secure the undecided, in order to win the battle (Brewer, 2008). The lines were quickly drawn between those who rebuff all claims to validity, protection, and acceptance of gays and lesbians with those embracing gays and lesbians as full members of a pluralistic society.

Advocates of same-sex marriage argue that denying gay and lesbian couples the right to be legally married infringes on their Equal Protection and Due Process rights, and labels them as inferior. Its opponents offer a variety of religious arguments, including the notion that same-sex marriage infringes on religion by altering the definition of marriage. Craig, Martinez, Kane, and Gainous (2005) argue that the American public is literally of "two minds" concerning same-sex marriage. Even with these polarized positions, public opinion has moved rapidly in support of same-sex marriage over the past 12 (Shear & Stolberg, 2011). This begs the question: What accounts for this striking shift in public opinion for same-sex marriage? How is it that in the span of just 12 years, public opinion in the United States can shift from majority opposition to majority support? Understanding the answer to this complex question is critical to better comprehend the remarkable swing in public opinion supporting same-sex marriage.

One of the most likely causal reasons is what is typically characterized as the "social value change" (Inglehart, 1997). This concept is based on an array of sociological arguments suggesting that large-scale societal transformations in the post–World War II era, including rising wealth, shifting work environments, and the breakdown of traditional nuclear family structures have led to a new "postindustrial" moment in time (Inglehart, 2008). Individuals growing up during these times are exposed to new ideologies so that general opinion can sometimes come to mirror these new ideologies. Applied to the realm of gay and lesbian civil rights, this new value orientation implies increased support for novel rights and recognition claims such as same-sex marriage.

The social changes around sexual orientation including the greater public visibility of gays and lesbians and exposure through mass media may also cause more positive attitudes toward same-sex marriage. The central dynamic of the cultural realignment surrounding same-sex marriage is not merely that different public values create diverse public opinions. These opposing viewpoints, rather, elucidate the institutionalization and politicization of two diametrically opposed cultural structures (Baunach, 2011; Smith, 2007). Each side functions inside its own collection of deeply held values, interests, and beliefs. At the heart of each are two distinct perceptions of ethical authority—two dissimilar ways of perceiving reality, of categorizing experience, and of making just conclusions (Becker & Scheufele, 2011). How these opposing arguments are framed will have an impact on the public attitudes.

Public Opinion

Around the world, attitudes about gays and lesbians and support for same-sex marriage differ considerably. Same-sex marriage is permitted in 10 countries such as Canada, Belgium, Spain, South Africa, and the Netherlands. Nonetheless, persons can be executed for being gay, lesbian, or transgendered in Iran, Mauritania, the Republic of Sudan, Saudi Arabia, and Yemen (Glass, 2011). The cultural, religious, legal, and political differences across countries play a significant role in forming attitudes about homosexuality. Public support for same-sex marriage has increased steadily in the United States for more than a decade, with supporters achieving a slim majority in 2011 (Silver, 2011). This is an unusually extensive movement toward the positive direction. When DOMA was passed by Congress and signed into law by President Clinton in 1996, only 25% of the public supported same-sex marriage. The chart below represents the attitudes favoring and opposing same-sex marriage from opinion polls starting in 2000. As Figure 8.1 demonstrates, support for same-sex marriage was mostly headed on a steady increase reaching above 50% in 2011.

What helps to explain this considerable swell in support? The literature concerning attitude formation has an extensive history of empirical research from which three particular areas of influence have been examined. They are contact factors, which include changes in a society's exposure directly to those involved in the issue (Lewis, 2007); demographic factors such as age, ideology, gender, race, and education (Nevitte, Blais, Gidengil, & Nadeau, 2000); and attitudinal factors such as transformation in the beliefs, attitudes, and values around the issue (Fletcher & Howe, 2000). In order to gain a better understanding of the various factors influencing attitudes about same-sex marriage, this literature review includes studies for each of these three broad areas.

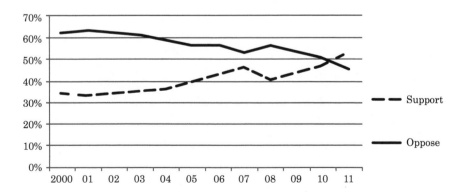

Figure 8.1. Changing Attitudes on Same-Sex Marriage.

Contact Factors

Research suggests that greater rates of personal contact with someone who is gay or lesbian increases support for same-sex marriage
(Becker & Scheufele, 2011; Lewis, 2007). In addition, the quantity of
personal or social interaction is relevant. The closer the connection
such as having a close family member or friend who is gay or lesbian,
as opposed to a work colleague or associate, the more noticeable the
impact on public opinion (Becker & Scheufele, 2011; Brewer, 2008;
Mohipp & Morry, 2004). In other words, the closer the social link
between a person and his or her gay or lesbian point of connection,
the more noteworthy the impact on attitudes (Pettigrew & Tropp,
2006). Becker and Scheufele (2011) contend that while social contact
is more powerful in influencing the attitudes of younger rather than
older voters, social contact is being more and more central for older
groups as well. The importance of social contact is also believed to
have contributed to shaping the votes of Republican and Democratic
legislators in New York during the struggle to legalize same-sex marriage (Barbaro, 2011). The impact of demographic factors on same-sex
marriage has also been studied a great deal.

Demographic Factors

Another area of research examining attitude formation about same-
sex marriage concerns demographic characteristics such as age
(Adamczykad & Pitt, 2009; Anderson & Fetner, 2008), education
(Ohlander, Batalova, & Treas, 2005; Treas, 2002), gender (Edgell &
Docka, 2007; Herek, 2002), ideology (Loftus, 2001; Rimmerman &
Wilcox, 2007), socioeconomic status (Morrison, Parriag, & Morrison,
1999), and race (Sherkat, DeVries, & Creek, 2010). Research indicates
in general that younger people, individuals with a greater level of
education, and a higher socioeconomic status report greater support
for gay and lesbian civil liberties (Lewis, 2003; Negy & Eisenman,
2005). In particular, studies about gender have routinely found that
heterosexual men have more negative attitudes toward gay men and
lesbians compared to heterosexual females (Finlay & Walther, 2003).
This might be due to the fact that men find homosexuality more
threatening (Davies 2004; Whitley, 2001).

The examination of ideology also clearly suggests that liberal
Democrats are more supportive of same-sex marriage than conservative Republicans, particularly as the "family values" agenda of social

conservatism has develop into a more dominant aspect of political conservatism (Kaufmann, 2002). Persily, Egan, and Wallsten (2006) find that political ideology is an increasingly powerful predictor of support for same-sex marriage, with support rising much faster for liberals than conservatives. Brewer (2008) also discovered that ideology and partisanship may be a strong reason for how individuals view same-sex marriage. Using ANES data, he determined that liberals and conservatives were in disagreement on the issues of gay and lesbian rights, including nondiscrimination in the workplace, gays in the military, and same-sex marriage. Specifically, he found that conservative Republicans were more likely to oppose gay rights than liberal Democrats.

Concerning race, African Americans and Asians tend to be less accepting of gays and lesbians than Whites (Davies, 2004; Lewis, 2003); while Latinos and non-Hispanic Whites do not appear to differ significantly (Bonilla & Porter, 1990). Additional research has demonstrated that even after controlling for intervening variables such as church attendance, moral traditionalism, and living in the South, African Americans are still more opposed to same-sex marriage than Whites (Egan, Persily, & Wallsten, 2008). The majority of African Americans hold affiliations in Baptist and other sectarian denominations, such as the Church of God in Christ, and African Americans have the highest rates of religious participation of any subgroup within the American population (Sherkat, 2002; Hunt & Hunt, 2001).

Sherkat et al. (2010), examined racial differences in support for same-sex marriage using General Social Surveys from 2004 to 2008. They examined whether the rising gap between Whites who were more likely in support for same-sex marriage and African Americans who were less likely to be in support is a function of religion. They concluded that religion did impact their results. The racial divide was a function of African American's connection to sectarian Protestant religious denominations and high rates of church attendance (Sherkat, DeVries, & Creek, 2010). Fifty percent of the difference between Whites and African Americans in their support for same-sex marriage was explained by differences in religious affiliation (Sherkat, DeVries, & Creek, 2010). While only 30% of White Americans identify with conservative Protestant denominations, over 63% of African Americans affiliate with Baptist or other sectarian groups (Sherkat, 2002). The remaining 50% is explained by African Americans' high rates of religious attendance. There have also been a number of studies which examine the impact of attitudinal factors on same-sex marriage.

Attitudinal Factors

The opposition to same-sex marriage by several prominent religious denominations is diminishing. For example, Episcopalians and Unitarian Universalists have shown majority support for same-sex marriage (Pew Forum on Religion and Family Life, 2010). In 2010, the Episcopalian Church in the United States ordained their second openly gay bishop (Goodstein, 2010). The Anglican Church in Africa, however, is adamantly opposed to same-sex marriage. There is a substantial amount of literature examining attitude formation in relation to gay and lesbian civil rights and religion (Burdette, Ellison, & Hill, 2005; Pearl & Galupo, 2007; Rowatt, LaBouff, Johnson, Froese, & Tsang, 2006). There are also studies that examine religiosity (Froese, Bader, & Smith, 2008; Lemelle, 2004; Lewis, 2003), religious denomination (Finlay & Walther, 2003; Greeley & Hout, 2006; Koch & Curry, 2000), images of God (Froese & Bader, 2008) and national religious culture (Adamczyk & Felson, 2006; Moore & Vanneman, 2003).

Olson, Cadge, and Harrison (2006) examined same-sex marriage and how religion influences public opinion on this issue. Utilizing the information from a telephone survey conducted by Greenberg Quinlan Rosner Research, Inc. in 2004, the authors used a multiple logistical regression as their methodology. The authors discovered variance within an assortment of religious affiliations and found that someone of the Jewish faith and mainstream Christianity were the largest indicators influencing support for same-sex marriage. They concluded that religion is very strong in effecting public support for same-sex marriage. They also found that those in opposition to same-sex marriage objected to allowing the government to recognize same-sex marriages because of moral reasons (Olson et al., 2006). Although the research discovered religious variance concerning same-sex marriage, the analysis did not examine why certain religions approve of same-sex marriage, while others are opposed.

Concerning denominational status some studies find members of conservative Protestant denominations against same-sex marriage (Finlay & Walther, 2003), with Baptist and other fundamentalist Protestants demonstrating a greater likelihood to oppose same-sex marriage than Catholics and people of the Jewish faith (Fisher, Derison, Polley, Cadman, & Johnston, 1994; Lewis, 2003). There is also literature on significant opposition to gay and lesbian rights broadly by Protestant Evangelical denominations (Burdette, Ellison, & Hill, 2005; Tuntiya, 2005; Fulton, Gorsuch, & Maynard, 1999; Wilcox & Jelen, 1990). Reimer and Park (2001) found conservative Protestants were less prepared to approve of civil rights to marginalized groups (including gays and lesbians) than were Mainline Protestants or Catholics. The terms *conservative* Protestants or *fundamentalist* Protestants are used interchangeably in the literature to signify Evangelical Protestants. It is interesting that even though Catholic doctrine strongly disapproves of homosexuality and same-sex marriage, lay Catholics are less opposed to same-sex marriage than conservative Protestants (Bendyna, Green, Rozell, & Wilcox, 2001). Mainline Protestants are more liberal, and some denominations no longer attack homosexuality as immoral. Finally, any religious affiliation strengthens the probability of having negative attitudes toward gays and lesbians, even when individuals are affiliated with denominations that are tolerant of gays and lesbians (Lemelle, 2004; Walls, 2010).

In general, religiosity and frequency of church attendance are associated with greater disapproval of homosexuality and less support for same-sex marriage. Brumbaugh, Sanchez, Nock, & Wright, (2008) found that religiosity, measured by an eight-item Likert scale on attendance at religious services, led to a significant role in accounting for opposition to same-sex marriage when correlates of attitudes toward divorce, political conservatism, condemning family breakdown on selfishness, and opinions about covenant marriage were incorporated as controls. Whitehead (2010) also used religious service attendance, religious belief, and religious affiliation to examine attitudes about gay marriage. She found that people who attended religious services more frequently were 16% less likely than those who did not attend religious services to agree with same-sex marriage.

Studies focused on attribution theory have also found an influence on attitudes about same-sex marriage. Those individuals who believe that being gay or lesbian is the result of biology are more likely to be in support of same-sex marriage than those attributing someone's sexual orientation as a choice (Haider-Markel & Joslyn, 2008; Wilcox & Norrander, 2002; Wood & Bartkowski, 2004). Haider-Markel and Joslyn (2008) found that those viewing homosexuality as not related to biology are much less likely to support same-sex marriage. They concluded that attribution theory concerning gays and lesbians is a very strong predictor of support for same-sex marriage.

There has also been a great amount of research searching for evidence that the Supreme Court has an impact on public opinion (Kritzer, 2005). The results in the literature concerning the influence of elite institutions such as the courts on public opinion is somewhat mixed overall (Hoekstra, 2003; Klarman, 1994; Rosenberg, 1991). However, more recently evidence has been increasingly demonstrating that the Supreme Court is having some influence on public opinion (Clawson, Kegler, & Waltenburg, 2001; Clawson & Waltenburg,

2003; Friedman, 2009; Giles, Blackstone & Vining, 2008; Grosskopf & Mondak, 1998; Hoekstra, 2003; Marshall, 2008; McGuire & Stimson, 2004).

Scholars contend that court decisions can lead to one of three results about public attitudes including: public "legitimacy," which is shifting support in the direction of the court's decision; "backlash," which are objections to a decision simply because the court has issued it; and "polarization," which is shifting views amongst different subgroups comprising "the public" (Gibson, 2007). In particular, legitimacy theory suggests that the general public trust courts more than other institutions because they perceive judges to be impartial decision-makers who are separate from politics (Dahl, 1957; Murphy, Tanenhaus, & Kastner, 1973; Gibson, Caldeira, & Baird, 1998). An implication of legitimacy theory is that citizens are more likely to accept government policies when they are attributed to courts than to other institutions (Clawson et al., 2001; Gibson, Caldeira, & Spence, 2005). The public's support is important, particularly when it comes to issues such as the legalization of same-sex marriage, because public opinion is more likely to influence the development of what is seen as "morality" policies than more routine government policies (Lowi, 1972; Hwang & Gray, 1991; Haider-Markel & Meier, 1996). The literature on court influence of public opinion is almost non-existent as it relates specifically to same-sex marriage. There have been a few studies within the United States (Egan & Persily, 2008, 2009).

Egan and Persily (2008) examined attitude shifts in response to state court decisions that provided legal recognition of same-sex marriage. Using polling data from CNN, Gallup, and Pew about whether same-sex marriage should be legalized, they found that in states where same-sex marriage cases have reached the highest court within the state, residents support same-sex marriage at greater levels than in states without court decisions. They also examined three states that at the time of the research had positive-gay and -lesbian decisions in place the longest, which included Massachusetts, Vermont, and New Jersey. In these states, citizens had greater increases in support of same-sex marriage than the national average. There were two states, Connecticut and Iowa, where high courts had more recently legalized same-sex marriage and the study found that it was too early to determine whether those rulings would demonstrable influence public opinion. The authors also observed that the *Lawrence* decision produced something of a short-term backlash that disrupted increasing support for gay and lesbian rights generally, but levels recovered by 2005. They finally thought that it was reasonable to assume that the *Lawrence* decision perhaps accelerated legal change in some states in a direction agreeable to legal recognition of gay and lesbian relationships because citizens become comfortable to such court decisions over time.

It is important to note that there was a significant backlash of the Iowa decision. Two of the Iowa Supreme Court justices who participated in the unanimous 2009 ruling that Iowa could not deny marriage licenses based on sexual orientation, were removed from office after judicial retention elections (Schulte, 2010). Each of the three justices received approximately 45% of the vote, making this the first time associates of the state's high court had been rejected by voters (Sulzberger, 2010). Their removal followed vigorous campaigning by groups opposed to same-sex marriage including the National Organization for Marriage. However, Justice David Wiggins who was also part of the majority opinion granting same-sex marriage won retention during the 2012 retention election, which could demonstrate a shift of public opinion within the state of Iowa.

Most of these studies fail to include an examination of the prominent court decisions that started to frame the issues of gay and lesbian civil rights in terms of equality. The impact of these court cases needs to be studied in order to have a more comprehensive understanding of attitude shifts by the general public. In the next section the theoretical underpinnings of framing with an emphasis on how it relates to same-sex marriage will be discussed.

Theoretical Background on Framing

Research on framing can be found within the social and cognitive sciences (Bateson, 1972; Goffman, 1974; Tversky & Kahneman, 1981), communication and media studies (Pan & Kosicki, 1993; Scheufele, 1999), and various subfields in political science (Schon & Rein, 1994; Triandafyllidou & Fotiou, 1998). The use of framing has become a widespread method employed by groups to provide authority to organize supporters for their positions (Benford & Snow, 2000; Snow & Benford, 1992; Tarrow, 1992). As applied to the issue of same-sex marriage, those groups in support engage in framing strategies centered firmly on the notion of equality (Gallagher & Bull, 2001), while the opposing groups generally implement framing strategies also situated within the context of morality (Brewer, 2002; Rimmerman, Wald, & Wilcox, 2000).

There are variations in the literature about an appropriate and comprehensive definition of framing (Druckman, 2001), but attempting to examine and justify one definition over another is beyond the scope of this chapter. For the purposes of this discussion, a frame establishes what considerations are significant to opinion making about a particular issue. Exposure to a frame, in theory, should modify the balance of thoughts individuals recall as they determine their opinions on specific issues. As a result, those connected to dissimilar framings of an issue could be different in the opinions they communicate on that issue. According to Chong and Druckman (2007), "(f)raming refers to the process by which people develop a particular conceptualization of an issue or reorient their thinking about an issue" (Chong & Druckman, 2007, p. 104). When developing a judgment on a public issue, like the extension of legal recognition for same-sex couples, Chong and Druckman (2007) argue that an individual will evaluate the comparable values of rival beliefs and positions. Framing works by shifting one's core belief to impact the individuals' conceptualization and assessment of public issues. Frames can shift this calculus "by making new beliefs available about an issue, making certain available beliefs accessible or making beliefs applicable or 'strong' in people's evaluations" (Chong & Druckman, 2007, p. 111). Frames in effect develop out of cooperative attempts to understand and comprehend issue problems, and they help people "locate, perceive, identify, and label" their experience (Goffman, 1974, p. 21).

The differences in opinion formation that result are known as "framing effects" (Druckman, 2001). If framing effects work by changing the general significance of the attitudes that determine opinionation, then influential effects operate by altering the substance of those similar beliefs (Nelson & Oxley, 1999). The exposure to a one-sided aspect of a framing strategy on an issue that is biased in one direction can, given certain conditions, induce individual-level opinion change. In the perfect opinion circumstance, the information stream establishes new attitudes that become prominent deliberations throughout the development process. If these new beliefs truly are new to the individual that is, if they differ in direction from preexisting beliefs the balance of considerations an individual holds on a given issue is altered, and opinion change is a likely result (Chong & Druckman, 2007). Successful persuasion, then, involves the introduction of novel beliefs concerning a given issue that become the basis of an altered opinion concerning that issue.

What do the theoretical underpinnings of framing mean in the case of attitude formation and same-sex marriage? As the following examination illustrates, in the resulting debates these two diametrically opposed factions are communicating beyond each other rather than really engaging in a discourse that may lead to conciliation or a new consideration. In order to frame the issues in the most effective way for their faction, they must stay in their separate spheres. To argue in their opponent's sphere is to lose the ideological strength of their framing strategy and thus weaken their own position. On the surface, then, framing and persuasion processes would appear to enjoy just about unlimited potential to shape public opinion. And, indeed, their effects could be great (Zaller, 1996). In relation to judicial activity, there is some support in the literature that these court decisions have had a direct and persuasive impact about gay and lesbian civil rights on individuals. We have both empirical (Baunach, 2011; Egan & Persily, 2009; Druckman, 2001) and theoretical reasons (Lupia & McCubbins, 1998; Smith, 2007) for determining that many people will accept the views of the courts and incorporate them in forming of their own opinions. Based on this premise, the remainder of the chapter will discuss how the courts framed the issue concerning gay and lesbian civil rights and same-sex marriage.

Courts Framing of Same-Sex Civil Rights in *Lawrence*

Even though the *Lawrence* case was not directly presented with a question about the constitutionality of same-sex marriage, by framing the issue as one where gay and lesbian couples were entitled to equal treatment to that enjoyed by opposite sex couples, the court held that the value of equality deserved the same level of respect and dignity. The majority in *Lawrence* held that intimate consensual sexual behavior was included within the liberty interest protected by substantive due process under the 14th Amendment. Four of the 13 sodomy statutes on the books at the time *Lawrence* was litigated applied only to same-sex sodomy, and the remainder opposite-sex statutes were seldom if ever enforced. *Lawrence* explicitly overruled *Bowers v. Hardwick*, 478 U.S. 186 (1986), which had upheld laws that criminalized sodomy had viewed the liberty interest too narrowly. Justice Kennedy framed his criticism of *Bowers* by observing that the longtime condemnation of homosexuality "has been shaped by religious beliefs" (Lawrence, 2003, p. 571). The Court noted that the criminal penalties imposed on violators of the law would result in a kind of scarlet letter, "with all that imports for the dignity of the persons charged" (Lawrence, 2003, p. 575). The *Lawrence* majority clearly moved away from the morality frame and discussed the issues related to gay and lesbian individuals and their families in terms of equality and respect. The language refused to rely on outdated stereotypes put forth by the state and instead talked about the legitimacy of same-sex couples and their lives. The majority in

Lawrence also suggested that the liberty-based dignity claim could be claimed more often in the future.

Justice Kennedy's framing of the issue in terms of equality and dignity of gay and lesbian persons with such broad implications drew sharp criticism from his conservative colleagues based in part of how they framed the issue as encompassing that of pure morality. In the United States, religious hatred toward gays and lesbians cloaked in the argument of morality remains a potent and central foundation of cultural and political currency. With modernization came secularity in most of the industrialized West, the United States underwent a divergent trend. Even as the nation entered the twenty-first century, it persisted through some religious denominations to cultivate intolerance for gays and lesbians. The morality frame characterizes the behavior of gays and lesbians to be wrong and undeserving of social acceptance and government support (Eskridge, 2000; Reimer, 2003). When gays and lesbians are protected from discrimination through laws, for example, the morality frame characterizes them as "special rights," implying additional protections and privileges outside the rule of law. The center of the morality frame is based on the inequality of homosexual and heterosexual relationships, identity and behavior. This morality frame is sometimes advocated by members of the judiciary and their opinions.

Justice Scalia joined by Chief Justice Rehnquist and Justice Thomas argued in dissent of *Lawrence* that *Bowers* should have been retained and that the only rights that are fundamental and should be protected under the constitution are deeply rooted in this nation's history and tradition. According to his evaluation—the view of history supported the narrow holding of *Bowers*—there was no fundamental right to engage in homosexual sodomy. Justice Scalia framed the issue in morality terms by stating that:

> Many Americans do not want persons who openly engage in homosexual conduct as partners in their business, as scoutmasters for their children, as teachers in their children's schools, or as boarders in their home. They view this as protecting themselves and their families from a lifestyle that they believe to be immoral and destructive (Lawrence, 2003, p. 602).

Scalia's dissent argues that preserving public morality is a rational basis for the Texas sodomy law and not allowing morality to be a legitimate consideration by the state; this makes it possible to strike down laws against adult incest, prostitution, masturbation, adultery, fornication, and bestiality (Lawrence, 2003, p. 590). Scalia's dissenting opinion is fashioned in a way to continue the oppression of gay and lesbian individuals and their families within society.

Scalia concluded that the majority in *Lawrence* could ultimately lead to the Supreme Court's endorsement of gay marriage nationwide, and he observed that "today's opinion dismantles the structure of constitutional law that has permitted a distinction to be made between heterosexual and homosexual unions, insofar as formal recognition in marriage is concerned" (Lawrence, 2003, p. 604). Scalia would argue that same-sex marriage should be determined by the people and if they are morally opposed to such a union that is perfectly acceptable under the Constitution.

Comparatively, the majority opinion written by Justice Anthony Kennedy, who was joined in his opinion by Justices Stevens, Souter, Ginsburg, and Breyer, framed the issue as one for equality and dignity for gay and lesbian couples and families. Kennedy's opinion framed the rights for gays and lesbians as one which should include both equality and liberty: "Equality of treatment and the due process right to demand respect for conduct protected by the substantive guarantee of liberty are linked in important respects, and a decision on the latter point advances both interests" (Lawrence, 2003, p. 567). Kennedy knew that not including both equality and liberty under due process as part of the formulation for determining gay and lesbian civil rights would leave the door open for continued discrimination. Kennedy's focus on equality, however, brings American constitutional jurisprudence more in line with the mainstream of the world's democracies that recognize not only the importance of individual dignity and equality but the significance of defending it as a judicially enforceable constitutional right. Liberty and equality were framed by Kennedy to be two sides of the same coin providing gays and lesbians the dignity they deserve and the protections they are guaranteed to have under the Constitution.

While the majority in *Lawrence* concentrated on several aspects of human dignity, it explained that respecting individual dignity required permitting individuals the right to make choices about their sexuality without intervention by the government. As the Court explained, "Adults may choose to enter upon this [gay or lesbian] relationship in the confines of their homes and their own private lives and still retain their dignity as free persons" (Lawrence, 2003, p. 567). This dignity displays is part of an inherent trait that all human beings deserving. The majority associates equality and dignity with the respect owed to the core characteristics of an individual's personality and the right to be free from government interference

with the expression of those characteristics. Under the liberty formulation acknowledged by the *Lawrence* majority, dignity appears to
be identified as an indicator of value granted to individuals on the
position of their status as a human being. In other words, humans
command respect for their dignity rights for no reason other than
their existence. The Court, in this instance, connected this argument
for dignity and equality of gay and lesbian individuals within the
14th Amendment's liberty clause that exemplify this extra-positive
source of the law. The next section will examine how the court in
Goodridge framed the issue of same-sex marriage.

Courts Framing of Same-Sex Marriage in *Goodridge*

Shortly after the Supreme Court decided *Lawrence*, the Massachusetts Supreme Court ruled, in *Goodridge v. Department of Public
Health*, that Massachusetts state law prohibiting gay marriage was
unconstitutional. The court recognized that civil marriage in Massachusetts has always been "a wholly secular institution," and the status
affords couples "enormous private and social advantages" (Goodridge,
2003, p. 954). Along with the personal benefits of "mutuality, companionship, intimacy, fidelity, and family," civil marriage also provides
important public rights under the laws of the Commonwealth, including income tax filing, property ownership through tenancy by the
entirety, certain intestacy rights, the right to share medical policies
and other insurance benefits, the right to equitable division upon
divorce, alimony rights, the right to bring wrongful death and loss
of consortium claims, and spousal privilege (Goodridge, 2003, pp.
954–956). By focusing on the right and principle of equal treatment
and the importance of individual autonomy guaranteed by the Massachusetts Constitution, the court held that the Commonwealth cannot
refuse an individual the "protections, benefits and obligations" conferred by civil marriage solely because that person wishes to marry
an individual of the same sex.

The *Goodridge* decision was based on the principle that dis-
allowing same-sex couples the right to marry failed rational basis
review for both equal protection and due process under the state
constitution. Rather than reach a decision on many of the claims
requiring strict judicial scrutiny, the court determined it did not need
to examine those issues because, as in *Romer*, the discrimination of
concern failed to satisfy even rational basis review (Romer, 1996,
pp. 631–332). The Court in *Romer* struck down a voter-approved
amendment to the Colorado Constitution on equal protection grounds

that would have prohibited state and local governments from adopting measures protecting lesbians, gay men, and bisexuals from discrimination. In Massachusetts, for due process claims, rational basis analysis requires that statutes "bear a real and substantial relation to the public health, safety, morals, or some other phase of the general welfare" (Goodridge, 2003, p. 960). For equal protection challenges, the rational basis test requires that "an impartial lawmaker could logically believe that the classification would serve a legitimate public interest that transcends the harm to the members of the disadvantaged class" (Goodridge, 2003, p. 960). This is usually a very easy standard for the state to meet which usually means the court will defer to the legislature but not in this case.

The framing of equality was more nuanced for the court and was based on how the majority responded to the justifications put forth by the Department of Health to support the denial of same-sex marriage. The court held that the reasons of procreation, child rearing, and conserving resources were all assumed to be legitimate interests. While taking the Commonwealth at its word, the court examined the state's related regulations and laws about procreation, child rearing, and resource conservation. It then examined whether the Commonwealth's denial of marriage rights actually advanced the interests of the state. The court held that the state interests advanced and the exclusion of same-sex couples had no real or substantive connection to one another and therefore did not meet the lowest standard of rational basis.

In terms of procreation, the court concluded that Massachusetts laws never advantaged procreative heterosexual intercourse by married spouses over all "other means of creating a family," because fertility is not a condition for marriage or grounds for divorce, and consummation is not required to validate a marriage (Goodridge, 2003, p. 961). The court acknowledged that any denial of same-sex marriage based on procreation allows official approval of a stereotype that same-sex relationships are inherently unstable and inferior to opposite-sex relationships. The court was not willing to support such a premise because the issue of equality and dignity of its citizens was at stake.

The court also rejected the state's argument that limiting marriage to opposite-sex couples would guarantee that children are raised in the "optimal" setting. The court found no evidence and no rational reasons that excluding same-sex couples from the institution of marriage would increase the number of opposite-sex couples who would marry and raise children. The court also stated that while the ban on same-sex marriage failed to raise the security for children of opposite-sex married couples, it also increased the number of less than optimal family settings by exposing children of same-sex couples to the insecurity of being raised outside the protections and benefits conferred through civil marriage. In the end, the court reasoned that if marriage is a good setting for raising children, then it is good for the children of same-sex couples as well. The court was affirming the respect and dignity of gay and lesbian families.

Finally, the state assumed same-sex couples to be more economically autonomous than heterosexual married couples and maintained that the legislature's goal in saving limited state and private monetary assets validates not including same-sex couples from civil marriage. The court rejected this claim as a false statement, recognizing that numerous same-sex couples, including most of the plaintiffs in the *Goodridge* case, already took care of children and other dependents and were not automatically in less need of or disqualified from government and private assistance. Even if the Department sought to argue that same-sex couples categorically need less financial assistance than opposite-sex couples, the court would not accept this argument because receipt of many public and private financial benefits is not conditioned upon demonstration of financial dependence on a spouse or partner. These benefits are granted merely on the condition of marriage, an option which the State of Massachusetts, through the Department of Public Health, has definitely foreclosed to same-sex couples.

The dissenting opinions were also nuanced in their approach and did not include the morally charged language used by Justice Scalia in the *Lawrence* dissent. Their responses in part attempted to justify the damaging stereotypes put forth by the Department of Health. Justice Cordy declared that "the Legislature could rationally conclude that it furthers the legitimate State purpose of ensuring, promoting, and supporting an optimal social structure for the bearing and raising of children" (Goodridge, 2003, p. 998). He was very willing to support the notion that children would be happier and healthier with opposite sex parents even though this is not accurate.

Justice Sosman paralleled this support of negative stereotypes by concluding that:

[a]bsent consensus on the issue (which obviously does not exist), or unanimity amongst scientists studying the issue (which also does not exist), or a more prolonged period of observation of this new family structure (which has not yet been possible), it is rational for the Legislature to postpone any redefinition of marriage that would include same-sex

couples until such time as it is certain that redefinition will not have unintended and undesirable social consequences (Goodridge, 2003, p. 982).

Even with all of the definitive studies and evidence which demonstrate no tangible differences between opposite sex parents and same-sex parents, Justice Sosman attempts to leave that door open by implying that either more research needs to be completed or there needs to be continued observation for clarity. This type of analysis is much more insidious than the dissent in *Lawrence* by attempting to justify blatant discrimination through the use of misinformation about gay and lesbian families.

Each of these stereotypes argued by the Department of Health was rejected forcefully by the majority of the court as not meeting the minimum standard of rational basis required by the state constitution. This is an unusual result because the state is usually able to meet such a weak level of judicial review. The court reaffirmed the underlying principles of *Lawrence* by framing the issue as one of equality for gay and lesbian couples and their families. These decisions have become woven into the fabric of the United States culture and society.

Conclusion

The gay and lesbian civil rights movement has been struggling against oppression. As part of a marginalized group within the United States, gays and lesbians have been fighting for social justice in society and every area of the law. Each side of the debate over gay and lesbian civil rights has its own collection of strongly held values, interests, and beliefs. Even with this fervent and persistent opposition, the positive shift toward supporting same-sex marriage over the past 12 years is incredible. The support for same-sex marriage in the United States has moved in a positive direction and reached a majority in 2011. This chapter attempted to demonstrate that the framing of the issue by the courts as an issue of equality should be included as one of the influential factors in the shift of attitudes favoring same-sex marriage. The strategy was based on the belief that gay and lesbian relationships were entitled to the same legal protections to that enjoyed by opposite sex couples. In the early part of the twenty-first century, the Supreme Court echoed this board principle in the *Lawrence* decision which was then fortified through a novel approach in *Goodridge*.

The context of the same-sex marriage debate impacts the ways in which information of gay and lesbian life is perceived and understood. When the issue is characterized as only based in religious morality, it repositions gay and lesbian individuals and their families outside the realm of the courts, which can lead to further erosion of public support. This framing of the issue as one inherently connected to equality is making its way into the public sphere. As a result, national opinion has shifted toward greater acceptance of gays and lesbians and same-sex marriage. It seems that this paradigm shift away from moral religious-based arguments to a more equal rights–based discourse, combined with public opinion swings, indicates the appearance of a new, more progressive era of same-sex marriage support.

References

Adamczyk, A., & Felson, J. (2006). Friends' religiosity and first sex. *Social Science Research, 35,* 924–947.

Adamczyk, A., & Pitt, C. (2009). Shaping attitudes about homosexuality: The role of religion and cultural context. *Social Science Research, 38*(2), 338–351.

Andersen, R., & Fetner, T. (2008). Cohort differences in tolerance of homosexuality: Attitudinal change in Canada and the United States, 1981–2000. *Public Opinion Quarterly, 72,* 311–330.

Badgett, M. V. L. (2003). *Money, myths, and change: The economic lives of lesbians and gay men.* Chicago, IL: University of Chicago Press.

Badgett, M. V. L. (2006). Supporting families, saving funds: An economic analysis of equality for same-sex couples in New Jersey. Rutgers Journal of Law and Public Policy, Vol. 4, No. 1.

Barbaro, M. (2011, June 25). Behind N.Y. gay marriage, an unlikely mix of forces. *New York Times.* Retrieved from: http://www.nytimes.com/2011/06/26/nyregion/the-road-to-gay-marriage-in-new-york.html

Bateson G. (1972). *Steps to an ecology of the mind.* New York: Ballantine.

Baunach, D. M. (2011). *Decomposing trends in attitudes toward gay marriage, 1988–2006. Social Science Quarterly, 92,* 346.

Becker, A. B., & Scheufele, D. A. (2011). New voters, new outlook? Predispositions, social networks, and the changing politics of gay civil rights, *Social Science Quarterly, 92,* 324–345.

Becker A. B., & Scheufele D. A. (2009). Moral politicking: Public attitudes toward gay marriage in an election context. *International Journal of Press/Politics, 14*(2), 186–211.

Bendyna, M. E., Green, J. C., Rozell, M. J., & Wilcox, C. (2001). Uneasy alliance: Conservative Catholics and the Christian right. *Sociology of Religion, 62,* 51–64.

Benford, R. D., & Snow, D. A. (2000). Framing processes and social movements: An overview and assessment. *Annual Review of Sociology, 26,* 611–639.

Bonilla, L., & Porter, J. (1990). A comparison of Latino, Black, and non-Hispanic White attitudes toward homosexuality. *Hispanic Journal of Behavioral Science, 12*(4), 437–452.

Brewer, P. R. (2008). *Value war: Public opinion and the politics of gay rights.* Lanham, MD: Rowman & Littlefield Publishers.

Brown, S. L. (2000). The effect of union type on psychological well-being: Depression among cohabitators versus marrieds. *Journal of Health and Social Behavior, 41,* 241–255.

Brumbaugh, S. M., Sanchez, L. A., Nock, S. L., & Wright, J. D. (2008). Attitudes toward gay marriage in states undergoing marriage law transformation. *Journal of Marriage and Family, 70,* 345–359.

Burdette, A. M., Christopher G. E., & Hill, T. D. (2005). Conservative Protestantism and tolerance toward homosexuals: An examination of potential mechanisms. *Sociological Inquiry, 75,* 177–196.

Cherlin, A. J. (2004). The deinstitutionalization of American marriage. *Journal of Marriage and Family, 66,* 848–861.

Chong, D., & Druckman, J. (2007). A theory of framing and opinion formation in competitive elite environments. *Journal of Communication, 57*(1), 99–118.

Clawson, R. A., Kegler, E., & Waltenburg, E. N. (2001). *The legitimacy-conferring authority of the U.S. Supreme Court: An experimental design. American Politics Research, 29*(6), 566–591.

Clawson, R. A., & Waltenburg, E. N. (2003). Support for a Supreme Court affirmative action decision: A story in black and white. *American Politics Research, 31*(3), 251–279.

Craig, S. C., Martinez, M. D., Kane, J. G., & Gainous, J. (2005). Core values, value conflict, and citizens' ambivalence about gay rights. *Public Research Quarterly, 58,*.5–17.

Dahl, R. A. (1957). Decision-Making in a Democracy: The Supreme Court as a national policy-maker. *Journal of Public Law, 6*(2), 279–295.

Davies, M. (2004). Correlates of negative attitudes toward gay men: Sexism, make role norms and male sexuality, *The Journal of Sex Research, 41*(3), 259–266.

Davis, J. A. (1992). Changeable weather in a cooling climate atop the liberal plateau: Conversion and replacement in forty-two general social survey items, 1972–89. *Public Opinion Quarterly, 56*(3), 261–306.

Druckman, J. N. (2001). On the limits of framing effects: Who can frame? *Journal of Politics, 63,* 1041–1066.

Edgell, P., & Docka, D. (2007). Beyond the nuclear family? Familism and gender ideology in diverse religious communities. *Sociological Forum, 22*(1), 26–51.

Egan, P., Persily, N., & Wallsten, K. (2008). *Gay rights: Public opinion and constitutional controversy.* New York: Oxford University Press.

Egan, P., & Persily, N. (2009). Court decisions and trends in support for same-sex marriage. *The Polling Report, 25,* 15.

Emerson, M. O., & Hartman, D. (2006). The rise of religious fundamentalism. *Annual Review of Sociology, 32,* 127–144.

Epstein, L., & Knight, J. (1998). *The choices justices make.* Washington: CQ Press.

Eskridge, W. N., Jr. (2000). No promo homo: The sedimentation of anti-gay discourse and the channeling effect of judicial review. *New York University Law Review, 75,* 1327–1411.

Finlay, B., & Walther, C. S. (2003). The relation of religious affiliation, service attendance, and other factors to homophobic attitudes among university students. *Review of Religious Research, 44,* 370–393.

Fiorina, M. P. (2005). *Culture War? The Myth of a Polarized America.* New York: Pearson Longman.

Fisher, R. D., Derison, D., Polley, C. F., III, Cadman, J., & Johnston, D. (1994). Religiousness, religious orientation, and attitudes toward gays and lesbians. *Journal of Applied Social Psychology, 24,* 614–630.

Fletcher, J., & Howe, P. (2000). Public opinion and the courts. *Choices, 6*(3), 4–57.

Friedman, B. (2009). *The will of the people: How public opinion has influenced the Supreme Court and shaped the meaning of the constitution.* New York: Farrar, Straus and Giroux.

Froese, P., Bader, C., & Smith, B. (2008). Political tolerance and God's wrath in the United States. *Sociology of Religion, 69*(1), 29–44.

Fulton, A. S., Gorsuch, R. L., &. Maynard, E. A. (1999). Religious orientation, antihomosexual sentiment, and fundamentalism among Christians. *Journal for the Scientific Study of Religion, 38,* 14–22.

Gallagher, J., & Bull, C. (2001). *Perfect enemies: The battle between the religious right and the gay movement.* Lanham, MD: Madison Books.

Gibson, J. L., Caldeira, G. A., & Baird, V. A. (1998). On the legitimacy of National High Courts. *American Political Science Review, 92,* 343–358.

Gibson, J. L., Caldeira, G. A. & Spence, L. K. (2005). Why do people accept public policies they oppose? Testing legitimacy theory with a survey-based experiment. *Political Research Quarterly, 58*(2), 187–201.

Gibson, J. L. (2007). The legitimacy of the U.S. Supreme Court in a polarized polity. *Journal of Empirical Legal Studies, 4*(3), 517–523.

Giles, M. W., Blackstone, B. & Vining, R. L. (2008). The Supreme Court in American democracy: Unraveling the linkages between public opinion and judicial decision making. *Journal of Politics, 70*(2), 293–306.

Glass, C. M., Kubasek, N., & Kiester, E. (2011). Toward a 'European Model' of same-sex marriage rights: A viable pathway for the U.S.? *Berkeley Journal of International Law, 29,* 132.

Goffman E. (1974). *Frame analysis: An essay on the organization of the experience.* New York: Harper Colophon.

Goodstein, L. (2010, March 17). Episcopalians confirm a second gay bishop. *New York Times.* Retrieved from: http://www.nytimes.com/2010/03/18/us/18bishop.html

Greeley, A., & Hout, M. (2006). *The truth about conservative Christians: What they think and what they believe.* Chicago, IL: University of Chicago Press.

Grosskopf, A., & Mondak, J. J. (1998). Do attitudes toward specific Supreme Court decisions matter? The impact of Webster and Texas v. Johnson on public confidence in the Supreme Court. *Political Research Quarterly, 51,* 633–654.

Haider-Markel, D. P., & Joslyn, M. R. (2008). Beliefs about the origins of homosexuality and support for gay rights: an empirical test of attribution theory. *Public Opinion Quarterly, 72,* 291–310.

Herek, G. (2002). Gender gaps in public opinion about lesbian and gay men. *Public Opinion Quarterly, 66,* 40–66.

Herek, G. M., & Capitanio, J. P. (1995). Black heterosexuals' attitudes toward lesbians and gay men in the United States. *The Journal of Sex Research, 32,* 95–105.

Herek, G. M., & Allen, T. J. (2007). When does heterosexuals' contact with sexual minorities reduce sexual prejudice? Paper presented at the Annual Meeting of the American Psychological Association, San Francisco, CA. August 17–20.

Hoekstra, V. J. (1995). The Supreme Court and public opinion change: An experimental study of the Court's ability to change opinion. *American Politics Quarterly, 23,* 109Í129.

Hoekstra, V. J. (2003). *Public reaction to Supreme Court decisions.* New York: Cambridge University Press.

House Judiciary Committee Report for the Defense of Marriage Act, see H. R. REP. No. 104-664 (1996), reprinted in 1996 USCCAN, pp. 2905–2947.

Hunt, L. L., & Hunt, M. O. (2001). Race, region, and religious involvement: A comparative study of Whites and African Americans. *Social Forces, 80,* 605–631.

Hwang, S.-D., & Gray, V. (1991). External limits and internal determinants of state public policy. *Western Political Quarterly, 44,* 277–298.

Inglehart, R. (1997). *Modernization and postmodernization.* Princeton, NJ: Princeton University Press.

Inglehart, R. (2008, January–March). Changing values among Western publics from 1970 to 2006. *West European Politics, 31*(1–2), 130–146.

Kaufmann, K. M. (2002). Culture wars, secular realignment and the gender gap in party identification. *Political Behavior, 24,* 283–307.

Kite, M. E., & Whitley, B. E. (1996). Sex differences in attitudes towardshomosexual persons, behavior, and civil rights: A meta-analysis. *Personality & Social Psychology Bulletin, 22,* 336–353.

Klarman, M. J. (1994). How Brown changed race relations: The backlash thesis. *Journal of American History, 81*(1), 81–118.

Koch, J. R., & Curry, E. W. (2000). Social context and the Presbyterian gay/lesbian debate: testing open-systems theory. *Review of Religious Research, 42,* 206–214.

Kritzer, H. M. (2005). The American public's assessment of the Rehnquist court. *Judicature, 89*, 168–176.

Lee, K. M. Y. (2010). *Equality, dignity, and same-sex marriage: A rights disagreement in democratic societies.* Leiden, The Netherlands; Boston, MA: Martinus Nijhoff Publishers.

Lemelle, A. J., Jr. (2004). African American attitudes toward gay males: Faith-based initiatives and implications for HIV/AIDS services. *Journal of African American Studies, 7*, 59–74.

Lewis, D. C. (2011). Direct democracy and minority rights: Same-sex marriage bans in the American states. *Social Science Quarterly, 92*(2), 364–383.

Lewis, G. B. (2003). Black-White differences in attitudes toward homosexuality and gay rights. *Public Opinion Quarterly, 67*, 59–78.

Lewis, G. B. (2005). Thinking about gay marriage: Putting the moral condemnation back in morality policy. *Paper presented at the Annual Meeting of the Association for Public Policy Analysis and Management,* Washington, DC. November 3–5.

Lewis, G. B. (2007). The friends and family plan: Assessing the impact of knowing someone gay on support for gay rights. *Paper presented at the Annual Meeting of the American Psychological Association,* San Francisco, CA. August 17–20.

Lofton, K., & Haider-Markel, D. P. (2007). The politics of same-sex marriage versus the politics of gay civil rights: A comparison of public opinion and state voting patterns. In C. A. Rimmerman & C. Wilcox (Eds.), *The politics of same-sex marriage* (pp. 313–340). Chicago: University of Chicago Press.

Loftus, J. (2001). America's liberalization in attitudes towards homosexuality, 1973–1998. *American Sociological Review, 66*, 762–782.

Lowi, T. J. (1972). Four systems of policy, politics, and choice. *Public Administration Review, 32*, 298–310.

Lupia, A., & McCubbins, M. D. (1998). *The democratic dilemma: Can citizens learn what they need to know?* Cambridge: Cambridge University Press.

Marshall, T. R. (2008). *Public opinion and the Rehnquist court.* Albany: State University of New York Press.

McGuire, K. T., & Stimson, J. A. (2004). The least dangerous branch revisited: New evidence on Supreme Court responsiveness to public preferences. *Journal of Politics, 66*(4), 1018–1035.

McVeigh, R., & Diaz, M.-E. D. (2009). Voting to ban same-sex marriage: Interests, values, and communities. *American Sociological Review, 74*, 891–915.

Mistler, S. (January 26, 2012). It's on: Same-sex marriage supporters give it another try. *Lewiston Sun Journal.* Retrieved from: http://www.sun-journal.com/comment/91821

Moats, D. (2004). *Civil Wars: The battle for gay marriage.* New York: Harcourt.

Mohipp, C., & Morry, M. M. (2004). The relationship of symbolic beliefs and prior contact to heterosexuals' attitudes toward gay men and lesbian women. *Canadian Journal of Behavioural Science, 36*(1), 36–44.

Moore, L. M., & Vanneman, R. (2003). Context matters: Effects of the proportion fundamentalists on gender attitudes. *Social Forces, 82*, 115–139.

Morrison, T. G., Parriag, A. V., & Morrison, M. A. (1999). The psychometric properties of the homonegativity scale. *Journal of Homosexuality, 37*, 111–126.

Murphy, W. F., Tanenhaus, J., & Kastner, D. L. (1973). *Public evaluations of constitutional courts: Alternative Explanations*. London: Sage.

Negy, C., & Eisenman, R. (2005). A comparison of African American and White college students' affective and attitudinal reactions to lesbian, gay, and bisexual individuals: An exploration study. *The Journal of Sex Research, 42*, 291–298.

Nelson, T., & Oxley, Z. (1999). Issue framing effects and belief importance and opinion. *Journal of Politics, 61*, 1040–1067.

Nevitte, N., Blais, A., Gidengil, E., & Nadeau, R. (2000). *Unsteady State: The 1997 Canadian Federal Election*. Don Mills: Oxford University Press.

Ohlander, J., Batalova, J., & Treas, J. (2005). Explaining educational influences on attitudes toward homosexual relations. *Social Science Research, 34*, 781–799.

Olson, L. R., Cadge, W., & Harrison, J. T., (2006). Religion and public opinion about same-sex marriage. *Social Science Quarterly, 87*, 340–360.

Pan Z, & Kosicki G. M. (1993). Framing analysis: An approach to news discourse. *Political Communication, 10*, 55–75.

Pearl, M. L., & Galupo, M. P. (2007). Development and validation of the attitudes toward same-sex marriage scale. *Journal of Homosexuality, 53*(3), 117–134.

Persily, N., Egan, P., & Wallsten, K. (2006). Gay marriage, public opinion and the courts. Public Law Working Paper No. 06-17. Retrieved from: http://papers.ssrn.com/sol3/papers.cfm?abstract_id=900208

Pettigrew, T. F., & Tropp, L. R. (2006). A meta-analytic test of intergroup contact theory. *Journal of Personality and Social Psychology, 90*(5), 751–783.

Pew Forum on Religion and Public Life. (2010). Gay marriage and homosexuality. Retrieved in 3/10/2011 from: http://pewforum.org/Gay-Marriage-and-Homosexuality/Religious-Groups-Official-Positions-on-Same-Sex-Marriage.aspx/

ProCon.org. State level marriage equality. ProCon.org, Retrieved from: http://gaymarriage.procon.orgPrice, V., & Tewksbury, D. (1997). News values and public opinion: A theoretical account of media priming and framing. In G. A. Barnett & F. J. Foster (Eds.), *Progress in Communication Sciences* (pp. 173–212). Greenwich, CT: Ablex.

Ratcliff, J. J., Lassiter, G. D., Markman, K. D., & Snyder, C. J. (2006). Gender differences in attitudes toward gay men and lesbians: The role of motivation to respond without prejudice. *Personality and Social Psychology Bulletin, 32*(10), 1325–1338.

Reimer, S. (2003). *Evangelicals and the continental divide*. Montreal, QC & Kingston, ON: McGill-Queen's University Press.

Reimer, S., & Park, J. Z. (2001). Tolerant (In)civility? A longitudinal analysis of White conservative Protestants' willingness to grant civil liberties. *Journal for the Scientific Study of Religion, 40*, 735–745.

Rimmerman, C., Wald, K., & Wilcox, C. (2000). *The politics of gay rights.* Chicago: University of Chicago Press.

Rimmerman, C. A., & Wilcox, C. (2007). *The politics of same-sex marriage.* Chicago: University of Chicago Press.

Romer v. Evans, 517 U.S. 620 (1996).

Rosenberg, G. (1991). *The hollow hope. Can courts bring about social change?* Chicago: The University of Chicago Press.

Rowatt, W. C., LaBouff, J., Johnson, M., Froese, P., & Tsang, J. (2009). Associations among religiousness, social attitudes, and prejudice in a national random sample of American adults. *Psychology of Religion and Spirituality, 1*, 14–24.

Scheufele D. A. (1999). Framing as a theory of media effects. *Journal of Communication, 49*, 103–122.

Schon D. A., & Rein M. (1994). *Frame reflection: Toward the resolution of intractable policy controversies.* New York: Basic Books.

Schulte, G. (2010, November 3). "Iowans dismiss three justices." *Des Moines Register.*

Shear, M. D., & Stolberg S. G. (2011, June 29). Gay marriage seems to wane as conservative issue. *The New York Times.* Retrieved from: http://www.nytimes.com/2011/02/25/us/politics/25marriage.html?_r=1&hp

Sherkat, D. E. (2002). African-American religious affiliation in the late twentieth century: Trends, cohort variations, and patterns of switching, 1973–1998. *Journal for the Scientific Study of Religion, 41*, 485–494.

Sherkat, D. E., Kylan D., & Creek, S. (2010). Religion, race and support for same-sex marriage. *Social Science Quarterly, 91*, 80–98.

Sherkat, D. E., Williams, M. P., Maddox, G., & De Vries, K. M. (2011). Religion, politics, and support for same-sex marriage in the United States, 1988–2008. *Social Science Research, 40*(1), 167–180.

Silver, N. (2011, June 29). The future of same-sex marriage ballot measures. *The New York Times.* Retrieved from: http://fivethirtyeight.blogs.nytimes.com/2011/06/29/the-future-of-same-sex-marriage-ballot-measures

Smith, M. (2007). Framing same-sex marriage in Canada and the United States: Goodridge, Halpern and the national boundaries of political discourse. *Social & Legal Studies, 16*, 5–26.

Snow, D. A., & Benford, R. D. (1992). Master frames and cycles of protest. In A. D. Morris & C. M. Mueller (Eds.), *Frontiers in social movement theory* (pp. 133–155). New Haven, CT: Yale University Press.

Stack, S., & Eshleman, J. R. (1998). Marital status and happiness: A 17-nation study. *Journal of Marriage and the Family, 60*, 527–536.

Sulzberger, A. G. (2010, November 10). Ouster of Iowa judges sends signal to bench. *New York Times.* Retrieved from: http://electionlawblog.org/archives/017823.html

Tarrow, S. (1992). Mentalities, political cultures, and collective action frames: Constructing meanings through action. In A. D. Morris & C. M. Mueller

(Eds.), *Frontiers in social movement theory* (pp. 174–202). New Haven, CT: Yale University Press.

Treas, J. (2002). How cohorts, education, and ideology shaped a new sexual revolution on American attitudes toward non-marital Sex, 1972–1998. *Sociological Perspectives, 45*(3), 267–283.

Tuntiya, N. (2005). Fundamental religious affiliation and support for civil liberties: A critical examination. *Sociological Inquiry, 75,* 153–176.

Tversky, A., & Kahneman, D. (1981). The framing of decisions and the psychology of choice. *Science, 21*(1), 453–58.

Tygart, C. E. (2002). Legal rights to homosexuals into the areas of domestic partnerships and marriages: Public support and genetic causation attribution. *Education Research Quarterly, 25*(3), 20–28.

United States Government Accountability Office, GAO-04-353R Defense of Marriage Act (2004). Retrieved from http://www.gao.gov/new.items/d04353r.pdf.

Walls, N. E. (2010). Religion and support for same-sex marriage: Implications from the literature. *Journal of Gay and Lesbian Social Services, 22,* 112–131.

Werum, R., & Winders, B. (2001). Who's "in" and who's "out": State fragmentation and the struggle over gay rights, 1974–1999. *Social Problems, 48,* 386–410.

Whitehead, A. L. (2010). Sacred rites and civil rights: Religion's effect on attitudes toward same-sex unions and the perceived cause of homosexuality. *Social Science Quarterly, 91*(17), 63–74.

Whitley, B. E., Jr. (2001). Gender-role variables and attitudes toward homosexuality. *Sex Roles, 45,* 691–721.

Wilcox, C., & Jelen, T. (1990). Evangelicals and political tolerance. *American Politics Research, 18,* 25–46.

Wilcox, C., & Norrander, B. (2002). Of moods and morals: The dynamics of opinion on abortion and gay rights. In B. Norrander & C. Wilcox (Eds.), *Understanding public opinion* (pp. 121–147). Washington, DC: CQ Press.

Wilgoren, D., Backon, P., Jr. (2010). "Obama to sign DADT repeal before big, emotional crowd," *Washington Post.* Retrieved from http://www.washingtonpost.com/wp-dyn/content/article/2010/12/22/AR2010122201888.html

Wood, P. B., & Bartkowski, J P. (2004). Attribution style and public policy attitudes toward gay rights. *Social Science Quarterly, 85,* 58–74.

Young, I. M. (1990). *Justice and the politics of difference.* Princeton, NJ: Princeton University Press.

Zaller, J. (1996). The myth of massive media impact revisited: New support for a discredited idea. In D. Mutz, P. Sniderman, & R. Brody (Eds.), *Political persuasion and attitude change* (Eds.), Ann Arbor: University of Michigan Press.

Zernike, K. (2012, February 17). Christie vetoes gay marriage bill. *New York Times.* Retrieved from: http://www.nytimes.com/2012/02/18/nyregion/christie-vetoes-gay-marriage-bill.html

CHAPTER NINE

Oppression's Three New Faces

Rethinking Iris Young's "Five Faces of Oppression" for Disability Theory

Elizabeth Purcell

Introduction

Iris Marion Young's "Five Faces of Oppression" has become a staple in contemporary social and political philosophy. In her essay, she articulates and extends a Marxian account of oppression to include not only the exploitation facing women and racial minorities, but also to address four additional forms of oppression: marginalization, powerlessness, cultural imperialism, and violence. The purpose of the present essay is not to question what Young has succeeded in articulating, but rather, to add three new faces to her account.

I am motivated to interrogate Young's "Five Faces" because it does not seem to me that the problems facing people with disabilities are adequately addressed in what she argues in her essay. Because the spectrum of disability is so vast, ranging from physical impairment to cognitive disability, from impairments due to age to psychological illness and trauma, some "faces" of systemic oppression that people with disabilities face find no voice in Young's work. In particular, it seems to me that there are three such forms, though one of them at least is experienced by other oppressed groups such as racial minorities and nonheterosexuals as well. The first of these faces is Stigma, which concerns an "undesired difference." Persons with disabilities are *stigmatized* within a society. Stigma disvalues people with disabilities and does not grant them societal recognition, or if it does, it mis-recognizes them through stereotypes and poor representation. One example of this stigmatization is the medical gaze, which, though trained to aid people, often slides into viewing the "disabled" body as a body "with broken parts." A second face of oppression is Questioned Personhood. Currently, people with disabilities face educational and other forms of institutional oppression that question their status as persons at biological and psychological levels. For people with cognitive disability, for example, their personhood has come under scrutiny and has included a history of abuse and human experimentation. It is still not uncommon to find people, even academic philosophers, who routinely compare such people with nonhuman animals, such as chimpanzees, dolphins, or household dogs, thereby intentionally stripping these people of human dignity and any human rights that might serve to protect them. Last, the third form is Societal Incapacity. This form of oppression concerns the social and environmental factors that give advantages to people with "able" bodies, such as constructing buildings in which the only fire exits are via a stairwell. This form does not ensure capacities for all of its citizens within a given society, and thus systemically oppresses those the society has disregarded.

My hope is that these three new faces oppressing people with disabilities, namely Stigma, Questioned Personhood, and Societal Incapacity, strike one, at least intuitively, as serious and as deserving of more careful social reflection. I elaborate on them below. In the argument that follows, I need to demonstrate two points: first, that these three new faces are not accounted for with Young's framework; and second, that they are in fact forms of oppression and not merely discriminatory incidents. The latter task requires that I demonstrate that each of these three new faces has systemic implications, while the former requires that I show how they slip through Young's existing framework. In what follows, I begin with a more careful review of Young in order to assess to what extent each of her forms of oppression is capable of addressing these particular faces of oppression. Afterward, I turn to a more detailed account of these three new faces in order to show that they are in fact forms of oppression. It is my hope that by identifying these forms, new methods and plans of action can be developed for countering the particular forms of oppression that persons with disabilities face.

The Five Faces of Oppression

In order to address Young's five faces of oppression adequately, I first treat each of them separately and then consider them as overlapping forms of oppression. In "The Five Faces of Oppression," Young reconsiders the term *oppression* in its systemic and structural forms rather than as the violence and injustice some people suffer because a tyrannical power "intends to keep them down" (1990a, pp. 40–41). Her account of the five faces illuminates how oppression makes up much of our social experience. Furthermore, she argues that oppression is a systemic and structural problem latent within the major economic, political, and cultural institutions but is not simply reducible to institutions themselves.

A second point of conceptual clarification distinguishes oppression from discrimination. The concept "discrimination" refers to the "conscious actions and policies by which members of a group are excluded from institutions or confined to inferior positions" (ibid.). Oppression differs because it exists in absence of overt discrimination. Young (1990a) expands on the definition of oppression as follows:

> [t]he concept [of oppression] names the vast and deep injustices some groups suffer as a consequence of frequently unconscious assumptions and reactions of well-meaning people in ordinary interactions, media and cultural stereotypes, and structural features of bureaucratic hierarchy and market mechanisms, in short, the normal ongoing processes of everyday life (p. 41).

Oppression differs from discrimination because it concerns the often invisible barriers which immobilize a particular group of people. It is either structural or systemic and thus does not require that there is a correlated "oppressing" group for any specific group suffering oppression. Instead, for every oppressed group there is a corresponding *privileged* group within society.

With these conceptual distinctions in mind, I turn to the specific forms of oppression themselves. The first form Young describes is *exploitation*. Young draws here from Marx's theory of exploitation and then expands it to address issues of race and gender. The Marxian theory of exploitation answers the paradox of capitalism: "when everyone is formally free, how can there be class domination? Why does there continue to be class distinction between the wealthy, who own the means of production, and the mass of people, who work for them" (1990a, p. 48)? Capitalism systematically transfers the powers of the laborer to augment the power of the one who owns the means of production. Thus, the capitalist is able to maintain an "extractive power," which allows for the continual extraction of benefits from workers. This extractive power extends beyond the transfer of power: it also deprives workers of their sense of control and self-respect. It can also accumulate passively for the capitalist, so that he may not even be aware that he is the beneficiary of such oppression.

A similar kind of transfer of power may be seen to occur with respect to gender and race as well. In the case of gender, according to Young, there is a systematic transfer of powers from women to men. This systematic transfer takes place on two planes: (1) in the transfer of nurturing and sexual energies to men, and (2) in the transfer of powers in domestic labor as a form of capitalist exploitation. Young (1990a) writes:

> As a class, however, women undergo specific forms of gender exploitation—ways the energies and power of women are expended, often unnoticed and unacknowledged, usually to benefit men by releasing them for more important and creative work, enhancing their status or the environment around them, or providing men with sexual or emotive service (p. 51).

Likewise, a similar systematic transfer of powers occurs for race from non-Whites to Whites. One might recall, for example, how in the United States there is an imbalance of power for private household services and "menial" labor. These laborers are usually servants for business executives, government officials, and other high-status professionals. Young notes:

> [i]n our society there remains strong cultural pressure to fill servant jobs—like bell hop, porter, chamber maid, bus boy, and so on—with black and Latino workers (1990a, p. 52).

I believe this form of analysis does, in some respects, speak to the concerns of people with disabilities. Specifically, it seems to me that race, gender, and class exploitation intersect with the case of the dependency worker, or professional caregiver, for a person with a disability or (even) illness. The majority of care workers within the United States are women, and many of those women are of certain ethnic or racial minorities. These workers, specifically in the field of health-care, experience systemic exploitation. While they experience a transfer in power from their skill sets to those who employ them, they are often little remunerated and little respected. Much of their work goes "unseen" and unappreciated within society: they are often paid little, work long and exhausting hours, and take care of those with profound physical or psychological needs (Young, 2002, pp. 41–42).

Even granted this analysis, it does not seem to me that exploitation adequately addresses Stigma, Questioned Personhood, or Societal Incapacity. None of these difficulties concern the systematic transfer of value or power from one group to another, which is the hallmark of exploitation. While Young's account targets certain people with disabilities who are employed by the labor market, and as a result, are exploited, exploitation is not the only face of oppression these people experience. Certain people with disabilities may also experience societal incapacity and struggle to maneuver around their work space due to a building that has limited wheelchair accessibility. Likewise, they may experience stigmatization and exclusion from their work associates because of this lack of motility, such as being excluded from being on teams for company softball games.

Young's second face of oppression is *marginalization.* The "marginals" in society differ from those who are exploited, because marginals are the people the labor market does not employ. Many of those who are included in this group are certain racial minorities, elderly people, and people with disabilities (Young, 2000, p. 169). A large proportion of the United States population are marginals. Often these include: those who have been laid off from work and are struggling to regain employment, young people and people of color who cannot find first or second jobs, many single mothers with children, people with cognitive or physical disabilities, and Native Americans who live on reservations. Young (1990a) describes the oppression they experience:

> Because they are dependent on bureaucratic institutions for support or services, old people, poor people, and mentally or physically disabled people are subject to patronizing, punitive, demeaning, and arbitrary treatment by the policies and people associated with welfare bureaucracies (p. 54).

The forms of oppression that occur come both from the social service providers who enforce rules with which these "dependents" must comply and from medical and social service providers who insist on having a right to claim they know what is best for these dependents. Thus, part of this systemic oppression includes the suspension of rights to privacy, respect, and individual choice.

Here again, while I find Young's articulation of this kind of oppression insightful, neither stigmatization, nor the questioning of personhood, nor even societal incapacity concern the labor market directly. Such that concern with the labor market is constitutive of marginalization, I do not think marginalization is able to address these three specific difficulties facing persons with disabilities. In the specific case of people with cognitive disability such as mental "retardation" or dementia, these people would not only experience the oppression of marginalization from the labor force, but also the oppression of questioned personhood as well. Because they are viewed as "dependents" by the state they experience marginalization, but because they differ in psychological ability, their human dignity and moral status are questioned and discounted by various members of that state.

The third face of oppression Young articulates is *powerlessness*. This form of oppression can be witnessed in the social division of labor between the "middle class" and "working class" or professionals and nonprofessionals. This form of oppression concerns *status* rather than class. As Young says, "[b]eing a professional entails occupying a status position than non-professionals lack, creating a condition of oppression that non-professionals suffer" (1990a, p. 56). Powerlessness describes the lack of work autonomy that nonprofessionals experience: they have little opportunity to exercise creativity or judgment in their work, have little technical experience or authority, express themselves "awkwardly," and "do not command respect" (1990a, p. 56).

Powerlessness appears to address at least two of the new faces of oppression I am seeking to articulate. Questioned Personhood certainly looks like another sort of oppression, but perhaps Stigma could be construed as a kind of powerlessness. Some people with disabilities, depending on the impairment, do express themselves with difficulty. Yet, at the heart of the concept of powerlessness for Young, one finds that it stems from the advantages gained by people with professional class status. Powerlessness is, for her, clearly linked to class, and stigma is not. Even professionals with disabilities suffer from stigma. People with disabilities suffer a stigma that is similar to the stigma a Black person experiences with "Black Exceptionalism": no matter how much wealth this person has acquired and how much status he or she has achieved, he or she will always be "marked" or "branded" by his or her color. Societal Incapacity is also unaddressed by powerlessness, since this difficulty is not a class difficulty. Lacking wheelchair access is something that faces professionals and the working class alike, even if a member of the professional class may be able to afford a motorized wheelchair while a member of the working class may not.

The fourth face of oppression is *cultural imperialism*. While the first three forms operate according to power structures, this fourth form concerns both power and recognition. In cultural imperialism, one dominant perspective renders another perspective as Other and often as of less worth, as occurs, for example by stereotyping. At its heart, cultural imperialism "consists in the universalization of one group's experience and culture, and its establishment as the norm" (1990, p. 59). Not cognizant of what they are doing, the members of the dominant group project their own experiences as representative of humanity as such. The result is that victims of cultural imperialism are paradoxically only recognized as stereotypes and at the same time treated as invisible. According to Young, "[t]hose living under cultural imperialism find themselves defined from the outside, positioned, and placed by a system of dominant meanings they experience as arising from elsewhere, from those with whom they do not identify, and who do not identify with them" (1990a, p. 59).

This consciousness is double because the oppressed desires recognition within her society but is only stereotyped and marked as different or inferior. In response, this group tries to express itself as a subculture. One's consciousness is double because one finds oneself defined by two cultures—a dominant one and a subordinate one. Thus, this is the injustice of cultural imperialism: "that the oppressed group's experience and interpretation of social life finds no expression that touches the dominant culture, while that same culture imposes on the opposed group its experience and interpretation of social life" (Young, 1990, p. 60). An example of cultural imperialism is witnessed in the oppression of Deaf culture. Deafness, unlike other forms of disability, is not considered an impairment by those who are deaf. Rather, it is considered its own culture or subculture within American society, and has its own language, American Sign Language (Dolnick, 1993). Yet, this culture is almost always silenced, ignored, or unrecognized by a hearing community, which dominates the United States (or any other country).

While cultural imperialism is a face of oppression that affects people with disabilities, it does not oppress people with disabilities in the same way as Stigma, Questioned Personhood, and Societal Incapacity. Young herself describes the discrimination that people with disabilities face as sometimes being a form of cultural oppression, in her essay "Social Movements and the Politics of Difference," but then at other times in that essay she describes those with disabilities as "unhealthy" and thus different from "normal" pregnant women (1990b, p. 175). Likewise, for the status of work, she argues that "[t[he variability of condition of people with disabilities is huge, however, and many of those brought together under this label have nothing at all in common in the way of experience, culture, or identity" (2000, p. 171). Thus, Young's concern for those with disabilities moves beyond the idea of one culture oppressing another. For example, unlike Deaf culture, which is its own oppressed culture, people who suffer from terminal illnesses are not a culture. They form support groups and try to educate the public, but it is not a culture or subculture. People who are deaf have loudly proclaimed that they do not want to be "cured." In contrast, most of those with a terminal illness desire to be cured or to have relief from painful physical, emotional, or mental suffering. A prime example is a patient with Alzheimer's disease. The patient with Alzheimer's disease experiences tragedy not only alone, but with those who love her. A daughter may come home from work to find that her mother has "gone out for a walk" and gotten lost, unable to remember how to find her way home. Alzheimer's patients may not recognize their own danger: they may wander out into oncoming traffic, become lost in wooded areas, or start fires. These dangers for loved ones can cause terror for family members and caregivers who worry about their safety.

Researchers from the School of Nursing and Midwifery at Trinity College Dublin have identified the various forms of Stigma, Questioned Personhood, and Societal Incapacity facing those with Alzheimer's. According to Mary McCarron, the principal investigator, the challenges facing those with this disease include "social isolation, fragmented, unsuitable and poorly-resourced services, lack of information about the services available and the difficulty navigating a complex health and social care system in which services are often unresponsive to the real needs of people with dementia and their carers" (cited in Hunter, 2012). The patient with Alzheimer's experiences *Stigma* both from the public and from the health-care system. In the public eye, patients with this disease are viewed in terms of negative images, stereotypes, and fear. As a result, many individuals shun or are reluctant to engage patients with Alzheimer's. This stigmatization leads to further social isolation for those individuals suffering from the disease. Furthermore, from the health-care system, patients with Alzheimer's experience stigmatization in terms of policy and resource allocation: in most cases, their illness is not viewed as a priority for care. This stigma reverberates into the life of family members and caregivers who may experience anger, hurt, frustration, and shame when others witness difficult or "inappropriate" behavior in public, and they may feel guilt for being unable to meet a "perceived societal expectation to continue caring on an indefinite basis" (ibid.).

In addition to Stigma, a patient with Alzheimer's may experience *Societal Incapacity*. The individual with this disease experiences Societal Incapacity in three ways. First, she may experience a "loss of place" insofar as she encounters enforced isolation from being placed in certain living facilities and enforced social isolation due to a withdrawal of friends and family. Carers and loved ones describe themselves as being at risk for something similar because they are forced to redefine their life spaces and develop new roles (ibid.). Second, she may encounter institutional barriers when trying to "navigate the system" in health care. Oftentimes these services are found to be "fragmented, inadequate and inflexible and [have] failed to offer choice or meet their needs" (ibid.). Third, she may encounter "unsafe environments" that include environments unsuitable for her needs or dangerous for her. Caregivers also must worry about their loved one being subject to critical or hostile gazes from others in public places.

Finally, a patient with Alzheimer's may also endure *Questioned Personhood*. Her personhood status is questioned first by her society because she is deemed a "dependent," and with this designation, she loses certain rights she once had. She may also experience ageism and discrimination from a health care worker's patronizing actions (ibid.). Many times those with Alzheimer's are not treated with the loving care and respect that they deserve; instead, some have been referred to as "burdens" on family and society or interpersonally treated as children rather than adults.

Thus, while cultural imperialism does illuminate some facets of the oppression facing those with disabilities, it does not illuminate the three forms currently under consideration. The stigmatized are not uniformly a culture, and neither are those who have their personhood questioned or suffer from societal incapacity. McCarron and her research team have found that conceptualizing dementia in terms of disability has generated positive steps to advance measures to counteract these forms of oppression facing loved ones (ibid.).

The final face of oppression is systemic and legitimate *violence*. In this case, the oppressed group knows that they must fear violent, unprovoked attacks at random to their persons and property with the motive to "damage, humiliate, or destroy a person" (Young, 1990, p. 62). An example of this would be that any woman, because she is a member of the group "women," has a reason to fear rape. In the particular case of disability, "disabled women are raped and abused at a rate more than twice that of nondisabled women" (Davis, 2000, p. 332). People with disabilities are targets for such violence both in public places and in private institutions or group homes. Often, people with disabilities and deaf people are targets for verbal, physical, and sexual abuse. In general, much of this kind of violence surfaces in the form of hate crimes, hate speech, or psychological violence and often goes unpunished within a society.

This violence and marginalization may be the result of stigma in some cases, but I think it is clear that the systematically legitimated

forms of violence are one matter, while stigma is another. A similar point holds for Questioned Personhood. While this practice does
legitimate violence against people with disabilities, violence itself is
a different matter than the act of stripping human dignity from a
segment of the population for legal, political or ethical purposes.
Finally, Societal Incapacity does not appear to be addressed in any
direct fashion by violence.

While a person may experience any one of Young's faces individually, it is more likely that he or she will experience them in an
overlapping effect. Furthermore, it is possible that this person could
experience these three new faces in addition to Young's overlapping
framework as further dimensions of oppression. The overlapping of
these forms becomes apparent in numerous cases. For example, consider the case of a gay Black man who lives in a conservative Christian area in the South. In this area, he may struggle to find work
and be marginalized because of the racist and homophobic culture
in which he lives. Because of this, he may experience a sense of
powerlessness for being in a lower economic class than a Christian
White heterosexual male lawyer. He may also experience Cultural
Imperialism because of an overwhelming Christian homophobia that
may force him to hide or silence his homosexuality: he may not be
able to hold hands with his lover in public for fear of being chased
out of town. This fear is linked to the violence he may experience
or anticipate for being in an oppressive cultural area. But he also
experiences one of the three new faces as well: Stigma. Here, his
stigma is double because of racism and homophobia. This stigma,
because of the "branding" and negative values it attaches to his body,
that is, his sexual orientation and the color of his skin, may lead to
marginalization and violence.

In another example, these three new faces overlap with some
of Young's faces with the case of a woman diagnosed with a "disorder" along the "autism spectrum." Because she may not be able to
speak with ease, and jerks her hands or bangs her head in frustration, she experiences Stigma in her society because her body is not
an "able" body. This stigma may lead to marginalization insofar as
she is denied work because she may "scare" customers. Within the
United States, it is documented that workers with "autism" have a
combined unemployment and underemployment rate of around 90%
and only 56% in a study done in 2011 have graduated high school
(Wilkie, 2012). As a result she experiences powerlessness because she
is dependent on government programs and considered a "mooch" by
a professional class. But she may also experience Questioned Personhood: due to her "poor ability to express herself" and difficulty taking

exams, she may be diagnosed with "mental retardation" [*sic*]. If she is diagnosed as a "dependent" by the state, then she is denied certain rights but also her biological and psychological abilities are used as a way to deny her life intrinsic and equal worth with others within her society. Finally, she may experience societal incapacity in the educational system because she cannot speak "well" or sit still for long periods of time, and as a result her education must be taught within the home or by specialists.

The result of the foregoing, then, is that Young's account looks as though it needs to be augmented to address the concerns of people with disabilities. Still, one could argue that it may be the case that Young's account does not address these concerns because they are discriminatory rather that oppressive matters. It is in order to address this concern, then, that I turn to elaborate just what is at stake in Stigma, Questioned Personhood, and Societal Incapacity.

Disability and Oppression

In her analysis, Young articulates oppressive structures that operate according to power (the first three), recognition (the fourth), and violence (the fifth). My hope here is to bring three new faces of oppression to light that are not present in Young's account. These three new forms of oppression operate according to a "social framing" of the *able body* as a site of privilege. In order to make my case I shall draw rather freely from some of the existing narrative literature on disability.

Stigma and the "Broken Part" Narrative

The first form of oppression that occurs for people with disabilities is the phenomenon of *stigma*. In his work *Stigma*, Erving Goffman describes how the word *stigma* originates from the Greek practice of branding or marking slaves and criminals as well as from the wounds of saints in Christianity (1963, pp. 1–2) Stigma, according to Goffman, marks "different" physical or behavioral traits and devalues those traits. Thus, to stigmatize someone is to mark that person as different, abnormal, or deviant and assign negative values to their "difference."

Wolf Wolfensberger, in his Social Role Valorization theory, discusses a similar account of stigma for people with disabilities and who are in vulnerable positions in society. Throughout history, there has been the symbolic stigmatizing of roles and attached to this stigmatization are messages conveyed that devalue a person and reinforce certain perceptions or stereotypes about them. With this stigmatization, people with disabilities were cast into negative roles such as "wastes" or "rubbish," "objects of pity," "burdens of charity," or "non-human" (Race, Boxall, & Carson, 2005, p. 510).

What can be noted in both Goffman and Wolfensberger's accounts about stigma is its double function: it both designates or brands a person as *abnormal* and simultaneously *devalues* that person. What stigma assumes is the social framing of the "healthy" body as normal, and thus renders all other different bodies as *bad*. Although Young does use the term *stigma* to describe one of the challenges people with disabilities face, for her it operates according to discrimination rather than oppression. She has in mind Martha Minow's "dilemma of difference" concerning the discrimination people with disabilities face in the workplace (2000, pp. 169–170).

According to Goffman, however, stigma has a more overarching structure in society and thus, would be more indicative of oppression. Goffman describes three types of physical or behavioral characteristics which can be stigmatized: (1) physical disability, (2) individual behaviors such as addiction or certain sexual habits, and (3) race, religion, ethnicity, or gender. What stigma thus accomplishes is a move from the particular focus and oppression on the individual body, to an oppressive "social framing" of *the body*. This kind of oppression can also be found in the "white racial framing" of the body found in Joe Feagin's work *The White Racial Frame*. Oppressive framing of the body includes a "general worldview, oppressive ideas, terms, images, emotions, and interpretations" (Feagin, 2010, p. 3). The oppressive social frame of the body for people with disabilities is most evident in the *medical gaze*.

The medical gaze occurs between the medical practitioner and her patient. In this relation, the social framing of the body is assumed and that social frame is that the body should be a "healthy" or "finely operating" machine. Thus, any part of the body that does not align with this frame is deemed "unhealthy" or in "need of repair." As a result, the doctor is the only one who can "repair" or "fix" this body made up of "broken parts."

In her work *The Rejected Body*, Susan Wendell describes her personal experience of living with chronic fatigue syndrome and argues that this medical social framing is a form of able-bodied prejudice and oppression. She extends this criticism to other examples of illness and impairments. In particular, she cites the case of a deaf child born to hearing parents. Viewed from either the medical practitioner's or hearing community's point of view, the deaf child "suffers" from disability because of her inability to hear. Thus, everyone focuses his or her efforts in order to "normalize" the child. Yet, from another and equally warranted point of view, "the same child is [impaired] by hearing people's (often including her parents') ignorance of sign. In a Deaf, signing community, she is already normal, assuming that she has signing ability appropriate for her age" (1996, p. 29).

What we recognize from Wendell's description is that the stigmatization of the "disabled" body is to view it as a body with "broken parts." This is the perception of *able-bodied privilege*. What stigma obscures from view is that to live one's life as *dis-abled* whether with an impairment or illness is to have a shift in identity. It is to have an identity which is both un-recognized and misrepresented within society. What the medical gaze of the practitioner projects onto people with disabilities is a social narrative—a social construction that the "disabled" body is a body that has "broken down" or has "broken parts" that need to be fixed and need to be made whole again. It is this socially constructed "broken part narrative" that undergirds the stigmatization from able-bodied privilege.

The goal, then, from the perspective of the medical practitioner and the able-bodied community is to "cure" or return to normalcy these unruly bodies. One becomes a "hero" if one can overcome the broken part. As a result, the narratives which are recognized within society are the narratives of those who have overcome their "broken parts," rather than recognizing those who live as different. Joseph P. Shapiro in his work *No Pity* (1994), describes this narrative of a "hero" overcoming a "broken part":

Nondisabled Americans do not understand disabled ones. That was clear at the memorial service for Timothy Cook, when longtime friends got up to pay him heartfelt tribute. "He never seemed disabled to me," said one. "He was the least disabled person I ever met," pronounced another. It was the highest praise these nondisabled friends could think to give a disabled attorney who, at thirty-eight years old, had won landmark disability rights cases, including one to force public transit systems to equip their buses with wheelchair lifts. But more than a few heads in the crowded chapel bowed with an uneasy embarrassment at the supposed compliment. It was as if someone had tried to compliment a black man by saying, "You're the least black person I ever met," as false as telling a Jew, "I never think of you as Jewish," as clumsy as seeking to flatter a woman with "You don't act like a woman" (pp. 3–4).

The aim of people with disabilities is not to be pitied but to be validated and recognized. The narrative of able-bodied privilege that affects the "disabled body" is that the body is a body with "broken parts" that must be fixed, corrected, overcome, or returned to normalcy.

Because being able-bodied is valued as *good* within society, people with disabilities are stigmatized for having "bad" bodies. This form of stigma functions differently from normal practices of group solidarity insofar as these "broken" bodies are collectively devalued, and as a result, oppressed. According to Rosemarie Garland-Thomson, in her work *Extraordinary Bodies* (1997), "[s]tigma creates a shared, socially maintained and determined conception of the normal individual, sculpted by a social group attempting to define its own character and boundaries" (p. 31). Stigma, then, is paramount for the construction of normalcy within a given society: whatever is not "normal" is thus marked as inferior, unwanted, abnormal, or deviant. Marked or branded as *bodies with broken parts*, individual people with disabilities suffer a form of systemic oppression because they do not "conform" to an able-bodied society's social construction of normality. Thus, stigma of unruly bodies leads to violence, social stereotypes and lack of recognition. It is systemic because it is latent within the practice of a whole culture, is part of our social imaginary, and is even institutionalized in our medicine.

Questioned Personhood

While people with disabilities are stigmatized within society, those who have a form of cognitive disability face another form of oppression: *questioned personhood*. Some philosophers have called into question the "equal value and dignity of all human life" (Singer, 2010; McMahan, 2002). Their aim is to reconstruct our concept of "personhood," and with that human dignity, to provide a graduated form of moral status to humans and nonhuman animals. Although on the surface this seems like a noble attempt to recognize the dignity of certain species of nonhuman animals, it relies on a systemic form of oppression: namely, that those who are cognitively impaired should not qualify as "persons." The implications of questioning, or disqualifying, those with cognitive disability from the status of personhood are frightening.

Peter Singer, in his essay "Speciesism and Moral Status," compares the various skill sets of animals, like the great ape Koko, who have basic language skills and score between 70–95 on the IQ test, with people who have severe or profound mental "retardation" [*sic*] or severe dementia. His comparison draws from capacities listed with the American Association on Intellectual and Developmental Disabilities: (1) intellectual quotient (IQ); (2) the need for supervision; (3) capacity for speech; (4) following simple directions; and (5) social isolation. He uses these factors to compare humans with severe mental "retardation" with nonhuman animals such as apes, border collies, and gray parrots, which have these capacities and perform these specific tasks "more efficiently." After his comparison he asks: "can we justify attributing equal value to all human lives, while at the same time attributing to human life a value that is superior to all animal life" (2010, p. 335)?

Singer asks us to reconsider the statement "we" for the discussion of personhood. Rather than granting personhood to all biological humans, instead, he argues, we should "abandon the idea of equal value of all humans, replacing that with a more graduated view in which moral status depends on some aspects of cognitive ability, and that graduated view is applied both to humans and nonhumans" (2010, p. 338). This desire by some philosophers to "open up for discussion" the moral status of those with severe cognitive disability constitutes a form of oppression. Would we consider questioning someone's personhood today based on race, gender, or ethnicity? Why, then, is it socially acceptable to question the personhood of a person with disabilities? Beyond the ethical inequality here, the matter is patently systemic since a person's status as a person directly grants that person rights within existing political and legal institutions. Denying a person's status as a person is tantamount to directly subordinating that person in all such institutions. It is difficult to imagine a more directly oppressive practice. This form of oppression differs from practices concerning immigration and citizenship as well as tacit practices of racial segregation insofar as philosophers like Singer are drawing these distinctions based on biological and psychological differences rather than political status. To elaborate these points, I turn to consider a few cases that will, hopefully, "flesh out" the character of this oppression.

Questioning the personhood of someone's race in the United States was part of the horrific and oppressive history of slavery, which treated people who were slaves to be only worth three fifths of a person, and later continued in the practice of racial segregation (e.g., the case of the *Dred Scott* decision and the case of racial segregation in *Plessy v. Ferguson*). This same questioned personhood was used in the racist Tuskegee Syphilis Experiments in the United States and by Nazi Germany to experiment on and exterminate Jews, homosexuals, and people with mental illness or physical impairments. In the

1960s within the United States, one need only remember the atrocities of Willowbrook State School on Staten Island, New York, which was home to children with severe mental "retardation." Prior to the mid-1800s in the United States, those who were cognitively disabled were largely taken care of by their families and communities. After the mid-1800s, the "state institution" developed and its aim was to prepare the "feeble-minded" for "productive work" (Kittay, 2000, p. 66). During this time was witnessed a similar oppression of "able-bodied" Blacks who were deemed "feeble-minded" as well (Brosco, 2010, p. 40). But for the cognitively disabled and mentally insane, these particular institutions were terrible places to live. After World War II, there was rapid growth in the United States economy, and with it came the expansion of these institutions, but by the 1960s there were cutbacks and this greatly affected the quality of care at those institutions. At Willowbrook, children were covered in filth, and there was overcrowding and outbreaks of disease such as hepatitis. Furthermore, some of the children were subjected to human experimentation insofar as they were deliberately injected with hepatitis to "find a cure" (Boleyn-Fitzgerald, 2005, p. 411). It was not until 1965, when Robert Kennedy spoke out against Willowbrook, and by 1972, that Geraldo Rivera, in a televised exposé, awoke the national interest to the horrors that were taking place there. These horrors were the result of a society that did not give equal moral status, and with it human rights, to the cognitively impaired.

Questioning the personhood of the cognitively disabled is a systemic disvaluing of disability. This systemic disvaluing leads to oppressive practices such as abuses within institutions and opens the door for outright violations of human dignity. This form of systemic oppression is prevalent because many think that to be a "fully functioning" human being one needs to be "normal." What this kind of oppression does is base the dignity and value of human life on capacities rather than on human nature. Instead of respecting differences within humanity, it points to the generally held belief that "normal" humans are "worth more" than those who "cannot qualify."

Societal Incapacity

The final form of systemic oppression for people with disabilities that I would like to address is *societal incapacity*. This form concerns the physical environment or learning environments people with disabilities encounter. Many buildings and vehicles for transportation have either limited access or no access for people with physical impairments. Consider how in the Northeast in the United States or much of Europe, the majority of homes were built without the accommodation of a body with physical impairments. These homes include non-standard doorways, narrow staircases, and small bathrooms. Many of these homes would prove difficult or impossible to navigate for a person in a wheelchair. As a result, these structures and vehicles *dis-able* people with physical impairments and are thus a form of systemic spatial oppression. Similarly, many educational structures do not accommodate or accommodate poorly other forms of learning. As in the earlier example of the female diagnosed along the lines of autism spectrum disorder, an educational system may have trouble accommodating her different type of learning because it is difficult for her to communicate her thoughts orally.

Like Stigma and Questioned Personhood, Societal Incapacity is a form of oppression that also functions according to the social framing of the able body. The preferred social body is the able body, which determines the form of public and private buildings and learning environments. Although this social body is invisible, its residue is left on the architectural design and blueprints of any structure or educational institution. As a result, the able body creates the *standard* for spaces and modes of transportation and *standard* ways of learning. This *standard* becomes apparent when anyone who does not conform to it tries to move through this space or educational environment. Tobin Siebers, in his work *Disability Theory* (2008), describes his own home's lack of accessibility, which was built in 1939. He describes the wheelchair inaccessibility of his house as follows:

> All of my entry doors are too narrow, and they also have metal, unbeveled thresholds that a wheelchair user would need to "jump." Of course, if a wheelchair user were lucky enough to get into my house, it would still be impossible to use any of the bathrooms. The largest entry is the door to the master bedroom at 29 inches, but it is located on the second floor. The first floor half-bath has the smallest passage, 22.5 inches, and would not hold a wheelchair in any event. All of the toilets are too low for a wheelchair user, and there are no grab bars in any of the bathrooms. Nor could a wheelchair user sit easily at table in my house because the large table and small dining room leave little room to maneuver (pp. 87–88).

The Americans with Disabilities Act of 1990 requires state and local governments to make their programs and services accessible to people with disabilities, but many times city governments do not abide by this act. Some city governments try to take exemption from the ADA by arguing that they are a small entity and thus it is not necessary for them to make any changes. Similarly, many government organizations are housed in historic buildings. Often, the argument is made that these buildings are historically significant and as a result should not be modified. This lack of modification leads to inaccessible environments for many people with disabilities and disables their participation in civic life. Furthermore, city governments do not usually provide direct and equal access to 9-1-1 systems or similar emergency response systems for individuals who are deaf or hard of hearing and use TTY's (TDD's or text telephones) or computer modems. The result is that they enforce societal incapacity in public safety.

This sort of able-bodied privilege indicates on its flip side a systemic and structural oppression for those who lack "able" bodies. The able-bodied privilege of spaces and learning forms becomes apparent in their social construction: for those whose bodies do not conform, these spaces and educational structures present challenges and difficulties for actual living and functioning in their environment. Thus, these constructed buildings and vehicles for transportation as well as schools present oppression in the form of societal incapacity insofar as they enable some while *dis-abling* others.

Concluding Thoughts

Iris Young described five faces of oppression which overlap to systematically and structurally oppress people within a given society. What disability particularly teaches us is that there are three more faces of oppression that take place and overlap with Young's account. These three forms are *stigma, questioned personhood,* and *societal incapacity.* All three of these forms assume the social frame of a "normal" and most of the time "able" body. Thus, able-bodied privilege and value are given to some while oppression and dis-value are forced on others.

Stigma, in particular, marks the body of a person with disabilities as "broken." This branding not only results in ostracism, violence, and stereotyping but also encourages the desire to "repair" or "cure" this unruly body. Thus, stigma assumes both Foucauldian sovereign power and biopower: on the one hand, the physician holds ultimate authority over one's condition and on the other hand, one conforms to the self-regulatory desire to be cured of one's "broken parts." If one resists, then one is criticized or ostracized.

Questioned personhood presents a form of oppression which dis-values the moral status of those with cognitive impairments. By asserting a hierarchy of dignity, this form of oppression calls into question not only the practices of "disabled" bodies, but also their human rights. With a long history of violence and abuse in its past, the present-day practice of questioning one's personhood is a form of systemic oppression that afflicts those with severe or profound "mental retardation" and severe dementia. This form of oppression points to the able-bodied privilege that certain "normal" bodies are valued and thus "worth more" than those bodies that prove deviant.

Finally, societal incapacity is a form of oppression latent within one's environment. One finds one's environment either enabling or dis-abling. The fact that universal access to buildings and vehicles as well as access to accommodating learning environments is restricted or simply forgotten leads to a systemic oppression for people with physical impairments and other forms of learning. Curb cuts, ramps, elevators, and power doors are necessary spatial elements which have often been left out of designs or included as after thoughts in hard to reach places. Likewise, providing multiple forms of accessibility in learning environments such as captions in videos shown in class, extended time for exams or the assistance of a reader, scribe, or word processor for exams are often forgotten by educational systems or teachers in classrooms. The able-bodied privilege is one that assumes the "able body" as the "normal" body in social spaces and learning environments and designs housing, commercial buildings, vehicles, and schooling accustomed for this body.

With the analysis of these three new forms of oppression I hope that new sites of political change and resistance can be developed. The first site of political change might be bureaucratic. With the regulation and development of policies for integration in school systems and working environments, people with disabilities will become less subject to stigma and isolation. The second site of political change might be economic: more structures should be constructed with the aim of universal access, and this should include the addition of more businesses developing products with "different" bodies in mind.

The final site of political change is perhaps better understood as a task for new research, a new problematic in social and political philosophy. I raise this point because, one must recall, Young's original essay was only the second chapter within a larger work on the politics of difference, a political conception of justice that sought to move beyond the standard debates concerning redistributive paradigms (as one finds in John Rawls's thought, for example). I put the matter as follows: with these three new faces of oppression, does disability not call into question our current theories of justice, and challenge us to expand our theories or develop novel ones for the future? Quite specifically, one notes that Young's later work addressed the topic of difference and oppression at a global level, but she never addressed the faces of oppression discussed in the present essay. Minimally, then, a similar reconfiguration of Young's thought at the global level is entailed by the foregoing.

More generally, the problematic that I believe is raised by the forgoing concerns a program for justice. Existing theories of justice turn on a commitment to a distributive or recognition-theoretic paradigm (e.g., John Rawls and Axel Honneth, respectively). It is not clear to me how the three new faces of oppression can be addressed by either of these models. Stigma concerns social recognition and not "primary goods" (Rawls, 2001, p. 58). Furthermore, since Rawls conceives of social cooperation as one that proceeds by mutual advantage, his basic framework seems inadequate to address the concerns of persons with disabilities (2001, p. 6). These people suffer oppression, but it is not at all clear that by helping them it will be to our mutual advantage—the loss in time and effort may never be remunerated. In a reciprocal way, Honneth's concern with recognition does not appear to be up to the task of addressing the *material needs* required to redress Social Incapacity. Finally, even newer accounts of justice that do specifically address disability, such as one finds in Martha Nussbaum's Capabilities Theory, seem to lack the resources to address oppression as its own problem. My suggestion here, then, is that perhaps people with disabilities might challenge philosophers to develop a new account of justice. In the spirit of Young, who challenged us to rethink our categories of oppression, my hope is to suggest that maybe three new faces of oppression can lead to innovation concerning the way we think about the relation of oppression and justice.

References

Boleyn-Fitzgerald, P. (2005). Experimentation on human subjects. In R. G. Frey & C. H. Wellman (Eds.), *A Companion to applied ethics* (pp. 410–123). Malden, MA: Blackwell.

Brosco, J. P. (2010). The limits of the medical model: Historical epidemiology of intellectual disability in the United States. In E. F. Kittay & L. Carlson (Eds.), *Cognitive disability and its challenge to moral philosophy* (pp. 27–54). Malden, MA: Wiley-Blackwell.

Davis, L. J. (2000). Go to the margins of the class: Hate crimes and disability. In L. P. Francis & A. Silvers (Eds.), *Americans with disabilities: Exploring implications of the law for individuals and institutions* (pp. 331–338). New York: Routledge.

Dolnick, E. Deafness as culture. (1993, September). *The Atlantic Monthly* (pp. 37–53).

Feagin, J. (2010). *The white racial frame: Centuries of racial framing and counter-framing.* New York: Routledge.

Goffman, E. (1963). *Stigma: Notes on the management of spoiled identity.* New York: Simon and Schuster.

Hunter, N. (2012, December 5). Alzheimer's: The problem of stigma. Retrieved from: http://www.irishhealth.com/article.html?id=10241

Kittay, E. (2000). At home with my daughter. In L. P. Francis & A. Silvers (Eds.), *Americans with disabilities: Exploring implications of the law for individuals and institutions* (pp. 64–80). New York: Routledge.

Kittay, E. (2005, October). At the margins of moral personhood. *Ethics 116*(1), symposium on disability, 100–131.

Kittay, E. (2010). The personal is philosophical is political: A philosopher and mother of a cognitively disable person sends notes form the battlefield. In E. F. Kittay & L. Carlson (Eds.), *Cognitive disability and its challenge to moral philosophy* (pp. 393–413). Malden, MA: Wiley-Blackwell.

McMahan, J. (2002). *The ethics of killing: Problems at the margins of life.* New York: Oxford.

Race, D., K. Boxall, & Carson, I. (2005). Towards a dialogue for practice: Reconciling social role valorization and the social model of disability. In *Disability and Society, 20*(5), 507–521.

Rawls, J. (2001). *Justice as fairness: A restatement.* Erin Kelly (Ed.). Cambridge: Harvard University Press.

Shapiro, J. P. (1994). *No pity.* New York: Random House.

Siebers, T. (2008). *Disability theory.* Ann Arbor: University of Michigan Press.

Singer, P. (2010). Speciesism and moral status. In E. F. Kittay & L. Carlson (Eds.), *Cognitive disability and its challenge to moral philosophy* (pp. 331–344). Malden, MA: Wiley-Blackwell.

Thomson, R. G. (1997). *Extraordinary bodies: Figuring physical disability in American culture and literature.* New York: Columbia University Press.

Young, I. M. (1990a). Five faces of oppression. In *Justice and the politics of difference* (pp. 39–63). Princeton, NJ: Princeton University Press.

Young, I. M. (1990b). Social movements and the politics of difference. In *Justice and the politics of difference* (pp. 156–183). Princeton, NJ: Princeton University Press.

Young, I. M. (2002). Autonomy, welfare reform, and meaningful work. In E. F. Kittay & E. K. Feder (Eds.), *The subject of care: Feminist perspectives on dependency* (pp. 40–60). Oxford, UK: Rowman and Littlefield.

Young, I. M. (2000). Disability and the definition of work. In L. P. Francis & A. Silvers (Eds.), *Americans with disabilities: Exploring implications of the law for individuals and institutions* (pp. 169–173). New York: Routledge.

Wendell, S. (1996). *The rejected body: Feminist philosophical reflections on disability.* New York: Routledge.

Wilkie, C. (2012, September 27). Young adults with autism seek out white-collar careers for first time. Retrieved from: http://www.huffingtonpost.com/2012/09/27/autism-employment-white-collar-jobs_n_1916611.html

CHAPTER TEN

Gender and the Politics of Invisible Disability

NANCY J. HIRSCHMANN

Disability is generally conceived as highly visible, clearly demarcated from the "normal," decidedly "other:" indeed, "the other other that helps make otherness imaginable" (Siebers, 2008, p. 48). But disabilities that we cannot or do not see are an important dimension of disability that philosophers and theorists need to think about. Though it may be true that "the question of nonvisible disability is emerging as a highly vexed, profoundly challenging concern" for disability scholars, such attention seems to be devoted to the various problems experienced by persons with invisible disabilities, while the notion of invisible disability itself has not been theorized to any great extent (Samuels, 2003, p. 244). Moreover, "*nonvisible* disability," which is the way the issue is generally construed, constitutes only one kind of "*invisible* disability," as I shall articulate below. By contrast, I argue there are different *ways* of being invisible that pertain less to the specific identity of the disability and more to the way that it is arranged, structured, considered, and treated. I here develop a typology of invisible disabilities, articulating the various ways in which disability is, or is made, invisible by social context, by social categories of gender, race, and sexuality, and by discriminatory attitudes toward disability. Invisibility can be used as an instrument to dominate and oppress people with disabilities, but it can also help provide tools to resist such oppression.

Gender and sexuality are important aspects of this invisibility. Gender norms particularly condition responses to women with disabilities so as to heighten invisibility, as in the case of men's pain complaints being given greater credibility (Hoffman & Tarzian, 2001, pp. 13–27). Not only may women "be at greater risk for pain-related disability than men . . . [they also] may be more vulnerable than men to unwarranted psychogenic attributions by health care providers for pain," and suffer from chronic pain from two to six times more than men (Unruh, 1996, p. 123). Additionally, "Women are more likely than men to experience disability from the same pain condition" (Greenspan, Craft, & LeResche, 2007, pp. 26–45). In other words, women experience a negative feedback loop: women are put in situations of greater vulnerability to pain by having their symptoms treated as emotional problems, resulting in less aggressive treatment, and thereby greater disability from pain. Perceptions of and reactions to pain are culturally produced in gendered ways that alter the physical experience, as the situation of gendered treatment thus heightens the physical condition. In other words, it is not simply biological bad luck that heightens some women's pain and disability; it is social power.

Feminism is relevant not just to the differences between men's and women's experiences, however; there are also important comparisons and intersections between disability and sexuality in the notion of "passing" and "coming out." Feminism, as experienced as it is with revealing the hidden dimensions of sexism that occupy the "normal background noise" of patriarchal society, also contributes to the framework for "seeing" what is invisible.

The idea of "invisibility" may seem self-evident: that which we cannot see, like H. G. Wells's "invisible man" (Wells, 1996). But I have in mind a wider understanding, perhaps captured more by Ralph Ellison's "invisible man"—"a man of substance, of flesh and bone" who "people refuse to see" (Ellison, 1995). Within disability, I argue, there are different configurations of invisibility that range from what one literally cannot see no matter how hard one tries, to what is hidden from view through an elaborate scheme of camouflage and hiding. Insofar as the former may seem "naturally" invisible, while the latter are "socially constructed" to be unseen, it is important to note that within disability as currently experienced, all forms of invisibility are political, and manifestations of language, interpretation, and social structure. This is true of disability more broadly construed, of course: the "social model" of disability states that while "impairments" may be biologically founded, they constitute "disabilities" only because of social arrangements, social norms, and a built environment that favor certain bodies and disadvantages others. Those social arrangements are a function of power.

I further suggest that the "invisibility" of many disabilities is a particular way in which power is expressed in the social construction of disability; the invisibility of disability is an additional function of social structure, a logical extension of the turning of impairment into disability. Identities and subjectivities are structured by how people are seen and perceived, based on body type, skin color, and physical characteristics: "Certain assumptions about the correlation between appearance and identity have resulted in an almost exclusive focus on visibility as both the basis of community and the means of enacting social change," Ellen Samuels notes (Samuels, 2003, pp. 236, 244). Martin Jay points out that vision is the central organizing category for comprehending and communicating about our world (Jay, 1993).

But what we actually "see" when we encounter other people is always filtered through conceptual categories, frameworks of comprehension, and expectations of "normality." This has particular implications for persons with disabilities, as Rosemarie Garland-Thomson's idea of the "normate" body dominates the common imagination— White, male, heterosexual, in perfect physical shape—even though few human beings live up to that ideal (Thomson, 1996). Lennard Davis similarly notes that disability is generally defined as the visual presentation of a difference that translates as distortion, abnormality, disfigurement (Davis, 1995, p. 12). Accordingly, persons with visible disabilities are often looked at with repulsion; impairments that have been turned into disabilities serve as a material reminder of human weakness, of the inevitability of the decay of the flesh, of mortality and our vulnerability to suffering. Disability is something to be feared; a fear that not only often misunderstands disability experience, but in turn, turns certain kinds of bodily differences *into* disabilities.

This fear is twofold. The first and obvious fear is the fear of becoming impaired or disabled (or ill, which many associate with disability) oneself. But this immediate fear signals a much deeper fear of what Butler has called the "undecidability" of the body; the notion that our bodies are not essentially given to us, but rather are in states of flux and uncertainty. She developed this notion in relation to sex, gender, and sexuality; heterosexual people view gays and lesbians, transsexuals, transgendered individuals, and indeed any challenge to the standard markers of sex and gender, with apprehension. The reason for this, she implies, stems from a fear of not knowing the self, of one's identity being called into question, that one might be, oneself, the very "other" that one fears (Butler, 1990; Butler, 1993).

Disability brings that flux into view even more clearly; regardless of whether I would view it positively (e.g., because I am "really" a man in a woman's body) or negatively (because I do not see myself that way), I am not going to suddenly wake up tomorrow with a penis. By contrast, I could wake up tomorrow with any range of serious medical problems or have an accident that creates serious mobility problems. Such things happen to people every day, and they are almost always perceived, at least at first, as unwelcome changes, as "other" to the "self" that I think I am. The apprehension of disabling impairment forces individuals to come to grips with the way the body changes and can change further without warning, betraying the self's conception of who and what one is. Keeping persons with disabilities invisible, or hidden from view, modulates such fear through the averted gaze. But in the return of the repressed, disability inevitably comes back even more powerfully than it began.

Before articulating the typology, however, I should offer a note on language. The preferred terminology in a great deal of disability studies is to deploy *impairment* to refer to a bodily state, whereas *disability* refers to how that state is penalized, disfavored, and hampered by social arrangements; my vision may be "impaired," but that impairment becomes a disability only in environments that are geared exclusively toward the sighted. Or I may have difficulty walking because my legs have an "impairment," but that becomes a disability only in contexts where I cannot have access to a wheelchair or my wheelchair's access is hampered by an awkward built environment. I try to follow that usage here, but at times I will use *disability* in a more inclusive sense to refer to difficulties that a body has within the current context without necessarily judging whether that context could be changed or whether the difficulty pertains to the body per se. That is, like Susan Wendell, I believe that some disabilities can be intrinsic to the body; for instance, she notes that chronic fatigue syndrome is defined by the notion that the sufferer is so weak and exhausted that he or she is unable to perform many "basic life functions," or able to do so only with difficulty, which is the usual definition of disability (EEOC, 2007, Wendell, 1996). For the most part, in fact, given the hostility of most built environments, workplaces, public places, and attitudes toward people with impairments, the term *disability* today can be taken to refer to a bodily state *and* a social one at the same time, and my usage at times reflects that fact. Additionally, I find *impairment* to be a more problematic term than *disability*, for it fundamentally contradicts one of the main ideas of disability studies, which is that disability should be seen as a difference rather than a disadvantage: my body is not "impaired," it is just different; but this difference may make it more difficult for me to engage in some activities, just as being female makes it more difficult for me to sing very low notes on a musical scale. However, I often use *impairment* to help the reader remember the basic distinction I have described, and when I use *disability* in a more inclusive sense the meaning should be apparent from the context in which the term is used.

Ways of Invisibility

The first, and most literal, kind of invisibility is *endemic invisibility*: that is, invisibility is not just unseen but *unseeable*, structured by the character of the illness or impairment per se. Learning disabilities are the most obvious example; the disability literally occurs inside the person's brain, and is hence not something that others can actually see. They can see only particular behaviors that the disability might generate, and these may be interpreted as something else, such as rudeness. Similarly, deafness cannot be seen unless the person wears hearing aids; signing might be a clue, but hearing people also sign. These are endemically invisible because by their nature they simply cannot be seen.

In *conditional invisibility*, the physical dimensions of the impairment are *difficult* to see, but not impossible; perhaps visibility is sporadic, as with epilepsy, or the signs are subtle, visible only in specific conditions. The symptoms of hypoglycemia—disorientation, profuse sweating—may be very obvious, but unless you know what you are looking at you are not likely to interpret them correctly, and instead think the person is inebriated or having a heart attack.

In *situational invisibility*, an impairment is literally visible, often highly so, but actively hidden or obscured by particular material conditions and policy choices that situate the person in a particular setting, such as persons who are institutionalized in a hospital or special care facility. Such situations may be desirable for the person affected, such as a person with Alzheimer's for whom living at home, where the familiar mingles with the unrecognized, can be upsetting, and who may be able to receive better care in a professional setting. But there is an obvious history of abuse associated with institutionalization, ranging from the "great confinement" of the eighteenth and nineteenth centuries to contemporary atrocities like Willowbrook (Porter, 1990; Tyor & Leland, 1984). In both negative and positive institutional situations, however, persons with disabilities are closed off from the public realm because of the ways in which social resources are allocated and social relations are organized. Institutionalization can be a way to avoid implementing changes in the structure of the social and political landscape that would be required for their full inclusion in the public sphere.

The most extreme form of this is *obliterative invisibility*, where the reluctance or refusal to see illness or impairment produces the figural or even literal obliteration of the individual, through death, including euthanasia and abortion. I support both abortion and the right to die, and I believe that women should have control over their own reproduction, even when it comes to aborting fetuses with impairments, though I recognize that that is a controversial position with disability studies. However, I also maintain it is important for feminists and nonfeminists alike to acknowledge that cultural pressure to adhere to the "normate" body often exaggerates the challenges of raising an infant with a disability and encourages the elimination of such fetuses. The flip side of this, of course, is state interference in reproduction, including forced sterilization, of women with disabilities (Davis, 1987; Seavilleklein, 2009; Cogdell, 2004; Thomson, 1998).

Epistemic invisibility, involves two forms: *Denial*, which involves the reluctance or even refusal of the able bodied to see, acknowledge, or accept disability even when it is clearly visible; and *epistemological invisibility*, caused by the failure of the medical community to diagnose a disability. Whereas denial-based invisibility is premised on the actual existence of an identifiable illness or disability that others ignore or do not believe, epistemological invisibility pertains to the existential character of one's physical situation. Fibromyalgia and chronic fatigue syndrome—conditions suffered overwhelmingly by women—were not recognized for many years as real medical problems. This creates an epistemically uncertain state for the affected person, to have her physical experience negated by another who is not having the experience but who sits in an authoritative position. It produces a level of self-doubt about one's own existence that makes one question one's own visibility in the empirical world (Wendell, 1996).

All of these forms of invisibility I have mentioned thus far help constitute *political invisibility*, which ranges from being unable to vote or run for office, if one is institutionalized or has no transport to the polls, to the lack of disability issues on public policy agendas, to the "representation" of disability perspectives by the nondisabled, ranging from social workers, to health providers, to social scientists, which is often filtered through inaccurate negative assessments of disability conditions that misconstrue what disabled people want and need, their ability to speak for themselves and participate. The resulting denial that disability issues are important enough to merit legislative attention is another form of epistemic invisibility. Multiple studies show that even though people with disabilities report levels of well-being and happiness roughly equivalent to those of people without disabilities, the latter routinely report that were they disabled, they would anticipate much lower levels of welfare and happiness. Nancy Weinberg indeed shows that able-bodied people simply *disbelieve* empirical evidence that people with disabilities are happy, much less that they would not prefer to be able bodied (Weinberg, 1988). This misrepresentation is often the political foundation for public policies. Such misrepresentation has particular resonance for women, who throughout history have been "represented" by men claiming to act in women's "best interests" but in reality shoring up men's privilege and power.

Whether through the inaccurate and paternalistic representation of disability perspectives by able-bodied agents through the distorting lens of the normate body, or the complete silencing of such perspectives through institutionalization and epistemic marginalization, political invisibility captures the essence of what is problematic about all the forms of invisibility I have articulated: namely the power relations that adhere in the relationship between those who experience illnesses and disabilities, and those who (currently) do not. Iris Young's "faces of oppression" (exploitation, marginalization, powerlessness, cultural imperialism, and violence) offers some useful conceptual tools. Certainly persons with disabilities experience the form of oppression she calls "marginalization," in which "a whole category of people is expelled from useful participation in social life" (1990, p. 53), and "cultural imperialism" which entails "the universalization of a dominant group's experience . . . and its establishment as a norm" (1990, p. 59) are particularly relevant to various forms of invisible disability I have already discussed. People with disabilities are marginalized and excluded from the public realm by institutionalization (situational invisibility); disability is understood, analyzed, and named by able-bodied people who "project their own experience as representative of humanity itself," cohering with epistemic invisibility (Young, 1990, p. 59). The lived reality of disability is denied by able-bodied people who seek to retain resources for themselves rather than redistribute them to pay for access and accommodation, thus ensuring "powerlessness," which Young equates to an economic category of nonprofessionalism, but which in my view dovetails well with political invisibility; insofar as "the powerless are situated so that they must take orders and rarely have the right to give them" (1990, p. 56), we can extend this conception from the workplace, where Young locates it, to the arenas of social welfare policy. And while her idea of "exploitation" cannot readily be experienced by those who are excluded from the workforce altogether, as people with disabilities often are, certainly her notion of "violence" is experienced by some persons with disabilities in institutional settings as well as on the street, in various forms of "obliterative disability."

Feminist theories like Young's show us that difference is a key political issue and a key threat to existing forms of power; were people with disabilities to be included in economic and political structures and give voice and power, current configurations of domination by the able bodied would be destabilized, as she suggests would be the case for men, Whites, and capitalists. But disability is one kind of "difference" that many people—including many feminists—do not want to include in the body politic. Even Young uses disability imagery in a way that many disability studies scholars find disturbing, such as her deployment of an "enabling conception of justice," which she contrasts with the "disabling constraints" of "oppression and domination"—imagery that could mesh with a social model of disability, but often does not (Young, 1990, p. 39). More clearly problematic is her claim in "Throwing Like a Girl" that patriarchy "handicaps" women's bodies (Young, 1980, p. 152). Although I agree with Young that because women are taught not to use their bodies effectively, they make themselves more vulnerable to injuries (see Chambers, 2007), throughout her essay she holds up able-bodied men as the standard from which women are disabled. For instance, strength is seen as an unalloyed good, but women's weakness is seen as a disability (see Thompson, 2002 for similar criticism). Such framework assumptions can turn even progressive theories seeking inclusiveness into exclusive mechanisms when it comes to persons with disabilities.

I believe, however, that a subversive deployment of invisibility has the potential to change our understanding of what sort of difference disability creates, one that needs to be more centrally incorporated into our understanding of politics. This deployment, perhaps ironically, involves *voluntary invisibility*, in which a person makes a choice to hide or dissemble about her disability. I call this ironic because up until this point in my essay, the reader might take me to be saying that invisibility is exclusively an instrument of oppression, in keeping with my discussion of Young, illustrating power in its crudest form of domination: the able bodied do not wish to see disability, and so they shut it away, or hide it, or deny it. Alternately, as with endemic invisibility, it may seem a neutral thing, it is nobody's "fault" that the disability cannot be seen; but making such disabilities visible, often by telling others of one's disability, can still lead to other forms of invisibility, particularly epistemic (particularly disbelief because one doesn't "look disabled"), that are a function of that same mode of power as oppression and domination.

Certainly oppression and domination are important modes of relationship between able-bodied people and people with disabilities that disability studies is devoted to uncovering, analyzing, and changing; and as I have shown, various forms of invisibility can be a tool for expressing such power. But in *voluntary invisibility*, the vectors of power take on a more complicated dimension and offer possibilities for resistance, redefinition, and identity. In this mode, the sick or disabled person seeks invisibility as a good in his or her life. As I just hinted, reasons for this choice could range from anxiety about social rejection to fear of professional repercussions, as companies are often (contrary to available evidence) afraid that such employees will cost them more money than nondisabled workers (Wendell, 1988; Watson 1998). Mothers of small children may hide their impairments because of the deeply held prejudice that they will not be able to cope with their responsibilities, resulting in losing their children (Lloyd 1992; Booth and Booth 1994; Morris and Morris, 1995; Olkon, 2009). A person with a disability may have privacy concerns, though this might be coupled with, or even motivated by, shame of his or her condition. Many of these reasons obviously dovetail with power as oppression or domination, in that the "choice" to be invisible results from a fear of being harmed. On a more nuanced plane, a person may also not wish to incorporate disability into his or her sense of who he or she is; as Wendell notes, "accepting [one's own] disability means making a deep change of identity" (Wendell, 1996, pp. 25–26).

There are thus many reasons why people who can "hide" their disabilities choose to do so. Yet it is most often treated by disability scholars as *passing*, a term that has pejorative connotations, as it often does within many segments of the gay community. Passing is seen as a "sign of the victim, the practice of one already complicit with the order of things, prey to its oppressive hierarchies" (Tyler, 1994, p. 212), or "a sign of assimilationist longing" (Samuels, 2003, p. 240). This negative reaction operates out of an understandable desire on the part of disability scholars and activists for acceptance of the bodily "difference" that disability entails, much as gay activists urged lesbians and homosexuals to come "out of the closet" to prove how "normal" and common it is to be gay.

From a political perspective, however, this reaction is itself problematic for persons with disability. In the first place, the negative view of voluntary invisibility ironically buys into the *nondisabled* view of disability: if disability really is "just a difference," not intrinsically a disadvantage, as disability activists and scholars want to argue, then I should be able to live my difference however I wish. The demand that a person with a disability "out" him- or herself is a tacit claim that the "difference" he or she embodies is of a certain kind; and that kind has to always already have been established by the dominant discourse.

Furthermore, becoming visible may involve a lot of work that a person who is already burdened by dealing with a context that is hostile to his or her bodily particularity cannot afford. It may subject the person to accusations of fraud because he or she does not fit the stereotype of disability, as when a person using a wheelchair stands up briefly to reach for something on a shelf. Siebers's writing on "masquerade" argues that individuals are disbelieved unless they heighten and exaggerate their disability's visibility (Siebers, 2008). But by making oneself hypervisible, one reinforces one's status as the other, who can then be categorized, controlled, and excluded—that is, made invisible in other forms. Overcoming one kind of invisibility (say, endemic) engenders another form of invisibility (epistemic). This is particularly true for women, for while illness and disability are associated with the feminine—weak, helpless, physically unable—femininity is also at odds with disability by challenging standard sexist norms of feminine beauty and sexual desirability (Lloyd, 1992; Samuels, 2002; Thomson, 1996; Wendell, 1996). For instance, male veterans from the two Gulf Wars who were amputees have tended to embrace high-tech prosthetic limbs as symbols of their warrior status, and aspired to return to the battlefield or engage in extreme sports, whereas female veterans felt more self-conscious about their appearance and often opted for the less functional but "normal" looking prostheses. They preferred to hide their disability, whereas the men sought to brandish their high-tech limbs as proof that they were better than ever (Linker, 2011).

Voluntary invisibility is not simply a defensive reaction to discrimination and stigma, however; it may also hold a powerful subversive potential. There is epistemological power in invisibility, as you deny the other the ability to construct you as she wishes, she must see you as you present and construct yourself. The choice to be invisible involves a retention of knowledge denied to the other; what Eve Sedgewick called "the epistemology of the closet" involves the duality of knowledge retained and expression suppressed (Sedgwick, 1990, p. 75). As Ralph Ellison's *Invisible Man* showed, invisibility creates abilities denied to the seen, abilities of movement and maneuvering that the dominant group not only cannot see, but fail to recognize until it is too late (Ellison, 1982).

This may seem counterintuitive, if not paradoxical, in terms of political action: How can someone who has chosen to hide her impairment or disability change anything unless she reveals what she is hiding? I do not wish to appear sanguine about constitutive power; for it always already presupposes the power of oppression as well. The woman who fears the state will take her child if she is seen as disabled; the HIV-positive colleague who fears ostracism; the dyslexic student who does not ask her professor for more time on an exam for fear she will be disbelieved and penalized: all operate within parameters defined by the able bodied. But voluntary invisibility also offers a political strategy of ambiguity and uncertainty as a way to unsettle the ability of the nondisabled to police the boundaries of their community. As Walker notes about lesbianism, "the passer, as a figure of indeterminacy, destabilizes identities predicated on the visible to reveal how they are constructed" (Walker, 2001, p. 10).

We start by claiming that disability is the universal norm; arguments for universal access tacitly employ such an idea, arguing that access should accommodate a wide variety of bodies, rather than thinking in terms of creating "special" accommodation for "abnormal" bodies. Ramps, to take the most common example, are not just important for people in wheelchairs, but are easier for people with canes and crutches, the elderly, and indeed can be negotiated by all able-bodied individuals as easily as stairs can.

Including the invisibly disabled body in this norm would take us further, because we cannot know what that body can and cannot do. When nondisabled people conjure up an image of a person who uses a wheelchair, or a blind person, or a Deaf person, they *think* that they know what such persons can and cannot do; and often they are wrong, as Georgina Kleege has so eloquently argued (Kleege, 1999). Such mistaken assumptions, however, can be used to shape laws, policies, and practices. For instance, workplace policies, supported by a Supreme Court and many lower courts hostile to the Americans with Disabilities Act (ADA), regularly misconstrue what employees with disabilities can and cannot do, making it impossible for plaintiffs to prevail in ADA cases (O'Brien, 2001). This situation prompted Congress, led by members who either had disabilities themselves, or family members with disabilities, to amend the act in 2009, greatly strengthening disability rights, though it is too soon to know how the courts will interpret the amendments (Feldblum, Barry, & Benfer, 2008). But schools, businesses, and social institutions regularly put up barriers to disability inclusion based on incorrect assumptions of what individuals with disabilities can and cannot do (Wendell, 1996). Buildings can be exempted by "grandfathering" from installing elevators and making other structural accessibility changes, but employers can nevertheless be resistant to providing ergonomic keyboards and chairs, telecommunication devices for deaf employees, and to hiring persons with cognitive disabilities; all instances that could possibly be remedied by the amended ADA but often only after costly and time-consuming lawsuits (O'Brien, 2003; Feldblum, Barry, & Benfer, 2008).

By contrast, knowing that a body is disabled without knowing what specific impairment(s) that body has could yield a different way of thinking that addresses disability concerns of universal access, while at the same time reminding those who are not disabled that they, too, could be become disabled, that we do not know the form that their disability might take, that the difference between disabled and nondisabled is not very great—and that maybe it's not so bad, not so "other." Recognition of the temporality of ability, the uncertainty of disability, the undecidability of the body, is vital to the full inclusion of individuals with disabilities in the body politic.

References

Booth, T., & Booth, W. (1994). *Parenting under pressure: Mothers and fathers with learning disabilities*. Buckingham, UK: Open University Press.

Butler, J. (1993). *Bodies that matter: On the discursive limits of "sex."* New York: Routledge.

Butler, J. (1990). *Gender trouble: Feminism and the subversion of identity*. New York: Routledge.

Chambers, C. (2007). *Sex, culture, and justice: The limits of choice*. University Park, PA: Pennsylvania State University Press.

Cogdell, C. (2004). *Eugenic design: Streamlining America in the 1930s*. Philadelphia, PA: University of Pennsylvania Press.

Davis, A. (1987). Women with disabilities: Abortion and liberation. *Disability, Handicap & Society, 2*(3), 275–284.

Davis, L. (1995). *Enforcing normalcy: Disability, deafness, and the body*. New York: Verso.

EEOC. (2007). Section 902 definition of the term disability. Published in the Federal Register (March 25, 2011), from http://www.eeoc.gov/laws/statutes/adaaa_info.cfm

Ellison, R. (1995). *The invisible man*. New York: Vintage.

Feldblum, C. R., Barry, K., & Benfer, E. A. (2008). The ADA Amendments Act of 2008, *Texas Journal on Civil Liberties & Civil Rights, 13*(187), 1–60.

Hoffman, D. E., & Tarzian, A. K. (2001). The girl who cried pain: A bias against women in the treatment of pain. *Journal of Law, Medicine & Ethics, 29*, 13–27.

Greenspan, J., Craft, R, LeResche, L., Arendt-Nielsen, L., Berkley, K., Fillingim, R., Gold, M., Holdcoft, A., Lautenbacher, S., & Mayer, E. (2007). Studying sex and gender differences in pain and analgesia: A consensus report. *Pain, 132*, S26–S45.

Kleege, G. (1999). *Sight unseen*. New Haven: Yale University Press.

Linker, B. (2011). *The roots of rehabilitation: Reconstructing disabled soldiers in World War I America*. Chicago, IL: University of Chicago Press.

Lloyd, M. (1992). Does she boil eggs? Towards a feminist model of disability. *Disability & Society, 7*(3), 207–221.

Morris, K., & Morris, J. (1995). Easy targets: A disability rights perspective on the 'children as careers' debate. *Critical Social Policy, 15*, 36–37.

O'Brien, R. (2001). *Crippled justice: The history of modern disability policy in the workplace*. Chicago, IL: University of Chicago Press.

O'Brien, R. (ed.). (2003). *Voices from the edge: Narratives about the Americans with Disabilities Act*. New York: Oxford University Press.

Olkon, S. (2009, December 20). Disabled mom fighting to keep her son. *The Chicago Tribune*.

Porter, R. (1990). Foucault's great confinement. *History of the Human Sciences, 3*(1), 47–54.

Samuels, E. (2002). Critical divides: Judith Butler's body theory and the question of disability. *NWSA Journal, 14*(3), 58–76.

Samuels, E. (2003). My body, my closet: Invisible disability and the limits of coming-out discourse. *GLQ, 9*(1–2), 233–255.

Seavilleklein, V. (2009). Challenging the rhetoric of choice in prenatal screening. *Bioethics, 23*(1), 68–77.

Sedgwick, E. K. (1990). *Epistemology of the closet*. Berkeley: University of California Press.

Siebers, T. (2008). *Disability theory*. Ann Arbor: University of Michigan Press.

Thomson, M. (1998). *The problem of mental deficiency: Eugenics, democracy and social policy in Britain*. Oxford, UK: Clarendon Press.

Thomson, R. G. (1996). *Extraordinary bodies: Figuring physical disability in American culture and literature*. New York: Columbia University Press.

Thomson, R. G. (2002). Integrating disability, transforming feminist theory. *National Women's Studies Association Journal, 14*(3), 1–32.

Tyler, C. (1994). Passing: Narcissism, identity, difference. *Differences, 6*(2/3), 212.

Tyor, P. L., & Bell, L. V. (1984). *Caring for the retarded in America: A history*. Westport, CT: Greenwood Press.

Unruh, A. M. (1996). Gender variations in clinical pain experience. *Pain, 65*(2–3), 123.

Walker, L. (2001). *Looking like what you are: Sexual style, race, and lesbian identity*. New York: New York University Press.

Watson, N. (1998). Enabling identity: Disability, self and citizenship. In T. Shakespeare (Ed.), *The disability reader: Social science perspectives*. London: Cassell.

Wells, H. G. (1996). *The invisible man*. New York: Oxford University Press.

Wendell, S. (1996). *The rejected body: Feminist philosophical reflections on disability*. New York: Routledge.

Weinberg, N. (1998). Another perspective: Attitudes on people with disabilities. In H. D. Yuker (Ed.), *Attitudes towards people with disabilities*. New York: Springer.

Young, I. (1980). Throwing like a girl: A phenomenology of female body comportment, motility, and spatiality. *Human Studies, 3*(2), 137–156.

Young, I. (1990). *Justice and the politics of difference*. Princeton, NJ: Princeton University Press.

CHAPTER ELEVEN

Stigmatized, Marginalized, and Ill

The Oppression of People With Serious Mental Illness

DIANE C. GOODING AND WILLIAM T. L. COX

Introduction

In the discussion of people struggling for equal access, dignity, and civil rights, people with serious and persistent mental illness constitute an often overlooked group. The authors assert that people with serious and persistent mental illness are a disenfranchised and disadvantaged group. The experiences of stigmatization, discrimination, and marginalization that most, if not all, seriously mentally ill (SMI) people face can be more generally classified as different types and levels of oppression. SMI people face oppression in housing, employment, health care, insurance, and social distancing—much like the oppression faced by other disenfranchised groups, such as ethnic/racial minorities and lesbian, gay, bisexual, and transgendered (LGBT) people. This oppression has mental health implications as well as physical health sequelae. As such, the oppression of people with serious and persistent mental illness is a public health issue as well as a social justice issue.

In the United States, 26.2% of the adult population experiences a mental disorder annually, and approximately 22% of those people (or 5.8% of all U.S. adults) have a severe mental illness (Kessler, Chiu, & Demler, 2005). About half of the people with severe mental illness are more seriously affected—in other words, have serious and persistent mental illness (SMI) (NAMHC, 1993; U.S. Department of Health & Human Services, 2011). People in the SMI category include the approximately 0.5% of the population who receive Social

Security disability benefits for mental health–related reasons (NAM-HC, 1993; U.S. Department of Health & Human Services, 2011). For the purposes of this chapter, we define serious and persistent mental illness (SMI) as any of the following diagnoses: schizophrenia and schizophrenia-spectrum disorders, delusional disorder, bipolar disorder with or without psychosis, major depression with or without psychosis, obsessive-compulsive disorder, and borderline personality disorder. Some readers may question our choice of the wording "people with SMI" or "SMI people." Certainly other terms/labels could have been chosen. Some people with SMI prefer to be referred to as "psychiatric survivors" or "mental health consumers." However, the former term is perceived to be value-laden, that is, promoting the view that the field of psychiatry or the medical model is something to be survived, rather than something that can be viewed as one of the resources in one's recovery armamentarium. The latter term is perceived to be potentially misleading, in that not all people with serious mental illness are receiving mental health services; therefore, it is inaccurate to label them as "consumers." Moreover, the term "consumer" can be considered a hierarchical term, conferring a relatively lower status to the person who has a somewhat dependent relationship with the mental health system, by receiving services, and/or who takes or "gorges on the metaphorical meals served by 'the system,' i.e., supervised living facilities, financial subsidies such as SSI and SSDI, etc." (Marrone & Golowka, 1999). For many years people with serious and persistent mental illnesses were referred to by the pejorative term "CMI," or "chronically mentally ill," implying to some that such individuals are treatment failures. Clearly, from a humanistic and a scientific perspective, we find such a term unacceptable. Another term that could have been used is "people with psychiatric disabilities." However, not all people with mental illness would consider themselves as having an impairment, though they might still meet the ADA definition. "The ADA definition recognizes disability to exist under any of the following criteria: "(a) a physical or mental impairment that substantially limits one of the major life activities (walking, speaking, breathing, seeing, hearing, learning, working, performing manual tasks, or caring for oneself); (b) a record of such impairment; or (c) being regarded as having such an impairment" (ADA, 1990). It also recognizes that impairment may or may not be disabling, depending on circumstances and environment" (Robert, 2003, p. 138).

In sum, for various reasons we preferred to use the term that we felt was most respectful and also consistent with the terms and operational definitions adopted by the National Advisory Mental Health

Council (1993). In addition to their psychiatric symptoms and any of the side effects of their treatments, people with SMI also have to face stigma associated with mental illness. We will now define stigma and explore the different types of stigma, then discuss the role stigma plays in the lives of people with SMI.

Defining Stigma

There is a considerable literature on stigma, beginning with Goffman's (1963) classic analysis. The term *stigma* refers to any mark or attribute that is not inherently meaningful in itself, but has significance attached to it through some shared social process. Stigma is therefore an inherently interpersonal construct. Through a shared understanding, both the person with the attribute ("the stigmatized") and the people without the attribute (called either "normal" or "the nonstigmatized") are aware that the attribute involves a negative or devalued quality (Miller & Major, 2000; Herek, 2004). Thus, the stigma does not simply identify the person who bears it as different from others; the deviation marked by the stigma has been deemed discrediting, rendering the person deserving of derision (Link & Phelan, 1999, 2001; Herek, 2004). According to sociologists Link and Phelan (2001), in order for the stigma to have negative consequences, two conditions are necessary: (1) there must be some difference or deviation that is noted as relevant and labeled as such; and (2) the stigmatizing group has to be in a more powerful position than the stigmatized group. The stigma, then, becomes the basis for assigning certain people and groups an undesirable social status, less power, less access to resources, as well as a justification for their social rejection and discrimination (Link & Phelan, 2001; Camp, Finlay & Lyons, 2002; Herek, 2004). The stigmatized attribute tends to become the dominant characteristic by which the person is identified and perceived (Camp, Finlay, & Lyons, 2002; Herek, 2004).

In addition to the public stigma (i.e., the reactions of the general public toward the stigmatized group) discussed above, there is self-stigma. Self-stigma, which is also referred to as self-devaluation (Goffman, 1963) or "internalized stigma" (Thoits, 2011), is defined as the internalization of the negative attitudes and social responses that others have toward them (Corrigan & Watson, 2002; Corrigan & Calabrese, 2005). Stigmatized people are often threatened by their awareness of others' negative stereotypes about them. However, the experience of being a member of a stigmatized group can be a major threat to one's self-esteem (Miller & Major, 2000). Examples of self-stigmatization include feelings of shame, being secretive, avoiding and/or limiting one's interactions with others.

In social psychology, stereotypes, prejudice, and discrimination are regarded as the cognitive, affective, and behavioral components of stigma, respectively (Rüsch, Angermeyer, & Corrigan, 2005). Stereotypes are cognitive associations with or beliefs about a group, whereas prejudice involves endorsement of those beliefs and/or emotional reactions toward the group. Discrimination is a behavior response to prejudice and stereotyping (Corrigan, 2000). In a more recent conceptualization of stigma, Rüsch and colleagues (2005) propose that stereotypes and prejudice alone are not sufficient for stigma. Rather, the three components of stigma must be present within the context of a power differential, whereby the stigmatizing group has greater social, economic, and political power than the stigmatized group. This conceptualization reflects a combination of Corrigan's (2000) social psychological model of stigma and the Link and Phelan (1999, 2001) sociological model of stigma.

Stigmas differ in various ways, including visibility and controllability. Stigma varies in the extent to which it sets a person apart, because the person with the attribute can vary in terms of how strongly they are associated with the undesirable characteristic(s), and therefore, with the resulting negative response (Link & Phelan, 1999). Stigmas that are chronic and visible bodily features, such as physical disabilities and membership in devalued ethnic/racial groups, are associated with a greater likelihood of eliciting strongly negative reactions across a broad range of contexts (Miller & Major, 2000). In contrast, other stigmatized conditions or identities that may be concealed, such as homosexuality, may have a less pervasive impact on social interactions. Mental illness is a condition, a part of an identity, or both that may be concealed; nonetheless, people with SMI as well as researchers assert that mental illness stigma is an especially pervasive and pernicious stigma (Hinshaw & Cicchetti, 2000; Wahl, 1999; Wahl & Harman, 1989). Mental illness stigma will be discussed in the section that follows.

Mental Illness Stigma

Unless a person is exhibiting grossly disorganized behavior or expressing delusional thoughts, one cannot typically "tell" that a person has a serious mental illness. Nonetheless, mental illness is a highly stigmatized attribute that can elicit a response on the basis of having received psychotherapy or counseling, been prescribed a psychiatric medication, received a diagnosis ("labeled"), and/or been hospitalized for psychiatric reasons. Once a person is associated with the label of "SMI," they are also vulnerable to being stigmatized, that is, associated with stereotypes about mental illness, and subject to prejudice against people with SMI.

Overall, people with mental illness are portrayed as dangerous, unpredictable, and unsociable (Signorelli et al., 1989; Link & Phelan, 1999; Wahl, 1995; Corrigan, Markow, & Watson, 2004; Corrigan, Watson, & Burne, 2005; Harper, 2009). Indeed, analyses of television, film, and print media indicate that stereotypes and stigmatizing attitudes regarding mental illness are rampant—according to the media, people with SMI are "psycho killers" who strike without warning, they are truthsayers, they are incompetent, with innocent, childlike perceptions of the world, or they are rebellious, free spirits. A common stereotype regarding mentally ill women is that they are hypersexual, moody, and unpredictable (Wahl, 1995; Rüsch et al., 2005; Harper, 2009).

A history of outpatient psychiatric care is less stigmatizing than a history of inpatient treatment (Leete, 1992). Some forms of mental illness are more stigmatized than others. More severe mental illnesses such as schizophrenia, are highly stigmatized (Sheppard, 2002, Guimon, 2010). Mental illnesses that are accompanied by behavioral disturbances, especially violence or bizarreness, are associated with stigma and social rejection (Nieradzik & Cochrane, 1985; Leete, 1992). Yet many patient surveys and interviews (c.f. Wahl, 1999; Roeloffs et al., 2003) reveal that mental illness stigma is also a major concern among people with major depression, despite the fact that compared to other severe mental disorders, depression may yield fewer observable symptoms and hospitalizations.

Stereotypes about mental illness are associated with attitudes regarding the treatment of people with SMI. Those who view people with SMI as victimized by their illness are more likely to feel pity, which is associated with "benevolence stigma" (Corrigan, Watson, Byrne, et al., 2005). In contrast, people who regard people with SMI as dangerous and unpredictable are more likely to be fearful and endorse social restrictiveness (Stuart & Arboleda-Flórez, 2001; Corrigan et al., 2002).

One of the common stigmatizing attitudes about people with SMI is that they are personally responsible for their impairments (Corrigan et al., 2002). Compared to people with physical illness, people with mental illness are more likely to be viewed as responsible for causing their illness, though the assumption of responsibility is somewhat less for schizophrenia (Rüsch et al., 2005). Some research suggests that framing mental illness in biological terms may reduce the likelihood to blame people for their mental illness, but it also makes people more pessimistic regarding their chances for recovery (Corrigan, Watson, Byrne, & Davis, 2005). Perhaps the most harmful of all stigmatizing attitudes for people with SMI is that they are dangerous (Corrigan et al., 2002; Marie & Miles, 2008). Research suggests that public attitudes toward the SMI population have become more stigmatizing recently; a representative U.S. population sample in 1996, was 2.5 times more likely to endorse the notion of a dangerous stigma than a comparable group in 1950 (Rüsch et al., 2005). We assert that mental illness stigma is oppressive. This assertion will be considered in greater detail in the sections that follow.

The Treatment of SMI People Viewed Through the Framework of Oppression

In her classic work, Young (2002) proposed criteria for determining whether people and groups are oppressed. According to Young, the five faces of oppression include: exploitation, marginalization, powerlessness, cultural imperialism, and violence. The presence of any of these five conditions is sufficient for considering a person or group oppressed. In the discussion of oppressed people struggling for equal access, dignity, and civil rights, people with SMI constitute an often overlooked group. However, the experiences of stigmatization, discrimination, and marginalization that most, if not all, SMI people face can be more generally classified as different types and levels of oppression. In the sections that follow, we will document the arenas in which people with SMI have been oppressed, using Young's framework. We will also compare the oppression that SMI people experience with that of other historically disadvantaged and disenfranchised groups.

The Marginalization of People With SMI

According to Young (2002), marginalization is the most dangerous form of oppression. Groups who experience marginalization are those who experience some degree of social exclusion, which is broadly defined to signify the lack of participation in mainstream social, cultural, economic, and political activities (Morgan, Burns, Fitzpatrick, et al., 2007). People with SMI are one of the most socially excluded groups in society (Johnstone, 2001; Sayce, 2001; Morgan et al., 2007).

There are various ways in which people with SMI are excluded from having full membership in the broader community.

People with SMI are barred from participation in mainstream citizenship on multiple dimensions, namely, level of social engagement, financial status, and housing status. This marginalization not only occurs at multiple levels of exclusion, it is also reinforced at multiple levels of interaction (e.g., at the level of individual, group/community, and institutional interactions). People with SMI typically have less "social capital" (e.g., social connections) than members of the general population. People with SMI tend to have smaller social networks, and fewer close relationships (MacDonald, Sauer, & Howie, 2005; Thoits, 2011). Although for some patients with SMI, the smaller size of their social networks may reflect part of their illness symptomatology (e.g., social anhedonia), for many others, it is more typically a secondary effect of their illness (e.g., social isolation), social stigma (e.g., social avoidance by others), or both. The comparative lack of social capital observed among the SMI population is thought to contribute to their social exclusion (Morgan et al., 2007).

Society typically deals with something frightening or distressing by distancing themselves from it; the perception of SMI people as dangerous and frightening has contributed to the "othering" or ostracism of mentally ill people (Fink & Tasman, 1992; Hinshaw & Cicchetti, 2000; Jorm & Griffiths, 2008). The social avoidance and/or rejection of people with SMI can be measured in terms of social distance. Social distance is defined as the degree of closeness desired by a respondent in terms of a hypothetical person (Hinshaw & Cicchetti, 2000). Studies indicate that members of the general public are less likely to freely interact with people labeled with SMI, preferring to maintain their distance (Corrigan, Rowan, et al., 2002). In a study of community attitudes toward people with schizophrenia, social distance increased as the level of intimacy in the relationship increased. More people were uncomfortable working on the same job with a person with schizophrenia than simply having a conversation with a person with schizophrenia. However, one in five respondents reported that they would be unable to maintain a friendship with, nearly one in two would be unable to room with, and three in four would be unable to marry, a person with schizophrenia (Stuart & Arboleda-Flórez, 2001). Other research confirms that compared to the general population, people with SMI are less likely to be successful in finding or maintaining sexual, romantic, and longer-term intimate relationships (Wright, Perry, & Foote-Ardah, 2007).

Although concerns regarding dangerousness have contributed to the social rejection of people with SMI, studies have also indicated that simply being associated with the label of a mental illness, or admitting having a mental illness, would result in stigmatization. There is evidence of such mental illness stigma in the workplace. In one study, many people believed that admitting a psychological problem would result in fewer interactions with coworkers and changes in their coworkers' confidence in their abilities (Britt, 2000). People with SMI have revealed concern about the potential effects of disclosure of their illness on factors such as promotion and professional development (Britt, 2000; Coleman, 2012). In one study of service members (Britt, 2000), the service members believed that admitting a psychological problem in the military would be more stigmatizing than admitting a medical problem. For example, 61% of the survey respondents agreed or strongly agreed that admission of a psychological problem would harm their career, compared to 43% who felt that way about admission of a medical problem. Twice as many (45% vs. 22%) of participants agreed or strongly agreed that admitting a psychological problem would cause their coworkers to spend less time around them, compared to admitting a medical problem.

Robert (2003) conducted a series of in-depth interviews of government employees with disabilities (including psychiatric and psychosocial) in the implementation phase of the Americans with Disabilities Act (ADA). The employees were at all levels of the job hierarchy below management level. The common theme in the employees' interviews was reports of alienation and harassment at work. Most of the employees interviewed reported alienation, both physically through segregation and social isolation, and from the actual work in which they were supposedly hired to participate. Most of the employees with psychiatric disabilities reported both subtle and blatant harassment, including jokes, needling, name-calling, innuendo, rudeness, sabotage, inappropriate questioning, and insensitive remarks. Robert (2003) observed that although there was compliance with ADA, the employees with emotional/mental disabilities were concentrated at the bottom of the occupational hierarchy. Unfortunately, a more recent study, based on a series of focus group meetings of people with histories of psychiatric hospitalizations, revealed that SMI people continue to experience mental illness stigma when dealing with employment situations (Forchuk et al., 2006).

Among the SMI population, unemployment is typically more common than underemployment. Especially following a psychiatric hospitalization or acute episode of illness, many people report being laid off, losing their jobs, or both due to excessive absences and finding it difficult to obtain new employment (Wahl, 1999). Ironically enough, some mental health professionals may be engaging in stigmatizing behaviors and unwittingly contributing to the marginalization of SMI people. Marrone and Golowka (1999) assert that by discouraging mentally ill people from seeking employment, or presenting employment as a choice rather than as a responsibility, rehabilitation professionals are actually perpetuating stigma. Many rehabilitation professionals as well as other mental health professionals may dissuade people with SMI from seeking employment, or may assume a relative neutral stance regarding patients' announcement that they have chosen not to work due to fears that it may be too overwhelming, too stressful for them, or both. The overprotectiveness of these professionals can be interpreted as an example of benevolent, rather than hostile stigma; nonetheless, Marrone and Golowka (1999) regard it as a form of oppression, because it prevents people with mental illness from being seen and treated like other contributing members of society.

Employment, whether paid or voluntary, is important because it assists people in developing social networks, thereby providing a context for establishing and maintaining instrumental as well as emotionally supportive relationships (Ruesch et al., 2004). Moreover, in our society, we identify ourselves by what we do, so having a job of some sort is critical to our social roles (Marrone & Golowka, 1999). "A major component of the civil rights movements in the U.S.—whether focusing on racial equality, gender, age, sexual orientation issues, the union movement, or the ADA—has been around freedom to gain access to, not freedom from, employment" (Marrone & Golowka, 1999, p. 188). Hence, employment for people with SMI is viewed as one of the necessary steps in the process of overturning the "stigma of difference" (Johnstone, 2001).

Several researchers (e.g., Morgan et al., 2007) maintain that much of the marginalization experienced by those with SMI is a function of societal responses. On the other hand, others (e.g., Sayce, 2001; Wright & Kloos, 2007; Mattsson, M., Topor, A., Cullberg, J., & Forsell, 2008) regard the marginalization as a reflection of a more complex psychological and sociopolitical process. "We can conceptualize social exclusion in relation to mental health service users specifically as the interlocking and mutually compounding problems of impairment, discrimination, diminished social role, lack of economic and social participation and disability" (Sayce, 2001, p. 122). Data seem to support this assertion, including observations that certain demographic factors affect the extent of social rejection; SMI males are more rejected than females, and the lower the social class, the more likely a person with SMI is to be excluded from the community (Leete, 1992). The prevalence of homelessness among the SMI population also buttresses support for Sayce's assertion.

Estimates of the percentage of the adult homeless population who have some type of SMI range from 20% to 37% (Federal Task Force on Homelessness and Severe Mental Illness, 1992; Torrey, 1997). According to the National Coalition for the Homeless (2005), a small percentage (approximately 6%) of the SMI population is homeless at any given point in time. The continued presence of SMI people among the homeless population has been attributed to deinstitutionalization, coupled with premature and unplanned discharge due to managed care, and/or either inadequate supportive aftercare or denial of services (National Coalition for the Homeless, 2005). The disproportionate number of people with SMI among the homeless population is a reflection of both marginalization and exploitation.

The Exploitation of People With SMI

The issue of unequal access to and distribution of resources is central to Young's concept of exploitation; this inequity must be group based and structurally persistent. Discrimination, which social psychologists regard as the behavioral component of stigma, is defined as the differential and negative treatment of people on the basis of their group membership, such as race, ethnicity, or gender (Smedley & Smedley, 2005). Typically, discrimination limits one's access to resources such as health care, housing, education, and employment. Although discrimination against the SMI appears nearly ubiquitous, in this section we will focus on the ways in which people with SMI are exploited in housing and health care.

People with SMI, like other disenfranchised groups such as the elderly or people living below the poverty line, are more likely to live in housing that they do not prefer or desire (Sylvestre, Nelson, & Sabloff,, 2007; Guimon, 2010). One of the major barriers to finding independent housing for people with SMI is poverty (Sylvestre et al., 2007). One could argue that their poverty status is a result of their unemployment or underemployment and thereby a more distal product of mental illness stigma. However, an even more proximal and formidable barrier to housing access is prejudice against SMI people. Overall, people with SMI, like members of racial and ethnic minority groups, are restricted in terms of where they can live due to discriminatory practices.

Studies of home mortgage lending, rental applications, housing practices, and residential segregation have consistently documented housing discrimination against racial and ethnic minority groups (Smedley & Smedley, 2005). Similarly, barriers of income and housing discrimination by individual housing providers result in restricted access to housing for the SMI population. Despite the availability of Section 8 certificates (i.e., certificates that enable people to pay a fixed proportion of their income for a rental unit) and other programs where the rent is adjusted to income level, enabling SMI people to have access to typical rental units, studies in North America indicate that landlords are less likely to rent a room or apartment to a person who discloses a history of mental illness (Corrigan et al., 2002; Rüsch et al., 2005; Forchuk, Nelson, & Hall, 2006; Sylvestre et al., 2007). In 1988, the Fair Housing Act, 42 U.S.C. §§ 3601–3631, was amended to specifically prohibit discrimination on the basis of disability, 20 years after the Civil Rights Act of 1968 prohibited housing discrimination against racial/ethnic minorities. However, nonprofit organizations, mental health organizations, or both continued to encounter difficulty when attempting to establish halfway houses or other arrangements for people with SMI in residential communities; this is referred to as the Not-in-My-Backyard (NIMBY) response. The group discrimination (NIMBYism) practiced by neighborhoods against supportive housing programs for people with SMI is similar to that seen in response to applications for low-income housing, housing for elderly residents, and people with physical and/or developmental disabilities.

There is considerable evidence of exploitation of the SMI population, particularly in the form of structural discrimination, in the health care system. The term *structural discrimination* is used to refer to rules, policies, and procedures of private and governmental institutions that restrict the access, rights, and opportunities of people based on stigmatized group membership (Link & Phelan, 2001; Corrigan et al., 2004). The health care system is an area in which the intersectionality of various oppressions can be seen; in addition to the overall inadequacy of access to mental health care plaguing the SMI population, there are gross racial and ethnic disparities in the availability of and access to mental health services. That is, despite the similarity in the prevalence of SMI across ethnic/racial groups, minorities have more unmet mental health needs (U.S. Department of Health and Human Services, 2001; Smedley & Smedley, 2005; Mishra, Lucksted, & Gloia, 2009). Inequitable health insurance coverage is another example of structural discrimination against the SMI population. The National Advisory Mental Health Council brought this institutional discrimination to light in 1993, when it published a report comparing the health insurance coverage for SMI with that of other illnesses. For example, the hospital coverage for mental illness was more restrictive (e.g., limited to 30–60 days annually) than for other types of illness (e.g., 120 or unlimited days).

Fewer outpatient treatments were covered for psychiatric care, and there were larger copayments than for nonpsychiatric medical treatment (National Advisory Mental Health Council, 1993). In 1996, the Domenici-Wellstone Mental Health Parity Act became a first step in national legislation that was intended to redress the inequitable practices in insurance coverage. However, the provisions in the Mental Health Parity Act allowed companies with 50 or fewer employees to be exempt from providing mental health coverage. This provision resulted in fewer financial resources being available for people affected by psychiatric illness, compared to people affected by medical illness. Thus, these policies yielded an unintentional consequence of discrimination against some people with SMI (Corrigan et al., 2004).

The Mental Health Parity and Addiction Equity Act of 2008 was intended to provide people with equal health insurance coverage for mental and physical health conditions. However, not all DSM-IV-TR (APA, 2000) diagnoses were required to be covered. Furthermore, although the federal law, which became effective January 2011, mandated that the health insurance for mental health, substance abuse, or both conditions had to be on par with medical-surgical coverage once the employer decided to cover mental health conditions, employers or other payers were not required to cover mental health conditions. Other inequities included the fact that there were not equal deductibles and/or copayments for treatment of mental illnesses compared to treatment of other chronic conditions, and visit limits were set for the former type of illnesses and not the latter. Unfortunately, then, this legislation did not appreciably alter the unequal distribution of health insurance resources; as such, the exploitation of people with SMI in terms of access to affordable health care continues. This exploitation is also a reflection of the powerless status of people with SMI.

The Powerless Status of SMI People

Young (2002) identifies powerless people as those people who have little or no role in terms of making decisions, using expertise, and/or dispersing authority. People who are powerless are regularly exposed to disrespectful treatment due to their status. When one listens to results from psychiatric patient focus groups or reviews findings based on surveys from SMI groups regarding their experiences of stigma, it is evident that powerlessness is a commonly perceived experience (Wahl, 1999; Hinshaw & Cicchetti, 2000; Forchuk et al., 2006). The status of SMI people satisfies the criteria for this aspect of oppression, because they are often subject to arbitrary treatment by the healthcare system as well as the legal system, and they lack the civil rights of many other citizens in our society. In this next section, we will discuss ways in which the stigma of mental illness and structural discrimination prevents the empowerment of people with SMI.

Like African Americans who experienced de jure discrimination of the Jim Crow laws, people with SMI frequently face structural discrimination in state legislation. Like African Americans, people with SMI were denied voting privileges, thereby further reducing their social status (Corrigan, Watson, Heyrman, 2005; Thornicraft, 2005; Bazelon Center for Mental Health Law, 2008). In 1993, the National Voter Registration Act, 42 USC §§ 1973 et seq., provided people with mental illness the express right to vote. Yet results of a 1999 survey of existing state laws revealed that approximately one third of the 50 states restricted the rights of a person with SMI to vote, serve jury duty, or hold elective office (Corrigan et al., 2005). Unfortunately, not much has changed in the ensuing years. In the United States, people with SMI have the right to vote as long as they comprehend what it means to vote (ADA, 42 U.S.C. Statute 12132, *Doe v. Roe* 156F. Supp. 2d 35 (D. Me. 2001). According to federal law, only a court can decide that a person is not competent to vote, though election officials, service providers, or both may attempt to block voter rights by imposing voter-competence requirements. Approximately, 15 states, along with the District of Columbia, have laws that sometimes deprive people with SMI of the right to vote. People who are "under guardianship" (i.e., due to an inability to care for themselves during an acute psychiatric episode) or judged "mentally incompetent" or "mentally incapacitated" are prevented from voting. As of August 2011, only 11 states have no disability-related restrictions on the right to vote (Judge David L. Bazelon Center for Mental Health Law, 2008).

In both the United States and Canada, losing custody of a child is more common for parents with SMI (Hollingsworth, 2004; Corrigan, Watson, Heyrman, 2005; Thornicroft, 2005). Identified factors associated with SMI people losing custody were: maternal mental illness, family income at or below the poverty line, compulsory admission to a hospital, and entry into a forensic treatment program (Hollingsworth, 2004; Thornicroft, 2005). Overall, however, Thornicroft (2005) maintained that parents with SMI lose custody of their children for reasons that would seldom be used for other parents. A survey of state legislative activity across the United States in 2002 revealed that there was a trend toward diminishing parental rights of people with a history of mental illness. It was estimated that approximately 50% of the states restrict child custodial rights of people with psychiatric disorders (Corrigan, Watson, Heyrman, 2005). "Parents with serious mental illness (SMI) are confronted with increased risk of involvement with the child welfare system and of having their children placed in out-of-home care. In fact, five states (Alaska, Arizona, California, Kentucky, and North Dakota) and Puerto Rico list mental illness or disability as grounds for not providing reasonable efforts toward reunification" (Hollingsworth et al., 2011, p. 53).

The risk of civil liberty violations is very high when one considers the treatment, hospitalization, incarceration, or both of people with SMI. Several issues are relevant here, including: Are people with SMI adequately protected from mistreatment and/or abuse while in care facilities? Is the person with SMI competent to have a role in their treatment planning? Can they make a rational decision regarding the right to decline treatment and/or choose between alternative treatments? How does society balance the rights of the individual with SMI and public safety? Mental health professionals, researchers, ethicists, and lawyers, as well as the SMI population, their advocates, and their loved ones continue to grapple with these issues. Historically, people with SMI have been vulnerable to arbitrary treatment, coercive treatment, or both when under the care of hospitals, institutions, jails, and prisons (Morrissey & Goldman, 1986).

In the past, forced restraints and/or forced seclusion were used as forms of intimidation and coercion by social service providers, members of the legal system, and health care staff. In 1999, the Compassionate Care Act was passed, which placed specific restrictions on the use of physical restraints, seclusion, and chemical restraints (i.e., psychopharmacological drugs) in any public or private health care facility or treatment center that received any federal assistance. The purpose of the legislation was to protect the rights of their SMI patients and residents, so that physical or mental abuse, corporal punishment, involuntary seclusion, or restraints could not be used for punishment or convenience. These federal regulations (42 CFR, Part 482) were later reinforced and finalized in 2006. While these regulations reflected a major advance in the protection of this population's civil liberties, there are other ways in which SMI people are still rendered relatively powerless.

Cook and Jonikas (2002) opined that "people with psychiatric disabilities are the only Americans who can have their freedom taken away and be institutionalized or incarcerated without being convicted of a crime. This widespread discrimination arises because of pervasive misconceptions about the dangerousness of people with psychiatric disorders, resulting in these individuals' being deprived of their civil rights in the name of treatment and public safety." (p. 89). Some mental health and legal professionals argue against the obligatory dangerousness criterion (ODC), a legislation that required that mentally ill people be given treatment without their consent *if and only if* they are determined to be a risk of harm/danger to themselves or others. Legislation including the ODC was first introduced in the United States in the District of Columbia in 1964 and in California in 1969. The dangerousness criterion was introduced in order to justify what was considered to be a restriction or loss of a person's autonomy. However, the ODC has been criticized as being unethical and discriminatory against people with mental illness because it allows for the involuntary treatment of many mentally ill people who will never become dangerous, in order to accurately predict and intervene in the few cases who will (Large, Ryan, Nielssen, 2008).

There is some question regarding whether the use of mandated community treatment orders (CTOs) are justifiable or whether they are wholly coercive. CTOs are legal mandates that force mentally ill people with a history of treatment noncompliance to undergo outpatient psychiatric treatment. The use of mandated treatment, which is also known as outpatient or community commitment, has the potential to be considered paternalistic, coercive, and/or disrespectful. At the very least, two key ethical principles, namely, autonomy and beneficence, are seemingly at odds when one considers the issue of CTOs (Snow & Austin, 2009). One could argue, however, that due to their psychiatric disorder, a person with SMI may lack the competence to understand: (a) the exact nature of the decision; (b) the relevant issues regarding the decision; and (c) the consequences of their decision. Moreover, outpatient commitment is regarded as the least restrictive alternative to hospitalization. Nearly all of the states in the United States use this legislation. A well-known example of legislation for CTOs is the New York law known as Kendra's Law (§ 9.60 of the Mental Hygiene Law), which is named after Kendra Webdale, a young woman who died after being pushed into the path of an oncoming subway train by a person with chronic and persistent schizophrenia. The schizophrenia patient was living in the community at the time but he was not receiving treatment for his illness. The law grants judges the authority to mandate treatment (including medication) on mentally ill people. If they are noncompliant, they face involuntary commitment to a treatment facility.

Under Wisconsin's "Fifth Standard for Civil Commitment," formally known as 1995 Wisconsin Act 292, Section 51.20(1) (a)2.e., a person with SMI can be involuntarily committed to treatment despite

the absence of a requirement of imminent dangerousness to oneself
or others. This criterion for commitment to treatment is reserved
for people who are so psychiatrically ill that they are incapable of
making an informed decision regarding medication or treatment.
As the legislation reads, someone can be placed in treatment if the
court determines that "there is a substantial probability that, if left
untreated, they will lack services necessary for their health or safety
and suffer severe mental, emotional, or physical harm, resulting in
the loss of their ability to function independently in the community
or resulting in the loss of cognitive or volitional control over their
thoughts or actions." The rationale for this legislation is to intercede
before further incapacity results in a loss of the ability to function,
which would presumably lead to further disability, possibly engen-
dering further adverse outcomes such as homelessness, self-harm, or
both. We believe that this action is an important, recovery-affirming
step, aimed at preventative intervention, which may ultimately serve
to preempt further marginalization and other stigmatizing outcomes
for an incapacitated person with SMI.

Despite the aforementioned examples of violations of civil liberties, people with SMI were relatively ignored by civil rights movements until the 1990s; they were not even included in forums on
disability rights. "This neglect was fostered by the stigmatized views
that individuals with psychiatric disorders were violent, volatile, and
unable to meaningfully participate in empowerment movements"
(Cook & Jonikas, 2002, p. 88). In a very real sense, the SMI group
has been so marginalized, stereotyped, and feared that they have
been rendered nearly unacceptable, even among other disenfranchised groups. This is a reflection of how extensively the stereotypes
about the SMI population have permeated the cultural consciousness
of North Americans. Ironically enough, despite the pervasiveness of
the stereotypes regarding people with SMI, due to cultural imperialism, society often refuses to acknowledge the individual with SMI.

Cultural Imperialism and the Invisibility of SMI People

"I am invisible, understand, simply because people refuse to see me"
(Ellison, 1952, p. 3). People with SMI not only recognize that their
own group perspective is invalidated by the dominant group, but they
also have the experience of Otherness created by specific experiences
not shared by the dominant group; this is an example of cultural
imperialism (Young, 2002). The recurrent message someone with SMI
receives from the dominant culture is that they are different, marked,

and inferior; like Ellison's protagonist in *Invisible Man*, they are rendered invisible. In earlier sections, we briefly summarized the most common stereotypes about people with mental illness, and we asserted that negative stereotypes regarding SMI were ubiquitous in our culture. Here, we expand on the process of labeling and discuss how structural discrimination from the private sector (i.e., the media) perpetuates the stereotyped and inferior images of the SMI population. We also consider how these stigmatizing portrayals may become internalized, and the consequences of that process.

The use of psychiatric medication can be stigmatizing because it can identify someone as having a mental illness. Diagnoses, however, serve as more official labels, which carry more potent cultural meanings, activate negative associations and connotations in diverse settings and are more difficult to dispute, ignore, and hide than informal labels (Link & Phelan, 1999). Once a person is labeled as having or having had a mental illness, either due to receiving a psychotropic medication or therapy, being hospitalized, or being diagnosed with a disorder, the person undergoes a shift in identity. Through a process of ideological hegemony people with SMI are inculcated with negative stereotypes, cultural myths, and "knowledge" about mental illness (Pyke, 2010; Gramsci, 1971). As Thesen (2001) described, "the experience of being reclassified from human being to psychiatric case is an absolute one, as others see you only as mentally ill, others can judge your experience as disqualifying, never qualifying" (p. 252).

The mass media provides the framework through which most North Americans view, perceive, and learn about the world; for some members of the public, this may be their primary source of information about psychiatric disorders and the people who are affected by them (Wahl, 1995; Safran, 1998). Analyses of television portrayals reveal that mentally ill characters are less likely to be physically attractive, have first and last names, and have ties to the community, such as friends, family, and neighbors (Signorelli, 1989; Wahl, 1995). Instead, mentally ill characters are more likely than other characters to commit violence or to be victimized; in one study of prime-time television dramas, 72.1% of the mentally ill characters (compared to 45.1% of all characters) were portrayed as murderers (Signorelli, 1989; Link & Phelan, 1999). Finally, as noted earlier, television as well as films typically portray mentally ill characters as "bad" or "evil," unemployed, and unsuccessful (Signorelli, 1989; Wahl, 1995; Harper, 2009). These repeated images serve to reinforce the sense that prejudicial attitudes and discriminatory behaviors toward SMI people are legitimate, justifiable, and culturally normative (Johnstone, 2001).

Like television and film, print media can also become social mechanisms for perpetuating stigma. Themes of newspaper articles can be used as a measure of structural stigma (Corrigan, Watson, Gracia et al., 2005). In a systematic study of 70 major newspapers across the United States, Corrigan and colleagues (Corrigan, Watson, & Gracia, 2005) found that themes related to dangerousness (e.g., violent crimes, danger to others, mental illness as legal defense, suicide) accounted for the largest proportion of stories related to mental illness during the periods studied. Consistent with reports by others (cf., Wahl, 1995), most of the newspaper stories were about violent crimes against others or legal defenses related to mental illness. Corrigan et al. (2005) concluded that compared to the rates reported in prior studies conducted at least ten years earlier, the number of articles portraying people with SMI as dangerous have decreased. Nonetheless, these types of articles remained the largest focus of the news media, and typically appeared in the front section of the newspaper; in contrast, news coverage of treatment for mental illness was more likely to be found either in the health section or the business section.

Stigmatized people are aware of the negative stereotypes and stigmatizing portrayals and are often threatened by them, even if they do not accept or believe them (Miller & Major, 2000). Invariably, SMI people recognize that they are evaluated more negatively and treated differently in their interactions with others. These experiences may compound feelings of "felt stigma" (i.e., shame regarding having the condition; Thornicroft, 2005). When stigmatized people are repeatedly affected by the differential perception and treatment of others and these stigmas may become internalized (i.e., turned against oneself); this is referred to as "internalized oppression" (Freire, 1970; Tappan, 2006), or more commonly, "self-stigma" (Rüsch et al., 2005). An analogous construct would be internalized racism, which is observed in ethnic/racial minority groups when they accept the negative societal beliefs and stereotypes that the dominant culture promotes (Williams & Williams-Morris, 2000). Examples of self-stigma in a person with SMI would include believing that they are incompetent due to their mental illness, or having a negative emotional reaction such as shame, low self-esteem or a sense of low self-efficacy (Rüsch et al., 2005; Kranke, Floersch, & Townsend, 2010). As a result of self-stigma, someone with SMI might not pursue employment or educational opportunities, or might shy away from relationships in order to avoid disclosure.

The differential way in which language is used to refer to people with SMI reflects the extent of their "Otherness." Although physi-

cians, nurses, and psychologists would not think of referring to a
person with cancer as "a cancer," it is not uncommon to hear the
same professionals refer to a person with schizophrenia as "a schizophrenic," as though they were not people! As others (Link & Phelan,
2001; Rüsch et al., 2005) have pointed out, by using "people first"
language, we are acknowledging that the person affected by mental
illness is still one of "us," rather than one of "them." Like a person
with cancer, the person with SMI would remain one of "us," a person who has an attribute (schizophrenia), thereby remaining part of
our community, rather than becoming the attribute (the disease). In
the twenty-first century, it remains a struggle to train the mental
health community, as well as the general public, to refer to people
with SMI using "people first" language. Just as being referred to in
dehumanizing or "othering" terms deprives one of their dignity, so,
too, does living under the specter of violence.

The Spectra of Violence and the SMI Population

When Young (2002) describes the oppression of violence, she includes
the threat of victimization as well as direct victimization. Members of
oppressed groups share the stress and burden of the daily awareness
that they are vulnerable to assault due to their group membership.
"Just living under such a threat of attack on oneself or family, or
friends deprives the oppressed of freedom and dignity, and needlessly
expends their energy" (Young, 2002, p. 66). We would broaden Young's
concept of violence to include what Sue, Capodilupo, & Torino (2007)
refer to as microassaults. Although the concept was developed by
Sue and colleagues (2007) to describe one of the types of daily verbal, behavioral, and/or environmental indignities that convey hostile,
derogatory, or negative racial attitudes toward racial/ethnic minorities, this particular type of microaggression can also be observed
in interactions with SMI people. When in the general community,
many people with serious and persistent mental illness are subject
to "violent verbal or nonverbal attacks that are consciously intended
to hurt them through name-calling, avoidant behavior, or purposeful
discriminatory actions" (p. 278).

SMI women are at greater risk for sexual victimization than
women in the general population; like other women, these women
are at an increased risk of being victimized by their partners (Wood
& Edwards, 2005). A review of extant studies conducted by Friedman
and Loue (2007) indicated that reports of intimate partner violence

against SMI females ranged between 24% and 49% of female psychiatric patients. Surprisingly, the rates among female psychiatric outpatients were similarly high (23% to 50%). One consistent finding across studies was that having a diagnosis of schizophrenia increased the woman's risk of being victimized by a partner. It is possible that the social isolation experienced by these SMI females renders them particularly vulnerable to being victimized.

The print media has historically focused on violent acts committed *by* members of the community who have mental illness histories. It is rare to observe media coverage regarding the criminal victimization *of* people experiencing mental illness. Yet studies indicate that people with SMI, regardless of gender, are 2.5 times more likely to be victims of violent crime than the general population (Hiday, Swartz, & Swanson, 1999; Council of State Governments Justice Center, 2007). Visible symptoms of mental illness, which may result in behavior or mannerisms that appear bizarre or strange, may result in defensive responses, hostile responses, or both from others (Hiday et al., 1999; Wood & Edwards, 2005). One study of 172 schizophrenia outpatients (Brekke, Prindle, & Bae, 2001) revealed that, contrary to stereotypes and media portrayals, these people were at least 14 times more likely to be victims of a violent crime than to be perpetrators of one.

Some of the SMI population's greater vulnerability to violence may be attributable to the fact that they are more likely to be homeless, or live in poorer, more crime-ridden areas. However, even when compared to university students, who were living similar lifestyles (e.g., urban, low SES, and transient/rental housing), researchers (Wood & Edwards, 2005) observed that the mentally ill patients experienced significantly more criminal victimization. Thus, lifestyle alone cannot account for the SMI group's higher rates of victimization.

People working in law enforcement as well as lawyers typically receive little or no specialized training regarding how to elicit information from people with SMI. Furthermore, damaging stereotypes about people with SMI may place them at higher risk for violence because those stereotypes serve to encourage and/or reinforce the notion that the "crazy" victims will not be believed, even if they do report the crime. That is, mentally ill patients may be regarded by perpetrators of crimes as easy targets because they are less likely to be considered credible (Woods & Edwards, 2005; Council of State Governments Justice Center, 2007). The SMI population's heightened vulnerability to violence is not only an aspect of their experience of oppression, it is a reflection of a social injustice.

The Oppression of SMI People as a Social Justice Issue

Social justice is broadly defined as the process in which all members of society are afforded equal access to opportunities, goods and services, equal treatment and participation in decision making, and equal value (Asumah & Johnston-Anumonwo, 2002). As illustrated above, people with SMI are not granted the same access to health care, insurance, and housing as people without the label or designation of mental illness. SMI people may be barred from voting, child rearing, and, as the research indicates, they are considered less desirable as partners, neighbors, and employees. These inequities appear to be group based and structurally persistent; as such, the treatment of people with SMI is a social justice issue. People with SMI face both individual discrimination and institutional discrimination. People with SMI are rendered powerless through various forms of structural discrimination. People with SMI lack decision-making power, and are subject to arbitrary treatment by the legal or health care systems. They are also vulnerable to damaging and pejorative labels and definitions by others (most notably, the media), and have fewer opportunities for self-definition. Economically, politically, interpersonally, and professionally, then, people with SMI are a disenfranchised and disadvantaged group. People with SMI are among some of the most marginalized members of our society. They experience social avoidance, exclusion, or both. Finally, they may be more vulnerable to violence, and many live under the threat of attack. Thus, due to these experiences that people with SMI typically face, they are an oppressed group. The social injustice stems from mental illness stigma, which incorporates issues of poverty, homelessness, and a gross power differential between the discredited and the dominant segments of society who participate in the discrediting. Indeed, the oppression which SMI people experience bears many similarities to the oppression that other disenfranchised groups, namely, people with physical disabilities, ethnic/racial minorities, and lesbian/gay/bisexual/ transgendered (LGBT) people, are struggling with or have struggled with in the past. Although we have presented mental illness stigma and its impact on people with SMI within the framework of social injustice, the oppression also presents a serious public health problem.

The Oppression of SMI People as a Public Health Issue

Many (e.g., Corrigan & Penn, 1997) assert that people with SMI suffer mental illness stigma that is at least as harmful as the mental illness itself. Indeed, in 1999, the U.S. Surgeon General, David Satcher, MD, declared that stigma was "the most formidable obstacle to future progress in the arena of mental illness and health" (U.S. Department of Health and Human Services, 1999, p. 3). Although we believe that most if not all of the disorders classified as serious and persistent mental illnesses have genetic and epigenetic origins, it is also evident that mental illness stigma is associated with several negative mental health–related outcomes. Everyday discrimination (i.e., treated with less respect than others, interpersonal slights in restaurants or stores), is related to psychological distress (Essed, 1991); similarly, we would assert that the cumulative effect of repeated exposure to microaggressions (as defined in Sue et al., 2007) would be related to psychological stress. The experience of discrimination and other stigma-related stressors is associated with psychological distress, depression, and anxiety in groups of African American people (Landrine & Klonoff, 1996; Williams & Williams-Morris, 2000), and LGBT people (Herek, 1991), as well as in a national probability sample including both Blacks and Whites (Kessler, Mickelson, & Williams, 1999). These stressors are also associated with lower self-esteem (Broman, 1997). Several studies suggest that people with SMI, who are acutely aware of mental illness stigma, also display lowered self-esteem (Link & Phelan, 2001; Corrigan, Watson, Byrne et al., 2005; Rüsch et al., 2005; but see Camp, Finlay, & Lyons, 2002). We assert that oppression has a deleterious effect on one's mental health, leading to the development of various psychological symptoms and exacerbating SMI people's already existing mental illness (Corrigan & Penn, 1997; Hinshaw & Cicchetti, 2000; Van Zeist, 2009).

Prior research on other oppressed groups indicate the adverse effects of stigma-related stressors on physical health outcomes (Williams & Williams-Morris, 2000; Friedman, Williams, & Singer, 2009; Williams, Neighbors, & Jackson, 2008). Indeed, there is increasing evidence (Felker, Yazel, & Short, 1996; Lawrence, Kisely, & Pais, 2010) indicating that relative to age- and sex-matched peers, people with SMI have greater physical illness morbidity and mortality. These data are similar to those indicating the shorter life expectancies and higher illness morbidity rates of African American people (Flacke, Amaro, & Jenkins, 1995).

There is ample evidence showing that mental illness stigma adversely affects help-seeking behavior. Due to the stigma, many people try to conceal the mental illness as long as possible, which often delays or deters them from seeking help (Hinshaw & Cicchetti, 2000; Granbois, 2005; U.S. Department of Health & Human Services, 2001; Thesen, 2001; Corrigan, Watson, & Byrne, 2005; Wang

Berglund, & Olfson, 2005; Corcoran, Gerson, & Sills-Shahar, 2007). The association between mental illness stigma and treatment delay is especially marked in the African American community. Studies indicate that African Americans are more concerned with stigma than other ethnic groups in the United States. Additionally, African American people are more likely to endorse stigmatizing beliefs regarding people with psychiatric disorders (Franz, Carter, & Leiner, 2010). The double stigma of mental illness and minority status may make American Indian/Alaskan Natives as well as African Americans even more reluctant to seek mental health treatment (Smedley, Stith, & Nelson, 2003; Granbois, 2005). This is significant, because delays in treatment may be associated with poorer prognosis. Thus, stigma makes recovery from SMI more difficult. The experience of social oppression for an African American person with SMI must be especially burdensome and troubling; studies have indicated that these mentally ill African American participants had difficulty distinguishing whether the prejudicial responses they were met with were the result of their race or their mental illness (Armour, Bradshaw, & Roseborough, 2009). As one can imagine, the additional overlay of pre-existing racial discrimination intensifies the mental illness stigma, thereby creating a greater barrier to recovery (Tew, 2011).

The stigma attached to mental illness is also a deterrent to medication compliance (Hinshaw & Cicchetti, 2000). Studies (e.g., Hodgkin, Volpe-Vartanian, & Alegria, 2007) indicate that mental illness stigma is one of the factors related to patients' discontinuation of their antidepressant use. Many people reject the use of their antidepressants in order to avoid the label of "psychiatric patient." Research (Sirey, Bruce, & Alexopoulos, 2001) has indicated a robust association between higher perceived stigma and medication noncompliance, even after the effects of perceived illness severity had been accounted for. This means that even when someone had sought mental health services and was receiving treatment, the fear of stigma was sufficiently powerful to deter them from initiating or adhering to antidepressant drug therapy. Other studies (cf. Weiden, Olfson, & Essock, 1997) have indicated similar findings for patients with schizophrenia and antipsychotic medications. In the next section, we summarize our observations regarding the oppression of people with SMI.

Ending the Oppression of People With SMI

In summary, the oppression of people with serious and persistent mental illness is both a social justice issue and a public health issue.

It is incumbent on us as a society to acknowledge this oppression and to work toward eradicating this insidious injustice.

> The gross injustice faced by people with mental health problems and mental disorders is not merely an abstraction; it is a lived reality and one that is frequently characterized by an intense and lonely struggle to survive and to 'find one's way back' to a world of meaningful human connection, intimacy, and shared identity. (Johnstone, 2001, p. 201)

There are several ways in which we can work, individually and collectively, to help to make the invisible visible. Currently, many people with SMI live in but apart from the community; there are some structural as well as individual changes that can be introduced in order to help facilitate their social integration.

On a structural level, better legal protection against discrimination and enforcement of the legislation would be paramount. Moreover, if individuals with SMI had viable opportunities for employment, whether paid or voluntary, they would be better able to become integrated into their communities. The types of positions that could be made available range from volunteer jobs such as assisting with Meals on Wheels and pet sitting to sorting mail and dishwashing or clerical work in an academic setting. The employment would not only enable them to feel that they were contributing in a meaningful way to their community, but it would also provide them with opportunities to interact with nonpsychiatrically ill persons. Social integration is a key component of community integration (Gooding, 2014). Having opportunities for forging supportive and reciprocal relationships is also important. Social clubs and religious organizations could hold support groups for members with mental illness, or offer a "befrienders group," to help assist new members to meet others. Civic groups and other neighborhood organizations could adopt the goal of becoming better informed about mental illness and working toward reducing and/or eradicating mental illness stigma. Reducing social distancing attitudes and mental illness stigma would be invaluable in terms of facilitating the social integration of people with SMI. Indeed, as discussed earlier, one of the primary contributors to the oppression of people with SMI is mental illness stigma. After reviewing the research literature, case studies, first-person accounts, and focus group transcripts we assert that the single act that could have the most proximal effect on an individual with SMI's perceived sense of oppression would be to reduce the level of stigma that they experience.

References

Americans With Disabilities Act of 1990, 42 U.S.C. 12101, et seq.

Armour, M., Bradshaw, W., & Roseborough, D. (2009). African Americans and recovery from severe mental illness. *Social Work in Mental Health, 7*(6), 602–622.

Asumah, S. N., & Johnston-Anumonwo, I. (2002). Grounding our terms, ideas, and concepts. In S. N. Asumah & I. Johnston-Anumonwo (Eds.), *Diversity, multiculturalism, and social justice.* Binghamton, NY: Global Academic Publishing, pp. 3–30.

Brekke, J., Prindle, C., Bae, S. W., & Long, J. (2001). Risks for individuals with schizophrenia who are living in the community. *Psychiatric Services, 52*(10), 1358–1366.

Britt, Thomas W. (2000). The stigma of psychological problems in a work environment: Evidence from the screening of service members returning from Bosnia. *Journal of Applied Social Psychology, 30*, 1599–1618.

Broman, C. L. (1997). Race-related factors and life satisfaction among African Americans. *Journal of Black Psychology, 23*(1), 36–49.

Camp, D. L., Finlay, W. M. L., & Lyons, E. (2002). Is low self-esteem an inevitable consequence of stigma? An example from women with chronic mental health problems. *Social Science and Medicine, 55*, 823–834.

Coleman, M. A. (2012). Up for tenure, facing depression. *Inside Higher Ed.* (January 11). Retrieved from: http://www.insidehighered.com/advice/2012/01/11/essay-dealing-depression-while-tenure-track

Cook, J. A., & Jonikas, J. A. (2002). Self-determination among mental health consumers/survivors: Using lessons from the past to guide the future. *Journal of Disability Policy Studies, 13*(2), 87–95.

Corcoran, C., Gerson, R., Sills-Shahar, R., Nickou, C., McGlashan, T., Malaspina, D., & Davidson, L. (2007). Trajectory to a first episode of psychosis: A qualitative research study with families. *Early Intervention Psychiatry, 1*, 308–315.

Corrigan, P. W. (2000). Mental health stigma as social attribution: Implications for research methods and attitude change. *Clinical Psychology Science and Practice, 7*, 48–67.

Corrigan, P. W. & Calabrese, J. D. (2005). Strategies for assessing and diminishing self-stigma. In P. W. Corrigan (Ed.), On the stigma of mental illness: Practical strategies for research and social change, pp. 239–256. Washington DC: American Psychological Association.

Corrigan, P. W, Markowitz, F. E., & Watson, A. C. (2004). Structural levels of mental illness stigma and discrimination. *Schizophrenia Bulletin, 30*(3), 481–491.

Corrigan, P. W., & Penn, D. (1997). Disease and discrimination: Two paradigms that describe severe mental illness. *Journal of Mental Health, 6*(4), 355–366.

Corrigan, P. W., Rowan, D., Green, A., Lundin, R., River, P, Uphoff-Wasowski, K., White, K., & Kubiak, M. A. (2002). Challenging two mental illness stigmas: Personal responsibility and dangerousness. *Schizophrenia Bulletin, 28*(2), 293–309.

Corrigan, P. W., & Watson, A. C. (2002). The paradox of self-stigma and mental illness. *Clinical Psychology: Science and Practice, 9,* 35–53.

Corrigan, P. W., Watson, A. C., Byrne, P., & Davis, K. E. (2005). Mental illness stigma: Problem of public health or social justice? *Social Work, 50*(4), 363–368.

Corrigan, P. W., Watson, A. C., Gracia, G., Slopen, N., Rasinski, K., & Hall, L. L. (2005). Newspaper stories as measures of structural stigma. *Psychiatric Services, 56*(5), 551–556.

Corrigan, P. W., Watson, A. C., Heyrman, M. L., Warpinski, A., Gracia, G., Slopen, N., & Hall, L. L. (2005). Structural stigma in state legislation. *Psychiatric Services, 56,* 557–563.

Council of State Governments Justice Center (2007). *Violence against women with mental illness.* New York: Council of State Governments Justice Center.

Ellison, R. (1952). *Invisible man.* New York: Vintage Books.

Essed, P. (1991). *Understanding everyday racism.* Newbury Park, CA: Sage.

Federal Task Force on Homelessness and Severe Mental Illness (1992). *Outcasts on Main Street: A report of the Federal Task Force on Homelessness and Severe Mental Illness.* Delmar, NY: National Resource Center on Homelessness and Mental Illness.

Felker, F., Yazel, J. J., & Short, D. (1996). Mortality and medical morbidity among psychiatric patients: A review. *Psychiatric Services, 47,* 1356–1363.

Fink, P. J., & Tasman, A. (1992). Introduction. In *Stigma and mental illness* (Ed.), P. J. Fink, & Tasman, A., Stigma and mental illness. Washington, DC: American Psychiatric Press.

Flacke, J. M., Amaro, H., Jenkins, S. W., Kunitz, S., Levy, J., Mikon, M., & Yu, E. (1995). Panel I: Epidemiology of minority health. *Health Psychology, 14,* 592–600.

Forchuk, C., Nelson, G., & Hall, G. B. (2006). "It's important to be proud of the place you live in": Housing problems and preferences of psychiatric survivors. *Perspectives in Psychiatric care, 42,* 42–52.

Franz, L., Carter, T., Leiner, A. S., Bergner, E., Thompson, N. J., & Compton, M. T. (2010). Stigma and treatment delay in first-episode psychosis: a grounded theory study. *Early Intervention Psychiatry, 4,* 47–56.

Freire, P. (1970). *Pedagogy of the oppressed.* New York: Continuum.

Friedman, E. M., Williams, D. R., Singer, B. H., & Ryff, C. D. (2009). Chronic discrimination predicts higher circulating levels of E-selection in a national sample: The MIDUS study. *Brain, Behavior, and Immunity, 23*(5), 684–692.

Friedman, S. H., & Loue, S. (2007). Incidence and prevalence of intimate partner violence by and against women with severe mental illness. *Journal of Women's Health, 16*(4), 471–480.

Gilbert, P., & Allen, S. (1998). The role of defeat and entrapment (arrested flight) in depression. *Psychological Medicine, 28,* 585–598.

Goffman, E. (1963). *Stigma: Notes on the management of spoiled identity.* Englewood Cliffs, NJ: Prentice Hall.

Gooding, D. C. (in press). Social integration. In A. Scull & J. G. Golson (Eds.), *Cultural sociology of mental health: An A-to-Z guide.* San Diego, CA: SAGE Reference Publishing.

Guimon, J. (2010). Prejudice and realities in stigma. *International Journal of Mental Health, 39,* 20–43.

Gramsci, A. (1971). *Selections from the Prison Notebooks of Antonio Gramsi.* (Q. Hoare & G. N. Smith, Ed. & Trans.). New York: International Publishers.

Grandbois, D. (2005). Stigma of mental illness among American Indian and Alaska Native Nations: Historical and contemporary perspectives. *Issues in Mental Health Nursing, 26,* 1001–1024.

Harper, S. (2009). *Madness, power, and the media: Class, gender, and race in popular representations of mental distress.* New York: Palgrave Macmillan.

Herek, G. M. (1991). Stigma, prejudice, and violence against lesbians and gay men. In J. C. Gonsiorek & J. D. Weinrich (Eds.), *Homosexuality: Research implications for public policy* (pp. 60–80). Thousand Oaks, CA: Sage.

Herek, G. M. (2004). Beyond "Homophobia": Thinking about sexual prejudice and stigma in the twenty-first century. *Sexuality Research & Social Policy, 1*(2), 6–24.

Hiday, V. A., Swartz, M. A., Swanson, J. W., Borum, R., & Wagner, R. (1999). Criminal victimization of persons with severe mental illness. *Psychiatric Services, 50*(1), 62–68.

Hinshaw, S. P., & Cicchetti, D. (2000). Stigma and mental disorder: Conceptions of illness, public attitudes, personal disclosure, and social policy. *Development and Psychopathology, 12,* 555–598.

Hodgkin, D., Volpe-Vartanian, J., & Alegria, M. (2007). Discontinuation of antidepressant medication among Latinos in the U.S. *Journal of Behavioral Health Services Research, 34,* 329–342.

Hollingsworth, L. D. (2004). Child custody loss among women with persistent severe mental illness. *Social Work Research, 28,* 199–209.

Hollingsworth, L. D., MacFarlane, P., & Rassi, S. L. (2011). Is the life history calendar a valid measure of child custody loss among birth mothers with serious mental illness? *Social Work Research, 35,* 53–57.

Johnstone, M.-J. (2001). Stigma, social justice, and the rights of the mentally ill: Challenging the status quo. *Australian and New Zealand Journal of Mental Health Nursing, 10,* 200–209.

Jorm, A. F., & Griffiths, K. M. (2008). The public's stigmatizing attitudes towards people with mental disorders: How important are biomedical conceptualizations. *Acta Psychiatrica Scandinavica, 118,* 315–321.

Judge David L. Bazelon Center for Mental Health Law and National Disability Rights Network (NDRN) (2008). *VOTE. It's your right: A guide to the voting rights of people with mental disabilities.* Washington, DC: Bazelon Center for Mental Health Law.

Kessler, R. C., Chiu, W. T., Demler, O., & Walters, E. E. (2005). Prevalence, severity, and comorbidity of 12-month DSM-IV disorders in the National Comorbidity Survey Replication. *Archives of General Psychiatry, 62*, 617–627.

Kessler, R. C., Mickelson, K. D., & Williams, D. R. (1999). The prevalence, distribution, and mental health correlates of perceived discrimination in the United States. *Journal of Health and Social Behavior, 40*(3), 208–230.

Kranke, D., Floersch, J., Townsend, L., & Munson, M. (2010). Stigma experience among adolescents taking psychiatric medication. *Children and Youth Services Review, 32*, 496–505.

Landrine, H., & Klonoff, E. A. (1996). The schedule of racist events: A measure of racial discrimination and a study of its negative physical and mental health consequences. *Journal of Black Psychology, 22*(2), 144–168.

Large, M. M., Ryan, C. J., Nielssen, O. B., & Hayes, R. A. (2008). The danger of dangerousness: why we must remove the dangerousness criterion from our mental health acts. *Journal of Medical Ethics, 34*, 877–881.

Lawrence, D., Kisely, S., & Pais, J. (2010). The epidemiology of excess mortality in people with mental illness. *Canadian Journal of Psychiatry, 55*(12), 752-–760.

Leete, E. (1992).The stigmatized patient. In P. J. Fink & A. Tasman (Eds.), *Stigma and Mental Illness*. Washington, DC: American Psychiatric Press.

Link, B. G., & Phelan, J. C. (1999). Labeling and stigma. In C. Aneshensel & J. C. Phelan (Eds.), *Handbook of the sociology of mental health*. Springer Publishing: New York.

Link, B. G., & Phelan, J. C. (2001). Conceptualizing stigma. *Annual Review of Sociology, 27*, 363–385.

MacDonald, E., Sauer, K., Howie, L., & Albiston, D. (2005). What happens to social relationships in early psychoses? *Journal of Mental Health, 14*(2), 129–143.

Marie, D., & Miles, B. (2008). Social distance and perceived dangerousness across four diagnostic categories of mental disorder. *Australian and New Zealand Journal of Psychiatry, 42*, 126–133.

Marrone, J., & Golowka, E. (1999). If work makes people with mental illness sick, what do unemployment, poverty, and social isolation cause? *Psychiatric Rehabilitation Journal, 23*(2), 187–193.

Mattsson, M., Topor, A., Cullberg, J., & Forsell, Y. (2008). Association between financial strain, social network, and five-year recovery from first episode psychosis. *Social Psychiatry and Psychiatric Epidemiology, 43*, 947–952.

Miller, C. T., & Major, B. (2000). Coping with stigma and prejudice. In T. F. Heatherton, R. E. Kleck, M. R. Hebl, & J. G. Hull (Eds.), *The Social Psychology of Stigma*. New York: Guilford Press, 243–272.

Mishra, S. I., Lucksted, A., Gloia, D., Barnet, B., & Baquet, C. R. (2009). Needs and preferences for receiving mental health information in an African American focus group sample. *Community Mental Health Journal, 45,* 117–126.

Morgan, C., Burns, T., Fitzpatrick, R., Pinfold, V., & Priebe, S. (2007). Social exclusion and mental health: Conceptual and methodological review. *British Journal of Psychiatry, 191,* 477–483.

Morrissey, J. P., & Goldman, H. H. (1986). Care and treatment of the mentally ill in the United States: Historical developments and reforms. *Annals of the American Academy of Political and Social Science, 484,* 12–27.

National Advisory Mental Health Council. (1993). Health care reform for Americans with severe mental illnesses: Report of the National Advisory Mental Health Council. *American Journal of Psychiatry, 150,* 1447–1465.

National Coalition for the Homeless. (2005, July). Mental illness and homelessness. *NCH Fact sheet #5.* Washington, DC. Retrieved from: http://www.nationalhomeless.org. Nieradzik, K., & Cochrane, R. (1985). Public attitudes towards mental illness—the effects of behaviour, roles, and psychiatric labels. *International Journal of Social Psychiatry, 31,* 23–33.

Pyke, K. D. (2010). What is internalized racial oppression and why don't we study it? Acknowledging racism's hidden injuries. *Sociological Perspectives, 53*(4), 551–572.

Robert, P. (2003). Disability oppression in the contemporary U.S. capitalist workplace. *Science and Society, Summer, 67*(2), 136–159.

Roeloffs, C., Sherbourne, C., Unützer, J., Fink, A., Linqi, T., & Wells, K. B. (2003). Stigma and depression among primary care patients. *General Hospital Psychiatry, 25,* 311–315.

Ruesch, P., Graf, J., Meyer, P., Rossler, W., & Hell, D. (2004). Occupation, social support and quality of life in persons with schizophrenic or affective disorders. *Social Psychiatry and Psychiatric Epidemiology, 36,* 13–19.

Rüsch, N., Angermeyer, M. C., & Corrigan, P. W. (2005). Mental illness stigma: Concepts, consequences, and initiatives to reduce stigma. *European Psychiatry, 20,* 529–539.

Safran, S. P. (1998). The first century of disability portrayal in film: an analysis of the literature. *Journal of Special Education, 31*(4), 467–479.

Sayce, L. (2001). Social inclusion and mental health. *Psychiatric Bulletin, 25,* 121–123.

Sheppard, M. (2002). Mental health and social justice: Gender, race, and psychological consequences of unfairness. *British Journal of Social Work, 32,* 779–797.

Signorielli, N. (1989). The stigma of mental illness on television. *Journal of Broadcasting & Electronic Media, 33*(3), 325–331.

Sirey, J. A., Bruce, M. L., Alexopoulos, G. S, Perlick, D. A., Friedman, S. J., & Meyers, B. S. (2001). Perceived stigma and patient-rated severity of illness as predictors of antidepressant drug adherence. *Psychiatric Services, 52,* 1615–1620.

Smedley, A., & Smedley, Brian D. (2005). Race as biology is fiction, racism as a social problem is real. *American Psychologist, 60*(1), 16–26.

Smedley, B. D., Stith, A. Y., & Nelson, A. R. (eds.). (2003). *Unequal treatment: Confronting racial and ethnic disparities in health care*. (Committee on Understanding and Eliminating Racial and Ethnic Disparities in Health Care, Institute of Medicine). Washington, DC: National Academies Press.

Snow, N., & Austin, W. J. (2009). Community treatment orders: The ethical balancing act in community mental health. *Journal of Psychiatric and Mental Health Nursing, 16*, 177–186.

Stuart, H., & Arboleda-Flòrez, J. (2001). Community attitudes toward people with schizophrenia. *Canadian Journal of Psychiatry, 46*, 245–252.

Sue, D. W., Capodilupo, C. M., Torino, G. C., Bucceri, J. M., Holder, A. M. B., Nadal, K. L., & Esquilin, M. (2007). Racial microaggressions in everyday life. *American Psychologist, May-June, 62*(4), 271–286.

Sylvestre, J. Nelson, G., Sabloff, A., & Peddle, S. (2007). Housing for people with serious mental illness: A comparison of values and research. *American Journal of Community Psychology, 40*, 125–137.

Tappan, M. B. (2006). Reframing internalized oppression and internalized domination: From the psychological to the sociocultural. *Teachers College Record, 108*(10), 2115–2144.

Tew, J. (2011). Social factors and recovery from mental health difficulties: A review of the evidence. *Social approaches to mental distress*. New York: Palgrave MacMillan.

Thoits, P. A. (2011). Resisting the stigma of mental illness. *Social Psychology Quarterly, 74*, 6–28.

Thesen, J. (2001). Being a psychiatric patient in the community: Reclassified as the stigmatized "other." *Scandinavian Journal of Public Health, 29*, 248–255.

Thornicroft, G. (2005). *Shunned: Discrimination against people with mental illness*. New York: Oxford University Press.

U.S. Department of Health and Human Services (2001). *Mental health: Culture, race, and ethnicity. A supplement to Mental health: A report of the Surgeon General*. Washington, DC: Author. Retrieved from: www.surgeongeneral.gov/library/bookshelf18/pressrel

U.S. Department of Health and Human Services (1999). *Mental Health: A report of the Surgeon General*. Rockville, MD: Author.

U.S. Department of Health and Human Services (2011). *Mental Health: A report of the Surgeon General*. Retrieved from: www.surgeongeneral.gov/library/mentalhealth/chapter2/sec2_1.html

Van Zeist, C. (2009). Stigmatization as an environmental risk in schizophrenia. *Schizophrenia Bulletin, 35*(2), 293–296.

Wahl, O. F. (1995). *Media madness: Public images of mental illness*. New Brunswick, NJ: Rutgers University Press.

Wahl, O. F. (1999). *Telling is risky business: Mental health consumers confront stigma*. New Brunswick, NJ: Rutgers University Press.

Wahl, O. F., & Harman, C. R. (1989). Family views of stigma. *Schizophrenia Bulletin, 15*, 131–139.

Wang, P. S., Berglund, P., Olfson, M., Pincus, H. A., Wells, K. B., & Kessler, R. C. (2005). Failure and delay in initial treatment contact in the National Comorbidity Survey replication. *Archives of General Psychiatry, 62*, 603–613.

Weiden P., Ollfson, M., & Essock, S. (1997). Medication noncompliance in schizophrenia: Effects on mental health service policy. In B. Blackwell (Ed.), *Treatment compliance and the therapeutic alliance: Chronic mental illness,* Vol. 5. Amsterdam, The Netherlands: Harwood Academic Press.

Williams, D. R., Neighbors, H. W., & Jackson, J. S. (2008). Racial/ethnic discrimination and health: Findings from community studies. *American Journal of Public Health, 93*(2), 200–208.

Williams, D. R., & Williams-Morris, R. (2000). Racism and mental health: The African American experience. *Ethnicity and Health, 5*(3/4), 243–268.

Wood, J., & Edwards, K. (2005). Victimization of mentally ill patients living in the community: Is it a life-style issue? *Legal and Criminological Psychology, 10*, 279–290.

Wright, E. R., Wright, D. E., Perry, B. L., & Foote-Ardah, C. E. (2007). Stigma and the sexual isolation of people with serious mental illness. *Social Problems, 54*(1), 78–98.

Wright, P., & Kloos, B. (2007). Housing environment and mental health outcomes. *Journal of Environmental Psychology, 27*(1), 79–89.

Young, I. M. (2002). Five faces of oppression. In S. N. Asumah & I. Johnston-Anumonwo (Eds.), *Diversity, multiculturalism, and social justice.* Binghamton, NY: Global Academic Publishing, pp. 35–71.

CHAPTER TWELVE

Rethinking United States Immigration Policy, Diversity, and the Politics of Exclusion

SETH N. ASUMAH AND MATTHEW TODD BRADLEY

Introduction

The bosom of America is open to receive not only the opulent and respectable stranger, but the oppressed and persecuted of all Nations and Religions; whom we shall welcome to a participation of all our rights and privileges.

—George Washington

Some uniculturalists worry about the current wave of immigration, thinking that today's immigrants are too different from Americans. Uniculturalists fear that the immigrants will not adapt to American customs; as a consequence, the character of American society will be transformed in ways that are unfamiliar and incompatible to today's residents.

—John Isbister

Immigration policy has long been controversial in the United States and has at times been used in openly racist ways. It has become even more controversial in the new century, as a plan proposed in Congress to both tighten border security and provide a path to citizenship for estimated 11–12 million undocumented aliens already present in the United States failed in 2007 amid opposition from both sides. . . . Afterwards, for the first time, the United States began to construct a fence along its border with Mexico to keep people out.

—John E. Farley

The discourse over the U.S. immigration policy in recent years like other "wedge" issues such as unemployment, racism, sexism, classism, and crime evoke cultural, racial, and socioeconomic disquietudes. Immigration issues, of late, have been made even more contentious with quasi-political parties and social movements like the Tea Party, and by state legislatures such as Alabama, Arizona, California, and New Mexico. Moreover, since the 2008 election (and reelection in 2012) of U.S. President Barack Obama, the stakes have been raised even higher, with his calls for "level-headedness" and "fairness" in any discussions regarding immigration. Nonetheless, the 2012 Republican Party presidential primary debates were submerged in name-calling over U.S. immigration policy as Mitt Romney accused Newt Gingrich for labeling him as anti-immigrant and Gingrich, former Speaker of the House, lashed back at Romney, former Massachusetts governor, about running an advertisement in which Gingrich called Spanish "the language of the ghetto" (Fox News Latino, 2012). Issues involving illegal Latino have topped the chart in those debates, yet a number of the Republican presidential candidates, including Newt Gingrich, had been too busy talking about voluntary deportation or what to do with 11 million undocumented grandmothers who may have lived in the United States all their lives—an important but not the most serious issue and perhaps, politicking with the topic by circumventing the most critical issues about U.S. immigration policy.. Thus, immigration issues have gained a centripetal position in policy debates because the number of foreign-born, non-European persons has reached the highest level in the United States' history. According to studies, the nation's immigrant population, both legal and illegal, reached 37.9 in 2007, making it one in every eight United States citizens an immigrant (Center for Immigration Studies, 2007, pp. 1–2). Nonetheless the characterization of Black and Brown people from Latin America, Africa, and Asia as depriving United States citizens of jobs, and tainting the American national ethos, culture, and norms is at best unfounded and at worst a uniculturalist agenda against new sojourners and multiculturalists.

It is indubitable that newer immigrants are coming to America in numbers that are only rivaled by that of the beginning of the twentieth century. It is also a truism that the immigrants who arrived in this country at the beginning of the century were overwhelmingly White Europeans, and now the majority of immigrants are non-Whites, they are Black and Brown persons from mostly "developing" countries.

The new immigration wave is generating a backlash of antagonism for reasons that are racial, ethnic, cultural, political, and partially economic. For all these reasons, indeed, there is an eminent need to re-examine the United States' immigration and naturalization policies. Nevertheless, the urgency to re-evaluate these policies is submerged in an unclear debate between advocates of *laissez entre* (free entry) and those who support strict scrutiny in immigration policy.

In the balance of this essay, we will argue that the immigration problem has not reached epidemic proportions yet, and the economic deprivation thesis is a façade developed by uniculturalists to reinvent the failed and unworkable "melting pot" idea in order to derail the efforts of multiculturalists in giving value, meaning, and respect to the diversity and national ethos of the United State. Also, we will present the argument that even though most of the recent immigrants have low skills and are far less educated than native-born Americans, neo-sojourners are assets to the underground economy and continue to accept jobs in areas that native borns refuse to accept.

Neo-sojourners, for the purpose of this chapter, are immigrants who arrived in the United States from 1990 onward. This part of the immigration argument is even more confusing because it transcends the limit of the liberal/conservative debate, where liberals are pro-multicultural and open door policy advocates, and conservatives are uniculturalists who want severe restriction on immigration. In this aspect, there are liberal trade unionists who believe that immigrants are used as instruments for lowering wage levels. Interestingly, conservative free-market enthusiasts and corporate elites remain some of the strongest supporters of increased immigration because they benefit from cheap labor the most. The immigration issue therefore is a mixed bag of labor economics, racism, ethnicity, nationality, multiculturalism, uniculturalism, facts/policy dichotomy, diversity in general and the future of America's national ethos. Thus, one cannot limit it to economic questions alone. All the other variables must be examined in order to fully comprehend the United States' immigration policy and why some analysts claim it is a failed policy. The problem is not of recent origin, even though the composition of immigrants and their places of origin changed in the latter part of the twentieth century. If from the 1880s America has pursued an unrealistic policy and has fallen victim to some philosophical "isms," then this is the time to face the realities of world conditions (including globalization) that continue to affect both legal and illegal immigration.

To support the arguments presented above, we will briefly track the historical perspectives of the United States' immigration policy, examine the economic argument, explain the relevance of legal, illegal, and humanitarian immigration and how they create the fact/

policy dichotomy, and then relate them to the multicultural/unicultural positions. The concluding paragraphs will attempt to provide some solutions to the problem of United States immigration policy. The impact of the past on present events cannot be ruled out. American history recounts the nature of United States immigration policy from the inception of this country. The succeeding section will therefore discuss how history has modeled or shaped the United States' immigration policy.

From Anglo Exclusivity to the
Arrival of Blacks and Brown People

Early in the history of the United States of America, Thomas Jefferson and other political leaders of the country recognized the benefit of large-scale immigration. This form of immigration provided cheap labor to build the nation, technology for reconstruction, and trade that provided fuel for the economy at that time. U.S. immigration policy followed an open door approach, where immigrants were not restricted from entering into this country. From 1875, the United States Congress instituted measures for excluding certain categories of people. Among these people were prostitutes, criminals, the disabled, and people who had the chance of becoming a public charge (Mitchell, 1992, p. 11). Many of these immigrant categories still remain on the books today as part of U.S. immigration law.

In a similar manner, the laws that applied to the groups mentioned above were extended to racial and ethnic groups also. The United States' first significant restrictions of free immigration were the Chinese Exclusion Act of 1882, and the Japanese Exclusion Act of 1907, which were examples of these racially based acts (AAC&U, 1994). Also, these acts were the results of the feeling among native-born Americans that Chinese laborers were racially inferior and must be restricted from entering this country (AAC&U, 1994). There was a similar sentiment about Japanese immigrants. The racially motivated acts later on generated economic implications. The Chinese Exclusion Act prohibited the entry of Chinese laborers for 10 years (Daniels, 1993); this ban was made permanent in 1902. Thus, Chinese were the first ethnic group to be excluded, in the so-called melting pot of America. Daniels (1993), further notes that it can be argued that the 1882 Exclusion Act was the hinge on which all future U.S. immigration policy rested on. Up until 1924, the once free and unrestricted immigration policy of the United States was systematically curtailed on economic, cultural, and political grounds. California workers claimed Asian workers who already faced discrimination here were paid poorly and employers gave preference to these poorly paid workers over native born workers in order to save money.

As the Japanese population in America rose to 72,000 by 1910, with more than 40,000 in California alone (Daniels, 1993), a strong appeal for a Japanese exclusion act was created by the U.S. Congress. With the growing Japanese military leading up to World War I, the U.S. government created a so-called Gentlemen's Agreement of 1907/1908, which curbed but did not stop the immigration of the Japanese. E. P. Hutchinson (1981) later aptly called a 1917 immigration law "an unmistakable declaration of a white immigration policy." The 1917 amendment excluded most Asian immigrants (except Japanese and Filipinos) under a barred zone provision. The 1924 Immigration Act dubbed "To Limit the Immigration of Aliens into the United States" was passed by the U.S. Congress and stood with no significant changes until 1943. With several appeals on previous Chinese immigrant policies, the liberalization of U.S. immigration laws did not occur until 1952–1965 (especially 1965, as it pertained to Black and Brown prospective immigrants).

In 1965, the Amendment to the Immigration and Naturalization Act (which sought to eliminate several highly discriminatory clauses of earlier immigration laws and to regulate the influx of immigrants by setting up a system of preference categories within the general quota) backfired on the United States with an unexpected increase of Black and Brown immigrants especially from Mexico, the Caribbean Basin, South Asia, and Southeast Asia (Report on the Americas, 1992). For instance, primarily as a result of the post-1965 Immigration Act, as of the 1990 census, the two largest Asian American ethnic groups are the Chinese and Filipinos. The 1965 act's emphasis on family reunification, had sought to ensure that the bulk of new immigrants would come from those regions that had already sent large numbers to the United States, primarily Europe, which meant not many Black and Brown immigrants.

What happened by the end of the 1800s and the early 1900s is repeating itself today. Conservative corporatists, ironically, fought to maintain immigration while liberal unionists were much against immigrants because of waged labor economics. Several laws were passed in 1921, 1924, and 1927. The main objective for these laws was to place a numerical limit to all migration. Nonetheless, the laws had Eurocentric preferences in that Western Europeans had a greater chance of receiving entry visas than people from other regions. Southern and Eastern Europeans were affected negatively by these laws because their political cultures and tradition were somewhat different from those of Europeans from the West. While a quota system was developed and applied to other regions of the world, Western Europe was exempted from this system. So, the National Origin Act of 1924 was designed to support Eurocentric immigration preferences while it discriminated against non-Europeans (AAC&U, 1994). If the policy affected eastern and southern Europeans, it did so because members of the Ku Klux Klan, the Progressive Party, and influential eugenicists formed an alliance to give an ethnic and religious meaning and justification to the policy's objective (AAC&U, 1994). Of course, the depression of the 1930s, with its economic implications, affected many immigrants. Even legal immigration was reduced by a startling 87% and over 400,000 persons were returned to Mexico as victims of a repatriation campaign that transpired between 1931 and 1939 (Hoffman, 1974). Even as over 400,000 Mexican Americans were being returned, the United States admitted over 85,000 European refugees (Hoffman, 1974). In the 1950s, the mean-spiritedness of McCarthyism influenced the immigration laws. Concomitant with the residue of the "Red Scare," the 1950 Internal Security Act made present and past membership in organizations defined as oppressive and totalitarian targets for exclusion. A reaffirmation of the discriminatory practices of the "national origin" system prevailed throughout the 1950s. In addition to these acts, the United States Congress created a complex system of favoring skilled workers, especially from European countries, relatives of United States citizens, and families of registered aliens in the country (Divine, 1957). During these times, as David Reiner (1985) carefully notes, health, literacy, and vagrancy regulations often served instead of quotas, enforcing congressional wishes to limit immigration from the Caribbean and Latin America.

The immigration policy of who was "fit" or "unfit" to settle in America remained in force until the Immigration and Naturalization Act of 1965 came into effect. This act served as one of the pillars of laws that would challenge past justification for denying people of color visas to the United States. The act, signed by President Johnson, was concomitant with world publicity and fanfare. Symbolism has always remained a good partner with American politics, so the act was signed at the base of the Statue of Liberty. The Jewish woman poet, Emma Lazarus, whose poem was used as the inscription at the base of the Statue, "Give me your tired, your poor, your huddled of masses yearning to breathe free . . . ," may have smiled in her grave during the signing of the 1965 Act. One should bear in mind the events that transpired in the early 1960s, especially 1964.

America, at this time, was becoming conscious and it was a critical time to re-examine its national ethos, race and ethnic relations. The 1965 Act abolished the National Origin system of 1924. For the first time, this law provided a ceiling on visas granted to Western Europeans. But as the number of legal immigrants grew because of a somewhat liberalized policy, illegal immigration also increased. America would then look for measures to tighten the process of gaining entry into the country. After several years of debate and politicking, the Immigration Reform and Control Act of 1986 came into effect.

This Immigration Reform and Control Act (IRCA), even though it did little to alter the overall framework of immigration policy, established the basis for dealing with illegal immigrants, many of whom were Brown, Black, and "Yellow" people. The IRCA was a compromise between the advocates of the rights of undocumented immigrants and minority groups, on the one hand, and those who believed that America has lost control over its borders, on the other hand. The first group wanted amnesty and nondiscriminatory practices in the workplace for immigrants. The second group wanted increased resources for the U.S. Border Patrol and sanctions on employers who hired illegal immigrants. While the IRCA was more concerned about illegals, the pool for legal citizens increased substantially between 1986 and 1990, until the 1990 Immigration Act was enacted.

Furthermore, furor over illegal immigration led to a series of congressional proposals that resulted in the Immigration Reform and Control Act (IRCA) of 1986 under the Reagan Administration (Hoffman, 1974). This law contained a limited regularization program in which undocumented aliens or illegals that could prove their continuous residence in the United States before January 1, 1982, and meet certain other strict eligibility criteria could legalize their status. The law also contained sanctions against employers who knowingly hired undocumented workers, and an extended guest worker program designed to ensure a continuing and abundant supply of cheap labor for agriculture (Hoffman, 1974). Such a scenario was another tool of social control which primarily benefitted agribusiness, but did little to ensure the political participation and integration of newer immigrants into American society.

A recent development in U.S. immigration policy was the Immigration Act (IMMACT) of 1990. This contribution was designed to reduce competition for visas and additional backlogs in the preference system (Yale-Loehr, 1991). IMMACT created a new selection procedure by increasing the annual worldwide numerical limit to 366,000 immigrants, revising the visa preference system, and implementing a three track system based on family ties, employment, or diversity (Yale-Loehr, 1991).

The 1990 Immigration Act could simply change the inscription at the base of the Statue of Liberty to "Give me your rich, your smart, and your movers and shakers," because it makes provision for the rich and powerful who are willing to invest a million dollars in a new business in America to gain easy entry into the country. The 1990 Act nonetheless increased the numbers of eligible immigrants, changed the priority categories, reduced the political and ideological grounds for deporting aliens, and made changes in all aspects of the United States' immigration laws.

Interestingly, the 1990 Act provided a section under "diversity." But the law's characterization of diversity was not the same as multiculturalists define it. The law's diversity only referred to adversely affected countries (Isbister, 1996, p. 67). Isbister (1996) correctly asserts:

These include many of the predominantly white countries of northern and Western Europe that once provided most of the American immigrants; those immigrants' flows are now so far in the past that the remaining kinship ties are too distant to allow for family reunification under U.S. law. Thanks mostly to Senator Kennedy's interest in the subject, fully 40 percent of the diversity visas were allocated to Ireland for the period 1992 through 1994. (p. 67)

Enough for diversity! Immigrants today mostly come not from Europe, but from the Third World, with Mexico sending most people to the United States. Mexico shares a 2,000-mile border with the United States, and it has sent people across its shifting northern border at least since the time that statistics were first gathered. From 1961 through 1993, over 4 million Mexicans arrived legally in this country (U.S. Immigration Fact Sheet, 1996). Most Mexicans came to the United States through California and Texas. Paradoxically, both California and Texas were formerly part of Mexico (Isbister, 1996, p. 67).

Central America and the Caribbean Islands have been also sending many more immigrants than ever. These immigrants come from such countries as the Dominican Republic, El Salvador, Guatemala, Haiti, the Bahamas, Nicaragua, and Cuba (U.S. Immigration Facts Sheet, 1997). The largest group of Asian immigrants, in recent times comes from the Philippines. Filipinos arrived here at the beginning of the twentieth century. When the United States annexed the Philippines after the Spanish/American War of 1898, the Filipinos were considered American nationals until they attained their independence on July 4, 1946, when visas were required of them.

A more recent immigration policy focused on how to effectively enforce United States' immigration laws. The architects of this policy were more interested in deporting undocumented aliens and tightening U.S. borders. The 1996 immigration policy required employers to be tougher on immigrants during their hiring practices. Verification of immigration status for prospective employees was a major part of this policy. Curbing the usage of fraudulent documents by immigrants was one aspect of the 1996 immigration policy. In addition, the policy enabled more border patrol agents to be hired for strengthening the enforcement of the laws especially between United States and Mexico and at the U.S.–Canadian borders.

Many attempts at creating a comprehensive immigration reform have failed and the 2007 major attempt is not an exception. The 2007 policy would have included five major essential areas: (1) security increase through the funding and hiring of 20,000 border patrol officers, new fences, and vehicle barriers at high crossing areas of U.S. borders; (2) creating procedures to expedite the process of permanent residency and citizenship for undocumented aliens through a new "Z-visa" system with a waiting period of eight years before obtaining a "green card.—yet these undocumented must return to the countries of origin and pay a fine of between $2,000 and $5,000 for beating the system and remaining in the United States illegally; (3) a guest-worker program under a new "Y-visa" would have been created to enable immigrants who would like to work and stay in the country for two years to do so legally; (4) the law would have eliminated dependent family members of U.S. citizens, except for spouses and children; and (5) the policy would have integrated the DREAM Act, which would have allowed undocumented immigrant children to complete college or render their services to the United States Department of Defense (Farley, 2012, p. 500).

Uniculturalists were the majority of law makers who killed the bill because they argued that the new policy would have granted amnesty to too many illegal immigrants and that would have been a bad signal for those who are attempting to enter the country illegally. Nevertheless, those who favored the bill argued that it was designed to temporarily repatriate undocumented immigrants who must pay a fine before their readmission to the United States. All in all, most United States citizens did not support the bill because they did not believe it would curb immigration and the state of U.S. economy and the new wave xenophobia and Islamophobia did not serve the bill favorably. Immigrants, both documented and undocumented, continue to make their way to the United States nevertheless. Yet as Belson and Capuzzo (2007) correctly note, the failure of the United States Congress to reach an agreement on a new immigration reform act has given incentives to especially anti-immigrant Border States within the Union to generate their own policies, which are generally xenophobic in nature. Below, in Table 12.1, we examine selected country data regarding immigrants to the United States, in the years, 2001, 2006, and the most recent data (2010).

The foreign-born labor force in the United States jumped from about 13% in 2000 to about 16% in 2007 (Organization for Economic Cooperation and Development (OECD), 2010). This increase can be partly explained in the growth of the Internet and e-commerce businesses, which require a highly skilled workforce, including engineers, software designers, and computer scientists. Many of these workers were emigrating from "developing" countries such as India and China. Thus, the rethinking of U.S. immigration policy began to take on even more pressing business needs and subsequently the economic implications of widening the net or loosening the immigration requirements for our economy, as it relates to supply and demand. Moreover, state governments have had to reconsider (or reconfigure) their politics of exclusion, while at the same time consider economic growth in their states, which means foreign investors and foreign-born brain power.

Table 12.1. Top 12 Origins of Immigrants to the United States

Country	2001	2006	2010
China	56,267	87,307	70,863
Cuba	27,453	45,614	33,573
Dominican Republic	21,195	38,068	53,870
Ethiopia	5,092	16,152	14,266
India	70,032	61,369	69,162
Jamaica	15,322	24,976	19,825
Mexico	205,560	173,749	139,120
Nigeria	8,253	13,459	13,276
Philippines	52,919	74,606	58,173
Russia	20,313	13,159	6,718
Ukraine	20,914	17,140	8,477
Vietnam	35,419	30,691	30,692

Source: From the United States Citizenship and Immigration Services and Department of Homeland Security, Office of Immigration Statistics, Washington, DC, 2010.

When we examine the 2001 data, there were increases in ethnic and racial foreign-born populations, some much more significant than others, for example, populations from Mexico and the Philippines far exceeded other parts of the world. As well, when we "fast forward" to 10 years later (2010), we see that foreign-born citizens comprised 36,750 of the entire United States population (U.S. Census Bureau, Current Population Survey, 2010). More specifically, foreign-born residents primarily emigrated from Latin America, especially Mexico (out of the 19,882 foreign-born citizens, over 11,615 came from Mexico). An additional 9,925 persons emigrated from the continent of Asia, 4,572 from the continent of Europe and another 2,371 emigrated from the continent of Africa. These findings suggest that "browning" and "yellowing" of America is continuing and that the politics of exclusion will continue to manifest in various public policies, whether those policies are as blatant as Arizona's recent legislation, only time will tell. By 2025, according to census projections, Blacks, Browns, and "Yellows" combined will balance out the White population in the United States. What would these projections do to policies and programs in a nation state that has never had those who were historically oppressed to have a greater say in policy formulation because of their numerical preponderance?

Brief Analyses/Interpretations of the Trends

As we continue to witness growth rates in Black, Brown, and "Yellow" subjects in the United States, there are parallel trends to New Reaganism, a type of highly decentralized state government interpretations of the 14th Amendment of the U.S. Constitution. That is, states are becoming much more "radical" in their approach in defining who is a legal resident of the said state, what constitutes requirements of that particular state and the types of enforcement mechanisms should be employed to halt the tide of these "other" people. Further, growing numbers of nativists are being attracted to social movements such as the Tea Party, which tout so-called American virtues, which de facto means that any foreigner should perhaps be much more scrutinized under the guise of "protecting our way of life," regardless of the federal interpretation of the 14th Amendment and federal laws prohibiting discrimination based on race, color, and national origin.

Neo-Reaganism also has judicial implications, such that the current make-up of the U.S. Supreme Court is much more likely to side with states' rights, which unfortunately harkens back to the days whereby civil rights and civil liberties take a backseat to "knee jerk" reactionary movements. While the number of foreign-born persons in the United States is at the apogee of all times, the share of the general populace that is foreign-born is much lower than it was throughout the 1870–1920 period—8% at the present and 15% in the 1920s (Passel and Fix, 1994). Since 1965, there have been 20 million people admitted to the United States, but 85% of them gained legal entry into the country (INS Facts Sheet, 1996). Therefore, the facts remain that most immigrants come to this country with the blessing of America. The characteristics of immigrants and their impact on the nation always find a place in the immigration debate. The following section looks at the qualities and values of neo-sojourners.

Characteristics of Neo-Sojourners

The prevailing argument about the shift in the origins of recent immigrants is that they do not bring the same "quality" of characteristics as their European counterparts. Using a conventional criterion such as education, one may realize that in the 1980s about one third of legal immigrants at the age 25 and over had college degrees compared to 20% of native-born Americans (Passel and Fix, 1994). Only one fourth of the legal immigrants had less than a high school diploma, a slightly higher number than that of the native population, and that is the trouble area.

Yet, in 2009, 9% of native-born United States citizens have less than high school education compared to 31% neo-sojourners. Twenty-eight percent of native-born citizens versus 22% of neo-sojourners are high school graduates; 33% of native-born U.S. citizens have some college education compared to 19% of neo-sojourners, and 20% native-

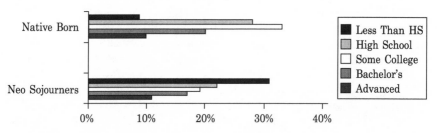

Figure 12.1. Educational Levels of Native-Born and Neosojourners, 2009. *Source:* From American Community Surveys, 2009. Decennial Censuses, Current Population Survey, 2011.

born United States citizens have acquired a bachelor's degree versus 17% of immigrants. In the area of advanced degrees, the numbers are almost even, but there are slightly more neo-sojourners with master's and doctoral degrees (11%) than U.S. citizens (10%).

If the 1980s possessed encouraging news for immigrants, the 1990s contained a sort of mixed baggage, and the 2000s are even worse. The United States' census figures show that both the immigrants and the native population had similar college or advanced degrees, and it is even better for those who arrived in the middle 1990s. Nonetheless, the picture is very bleak when it comes to low-level education. About 1.3 million people entered the United States with less than a high school education since 1990 (see chart, U.S. Census Bureau Data, 1996). In the 2009 Census data 31% of immigrants entered the United States with less than high school education. A case is presented that the low-level-educated immigrants also have low skills and are easy to submerge into a pool of poverty. But as Braining and Constable (1997) write: "Much of the current influx of poor immigrants stems from a 1986 amnesty law that legalized 2.68 million illegal aliens, who then sought to bring relatives" (p. 8).

If this trend continues for new immigrants, will the new citizens become marginalized and/or complacent in the political process? If this occurs, what friction and policies will the status quo "bestow" on the Black and Brown population just as they did and continue to do? For example, will we see more gerrymandering, and more "redlining" by financial institutions such as banks, who believe that such populations (Black and Brown) do not have the political will and political clout to challenge such mayhem?

Many low skilled neo-sojourners are caught in the service economy with dead-end jobs. Such jobs offer only minimal mobility upward. As indicated in the chart above, foreign born arriving after 1990 have a poverty rate of 33.3% compared to 12.9% of native born. Neo-sojourners arriving after 1990 have household incomes that fall 7% below those of native born. However, immigrants who arrived in the 1980s have comparable or significantly higher household income. According to the 1990 census, immigrants earned more than $285 billion in 1989, or about 8% of the total income the United States. This is the same percentage of the general immigrant population share of the total United States population (8%). Yet studies in 2007 indicate that it takes between 28 to 32 years for the average immigrant to match the earning levels of native-born United States citizen (Center for Immigration Studies, 2007). Thus, foreign-born immigrants tend to work three times harder to chase the American dream. Furthermore, immigrants who arrived here about 27 years ago are around 48 years old on the average, and 11 years older than their native-born cohorts. This calculation means these immigrants will generally not earn as much as the native born in their lifetime in the United States.

Nevertheless, immigrants arriving after 1970 pay a total of $70 billion in taxes, while using only $40 billion in public services (Passel and Fix, 1994). Immigrants therefore represent a net fiscal plus to the United States economy. They generate a total surplus of $30 billion to the United States economy. So, the charges that immigrants are a burden on the United States' economy are not quite correct. Even the unskilled and semiskilled immigrants help both the underground economy and aspects of the formal economy where native born would not seek employment. Opponents against immigration argue that immigrants do not pay their fair share in taxes, and they are parasites on the economy. Yet the story is not quite correct. The Advocates for Human Rights note: "Left out is the massive contribution to the economy made by immigrants: nationwide Hispanic business owners alone provided jobs of an estimated 1.5 million employees, had receipts of over $222 billion, and generated $36.7 billion payroll dollars in 2002 alone. In addition, the roughly 26 million immigrants now in the U.S. who arrived after the age of 18 represent a windfall of roughly $2.8 trillion to U.S. taxpayers" (Advocates for Human Rights, 2012).

An aspect of fiscal impacts of immigration that is particularly contentious is immigrants' use of public assistance. It is a truism that some immigrants receive welfare benefits, but it is important to distinguish between immigrants on the basis of how they gain entry into this country. Most illegal immigrants constantly run away from the law and they would be reluctant to go to the Department of Social Services to apply for welfare benefits. They just do not engage in activities that could easily reveal their illegal status. However, welfare use among immigrants is concentrated among refugees. Nonetheless, refugees are eligible for benefits from the very moment the United States government gives them permission to reside in this country. Nondocumented immigrants do not engage in activities that could easily reveal their illegal status. However, welfare use among immigrants is concentrated among refugees. Nonetheless, refugees are eligible for benefits from the very moment the United States government gives them permission to reside in this country.

Aside from refugees, elderly legal immigrants without sufficient social security benefits do depend on welfare. Welfare use among working-age immigrants between the ages of 15 and 64 is extremely low (Advocates for Human Rights, 2012).

Poverty Rate

Native/Foreign Born

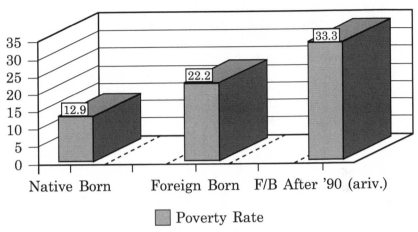

Figure 12.2. Poverty Rate. *Source:* From United States Citizenship and Immigration Services (formerly INS) Fact Sheet, 1996.

With the discussion above in mind, one would be puzzled about the economic deprivation thesis that immigrants are invading the American job market and are "taking" jobs away from native-born citizens. Such charges are not new. California workers accused Chinese immigrants of the 1800s of similar charges. The problem is that whenever the country fails to create job avenues, it is easier to put the blame on the defenseless immigrants. Passel and Fix (1994) firmly contend: "Recent worries over the economic impact of immigrants have been exacerbated by the failure of the U.S. economy to expand employment between 1989 and 1992. . . . of course, since 1992 the economy has grown rapidly and 1.7 million jobs were added in 1993 alone, so the view of immigrations effects may improve in the near future" (p. 153).

Also, studies using aggregate statistics attained from the United States Census Bureau indicate that immigrants have no meaningful job displacement effect on native borns. The same statistics indicate that immigrants have only a small effect on wages, varying from place to place, and depending on the vitality of the local economy of a particular area. In weak local economies, immigrants have a small negative effect on low-skilled native-born citizens, while in strong local economies, immigrants do increase economic opportunities for native borns.

Much of the debate has focused on wages, employment, and public finance. But as labor economist Vernon Briggs (1990) notes, America may well have been built by unskilled labor in the past, but employment needs are changing and the demand for unskilled labor is falling, just at the time when unskilled Blacks and Latino Americans are desperately looking for jobs. The arrival of large numbers of unskilled immigrants after 1990 only makes the task for the two minority groups harder. The public finance and wage aspects have been discussed in this essay and the evidence that immigrants are burdensome to public finance is not conclusive. Nevertheless, some states carry an uneven burden when immigration in the United States is concerned. The succeeding sections will examine why some states appear to be very much against the recent wave of immigrants into the United States.

Where Do They Go?

To fully answer the question, where do they go? the question of why they come to the United States must be tackled. In a way, the answer is obvious. Immigrants of today are no different from immigrants of yesteryears. The important answer here is that both earlier immigrants and recent ones left their homelands primarily to improve their socioeconomic well-being, raise their standard of living, and to provide more promising opportunities for their children. The attractiveness of the United States to immigrants is at least partly its prosperity. This pattern is not unusual, because England and many European countries during their times of prosperity have attracted immigrants too.

People move to the United States for a variety of reasons. Some immigrants leave their homeland for good; others leave for only a brief time. Some immigrants are from the poorest nations of the world, others from prosperous ones. The destinations of all immigrants are the final point of concern for this section of the essay. Ideological and cultural links are as important as economic ones so far as destinations are concerned. As communications and media links have expanded in Mexico and many Third World countries, immigrants from these areas have been drawn increasingly to the United States.

This type of immigration is influenced by sociocultural elements and the U.S. economy to which the immigrants move. Even though some immigrants reside in rural areas, the majority of today's immigrants come to the cities not rural areas. The leading states with immigrants arriving after 2000 include California with 27% of all immigrants, New York with 11%; Texas with 10%; Florida, 10%; New Jersey 5%; and the rest of the 44 states have only 39% combined (see The Immigration Chart, INS Facts Sheet, 2007). The top states that attract immigrants remain the same. California has 28%, New York, 12%; Texas, 9%; Florida, 9%; New Jersey, 5%; and Illinois, 5%. The rest of the United States accounts for 32% of all immigrants (Fix and Passel, 2002, pp. 179–203). The state of California has gained some relief from the 1990s, however, the states with the fastest-growing immigrant population are North Carolina, Georgia, Nevada, Arkansas, Utah, Tennessee, Nebraska, Colorado, and Arizona. More recently, states like Arizona and Nevada have seen 20–25% increases in their populations (which undoubtedly have included foreign-born persons) during the period of 2000–10 (U.S. Census, 2010).

If the State of California has taken the initiative in restricting immigrants from coming to the United States, it is because it shoulders much of the burden for the immigration problem. The six

The Immigration Chart

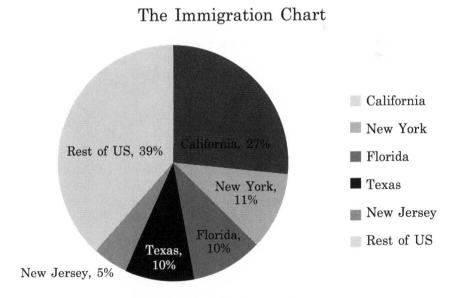

Figure 12.3. The Immigrant Chart: Top Five States Where Immigrants Reside.

leading states do need new strategies and federal grants to tackle their immigration problems. Even at the local level, the politics of diversity and immigration is even more transparent than years past. For example, Delray Beach, located in Palm Beach County in South Florida is a haven for Haitian immigrants. Approximately one third to one fourth of Delray Beach's 51,000 residents is from Haiti (Millman, 1997). Further, per capita, no city in America is more Haitian than Delray Beach (Millman, 1997). Despite the statistics above, the immigration problem has not reached epidemic proportions yet. The public frustration based on solely economic analysis is unfounded and must be transcended.

A combination of factors, including fear of ethnic conflicts, loss of a common language, culture, and national ethos have all increased the public's so-called frustration and have helped to create a new agenda for uniculturalists. Multiculturalists therefore naturally react to the position of uniculturalists on the immigration question. The next section will briefly examine the culture wars on immigration.

Multicultural America and Immigration

Unlike earlier immigrants for whom English was their linguae Francae, if one includes all the illegals, Spanish becomes the language of half of all recent immigrants. Spanish has become a de facto second language of America, and Latinos are beginning to develop political muscle. The frustration is again demonstrated by advocacy to end affirmative action in California. For example, California voters instituted Proposition 187 (known as Save Our State or SOS) in 1994, and more recently Proposition 209 (an antiaffirmative action measure in higher education). Proposition 187 was voted into law as a tool to deny publicly funded education, public health services (except for emergency care) to suspected illegal immigrants and their children (Orenstein, 1995). Many supporters of this measure believed that the illegal immigrants were the primary burden on the social welfare system of the state, yet statistics reveal otherwise, that illegal immigrants pay more in taxes than they consume in social services (Passel, Clark, & Griego, 1994). Ironically, tax-payers' money is being utilized to file the lawsuits that challenge the proposition. As a result of this measure (Proposition 187), not only are illegal immigrants denied basic human needs, but they are also denied the opportunity to participate in the political process to make necessary changes that will lessen their plight.

The U.S. border policies in recent years have all had one thing in common; they (policies) fail to stop illegal immigration. In fact, immigration continues to increase prodigiously, especially among Mexicans. The United States Census Bureau calculated that Mexican immigration quintupled between 1970 and 1988 (Gibney, 1989). Upward of nine million immigrants came to the United States in the 1980s, and somewhere between 200,000 and one million enter illegally each year; 55% of them are thought to be Mexican nationals (Gibney, 1989). The proximity of Mexico to the United States has presented a challenge that needs careful thinking for policy formulation. Mexico cannot be physically moved from its present location, and the United States cannot be reconstructed to change its current location, so the United States' foremost line of defense against illegal entry is to build a fence up and down the U.S.–Mexican border, another aspect of the politics of exclusion.

Fencing America's Borders and the Politics of Exclusion

The U.S. immigration policy to create a physical barrier between the United States and Mexico with a 670-miles concrete wall has generated another philosophical and diversity debate. The Secure Fence Act of 2006, which has been revised several times as follows: it separates the two nation states, divides United States public opinion about illegal immigration, and creates a philosophical debate about United States perception toward our neighbors to the south. As interlocutors of the border policy continue their debate, proponents of the policy have called the project a "fence," while opponents have labeled it a "wall." Whether it is a fence or a wall, the facts remain that the United States has built a structure that divides the United States and Mexico. The Associated Press opinion poll conducted in March 2008 indicated that Americans are split right in the middle about the 14-foot high border fence; 49% of those who were polled were in favor, and 48% were against it. Nevertheless, 55% of respondents maintain that the wall will not make a difference in deterring illegal immigrants (Public Affairs, 2008).

The states of Texas, New Mexico, Arizona, and California are sharing the 670-mile-fence with nearly half of it in the state of Arizona. About 370 miles of the immigration wall is aimed at stopping Mexicans who attempt to walk or sneak through the border, and the other 300 miles is to deter unauthorized vehicles from crossing the U.S.–Mexican border at the fence in the states mentioned above (Chertoff, 2008). Proponents of the fence maintain that it is not only deterrence to illegal immigrants, but it will also prevent terrorist from entering the United States through Mexico. Yet, James Carafano, a senior defense and counterterrorism analyst points out that the augment about the wall/fence stopping terrorist from entering the United States through Mexico is farfetched and unfounded. Carafano asserts, "Fixating, myopically on the wall is just bad public policy. . . . Looking for terrorists by standing watch on the border is stupid. It's looking for a needle in a haystack" (*Congressional Quarterly*, 2011, p. 184). It is indubitable that the wall's primary goal is to deter undocumented Mexicans in particular and illegal immigrants in general from entering the United States, opponents continue to argue that the terrorism argument is just a smoke screen in the politics of exclusion. Nevertheless, wall or no wall, the magnetic attraction of the United States to Mexicans will not stop until the quality of life in Mexico and especially the border towns has improved substantially. When people are desperate to improve their quality of life, they will do anything to make it happen. As most Mexican dwellers of the border towns will say, "show me a 12-foot wall and I will show you a 16-foot ladder."

An interesting but troubling observation is that national statistics reveal that the difference in the prefence and postfence apprehensions at border remain roughly the same, 1.2 million people in both 1992 and 2004 (Kariam, 2011, p. 185). This means we have to do more about immigration policy that would encourage our neighbors across the border to stay home instead of risking their lives and coming to the United States to be excluded and exploited. Furthermore, with the cost estimate of $47 billion to maintain the fence for the next 25 years (Kariam, 2012, p. 200), it makes sense to jointly develop a program for guest workers and attractive job avenues with the billions mentioned above. These programs could yield revenue from investment in jobs instead of being mean neighbors with a fence that psychologically screams at to the rest of the world, Keep Out!

Furthermore, if such policies continue to fail, what alternatives should the U.S. pursue? Or as Donato (1994) posits, "Understanding the consequences of immigration policy also entails study of the causes of policy formation." Donato (1994) further opines that further research in this area reconciles economic development with sociological insights about migration, which should enable practical policy reform (Donato, 1994). All segments of society must be able to fully integrate into United States society, which includes political participation.

Political participation in civil society is crucial for any society, especially a democracy such as the United States. An early proponent of political participation was Samuel Huntington. Although he is a giant in advocating political participation, he too practiced jingoism and ethnocentrism (just as U.S. immigration policy does) nicely when it came to immigrants, especially Latino immigrants (1993). For example, Huntington (1993) asserts that, "In the past, the United States has successfully absorbed millions of immigrants from scores of countries because they adapted to the prevailing European culture and enthusiastically embraced the American creed of liberty, equality, individualism, and democracy. Will this pattern continue to prevail as 50 percent of the population becomes Hispanic or nonwhite?"

Racism and political disenfranchisement coincide nicely with current U.S. immigration policy when it comes to Black and Brown prospects. There is a deeper sense of national disillusion, more than mere economics; a national identity crisis is causing what Peter Andreas (1994) calls a sort of bunker mentality and inciting xenophobic tendencies. As was mentioned previously, these same demagogues often overlook the many contributions of immigrants to the United States. Political participation by immigrant groups certainly helps to propel the governmental "machinery" at the local, county, state, and federal levels. But immigrants also contribute in more obvious, visible ways. As Millman (1997) finds out, Black and Brown immigrants reclaim urban neighborhoods, start family businesses, revitalize neglected industries and services, and raise their standard of living.

The African American "community" in the United States is undergoing major demographic changes because of immigration, which in turn highlights greater ethnic diversity and multicultural issues, but at the same time creates tremendous opportunities for policy makers. Various ethnic/racial groups make up large segments, in the African American "communities." For example, various groups from the Caribbean, South America, and Africa now occupy part of the Black "melting pot." The growth of these ethnic/racial groups is strengthening and challenging traditional American views of race, thereby creating new tensions in the society. However, Black immigrants find new challenges and obstacles to overcome as they settle in America. But, some find many resources, and strategies to survive and sustain themselves. This phenomenon of becoming valuable citizens in a multicultural country is not new to our neighbors across the border to the north, Canada. Why is the immigration issue in Canada not as contentious as the United States?

The Canadian Model of Immigration and Inclusiveness

In contrast to nebulous notions of inclusiveness in the United States' Constitution under the 14th Amendment, Canada's advocacy of inclusiveness is much more forthright. For example, the Canadian Multiculturalism Act (1985) explicitly states, "It is hereby declared to be the policy of the Government of Canada to: (a) recognize and promote the understanding that multiculturalism reflects the cultural and racial diversity of Canadian society and acknowledges the freedom of all members of Canadian society to preserve, enhance and share their cultural heritage; (b) recognize and promote the understanding that multiculturalism is a fundamental characteristic of the Canadian heritage and identity and that it provides an invaluable resource in the shaping of Canada's future; (c) promote the full and equitable participation of individuals and communities of all origins in the continuing evolution and shaping of all aspects of Canadian society and assist them in the elimination of any barrier to that participation; (d) recognize the existence of communities whose members share a common origin and their historic contribution to Canadian society, and enhance their development; (e) ensure that all individuals receive equal treatment and equal protection under the law, while respecting and valuing their diversity; (f) encourage and assist the social, cultural, economic and political institutions of Canada to be both respectful and inclusive of Canada's multicultural character; (g) promote the understanding and creativity that arise from the interaction between individuals and communities of different origins; (h) foster the recognition and appreciation of the diverse cultures of Canadian society and promote the reflection and the evolving expressions of those cultures; (i) preserve and enhance the use of languages other than English and French, while strengthening the status and use of the official languages of Canada; and (j) advance multiculturalism throughout Canada in harmony with the national commitment to the official languages of Canada" (Canadian Multiculturalism Act, R.S.C., 1985).

The progressive paradigm is enforced by federal institutions such as the Parliament, and the court system. Moreover, "It is further declared to be the policy of the Government of Canada that all federal institutions shall: (a) ensure that Canadians of all origins have an equal opportunity to obtain employment and advancement in those institutions; (b) promote policies, programs and practices that enhance the ability of individuals and communities of all origins to contribute to the continuing evolution of Canada; (c) promote policies, programs and practices that enhance the understanding of and respect for the diversity of the members of Canadian society; (d) collect statistical data in order to enable the development of policies, programs and practices that are sensitive and responsive to the multicultural reality of Canada; (e) make use, as appropriate, of the language skills and cultural understanding of individuals of all origins; and (f) generally, carry on their activities in a manner that is sensitive and responsive to the multicultural reality of Canada" (Canadian Multiculturalism Act, R.S.C., 1985).

One would expect the United States' stance on multiculturalism to be as strong as Canada's given the United States' diverse domestic population, and growing diversity with increasing numbers of workers relocating from countries such as India, Japan, and various African countries. These new workers are bringing their engineering, computer science, mathematical and technical skills to enhance our economy, and overall standard of living, which obviously benefits all Americans. As well, H-1B visas for high-skilled workers who wish to emigrate to the United States are 85,000 per annum, which is less than 10 years ago. H-1B is a nonimmigrant visa in the United States under the Immigration and Nationality Act. It allows U.S. employers to temporarily employ foreign workers in specialty occupations. Whether we are talking about the heartland (e.g., Kansas City, Missouri) of America, "Nationally and in the Kansas City area, demand for high-skilled science, technology, engineering and mathematics talent has grown over the last 10 years. Three-fourths of the Kansas City area's H-1B visa requests were for workers in those fields" (Stafford, 2012). Such federal (H-1B visas) limitations stymie U.S. industrial and manufacturing growth, because of the lack of competitive expertise in those occupational realms. "Canada, on the other hand, encourages high-skilled foreign-born worker relocation and has focused on offering cultural training programs for its skilled foreign-born workers" (Zakaria, 2012).

The Canadian model is certainly a useful framework for the United States to consider as we continue to move beyond the theoretical concept of a "melting pot" toward a "tossed salad" reality, whereby differences are not simply tolerated, but celebrated and enhanced in our cultural, social, political, and economic fabric.

The multicultural question is not a new phenomenon; it is only when uniculturalists confuse the issue with a sort of "melting pot" idea. With different immigrants, cultures, precepts, and norms, the American polity will not "melt" into one culture. We have to acknowledge the strength within our diversity and celebrate it. Multiculturalism would even increase in a world of vanishing borders, international mobility, the development of communication highways and cyberspace. With all these developments immigrants are finding it difficult to melt into the Anglo American hegemonic culture, something that is irritating to native-born Americans. Interethnic groups and intraethnic groups cannot rest on assumptions of uniformity if one wants to gauge which direction a policy application might take. De la Garza, Rodolfo, & Falcon (1993) summarize this myth of homogeneity among Latinos when they and others conclude that Latinos are not (just as other ethnic groups are not) united by an ethnic bond that distinguishes their policy preferences from those of other United States citizens. It would behoove policy analysts, comparativists, and other political participation researchers to strive to seek out internal and external differences if they are to begin to understand the dynamics and possibilities of increased immigration and its impact on political participation in the United States. More generally, issues of diversity will continue to be salient, as levels of globalization increase, which will be manifested in not only new immigrants in corporate America, but in academia and other facets of American society. Thus, not only America (but the world) will continue to become "flat." Failure to recognize the realities of today's immigration problems (and opportunities) as discussed above could only exacerbate the immigration problems.

Conclusion

The "people's bomb" has exploded and the world's population growth is a reality. The poverty in the "developing" countries and the United States prosperity produces a magnetic effect that attracts the poor, the disenfranchised, and the subjugated from other countries to the United States. The technologies enabling easy and swift immigration are real, and it is very important to develop strategies to confront the immigration wave, especially illegal immigration, instead of politicizing the issue on bases of economic and unicultural, xenophobic, hegemonic perspectives.

It is a dangerous mistake to view United States immigration policy as one monolithic policy and purpose. Legal immigration fulfills the purpose of linking families and bringing in skilled workers. Humanitarian admission grants asylum to immigrants and it satisfies political and religious purposes, a moral plus for the United States. Building a fence between the United States and Mexico which costs around $47 billion to maintain it for the next 25 years just sends a wrong message to the neighbors of the United States. Illegal immigration, the crucial category of immigrants, tends to push the immigration issue to a crisis level that upsets the public's sentiment about all immigrants. Recognizing that in a multicultural, multiethnic, multiperspective American society, the immigration debate must not be submerged in a unicultural, labor-economic perspective only, it must be examined in a multidimensional manner. As discussed above, the United States should begin taking lessons from its Canadian neighbors about how to handle multidimensional immigration policy.

References

The Advocates for Human Rights. (2012). Retrieved from http://www.theadvocateforhumanrights.org

American Association of Colleges and Universities (AAC&U). (1994). Diversity and democracy in higher education. Washington, DC: AAC&U Press.

American Community Survey. (2009). Educational attainment of U.S. born and foreign born residents. In *Just the fact: Immigrants and Education*, PPIC 2011. Retrieved from http://www.ppic.org/main/popup.asp?u=../content/images/Chart_ImmigrantsEd1.png&t=

Andreas, P. (1994). The making of Amerexico: (Mis)handling illegal immigration. *World Policy Journal 11*, 45–56.

Belson, K., & Kapuzzo, J. (2007, September 26). Towns rethink laws against illegal immigrants. *The New York Times* (September 26). Retrieved from: http://query.nytimes.com/gst/fullpage.htlm?res=940DE7D91331F935AC0A9619C8B63

Branigin, W., & Constable, P. (1997, May 26). A tidal wave of immigrants. *The Washington Post*, p. 8.

Briggs, V. (1990). Immigration policy and work force preparedness. *ILR Report, 28* (Fall).

Canadian Multiculturalism Act, R.S.C., 1985, c. 24 (4th Supp.). Center for Immigration Studies. (2007). Immigrants in the United States, 2077: A profile of America's foreign born population. Retrieved from: http://www.cis.org/immigrants_profile_2007

Chertoff, M. (2008). Testimony of the Department of Homeland Security. Retrieved from http://www.dhs.gov/xnews/testimony/testimony_1207933887848.shtm

Congressional Quarterly. (2011). *Issues in race and ethnicity*. Washington DC: CQ Press, p. 184.

Daniels, R. (1993). United States policy towards Asian immigrants: Contemporary developments in historical perspective. *International Journal, XLVII*.

Divine, R. (1957). *American immigration policy, 1994–1952*. New Haven, CT: Yale University Press, pp. 146–191.

Donato, K. M. (1994). U.S. policy and Mexican migration to the United States, 1942–92. *Social Science Quarterly, 75*(4), 705–729.

De la Garza, R. O., Falcon, C. F., Garcia, C., & Garcia, J. A. (1993). Attitudes toward U.S. immigration policy. *Migration World Magazine, 21*(2–3), 13–17.

Farley, J. E. (2012). *Majority-minority relations*, 6th ed. Boston, MA: Prentice Hall.

Fix, M., & Passel, J. S. (2002). Assessing welfare reform's immigrant provisions, Weil, A. & Finegold, K. (Eds.), *Welfare reform: The next act.* Washington, DC: Urban Institute Press.

Fox News Latino (2012, January 27). Latino leaders throw support behind Newt Gingrich. Retrieved from: http://www.latino.foxnews.com

Gibney, M. (1989). United States immigration policy and the huddled masses' myth. *Georgetown Immigration Law Journal, 3* (3).

Hoffman, A. (1974). Chapter 4. *Unwanted Mexican Americans in the Great Depression: Repatriation pressures, 1929–1939.* Tucson: University of Arizona Press.

Huntington, S. P. (1993). If not civilizations, what? *Foreign Affairs, 72*(5).

Hutchinson, E. P (1981). *Legislative history of American immigration policy, 1798–1965.* Philadelphia: University of Pennsylvania Press.

INS Facts Sheet, 1996. Retrieved from: http://www.uscis.gov/grahics/publications/factsheets/949.httm

Ipsos Public Affairs. (2008, March 3–5). *The Associated Press Poll.*

Isbister, J. (1996). *The immigration debate remaking America.* West Hartford, CT: Kumarim Press.

Kariam, R. (2011). America's border fence. *Congressional Quarterly Research, issues in race and ethnicity.* Washington, DC: QC Press.

Millman, J. (1997). *The other Americans: How immigrants renew our country, our economy, our values.* New York: Penguin.

Mitchell, C. (1992). *Western hemisphere immigration and United States foreign policy.* University Park: Penn State University Press, p. 11.

Orenstein, C. C. (1995). Illegal transnational labor: Mexicans in California and Haitians in the Dominican Republic. *Journal of International Affairs, 48*(2), 601–624.

Passel, J., & Fix, M. (1994). Myths about immigrants. *Foreign Policy, 95*, 153.

Passel, J. S., Clark, R. L., & Griego, M. G. y. (1994). How much do immigrants really cost? *Thomas Rivera Center Study.*

Reiner, D. (1985). *Still the golden door: The third world comes to America.* New York: Columbia University Press, p. 78.

Maria, T., Ricciardi, J., Bart, D., Sasson, S., Mahler, S., Jactaquin, C., Jimenez, M., Nathan, D., Frelick, B., Smith, R., Mines, R., Boccalandro, B., & Bart, S. (1992, July). Coming north: Latino & Caribbean immigration, NACLA report on the Americas, vol. 26, pp. 13–19. New York: NACLA.

Stafford, D. (2012, July 18). Survey finds familiar health, telecom, engineering firms among the area's leading employers of H-1B immigrants. *The Kansas City Star Newspaper.*

U.S. Census Bureau Data, 1996, 2000, 2002, 2010. Retrieved from: http://www.census.gov/main/

U.S. Immigration and Naturalization Services. Yearbook of immigration statistics, Office of Immigration Statistics. 1997 fact sheet. Washington, DC.

Yale-Loehr, S. (1991). *Understanding the Immigration Act of 1990*. Washington, DC: Federal Publications.

Zakaria, F. (2012, June 10). Global lessons: The GPS road map for making immigration work, CNN. globalpublicsquare.blogs.cnn.com

CHAPTER THIRTEEN

The Faces of Animal Oppression

LORI GRUEN

About 15 years ago, I wrote an article analyzing the connection between the oppression of women and the oppression of animals. I argued that nonhuman animals are oppressed in a myriad of ways and that examining the mutually reinforcing structures that support the oppression of nonhuman animals and the oppression of other groups is an important liberatory project (Gruen, 1993). These claims were, and continue to be, met with some skepticism. In response to one critic, I turned to Iris Young's "The Five Faces of Oppression" for intellectual support. Although Young never explicitly addressed the plight of other animals, her insights are instructive. Here I will return to the question of oppression beyond the species boundary, drawing on those insights to explore how it can be claimed meaningfully that nonhuman animals, like so many human groups that differ from those in positions of power and privilege, suffer from exploitation, marginalization, powerlessness, cultural imperialism, and violence and thus can be considered oppressed. When we understand the situation that individuals and groups are in as oppressive ones, then greater attention can be paid to rectifying the particular wrongs caused by oppression.

Animal Oppression

Humans have always interacted with nonhuman animals, and while contexts and relationships have changed, the structure of the relations have, arguably, stayed much the same. Humans dictate how nonhuman animals in human environments will fare. Given that human environments are continuously expanding, that human

behaviors—that is, emitting green house gases and polluting water
and air—cannot be contained in one geographical region, and that
we are encroaching on even the most remote places on earth, it is
not unreasonable to claim that virtually all nonhuman animals are
living in human-impacted environments. Most of our actions affect
them. Humans dominate and control the lives of nonhuman animals.
Humans oppress nonhuman animals. While some individual relationships may not look or feel like dominating and oppressive ones, the
structure of the relations are characterized by the forces of oppression. When we look at Young's categories of oppression we can see
how this is the case.

Young suggests that "the central insight expressed in the concept of *exploitation*" (Young 1990, p. 49) is that this type of oppression
occurs when one group systematically extracts the labor of another
to benefit themselves and not the laborer. Although the concept of
exploitation in traditional Marxist and more recent socialist-feminist
theory has been reserved for human laborers, it is not at all difficult
to expand the concept to include nonhumans. Consider the plight
of dairy cows, battery hens, and sows in factory farms. Intensively
reared dairy cows are so overworked that they begin to metabolize
their own muscle in order to continue to produce milk, a process
referred to in the industry as "milking off their backs." The cows are
milked by machine and often suffer from painful inflammation of the
mammary glands, or mastitis. Sows are confined for their entire lives
and repeatedly artificially inseminated so as to produce piglets who
are removed three weeks after birth, fattened up, and sold for consumption. In factory farms, sows spend most of their lives in crates
that are 7 feet long and 2 feet wide—they literally have no room to
move. Hens are kept in battery cages stacked tier on tier in huge
warehouses. Confined seven or eight to a cage, they too cannot move
or even spread one wing. Conveyor belts bring in food and water and
carry eggs away. The lives and bodies of female animals on factory
farms are completely controlled to produce the maximum amount
of product at the smallest cost to the producer. Factory farming, a
process in which over 5 billion animals annually in the U.S. alone
are intensively confined, manipulated, and ultimately slaughtered to
produce the greatest profit for the few agribusinesses that control the
market, not only exploits female animals' biological and reproductive
labor, but also denies all factory farmed animals their lives so that
some humans can profit. The animals are exploited and when their
labor is thoroughly extracted, they are killed.

Young's second category, *marginalization,* involves, in part,
separating one group and viewing them as dependent on the domi-

nant group. The conceptual structure of the human/animal divide, in mythology, in religion, in history, in art, and also in material terms, defines human as not animal, as above animal, as dominant over the animals. Human civilization and progress is measured by how far we humans have come from our animal ancestors. The group humans is framed by the nonhuman animals in the margins.

The marginalization of animals is not just conceptual or symbolic. It has direct and often devastating consequences on their lives. Consider those animals, particularly chimpanzees and orangutans, who are used in entertainment and commercials. Taken from their mothers at birth and raised to be comedic human stand-ins, infant apes are often kept alone and terrorized into performing. Dressed in human clothes, running amok in offices or shopping stores, these individuals are deprived of species-typical behaviors and community with others of their kind. When they become too big to handle (usually around puberty, between 6 and 8 years old) they are further marginalized, sent to roadside zoos and other substandard facilities, where they might spend the remainder of their lives; in the case of chimpanzees that can be as many as 50 years, alone in a small cage. Young suggests that even when marginals have their needs provided for, "injustices of marginality would remain in the form of uselessness [and] boredom . . ." (Young, 1990, p. 55). One need only visit one of the many unaccredited zoos or roadside exotic animal "farms" to see lives of uselessness and boredom, animals pace, rock back and forth, and look out at the world with what Jane Goodall has called "the thousand mile stare."

Young illustrates the oppressive nature of *powerlessness* by analyzing class injustices, yet much of what she argues can be extrapolated to the conditions under which nonhuman animals live. Those who are powerless are denied the opportunity and authority to make choices about their own lives, they are inhibited in the development of their own capacities, and they are subject to disrespectful treatment. Actual nonhuman animals are treated with disrespect in myriad ways, and one of the most poignant means of disrespecting humans is to compare them to a nonhuman animal. To be a nonhuman animal is to be a thing unworthy of respect. From zoos to feedlots, pet shops to laboratories, factory to fur farms, nonhuman animals are denied the most basic control over their lives. If they are allowed to reproduce, their infants are usually taken from them; they rarely have choices about when to eat, what to eat, or how much to eat; and very few have choices about basic movement—often they are forced to sit on cold concrete or other inappropriate substrate—and those who do live with others don't have the option of choosing with whom to interact. Even seemingly powerful animals in the wild are increasingly rendered incapable of doing what they might otherwise choose to do as habitat is being destroyed and they are more frequently meeting human animals who are certainly less physically powerful, but who have guns and other high-powered weapons that can be shot from jeeps, ships, and helicopters.

Though the majority of nonhuman animals are hunted and killed for economic reasons, many are killed, at least ostensibly, in the name of culture. Consider the case of the Makah Nation, the only Native American tribe that has a treaty right to hunt and kill whales. With the exception of a legal hunt that led to the death of a three-year-old gray whale in 1999, and the illegal hunt that mortally wounded a gray whale in the fall of 2007, the tribe had not hunted whales for over 70 years, but they are campaigning to be granted permission to do so again. Most Makah view the hunt as a way to reclaim their traditions and to provide the younger generation with the basis of identities that can help to shape their goals and aspirations (although some elder members of the Makah community view the hunt as a travesty). For the majority of the Makah, the cultural value of whale killing is crucial to their identities. While some Makah have suggested that the cultural values and the value of the whales can be simultaneously promoted in the hunt, it might also be claimed that the Makah are imposing their culture on the whales, much the way White Americans are imposing their cultural values on the Makah and other Native Nations. It represents a form of *cultural imperialism* that denies the very possibility that a whale's life may be valuable to her and her family, independent of the dominant culture's conception of that value (in the case of the Makah, they can only be considered a dominant culture in respect to the whales, certainly not within current U.S. society in which they are subject to cultural imperialism and marginalization).

In our personal lives, we can see the way cultural imperialism operates on the lives of our "domestic pets" or "companion animals." When humans bring nonhuman animals into their homes, the nonhuman animals are forced to conform to the human rituals and practices that exist there. Cats and dogs are often denied full expression of their natural urges when their "owners" keep them indoors or put bells around cats' necks to impact their success at hunting, or forbid dogs from digging or otherwise scavenging for food. While there are clearly reasons that can be given for imposing such restrictions on companion animals, and while there are also important benefits that are gained by both the companion animals and their human companions in domesticated relationships that are thoughtful and compassionate, the potential benefits do not erase the fact that they are forced to live by our cultural standards.

Finally there is the issue of *violence*. Young writes, "What makes violence a face of oppression is less the particular acts themselves, though these are often utterly horrible, than the social context surrounding them, which makes them possible and even acceptable. What makes violence a phenomenon of social injustice, and not merely an individual moral wrong, is its systemic character, its existence as a social practice" (Young, 1990, pp. 61–62). The assembly-line method of intensive agribusiness is violent from start to gruesome finish. During transport, many animals suffer broken bones, and some are crushed or suffocated by animals that cannot control their movement during shipment. Early on, chicks have their beaks cut off with hot blades so they don't peck each other in extremely cramped space; cattle and other animals are branded with hot irons to identify who's property they are; and pigs have their tails cut off so they won't be ripped off by other animals in the crowded conditions in which they spend their shortened lives. After they are transported again to slaughter, most are hung upside down while still conscious, then are jolted into unconsciousness before their throats are slit. Not all animals slaughtered are lucky enough to be unconscious as they bleed to death, however. While raising and slaughtering animals for food on factory farms is an extreme instance of oppressive violence, it is also a social practice that obscures, and in some instances authorizes, other forms of violence against nonhuman animals.

Though Young did not connect nonhuman animal oppression to human oppression, another feminist philosopher, Marilyn Frye, uses the oppression of nonhumans as a metaphor for human oppression:

> The experience of oppressed people is that the living of one's life is confined and shaped by forces and barriers which are not accidental or occasional and hence avoidable, but are systematically related to each other in such a way as to catch one between and among them and restrict or penalize motion in any direction. It is the experience of being caged in: all avenues, in every direction, are blocked or booby trapped. Cages. Consider a birdcage. . . . It is perfectly "obvious" that the bird is surrounded by a network of systematically related barriers, no one of which would be the least hindrance to its flight, but which, by their relations to each other, are as confining as the solid walls of a dungeon. . . . (Frye, 1983, pp. 4–5)

For billions of nonhuman animals, their cages and stalls and crates
and dungeons are not metaphors, but realities. Understanding that
their reality is an oppressive one can provide ways of thinking about
how to overcome oppression and begin to achieve justice for them.

Recognition and Oppression

The skepticism about applying the term *oppression* to nonhuman
animals, and perhaps even adopting Young's analysis of oppression
to describe our treatment of nonhuman animals, might be based
on the idea that in order to be oppressed one has to experience
oppression as oppression. Oppression is an experience that is sub-
jectively understood as limiting, harmful, frustrating, disrespectful,
and worse. Critics might contend that while the caged bird cannot
fly away, only humans can understand the structures that prevent
her flight. Nonhuman animals may be unable to do certain things in
virtue of the ways in which we exploit and marginalize them, strip
them of power and control, force them to live the way we want them
to live and are physically and psychologically violent toward them,
but they do not suffer from the extra knowledge that we are doing
these things to them because of who or what they are. They do not
experience oppression as an injustice against them.

Certainly the fact that humans can be aware of their oppression
represents an added feature of the injustice that oppression is for
them. Oppression denies individuals and groups the ability to pursue their way of life or to express themselves. Oppression operates
to systematically frustrate or deny a group of people the chance to
live their lives as their own, to be, as it were, the narrators of their
life stories. This way of understanding oppression has led some, for
example, Seyla Benhabib (2006, p. 441), to interpret Young as claiming that oppression represents a violation of the right to recognition.
Since nonhuman animals are not the kinds of beings who can be said
to formulate identities that would be the basis for a right to recognition, it would be a mistake to think of them as being oppressed.

However, oppression does not reduce to being denied the right
to recognition, in the case of humans or in the case of nonhuman
animals. Oppression can be measured objectively even if no member
of the group being oppressed themselves recognizes his or her oppression. This is particularly important in cases in which "internalized
oppression" or "false consciousness" or "adaptive preferences" may be
operating. The fact that there are such cases suggests that determining whether or not oppression is operating will require an objective

analysis of the context that goes beyond subjective assessment. In the case of women who may claim that their marginalization and their powerlessness do not constitute oppression, for example, we may want to determine who is benefiting from the practices that keep them marginal and powerless and who, as a group, is suffering from it. In many instances, though an individual woman may not identify her treatment as oppressive, the structures of oppression may nonetheless be present and those who perpetuate the structures continue to benefit from them, even in cases where the individuals being oppressed may also be said to benefit. For example, if becoming a sexual servant gets one out of conditions of horrible poverty, then there may be at least some benefit for the sex servant, but that doesn't mean the conditions in which she exists are not oppressive. There are those who benefit (the men) systematically and there are others (women) who may not themselves be sex servants but who nonetheless suffer from stereotypes, prejudices, and material hardship that are enabled by the structures that allow sexual slavery to exist. The importance of viewing oppression objectively is particularly clear in egregious cases of adaptive preference formation in which sex slaves view themselves as only worthy of being slaves and accept that they are getting what they deserve. In contexts in which the ability to think thoughts free of oppressive constructs is absent, it would be dangerous to understand oppression as a strictly subjective experience.

Indeed, Young does not argue that one has to see oneself as oppressed in order to be oppressed. She believes the criteria for oppression that she identifies "are objective. They provide a means of refuting some people's belief that their group is oppressed when it is not, as well as a means of persuading others that a group is oppressed when they doubt it" (Young, 1990, p. 64). In recognizing this, she provided us with tools to address oppression even in those contexts where it has distorted the very experiences of those who are oppressed. She has also, I believe, allowed for the possibility that others who she did not identify directly, such as nonhuman animals, may be oppressed.

One might object to the sensibility of the claim that nonhuman animals are oppressed, even objectively oppressed, because oppression is a social process that is exerted on groups and there is no social group that is "nonhuman animals." The category "nonhuman animal" itself is so large and variable that unlike human social groups there are no positive characteristics, identities, or affiliations that members of the group share. The group nonhuman animals seems to be based on a taxonomical distinction—the group consists of all animals that are not members of the species *Homo sapiens*. Within the group non-human animals, there are individuals as diverse as aardvarks and elephants, dolphins and cheetahs, mice and mountain goats, beings that have very little in common except for the classification as "not humans."

However diverse the group nonhumans actually is, and despite the importance in most contexts to attend to the diversity of interests and needs that the variety of species within the group nonhuman have, the larger category serves a central symbolic role in human social lives and in our self-understanding, as mentioned above. Given that the group has a social reality, even if not a meaningful biological or conceptual basis, it can be thought of as akin to the human social groups that are more often the subjects of discussions of injustice and oppression, for example, "People of color" or "LGBT." These human groups contain individuals and subgroups with very distinct interests, affiliations. and identities, yet, as Young notes, the larger groups are products of social processes, and so too is the group of nonhuman animals. Members of human groups may not "share a common nature," they are "multiple, cross-cutting, fluid and shifting" (Young, 1990, p. 48), but insofar as they are identifiable to those in positions of power, they can be subject to oppression. Unlike unified analyses of oppression, one of the virtues of Young's approach is that it recognizes that there are different kinds of groups that are constructed for different reasons in different contexts, and that oppression will operate differently given these social facts. This important recognition of difference provides a way of making sense of the oppression of nonhuman animals.

Perhaps the most forceful objection is that there are important differences, not in the analysis of nonhuman animal oppression and the oppression of human groups, but in the purposes or ends such an analysis is meant to achieve. Young's analysis of oppression is aimed, in part, at identifying forces that contribute to particular forms of injustice. Members of oppressed groups are denied the possibility of developing and exercising their capacities and are unable to express themselves and be heard in democratic, social deliberations. The goal of identifying oppression is to help construct institutional solutions that will enable members of oppressed groups to become full, equal participants in their social lives. It might be argued that these aspects of justice simply do not apply to nonhuman animals, and thus saying that nonhuman animals are oppressed either is metaphorical or means something very different than what Young had in mind.

In one sense, it is true that the goals that Young's antioppression analyses are meant to enable are not goals that nonhuman animals could share, even if they were desirable to them. Participating in decisions about the division of labor, reformulating social and cultural institutions to make visible previously oppressed groups' values, creating institutions that allow for full participation in social decision-making are liberatory ends for humans seeking justice, but they don't apply to nonhuman animals, even those that are living in human contexts. Nonetheless, I believe there is an important way that the shape of these ends for humans can help us to think about the shape of justice for nonhuman animals. The success of thinking in these ways will not only help clarify what antioppressive treatment might mean for the nonhuman animals themselves, but may also assist in pointing a way past what has become a fairly ugly divide within the social movement for animals. Let me turn specifically to this question.

The Significance of an Oppression Analysis for Nonhuman Animals

Much of the work that is directed at articulating the ethical and political importance of the plight of nonhuman animals, or at least the work that has gained the most attention, focuses on how an individual nonhuman animal's rights or interests have been violated or ignored. As sentient, feeling beings, as beings who can experience pleasures and pains, both physical and in many instances, psychological, they are, in important respects, no different from us. Since we can make claims on one another, whether verbal or not, when our interests or rights are in jeopardy, as ethically valuable beings like us, they too can make such claims. Nonhuman animals are morally considerable in virtue of the fact that they share with us the very capacities, most notably sentience, that we think make us morally considerable. To recognize these capacities as ethically salient only in humans is to engage in a form of "speciesism," which is akin to "racism" and "sexism" and other discriminatory attitudes. However, while animal advocates have identified speciesism as a form of prejudice, this has neither led to a unified analysis of the structures of power that speciesism represents and reinforces nor has the identification led to a consistent strategy for combating this prejudice.

There is a divide within the animal advocacy movement between those who are focused on ending suffering and those who are focused on ending the use of animals. Both positions are often referred to as "animal rights" positions, but they have been increasingly distinguishable as advocates of each position have taken issue with the other. Those who are primarily concerned with the pain and suffering nonhuman animals experience often adopt a utilitarian view—they are interested in minimizing unnecessary animal suffering and in practice that means they are opposed to most uses of nonhumans, particularly in the developed world. Those who are primarily interested in ending animal use call themselves "abolitionists"—they too are interested in ending animal suffering but are driven by the principle that opposes the use of nonhumans in all contexts. As abolitionist Gary Francione, who wants to rid the world of the use of animals for any purpose, including companionship, has written,

> our recognition that no human should be the property of others required that we abolish slavery and not merely regulate it to be more "humane," our recognition that animals have this one basic right [not to be property] would mean that we could no longer justify our institutional exploitation of animals for food, clothing, amusement, or experiments. (Francione, 2000, xxix)

Animal liberationist, Peter Singer doesn't see the contrast between abolition and regulation in such stark terms. He writes:

> It's absurd to say that because we do one thing that is arguably bad for [animals] therefore it doesn't matter what else we do to them and can just treat them as things. You might as well have said in the debate about slavery that we shouldn't have had laws to prevent masters beating their slaves because as long as they are slaves they are just things and you might as well beat them as much as you like [until slavery has ended]. (Leider, 2006)

The difference in the positions are more than just rhetorical; in practical terms they lead to different sorts of assessments of the problems nonhuman animals face.

One of the most contentious current issues is that of "cage-free" eggs. As I mentioned above, the battery system of egg production is exploitative, painful, and, I've argued, oppressive for hens. They are kept in small cages with six to eight other birds, none of them can stretch a wing, they are surrounded by tens of thousands of other hens also in small cages, and all the cages are stacked in rows in large, ammonia filled, dark sheds. Around the globe, an estimated 3.5 billion birds live under these terrifying, crowded, painful conditions until they are sent to slaughter after a year of egg production. In response to the awful reality these hens are forced to endure, animal campaigners and compassionate consumers have pushed for more humane conditions. In response to both changes in law and changes in demand, some egg producers have switched to "cage-free" systems. These cage-free systems take hens out of cages, but still keep thousands of them crammed in large, ammonia-filled dark sheds. The hens are still debeaked—a painful process that involves using a hot blade to cut through the complex horn, bone, and sensitive tissue of the hen's beak. This procedure often leads to deformities that prevent hens from eating, drinking, or preening normally. The purpose of debeaking is to minimize the damage caused when birds peck at each other in frustration, and the small space does not allow room for escape. The cage-free hens are also sent to slaughter after a year. Sometimes the hens can go outside of the shed, but the exits are very small and the sheds so crowded that the only hens that could get out would be those closest to the door.

There is no question that the move from the battery cage system of egg production to the cage-free system represents an improvement in the welfare of the hens, albeit a rather small improvement. For those concerned with animal suffering, even this small improvement represents a victory. So many hens suffer so horribly that improving the conditions even minimally amounts to a vast overall improvement, given that people are still eating eggs. For those opposed to any use of animals, cage-free systems of egg production work to prolong the violation of the rights of these animals as it makes people feel better about their abuse. Abolitionists point out that many people conflate "cage-free" with "cruelty-free" and they worry about the complacency that these small improvements encourage. While rarely admitting it publicly, many abolitionists think the chance of actually ending the use of animals is greater if the conditions in which they exist are worse.

By resisting discussion of improving animal welfare in "institutions of use" on principle, abolitionists are unable to address very practical issues of nonhuman animal well-being. Consider another example: presently there are an estimated 1,700–2,000 chimpanzees in captivity in the United States. These chimpanzees live in conditions ranging from naturalistic, group enclosures where they are given options about what to play with, what to eat, and who to spend time with, to sterile, solitary conditions in which everything they do is completely controlled by masked, gloved humans. For most captive chimpanzees, the conditions are somewhere in between. From the abolitionist perspective, these conditions are equivalent in that they all represent a violation of the chimpanzees' rights to be free.

However, since chimpanzees who have spent their lives in captivity cannot be released to the wild (and given that wild chimpanzees are under dire threats from habitat destruction and the "bushmeat" trade), there is an important question about what to do for captive chimpanzees who can live for 50 years or more. Abolitionists, insofar as they are unwilling to discuss improving conditions of "slavery" are unable to sensibly and consistently discuss what to do for these sensitive, captive individuals.

However, by recognizing these situations as oppressive, rather than merely as painful situations or, alternatively, as situations in which individual rights are violated, different practical solutions come into view. When combating oppression for human groups, one of the most important structures that requires interrogation is the market that both provides excuses for oppression and forces certain groups to suffer under oppressive working conditions because all too often they are denied any other options. Surely the economic system that allows for modest improvements in the conditions of hens, while continuing to make significant profits, can be pushed further. Given that there are many people in the world for whom access to protein is limited and would require killing animals, perhaps wild animals, it is important to consider models of symbiotic living and respectful use that might allow for nonoppressive egg consumption. As we also know from situations of human oppression, there are often contexts in which conflicts between the interests of various groups require compromises in order to eliminate oppression. What is necessary, often, is identifying ways to respectfully attend to the needs, interests, and desires of the members of the oppressed groups on their own terms. An absence of oppression does not always translate into either complete freedom or a life free from pain or distress. What we are after, as Young points out, is the possibility of developing one's capacities so that one can be, in some sense, a participant in a meaningful social life. If we extend these ends to captive chimpanzees, for example, we might find that attending to their particular needs for social and psychological engagement are centrally important to allowing them to live nonoppressed, yet nonetheless imprisoned lives. Chimpanzees appear to understand themselves as captives and humans as captors, but insofar as it is possible to treat them with respect, to provide them with the power to determine what they do with others of their kind, and to develop responsive and sincere relations with them while respecting their wild dignity, they may be able to live reasonably safe and meaningful lives.

Framing the discussion of animal liberation as one that is understood in terms of oppression provides for an importantly different, and arguably deeper, analysis of not only our current practices toward nonhuman animals but the ways such practices support unjust and harmful social and political structures, particularly structures of power. If we are to recognize and identify the oppression of nonhuman animals, then we may able to more readily see oppression in other contexts. There may be a perceptual as well as practical advantage to adopting an oppression analysis. For example, gender or racial hierarchies, in which White men are thought to be separate from and superior to White women and women of color share a similar structure to hierarchies that separate humans from other animals and justify human dominance over the allegedly inferior others. Linking people of color and all women with nonhuman animals reinforces the inferiority that serves as a justification for various forms of oppression. In speciesist social contexts (which is virtually every social context in the contemporary world), the nonhuman animal other serves as a marker of the "rightfully" oppressed. By comparing those who are to be oppressed or continue to be oppressed, oppressors can naturalize and justify oppressive structures. When we begin to identify the cruel and life-denying attitudes and practices that nonhuman animals are subject to as oppressive practices, we not only begin to explore ways to undermine their oppression, but oppression generally. Iris Young's analysis of the faces of oppression provides a valuable way to begin this long-overdue process.

Note

*This chapter was previously published in *Dancing with Iris* (2009), and it was reprinted with permission from Oxford University Press.

References

Adams, C. (1990). *The sexual politics of meat: A feminist-vegetarian critical theory*. New York: Continuum.

Adams, C., and Donovan, J. (Eds.). (1995). *Animals and women: Feminist theoretical explorations*. Durham, NC: Duke University Press.

Benhabib, S. (2006). In memoriam Iris Young 1949–2006. *Constellations* 13(4).

Collins, P. (1991). *Black feminist thought*. New York: Routledge.

Cuomo, C., & Gruen, L. (1997). Animals, intimacy and moral distance. In A. Ferguson & A. Bar On (Eds.), *Daring to be good*, pp. 129–142. New York: Routledge.

Donovan, J. (1990). Animal rights and feminist theory. *Signs 15*(2), 350–375.

Francione, G. (2000). *Introduction to animal rights*. Philadelphia: Temple University Press.

Frye, M. (1983). *The politics of reality: Essays in feminist theory.* Trumansburg, NY: Crossing Press.

Gaard, G. (ed.) (1993). *Ecofeminism: Women, animals, nature.* Philadelphia: Temple University Press.

Gruen, L. (1993). Dismantling oppression: An analysis of the connection between women and animals. In G. Gaard (Ed.), *Ecofeminism: Women, animals, nature,* pp. 60–90. Philadelphia, PA: Temple University Press.

Gruen, L. (1996). On the oppression of women and animals. *Environmental Ethics 18*(4), 441–444.

Gruen, L. (2003). The moral status of animals. In E. N. Zalta (Ed.), *The Stanford encyclopedia of philosophy.* Retrieved from: http://plato.stanford.edu/archives/fall2003/entries/moral-animal/

Leider, J. P. (2006, March 23). Animal rights activist Peter Singer explains his views. *The Minnesota Daily.*

Pollan, M. *The omnivore's dilemma.* New York: Penguin.

Singer, P., & Mason, J. (2006). *The way we eat.* New York: Rodale Press.

Young, I. (1988). The five faces of oppression. *Philosophical Forum 19*(4), 270–290.

Young, I. (1990). *Justice and the politics of difference.* Princeton, NJ: Princeton University Press.

PART III

Doing Diversity and Facing Global Challenges

CHAPTER FOURTEEN

The Tale of Two Worlds

Unpacking the Power of the Global North Over the Global South

GOWRI PARAMESWARAN

Author's note: While this essay attempts to provide a picture of exploitation transnationally, as with other forms of exploitation and privilege, it is important to acknowledge that there are intersections among communities based on class, race, and gender in terms of who benefits the most from the exploitation of the Global South by the Global North and who loses in this relationship. Colonialism and racism have an intertwined history, and White colonizers from the Global North richly reward some individuals and families in the Global South for acting as intermediaries in the process of colonizing the South. The latter live in opulence in the South, relegating the majority of the South to destitution and poverty. Similarly, there are communities here who have been relegated to the lowest social class, as jobs are moved to the Global South because of the corporate quest for lower wages and fewer government regulations. Men and women in the North are recruited to fight in wars aimed at furthering corporate interests even though they do not get to enjoy the fruits of the war and may even have to give up their lives for the privileged in their own nations.

The countries colored blue in the map below are collectively referred to as the Global North, while the countries in red form the Global South. The nations of the Global North are located in the temperate zones of the northern hemisphere (except for Australia and New Zealand), while the nations of the Global South are located in the tropical regions of the northern hemisphere and the southern hemisphere. The terms were coined by activists from the Global South who by giving themselves a name, wanted to forge a collective political and economic identity. The aim was to facilitate a struggle for more equal distribution of resources. Most of the world's population lives in regions that can be termed the Global South. Since about the 1500s, countries in the Global North colonized much of the South, thereby establishing dominion over its lands and resources. In the early years after nations in the Global South obtained independence from the North, the countries belonging to the North came together to create rules for world governance that kept power and resources in their own hands. They thus ensured an unequal distribution of wealth, resources, materials, and privileges that continues into the present day. Mainstream social sciences reinforced notions of superiority of European societies by classifying cultures in the Global South as backward and in need of civilizing influences, just like male scientists had argued a century earlier that women were not as capable as men.

I first read the article on unpacking racism by Peggy McIntosh when I was in graduate school, and have used it in my own classes as an instructor over the years. Readers cannot but be inspired by the simplicity of McIntosh's message and the deep truths that her list of privileges as a White person reveals about racism in our society. The privileges of the Global North over the Global South are

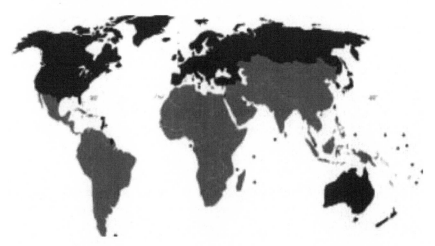

Figure 14.1. Map of the Global North (black) and the Global South (gray).

much harder to perceive than racism, sexism, and classism within our society, because many of us do not come across people or communities from the nations of the Global South except through the products we consume and the occasional news stories about the horrors of living there. I was born in India, part of the Global South. My family was advantaged within the context we lived in because we were Brahmin, one of the upper castes in a highly hierarchical society. I moved to the United States when I was 21, and since then have returned often to my native town in South India. When one travels across boundaries, the invisible privileges that one takes for granted become more visible.

Being a woman of color in the United States, and therefore marginalized, allows me to understand the many oppressions that communities from the lower castes experience in India. However, even though as a woman and as an Asian I am disadvantaged in some ways, I am conferred an important privilege as a result of my moving and settling down in the United States. I have become a citizen of the Global North. It is not easy to become a citizen in the nations that form the Global North for most people who live in the South, and my privileges came after a long and arduous process of obtaining a green card and later U.S. citizenship; I was allowed access to this exclusive club only because I had the skills resulting from an extensive education to offer to the United States.

Communities in both the North and South are negatively affected by the unequal distribution of wealth and access to resources between the most privileged of its citizens and its least powerful. It is thus important to acknowledge that there are powerful individuals and corporations in the South who benefit from this exploitation of the North over the South. However, the average citizen of the Global North still benefits from the unfair distribution of privileges that favor the North over the South. To people who live in the North, many of these privileges appear earned and therefore feel like a birthright.

The following is a partial list of benefits and privileges I enjoy that my family who still lives in the Global South does not enjoy. These privileges are interwoven with existing patriarchal power structures in the world of international politics and a masculine view of the world that takes for granted the rights of the rich over the poor and the powerful over the weak. Aggression and violence is the preferred weapon to maintain the hierarchy of dominance by the Global North over the South. Without a conscious exploration of these privileges, women in the Global South cannot enjoy the same rights as their brothers and sisters in the Global North.

As a Citizen of the Global North,
the Privilege of Life, Work, and Worth

1. I can choose to visit, live, and work in most places on earth. Since the currencies in the South are valued at a fraction of what the currencies in the North are valued at, it is easier for me to travel and take vacations in the nations of the South. With a U.S. passport, I am not scrutinized to the same extent as people from the Global South. My brothers and sisters living in the South will find it much harder to gain entry into the countries of the North.

2. My life is considered more valuable than people living in the nations of the South. Policy makers with global influence constantly make trade and business calculations based on this assumption. There are several examples that illustrate the devaluing of life in the South. Toxic waste in the North is routinely transferred to the South to be disposed of, even though this practice has enormous negative consequences on the health and the environment of people living in the South. Similarly experimental pharmaceutical products are often tested on people in the South, sometimes without meeting appropriate ethical stipulations that are routine in the North before being approved for consumption among people in the North.

3. I am considered a legitimate citizen of my country and bestowed full citizenship rights, while people from the Global South who cross the borders from the South to the North without appropriate government documentation are branded as "Illegal," thereby reducing them to less than human even though they may make similar contributions to society that I do. Most people who enter the North do so out of economic desperation caused by exploitation of the South, both historical and contemporarily, by governments of the North. The escape to places with better opportunities is constrained by punitive policing of the borders between the North and the South. When they are caught, they are treated as criminals, housed in prisons, and sent back. People in North Africa flee to Europe, while Mexicans and citizens of Latin American countries seek refuge in

North America. They contribute to the economic wealth of the nations that they reside in but live and work in exploitative conditions.

4. I have a disproportionate amount of resources devoted to exploring issues related to my health needs versus those of people from the South. There is a lot more resources devoted to research about diseases that I might suffer from than diseases more prevalent in the South. Only about 1% of medicines brought out by pharmaceuticals are devoted to diseases prevalent in the Global South. When research has led to the development of medicines for diseases like malaria or yellow fever that are prevalent in the South, it has often been because the nations of the North wanted to colonize the South or the medicines found have been side products of research to address diseases prevalent in the North.

Cultural Privilege

1. I can go to most places on earth and be assured that there are feature films, TV shows, books, and music available that I enjoy in the North. Movies and music that are products of Hollywood and other media capitals in the North are profitable all over the world. Books that win major prizes in the North are given due recognition in the Global South and translated into the many languages spoken in the South. Today, there are about seven media companies mainly located in the United States that own much of the world media outlets. Robert McChesney, the noted media critic, calls this global cultural domination by the United States the "Hollywood juggernaut," and compares it to the cultural assimilation within the United States that minority communities are subjected to. In recent years progressive community media groups in the Global South (and in marginalized communities in the North) have been fighting back by trying to organize for a more democratic popular media.

2. I do not have to travel outside of the North to view and experience the riches of ancient history from the

South. As the North colonized the South, many of the
ancient relics from the South were brought back to the
North and enjoyed by its citizens. Some nations in the
South are currently engaged in court battles in the
North to get those artifacts back. One famous example
is the demand for the return of the Rosetta Stone,
which Britain plundered from Egypt when it was still
ruling the country. Britain has consistently refused to
return it, even though according to a United Nations
1972 agreement artifacts are considered properties of
the nations of origin.

3. I am used as the yardstick to judge the mental health of
people living in the Global South, while their worldviews
about what constitutes a healthy individual are ignored
by the therapeutic community in the North. Thus, it
is considered "normal" and "healthy" when people hold
values of independence, assertiveness, and mastery over
the environment, while dependence, attributing primacy
to the group and to nature, are considered unhealthy
and "treatment worthy." Even though the prognosis for
diseases like depression and schizophrenia are best in
places like Zanzibar in Africa, where family members
do not associate mental health with being independent
and being in control, ideas from the Global North are
penetrating these communities and pharmaceutical
medicines from the North are offered as panaceas for
problems.

4. I can choose to ignore the cultural and religious beliefs,
celebrations, and social conventions in other countries
without it having a negative impact on my experiences
and work life, even when I am in the Global South.
People from the South have to acquaint themselves
about the cultural values and languages of the North,
even to get jobs in their own countries. One example
is the monopoly of the English language in business
and the impact that has on people in the Global
South. In developing countries like Philippines, India,
and China, in order to be employed at a professional
level, a candidate needs to know English or some
other European language. Employees are expected to
wear professional clothes that are dominant in the
North.

Economic privileges

1. I benefit directly and indirectly because of access to natural resources everywhere in the world. If other countries do not give them up readily, my government and others in the North consider it appropriate that they "persuade" them to exploit the resource for the good of the world. Governments of the North routinely topple governments, create unrest, and invade sovereign nations in the South in order to have access to minerals that can be used by corporations and researchers in the North. One current example is the Congo in Africa, considered perhaps the richest tract of land in the world. The country has been in the throes of civil war because the North funds rebel groups who have taken over some very mineral-rich land in Congo; the rebels then lease the captured land to mining companies based in the North who in turn give them weapons and finance them.

2. I can be assured that the rules of Global economics and international trade favor me over citizens of the South, since my government and others of the North have made the rules through organizations like the World Trade Organization (WTO). The WTO has the clout and the power to punish nations that do not abide by their economic regime set up by the North. The existing trade laws allow me to use disproportionate amounts of the earth's resources. One example is in the area of agriculture. The governments of the North subsidize their agricultural industries heavily and then force the nations of the South to buy farm products from the North. This impoverishes the rural population in the South and destroys local industries. At the same time, my need for cash crops like tea, coffee, sugar, and chocolate that can grow best in tropical climates have made farming communities in the South susceptible to starvation and have depleted water tables in those regions because of valuable local farming land being diverted to cash crop production that uses a lot of water.

3. I and my fellow citizens from the North benefit from the uneven flow of resources and wealth in favor of the North from the South. Most big banks and lending institutions

(i.e., Citibank, Chase, etc.) are located in the North. They lend to nations of the South charging high interest rates and demanding terms that are favorable to their own financial bottom-line. The financial resources then flow back to the corporations of the North. A second way in which money flows back to the nations of the North are through the profits that corporations make in the nations of the South. Some of the biggest global corporations (GE, GM, IBM, Microsoft, etc.) are located in the North. They set up businesses in the nations of the South, but the profits are sent back to their investors who live in the North. *Again, the largest beneficiaries are the wealthy who live in the North but they do pay taxes and consume goods produced in the North, thereby leading to better infrastructure and the availability of other services in the North that are unavailable in the South.*

4. I can expect to get paid a lot more for the work that I do compared to a worker who does the same work in the South. For instance, workers in the manufacturing sector earn $21.56 per hour in the United States, but only $2.61 in Mexico, and $2.58 in Brazil. While workers in a manufacturing plant in the North live in relative comfort, their brothers and sisters in the South live in shantytowns and in cardboard houses.

International Laws and Security

1. I and my fellow brothers and sisters from the North are much better represented in international institutions that make up the rules for war and peace. One example is the Security Council in the United Nations, whose permanent members are made up of countries from the North, except for China. Most issues related to war and peace are brought to the Security Council to be debated and ratified. My government can veto any resolution that the Security Council makes that it does not feel would benefit my nation or actively harm it. Thus, my government can choose to ignore international laws that it does not support, while punishing nations in the South for acting on similar principles. For instance, the

North has consistently voted to sanction nations that possess nuclear plants even if it is for peaceful purposes. When some nations like Iran, India, and North Korea developed nuclear programs in secret, the countries of the North punished them with sanctions even though most of the active nuclear weapons are located in the nations of the North, and private contractors located in the North have made huge profits selling nuclear technology to the South.

2. I am much better protected when it comes to legal rights as a citizen than a person from a nation of the South. My brothers and sisters who live in the South and who have never visited the North can be accused of committing a crime and can be convicted without due process by my government and others in the North. In the War on Terror, under the pretext of protecting me, the U.S. government secretly arrested suspects who were citizens of other nations as enemy combatants. Many of them were imprisoned indefinitely and interrogated in secret without U.S. laws being implemented appropriately. On the other hand, it is hard to bring a citizen of a nation in the North to justice. After the worst industrial accident in the history of the world that was perpetrated by a U.S. chemical company, Union Carbide (now Dow Chemical), in Bhopal, India, the Indian government has been trying unsuccessfully to get the CEO of Union Carbide sent to India for a trial for over three decades.

3. I have more military power to "protect" me than a citizen of the Global South. Much of the world's military might rests with the nations of the North, especially the United States and the European Union. The United States spends more on its military in general than the next 10 countries combined. The United States, Russian Federation, France, and the United Kingdom possess the most nuclear weapons of all of the nations in the world.

We in the North do not have to do much to earn these privileges. Our government does much of the policing and enforcing of these unjust global laws for us. The excellent roads, bridges, parks, museums, art houses, institutions of higher education and research universities, and other infrastructural amenities that we take for granted have been collectively obtained for our use by the national and transnational institutions that make this unequal transfer of wealth possible. It is also true that not all of us benefit equally from the unequal distribution of resources between the North and the South. Powerful corporations, agribusinesses, defense industries, the commercial entertainment industry, and mining interests are some of the biggest beneficiaries of the current trade regime. However, they are able to silence the voices of people in the South because of inaction on the part of citizens of the North who have the power to collectively object to this unequal distribution of privileges.

While much of the struggle for equal rights are being waged by citizens of the Global South, as we observed in earlier chapters, the privileged are invaluable allies in the fight against injustice. The average citizen of the North has a lot to gain by pushing for an equal distribution of global wealth. The current unjust trade and governing mechanisms were set up by vested interests in the Global North, with the collusion of the powerful and the wealthy in the Global South. Throughout the South we can see palatial mansions tended by innumerable servants, right next to shantytowns that lack basic access to safe drinking water and food or even functioning toilets. In the North, corporations have relocated factories and manufacturing units to the Global South on a massive scale, because of low wages prevalent in the South. The unequal world order that exists today destroys communities in both the North and the South. It would benefit everyone to upset the status quo of privileges.

Bringing the Global struggle home to our communities by engaging in action that benefits our brothers and sisters in the South helps strengthen our own local communities. There are many problems today that transcend the artificial borders between the North and the South; some examples of struggles that require our collective strength of action in both the North and in the South include:

1. Impending climate change due to industrial activity: Climate change affects us all by altering our environment, pushing the globe to experience extremes in weather leading to droughts and floods, and making large tracts of land unlivable in both the North and South.

2. Food and water security: In recent years industrial activity and industrial accidents (as recent events in the aftermath of the earthquake in Japan have demonstrated) have polluted our land, air, and water leading to toxins being leached into our food system on

a global scale. The unsafe products that we consume affect our individual and community health. Excessive exploitation of our farming land has led to a depletion of water sources. This phenomenon is especially visible in the South.

3. Wars for profit: The North spends an enormous amount of its financial resources building its military might to support the numerous wars engaged in by its governments. The wars are often about maintaining control over minerals and other resources that the North lacks, or to find new markets to sell products from the North. Sometimes the wars are overt, and at other times they are covert, with the North funding local militias or rebel groups in the South to fight other groups. The resources spent on the military can be better spent supporting local communities and improving health and educational infrastructures in the North. It benefits us all to work together for peace and justice in the world.

A worldview based on patriarchal values that emphasizes competition over cooperation, aggression over diplomacy, and negotiation and exploitation of nature over working with nature have lead us to a crucial fork in our collective history. These issues require all of us from the North and South to work together to resolve them. Feminist values offers us hope and faith in our collective strength to make a different world possible—a world where people from the Global North and Global South can share in the bounties of this earth equally and where the incredible benefits of modern technology can enhance life everywhere and not be used to exploit some communities.

Note

*This chapter was previously published in *Women: Images and Realities*, 5th Edition (2011), and it was reprinted with permission from McGraw-Hill.

References

Burgess, K. (2009, February 18). British toxic waste sent to Africa. *Times Online*. Retrieved from http://www.timesonline.co.uk/tol/news/uk/article5756601.ece

Clapp, J. (2002). WTO agricultural negotiations: Implications for the Global South. *Third World Quarterly, 27*(4), 563–577.

Konye, O. O. (2008, November). Egypt demands return of stolen artifacts from Europe and U.S. Retrieved from: http://www.afrik-news.com/article16460.html

Koyame, K., & Clark, J. (2002). The economic impact of the Congo War. In J. Clark (Ed.), *The African stakes of the Congo War.* New York: Palgrave-McMillan.

Grey, S. (2007, November 25). Flight logs reveal secret rendition. *The Sunday Times.*

Hargreaves, S. (2009). Global warming's biggest jerks. CNN Money. Retrieved from: http://money.cnn.com/galleries/2009/news/0912/gallery.global_warming/index.html

Jus Semper Global Alliance. (2010). Living wages north and south. Retrieved from: http://www.jussemper.org/Newsletters/Resources/Wage%20gap%20chartsa.pdf

Lowry, D. (September 23, 2013). Double standards on nuclear weapons. *The Guardian.* Retrieved from: http://www.theguardian.com/uk-news/2013/sep/26/double-standards-nuclear-weapons

McChesney, R. (2002). Global media, neo-liberalism and imperialism. *International Socialist Review, 52*(10). Retrieved from: http://www.thirdworldtraveler.com/McChesney/GlobalMedia_Neoliberalism.html

Milkias, P. (2010). Developing the global south. New York: Algora Publishing.

Norris, R. S., & Kristensen, H. M. (2006, August). Global Nuclear Stockpiles 1945–2006, *Bulletin of the Atomic Scientists,* 64–66.

Raja, K. (2008). The paradox of capital flows from south to north. Third World Network, September 2002. Retrieved on October 12, 2013 from: http://www.twnside.org.sg/title2/finance/twninfofinance20080805.htm

Shah, I. (2010, June 7). Bhopal's long injustice. *The Guardian.*

Silverstein, K. (1999, July 19). Millions for Viagra, pennies for diseases of the poor: Research money goes to profitable lifestyle drugs. *The Nation.*

Waters, E. (2010, January 8). The Americanization of mental illness. *The New York Times.*

Winn, P. (2010, December 26). Asia: Guinea pigs a plenty for drug companies. *Truthout.* Retrieved from: http://www.truth-out.org/asia-guinea-pigs-aplenty-drug-giants66279

CHAPTER FIFTEEN

Feeding the City and Financing the Family

Women Market Traders in Suva, Fiji

SUSAN DEWEY AND CEMA BOLABOLA

The Suva Municipal Market:
An Introduction and Overview

Markets, whether centrally organized or ad hoc in nature, provide a critical source of income generation for women throughout the Pacific Island region. This chapter—based on research in the Suva Municipal Market, one of the largest and oldest of all Pacific Island markets— provides an overview of challenges faced by female traders in the everyday course of their work and home lives. The authors argue that a number of forces, including gendered intrahousehold power dynamics and the low status of feminized labor, continue to marginalize women market traders and create an exploitative labor environment despite their significant contributions to Suva's economy.

An ample interdisciplinary body of literature demonstrates the absolute incorrectness of prevailing assumptions about women's informal sector work as undesirable, poorly paid, and unskilled. Indeed, many women earn considerably more in the informal sector and may enjoy more flexibility in their use of time than they would in other forms of work available to them (Anderson, 2008). Government elites and international organizations frequently undervalue the contributions made by market traders to national economies, leading the authors of one study to characterize the production and marketing of fresh food in Papua New Guinea as "one of the country's biggest success stories" (Bourke, 2005). Nonetheless, most women market traders throughout the Pacific Islands do not belong to formal organizations that advocate for their rights. Using the case study of the Suva Municipal Market in Fiji, this chapter explores some of the factors that inhibit women market traders from labor organizing to advocate for their rights.

Most definitions of *formal* and *informal exchange* stem from the state's level of involvement in particular forms of economic activity (Dallago, 1990), yet a number of anthropological texts have clearly illustrated that these lines are rarely clear in everyday lived experience (Castells and Portes, 1989; Dilley, 1992; Graeber, 2001; Hart, 1973). Research demonstrates that much of the labor characterized as informal trade, because it is untaxed and operates without a central supervising authority, is actually highly organized and exists partly in response to a lack of state engagement with the working poor (Ayittey, 2006; King, 2001; MacGaffey & Bazenguissa-Ganga, 2000; Hansen, 2000; Obukhova & Guyer, 2002; Meagher, 2010; Stoller, 2002). Market trade is perhaps the classic form of informal sector activity in that it is often untaxed and operates with minimal government intervention; in Fiji's municipal markets, traders pay a stall rental fee to the municipal authorities but are otherwise untaxed.

Recent anthropological analyses that address meanings ascribed to particular food commodities or other consumable goods in the Pacific Islands have illuminated the complex ways in which these meanings become intertwined with local and national identities, sexuality, and conceptions of modernity (Besnier, 2011; Gewertz & Errington, 2010; Wardlow, 2006). Some research regarding the impact of cash earned from market trade on rural producers who previously practiced subsistence agriculture finds that the introduction of a cash economy dramatically alters the gendered division of labor and related sex roles, with greater prestige attached to cash generation (Benediktsson, 2002; Feinberg, 1986; Mosko, 1999), while others contend that cash-for-goods exchanges are simply incorporated into previously subsistence-based groups' existing belief systems by utilizing multiple strategies to make sense of the use of cash (Curry, 2005; Sykes, 2007). One study of trade in Fiji has demonstrated that while increased involvement in the cash economy can benefit remote areas, it often comes at the expense of subsistence livelihoods that previously ensured a reliable food supply (Sofer, 2007). This is particularly relevant during a period in which the interim military government is embarking on a plan to reduce the amount spent on imported foods from just over U.S.$283 million to U.S.$59 million before 2012 (Vosamana, 2011).

A burgeoning feminist anthropological literature on market trade first began to emerge in the 1980s, as part of broader discussions regarding the impact of development projects on women. These studies established the cross-cultural frequency with which market trade is a feminized activity (Alexander & Alexander, 2001; Babb, 1998; Boserup, 1970; Chalfin, 2004; Clark, 2010, 1994; House-Midamba & Ekechi, 1995; Kapchan, 1996; Milgram & Brown, 2009; Seligmann, 2004). This literature is complemented by a related body of feminist scholarship from Papua New Guinea that focused on documenting the significant role played by women in exchange transactions, including market trade (Gewertz, 1977; Lederman, 2009; MacKenzie, 1991; Strathern, 1990; Weiner, 1976). This chapter thus builds on a growing body of anthropological literature that focuses on the social invisibility and low value ascribed to feminized labor cross-culturally, and in Fiji in particular (Carswell, 2003; Leckie, 2000a, 2000b; Mishra, 2008; Pollard, 1987; Rakaseta, 1995). This literature spans a wide array of topics that are united by their focus on women's more limited access to resources, formal education, and opportunities for upward mobility, and include literature on sex work, feminized labor migration, and caregiving activities (Cabezas, 2009; Katsulis, 2010; Kelly, 2008; Parrenas, 2008, 2010; Salzinger, 2003).

The origin of municipal produce markets organized and administered by a central authority with regulatory powers dates to the advent of the colonial period throughout the Pacific Island region (Connell & Lea, 2007), and in Fiji Dewey's research revealed that this system remains very much an extractive one through which the state, in the form of local government authorities, reaps an enormous profit while investing very little in market infrastructure. This is particularly significant given that Fiji's military government is currently in a state of financial crisis from which it is unlikely to emerge in the near future due to the loss of preferential trade agreements for sugar and a drop in tourism following the fourth coup (Serrano, 2007).

The Suva Municipal Market is the largest and most ethno-linguistically diverse venue for the exchange of agricultural products and cash in Fiji's capital city, Suva, the second most populous city in the entire South Pacific region. Several hundred traders sell from inside the market on any given Monday through Thursday, with this number swelling to over 2 thousand traders when functioning at full capacity on the weekend. Despite working in what many traders describe as less-than-ideal physical conditions, these women are a significant source of income for their families and for the rural villages in which many of them live. Even more significantly, income generated by their fees to the City Council, which regulates and oversees the market, provides Suva, Fiji's capital, with its second largest source of income after taxes. Market traders' substantial contributions to both City Council (through their stall fees) and their own families (through their earnings) put them in the position of providing the vast majority of Suva's food, a significant portion of its revenue, and, of course, a much-needed source of cash income for hundreds of families.

The market is located in Suva's central business district, where it was first constructed in 1950 (*Fiji Times & Herald*, 1950: p. 5). Records in the National Archives of Fiji indicate that rural farmers exchanged agricultural products for cash in Suva since at least 1882, when Suva became the national capital (*Suva Times*, 1885, p. 2). The first colonial ordinances concerning market trade date to 1891 (Legislative Council of Fiji, 1891), and, while elaborated on since that time, closely resemble current legislation governing the market (Suva City Council, 1990). Despite the significant time elapsed, current market-related regulations closely resemble their colonial predecessors in focusing primarily on the use of space in the market, items allowed for sale, and hours of operation.

Women constitute the vast majority of market traders in Suva, as is the case elsewhere in Fiji and most of the Pacific Island region. Women traders in the market come from all three of Fiji's major ethnic groups, with just over half of all traders self-identifying as indigenous Fijian, 40% as Indo-Fijian, and the remainder as Chinese; this demographic has remained relatively stable for at least 20 years (Dewey, 2011; Lateef, 1994) and mirrors Fiji's national ethnic composition (Government of Fiji, 2007). A quantitative survey carried out with several hundred traders by Dewey in 2011 revealed that significant demographic differences exist between traders who sell daily inside the market's physical structure, who are ethnically diverse and live closer to Suva, and those who sell on the weekends in the area surrounding the market and have traveled long distances from their homogenously indigenous Fijian interior villages to sell produce they have grown themselves. Most traders are the sole source of cash income for their household, and the average amounts earned in the market are well above the daily minimum wage earned in comparably skilled jobs, which is particularly telling because the majority of market traders have never engaged in any other income-generating activities, and over half have been involved in trading for over 10 years.

The market opens at 6:00 a.m., just before sunrise, and closes approximately 12 hours later on every day except Sunday. In order to begin trading inside the market, one must approach the Market Master, who is employed by the Suva City Council, which administers the market. The Council, as this local government entity is typically called, generates considerable revenue from the stall fees paid by market traders, which comprise the capital city's second-highest source of revenue after taxes (Suva City Council, 2008). Stall fees currently stand at Fiji dollars (FJD) $2.80 ($1.40 U.S.) per day for traders who sell inside the market structure; FJD $3.30 ($1.65 U.S.) per day for traders who sell outside the market or who sell seafood; FJD $3.60 ($1.80 U.S.) for dry goods; FJD $3.30 ($1.65 U.S.) per day for juice sellers; and FJD $20.25 ($10.12 U.S.) per week for bean or sweet cart vendors; and $56.25 per week for juice mall proprietors (Suva City Council, 2010). These prices, which prioritize the sale of fresh produce in order to promote local agriculture over imported foods, reflect the costs of various products. However, many vendors consistently remarked to Dewey during her fieldwork that they found these fees to be quite high.

Market traders display their produce on concrete tables provided by the Suva City Council inside the market. There is very little variation in the price of items throughout the market, and the vast majority of fruits and vegetables are sold by "heap" (*ibinibini*, in Fijian), which consists of the number of the particular fruit or vegetable that can be conveniently piled onto a small plastic plate. A "heap" of papaya, for instance, usually includes 4 medium-size fruits, while a "heap" of green chili peppers might include as many as 50 small peppers.

A quantitative survey Dewey conducted with nearly 2 hundred market traders in summer 2011 revealed that there are significant differences between those who sell goods from tables allocated to them from inside the market and those who lay their produce on the ground on the concrete verandah or unpaved area outside the market on Fridays and Saturdays. Those who sell outside the market travel much longer distances, often by carrier (as large transport trucks are known), often arriving in the early hours of dawn; whereas those who sell inside the market tend to live in Suva or its peri-urban outskirts, with an average commute time of 30 minutes or less by bus, taxi or, more rarely, private car. Approximately half of all traders are in their mid-forties and have an average of two school-age children, regardless of where they sell their produce, but similarities between these two populations stop there. Individuals who sell inside the market typically live closer to Suva, with an average commute time of just over 30 minutes, have more education and more years of trading experience, with approximately 30% of all traders working in the market for between 10 and 15 years.

According to Dewey's quantitative survey, 20% of those who sell inside have been trading at the Suva Market for more than 15 years. Approximately half of the inside traders report daily incomes of between FJD$50 and FDJ$100 ($25 to $50 U.S.), with this rising up to 2 hundred on Fridays and Saturdays. Traders who sell outside typically travel much longer distances, with just under half spending between one and a half and two hours to reach the market. Those who sell outside are also less formally educated, with a full 35% having completed no more than the U.S. equivalent of seventh grade. Outside traders have far fewer years of experience with market trading, with 30% selling between six to nine years, and one-fourth selling for four or five years. Just fewer than 60% of outside traders earn between $1 hundred and $2 hundred dollars on Fridays and Saturdays, the main days that they attend market from their rural homes. Women constitute the vast majority of sellers at the market, according to a June 2011 quantitative survey Dewey carried out with over 150 traders on all weekdays that the market is open. On Friday and Saturday, when rural traders predominate sales outside the market (and often traveling long distances to do so), the vast majority of traders are Fijian-speaking females. The demographic portrait of traders who regularly sell inside is more diverse, at approximately 75% female, and an ethno-linguistic breakdown among both women and men indicates that just over half of all traders speak Fijian as their mother tongue, and just under half speak Fiji Hindi as their mother tongue. A 1994 survey of approximately the same number of traders indicates that these numbers have remained relatively static (Lateef, 1994).

Challenges in the Workplace

Women market traders face a number of infrastructural and organizational challenges as they go about their work, which is the main source of cash income for many rural families. Despite their hard work and long hours, market trading remains a stigmatized, low-status occupation that many people in Fiji unfortunately view as a last resort for income generation. Market traders are not accorded the respect that they deserve as businesspeople, and do not receive many of the courtesies extended to other members of the city's business community. Most market traders Dewey spoke to during her research indicated that class privilege (and their relative lack of it) resulted in a situation that did not give them the same access to government elites as wealthy shop owners, most of whom are, not coincidentally, men. When Suva Central Farmers Association Prem Chandra complained to the press about what he regarded as unjust parking fees for vendors and farmers, he noted that "shopkeepers in other parts of Suva are provided loading/unloading areas free of charge by the Council. So why are the poor market vendors being penalized" (*Fiji Times*, 1996, p. 4)? This disparity was ongoing in 2011 during Dewey's fieldwork.

Women trading in the market face what can be serious risks to their health and safety through their long hours in a rather unhygienic environment. Women from the rural areas arrive as early as 10:00 p.m. the day before they plan to sell in the market, and arrange makeshift shelter for themselves using tarpaulins and bedding they have brought from their villages to create small sleeping areas on the market's cement verandah. While away, they typically leave their children with relatives who function as caregivers; Dewey's trip to a village from which many market traders come indicated that most women market traders have children who are older and thus easier to care for by women who remain in the village and do not go to market. These women are reluctant to leave the market prior to its opening due to fears that someone might steal their produce, which means that they must sit in groups until sunrise. During a 24-hour period the authors spent visiting the market at regular 2-hour intervals, they were struck by the vulnerability of women sleeping outdoors prior to the market's opening. Intoxicated groups of men frequently pass through the market from the nearby drinking establishments, and police presence in the late night hours they observed was either negligible or nonexistent.

Market traders have not always passively accepted these challenges, and there have been numerous instances of social justice activism. Charismatic Fijian businessperson Apolosi Nawai established the Fresh Produce Agency in 1915 as part of his efforts to organize Fijian agricultural producers into an association that would negotiate favorable terms of trade with European settlers (Heartfield, 2003, p. 39). Market vendors associations, which exist to convey traders' concerns to local government administrators, have been in existence since at least the early 1940s (*Pacific Islands Monthly*, 1942, p. 22), and a noble attempt to unite over 2 thousand market vendors and street traders into a centralized Fiji Municipal Market Vendors' Association took place in 1977 (*Fiji Times*, 1978, p. 11). Difficulties related to geographical distance and uniting such diverse groups precluded long-term national organizing, a problem that remains in place today. Market traders organizations remain divided between rural producers who sell at the market on the weekends, and those who live in or near Suva and buy primarily from wholesalers, which precludes cooperation and labor organizing.

At the time of writing, Suva Municipal Market vendors could choose between membership in the Suva Market Vendors Association, which caters to traders living in Suva and its suburbs, and the Rural Farmers' Representatives, comprised mainly of agricultural producers who travel longer distances to sell their goods in Suva (Suva City Council, 2011). Market vendor associations, as well as individual vendors, frequently petition the Suva City Council for repairs and improvements to the market's physical structure, permission to sell outside the market, hours of trading, the conditions of sales, and reductions in stall fees.

Shortly after Fiji's first and second coups, in 1987, the Suva City Council received a petition signed by 640 market vendors that requested improvements to the market facilities and a reduction in stall fees due to the economic trauma induced by the coups (Suva City Council, 1987a, p. 6). The Suva City Council refused, and in protest vendors stopped paying stall fees pending the receipt of a final response from the Council; within one month, the Council confirmed its decision that existing stall fees remain in place (Suva City Council, 1987b, p. 15). The Suva City Council clearly recognized the need to respond to vendors' demands, and at the February 1988 meeting of the Suva City Council, the Town Clerk presented a report outlining plans to reorganize the market and shelter all vendors (Suva City Council, 1988a). This decision, taken at least partially in response to vendors' strike action, culminated in the allocation of funds to construct a new, two-story market (Suva City Council, 1988b).

The new market, built around the existing market structure at a cost of $1.7 million, opened in January 1991. An article in Fiji's most widely read newspaper acknowledged the poor conditions of the previous market by noting "some Suva market vendors had the benefit of breaking away from tattered tarpaulins and rusted tin shacks when the top floor of the new market was opened for them" (*Fiji Times*, 1991, p. 3). Discussions regarding the need to replace its leaking, brittle asbestos roof that dated to the municipal market's opening in 1950 began just a year later (Suva City Council, 1992), but were not undertaken until 2009 despite numerous complaints of leakage and fears "that the roof could collapse anytime" (Suva City Council, 2005). *The Fiji Times* reported that most of the market vendors did not know what asbestos was, causing one market trader to opine, "If it can kill us, what can I do? This stall is my only means of earning a living" (*Fiji Times*, 2005, p. 2).

Tensions mounted again in the late 1990s, when representatives of the market vendors associations filed an injunction with the Suva High Court to prevent stall fee increases, arguing that they were both unjustified and unfeasible due to the high costs of living (*Fiji Times*, 1997, p. 3). In March 1998, following the accumulation of FJD$38 thousand (U.S.$19 thousand) in unpaid stall fees, 20 police officers and security hired by the Suva City Council forcibly removed vendors from the market, where they took up positions in protest in the surrounding market area (*Fiji Times*, 1998a, p. 1). To justify the Council's decision, Suva Mayor Dansukh Lal Bhika said, "vendors always claim that stall fees are too high. And they are always using this excuse to refrain from paying the amount of stall fees owed to the Council. We understand that cost of living is high. But the council also needs money to operate. That's what they don't understand" (*Fiji Times*, 1998b, p. 1).

Despite the SCC's closure of the market, the protest was a success in that the Suva City Council eventually agreed to defer the stall fee increases for three months and draw up a five-year plan with vendors for implementing future stall fees. The impacts of the strike were far-reaching, and by March 1998, the Suva City Council was technically insolvent and unable to service its debts, prompting director of Administration and Operations to inform each individual vendor of the amount owed, with the SCC vowing to close the market if any vendors associations interfered with repayment (Suva City Council, 1998). In response to the Suva City Council's decision to close the market for repairs following nearly a year of sporadic protests, Suva's Mayor conceded, "while I do not accept the illegal action by the market vendors, I sympathize with their claims and acknowledge that further improvement can be made to the Suva Market," promising to request the Suva City Council's permission to allocate repair funds (*Fiji Times*, 1999b). Fiji's third coup in 2000 created political and economic turmoil that precluded significant investment in the market.

The Suva City Council last increased stall fees in 2002, with proposed increases, in 2010, of 14% for inside traders and 10% for others. During discussions in 2004 regarding raising stall fees, the director of Administration and Operations acknowledged that the SCC would generate more revenue this way; councilors should "bear in mind that these vendors came from villages trying to make an honest living in a tough environment and it would not be proper to increase the same" (Suva City Council, 2004). In 2011, representatives from the Suva Market Vendors Association and the Rural Farmers Representatives approached the prime minister's office directly with their concerns, leading to a directive instructing the special administrator (akin to the position of mayor), director of Administration and Operations, and the Market Master to meet monthly with representatives from these associations regarding their concerns (Suva City Council, 2011).

Petitions and collective action by market vendors have clearly resulted in improvements to the Suva Municipal Market in years past, and yet significant challenges remain in terms of the everyday management of the market. As the following section will illustrate, these workplace issues are further complicated by challenges that many women market traders face in their home environment.

Challenges in the Home

Rural indigenous women market vendors live beyond the periphery of Suva city in rural villages and travel to market to earn an income. The situation of rural indigenous women market vendors are about hardship, heavy and multiple workloads, without appropriate labor-saving technology and face gender discrimination from all sectors of the family and community. Rural women face hardship in the form of having to manually do all work to support the family, the diminishing sources of fuel wood for cooking, the increasing distance walked to collect food and fuel wood, transportation, hours of work, absence of food preservation technology, and satisfying the conflicting demands of their time and hard-earned resources from family and community.

Rural women vendors as fishers and agriculturalists, face multiple challenges. They perform multiple production tasks to support the family and community economy and their work is not accounted for in national economic statistics. Village women are deemed part of the population of "economically unproductive" adults, and are classified as unemployed or underemployed. The production work of rural women vendors are carried out manually, they walk long distances under tropical heat and rain to harvest produce to meet domestic consumption and for the market. The multiple roles of rural women expose women to greater risk to their health, happiness, and well-being.

Rural women bear the brunt of prevailing standard of physical housing and development in rural villages. Though some rural villages of these women market vendors have had good standard housing and sanitation and water facilities, a majority of the villages of women continue to have substandard housing, sanitation, and water facilities. In such a situation, women's health and well-being are at increased risk as their workload is doubled under unhygienic and uncomfortable conditions. Indigenous rural women, though part of the Fiji community that owns 86% of the land resources, continue to have unequal access to resources in the home and in the community. Though they are legally registered as landowners, they only have usufruct rights to the land they occupy and use courtesy of their husbands, male relatives, or their children. Generally women marry outside their own landowning unit, since the indigenous Fijian community is patrilocal. Consequently, the women market vendors have no legal right to the land of their husbands or children. Rural women market vendors plant on land owned by a male relative or generally harvest wild foods from the land and sea of the community where they reside.

The land tenure system of communally owned indigenous land bars rural women from using land as collateral to access loans available from financial institutions (Aruntangai & Crocombe, 2000; Bolabola, 1986; Ward & Kingdon, 1995). Such a situation forces women into continuing dependence on male relatives for their utilization of land. Marriage is of no help to legalizing the rights of women to assets, especially land that belongs to their husbands' landowning units. In such a situation rural women become dependent on their male relatives, and unable to leave subsistence agriculture to set up non-agricultural microenterprise they continue in market vending activities. Apart from the lack of access to land resources, rural women face further persistent gender discrimination as they are deemed not to have the ability to engage in income-generation activities. Rural women do not have access to start-up capital or access to appropriate training for microenterprises. Rural communities do not perceive market vending as business enterprise, but rather a weekly activity that women carry out to earn an income.

Rural women vendors experience further discrimination that exclude them from participating in domestic and community decision-making process and leadership. As the indigenous Fijian community is patrilineal, rural women are considered to be without authority, based on their residence status, to participate in community decision-making process. At the domestic level, women are deemed unfit to make decisions that affect family income, even though their labor contributes to domestic and community income. Rural women are deemed good fund-raisers, but decision making to raise funds and designating the purpose is a male domain. Self-help village development projects have only been possible with the fund-raising efforts of rural women. Studies have revealed that indigenous males make 85% of the decisions, and women carry out 90% of the work necessary to implement actions in support of those decisions at family and village levels (Bolabola, 1986).

Village-based indigenous women have organized themselves into a nonprofit group that affiliates with a district and national association. The nonprofit group, Soqosoqo Vakamarama (Women's Cooperative), which started some 70 years ago, originally focused on training women to be better homemakers and mothers. The Soqosoqo Vakamarama was founded in 1924 as a Methodist organization, and presently plays an important role in fostering indigenous Fijian women's roles in traditional occupations, including trade and agriculture. Over the years the women's organization has neither supported women's programs designed to address gender equality nor the empowerment of women members in the decision making, economic livelihood, and access to resources and capital. In such a situation rural women as vendors feel good belonging to a national women's organization but look to other women's groups to meet and advocate for their development needs (Leckie, 2002).

Concluding Thoughts

There is a clear record of at least some amount of cooperation between the Suva City Council and the ethnically and socioeconomically diverse traders who carry out their activities in the Suva Municipal Market. Pacific Island markets must be acknowledged by local and national governments as significant sources of revenue. Market traders should be recognized as businesspeople in order to facilitate their access to credit, which has been an obstacle to many women engaged in trade (Sullivan & Ram-Bidesi, 2008). The work of market traders supplies local as well as global commodity chains (Benediktsson, 2002), and their careful investigations into ways to support themselves and their families should be recognized by local and national governments in order to help reduce some of the stigma associated with market trade (van der Grijp, 2002), and perhaps encourage further local agricultural production and sale.

Local and national government investment in infrastructural improvements to markets will benefit both traders and the communities that they supply. One Solomon Islands–based study recommended the improvement of road conditions to facilitate trade, as well as extending credit managed by a commercial bank into rural areas to support and encourage agricultural production (McGregor, 2005). Another study, based in Papua New Guinea, indicated that traders' lack of road transport negates any possibility for rural women to engage in trade, even if they have the desire (Hirsch, 1994). Market conditions in many Pacific Island countries require significant improvements to make them safe and hygienic places to work and sell. Making such improvements demonstrates institutional commitment to markets and to market traders, who generate a substantial source of income for local and national economies.

Pacific Island governments should engage in more active promotion of agricultural production and marketing, which could reduce some of the widespread preference for imported and processed foods, the consumption of which has seriously negative health consequences (Gewertz & Errington, 2010). Linking agricultural producers to tourism industry service providers would be particularly useful in countries like Fiji and Tahiti, which derive significant sources of income from tourism. Currently, many such service providers import food rather than utilizing local farmers' crops, which would be both wasteful and unnecessary if proper provisions were made for the exchange of produce and cash between these two parties (Taulealea, 2005).

With concerns about food security again becoming a priority throughout the world, governments can no longer afford to ignore the important roles played by women market traders in bringing affordable and high-quality produce to towns and cities. This is particularly true in the Pacific Islands, where climate change continues to create real and immediate threats to sustainable livelihoods. Now, more than ever, governments and policy makers need to work closely with market traders in order to determine ways to facilitate women's economic empowerment and poverty eradication measures while also ensuring a reliable supply of healthy local produce to Pacific towns and urban centers.

References

Alexander, J., & Alexander, P. (2001). Markets as gendered domains: The Javanese pasar. In L. Seligman (Ed.), *Women traders in cross-cultural perspective: Mediating identities, marketing wares* (pp. 47–72). Palo Alto, CA: Stanford University Press.

Anderson, T. (2008). Women roadside sellers in Madang. *Pacific Economic Bulletin, 23*(1), 59–73.

Ayittey, G. (2006). *Africa unchained: The blueprint for Africa's future.* New York: Palgrave Macmillan.

Babb, F. (1998). *Between field and cooking pot: The political economy of market women in Peru.* Austin, TX: University of Texas Press.

Benediktsson, K. (2002). *Harvesting development: The construction of fresh food markets in Papua New Guinea.* Ann Arbor, Michigan: University of Michigan Press.

Besnier, N. (2011). *On the edge of the global: Modern anxieties in a Pacific nation.* Palo Alto, CA: Stanford University Press.

Bolabola, C. (1986). *Fiji: Customary constraints and legal progress.* In C. Bolabola, D. Kenneth, H. Silas, M. Moengangongo, A. Fana'afi, &

M. James (Eds.), *Land rights of Pacific women* (pp. 1–66). Institute of Pacific Studies of the University of the South Pacific.

Boserup, E. (1970). *Women's role in economic development.* New York and London: Earthscan.

Bourke, R. (2005). Marketed fresh food: A successful part of the Papua New Guinea economy. *Development Bulletin, 67,* 22–25.

Cabezas, A. (2009). *Economies of desire: Sex and tourism in the Dominican Republic.* Philadelphia, PA: Temple University Press.

Carswell, S. (2003). A family business: Women, children and smallholder cane farming in Fiji. *Asia Pacific Viewpoint, 44*(2), 131–148.

Castells, M., & Portes, A. (1989). World underneath: The origins, dynamics, and effects of the informal economy. In A. Portes, M. Castells, & L. Benton (Eds.), *The informal economy: Studies in advanced and less developed countries* (pp. 11–37). Baltimore, MD: Johns Hopkins University Press.

Chalfin, B. (2004). *Shea butter republic: State power, global markets, and the making of an indigenous commodity.* New York: Routledge.

Clark, G. (2010). *African market women: Seven life stories from Ghana.* Bloomington: Indiana University Press.

Clark, G. (1994). *Onions are my husband: Survival and accumulation by West African market women.* Chicago, IL: University of Chicago Press

Connell, J., & Lea, J. (2007). *Urbanisation in the island Pacific.* London and New York: Routledge.

Curry, G. (2005). Doing "business" in Papua New Guinea: The social embeddedness of small business enterprise. *Journal of Small Business and Entrepreneurship, 18*(2), 231–246.

Dallago, B. (1990). *The irregular economy: The "underground" economy and the "Black" labour market.* Farnham, Surrey, UK: Ashgate Press.

Dewey, S. (2011). Markets and women's market trading in the Pacific Islands: An overview of social contexts and ongoing challenges. *Asian Women, 27*(3), 1–24.

Dilley, R., Ed. (1992). *Contesting markets: Analyses of ideology, disccourse and practice.* Edinburgh, UK: Edinburgh University Press.

Feinberg, R. (1986). Market economy and changing sex-roles on a Polynesian atoll. *Ethnology, 25*(4), 271–282.

Fiji Times & Herald, The. (1950, November 3). Suva's new market building to open tomorrow. *The Fiji Times & Herald,* p. 5.

Fiji Times, The. (2009, April 4). Market opening brings joy to vendors. *The Fiji Times,* p. 4.

Fiji Times, The. (2005, October 14). City residents face asbestos risk. *The Fiji Times,* p. 2.

Fiji Times, The. (1999a, September 2). City plans to close market for repairs. *The Fiji Times,* p. 4.

Fiji Times, The. (1999b, September 5). City may relocate vendors. *The Fiji Times,* p. 4.

Fiji Times, The. (1998a, March 3). City shuts market vendors out. *The Fiji Times,* p. 1.

Fiji Times, The. (1998b, March 4). Council Evicts Vendors. *The Fiji Times,* p. 1.

Fiji Times, The. (1997, July 17). Council gives vendors last chance. *The Fiji Times,* p. 3.

Fiji Times, The. (1996, September 5). Farmers protest Suva market car park. *The Fiji Times,* p. 4.

Fiji Times, The. (1991, January 3). Market opens. *The Fiji Times,* p. 3.

Fiji Times, The. (1978, August 28). Trade Briefs. *The Fiji Times,* p. 11

Gewertz, D., & Errington, F. (2010). *Cheap meat: Flap food nations in the Pacific Islands.* Berkeley: University of California Press.

Gewertz, D. (1977). From sago suppliers to entrepreneurs: Marketing and migration in the Middle Sepik. *Oceania, 48,* 126–140.

Graeber, D. (2001). *Toward an anthropological theory of value: The false coin of our own dreams.* New York: Palgrave Macmillan.

Hansen, K. (2000). *Salaula: The world of secondhand clothing and Zambia.* Chicago, IL: University of Chicago Press.

Hart, K. (1973). Informal income opportunities and urban employment in Ghana. *The Journal of Modern African Studies, 11,* 61–89.

Heartfield, J. (2003). "You are not a White woman!" Apolosi Nawai, the Fiji Produce Agency, and the trial of Stella Spencer in Fiji, 1915. *Journal of Pacific History, 38*(1), 69–83.

Herskovits, M. (1952). *Economic anthropology.* New York: Knopf.

Hirsch, E. (1994). Between mission and market: Events and images in a Melanesian society. *Man, 29*(3), 689–711.

House-Midamba, B., & Ekechi, F. (eds.) (1995). *African market women and economic power: The role of women in African economic development.* Boston, MA: Greenwood Press.

Kapchan, D. (1996). *Gender on the market: Moroccan women and the revoicing of tradition.* Philadelphia, PA: University of Pennsylvania Press.

Katsulis, Y. (2009). *Sex work and the city: The social geography of health and safety in Tijuana, Mexico.* Austin: University of Texas Press.

Kelly, P. (2008). *Lydia's open door: Inside Mexico's most modern brothel.* Berkeley: University of California Press.

King, K. (2001). Africa's informal economies: Thirty years on. *SAIS Review, 21*(1), 97–108.

Lateef, S. (1994). *Women market traders in Fiji.* Suva, Fiji: Fiji Association of Women Graduates.

Leckie, J. (2002). The complexities of women's agency in Fiji. In B. Yeoh, P. Teo, & S. Huang (Eds.), *Gender politics in the Asia-Pacific region* (pp. 156–180). New York: Routledge.

Leckie, J. (2000a). Women in post-coup Fiji: Negotiating work through old and new realities. In A. Akram-Lodhi & A. Haroon (Eds.), *Confronting Fiji futures* (pp. 178–201). Canberra, AU: Australian National University Press.

Leckie, J. (2000b). Gender and work in Fiji: Constraints to renegotiation. In A. Jones, P. Herda, & T. Suaali (Eds.), *Bitter sweet: Indigenous women in the Pacific* (pp. 73–92). Dunedin, NZ: University of Otago Press.

Lederman, R. (2009). *What gifts engender: Social relations and politics in Mendi, Highland Papua New Guinea.* Cambridge: Cambridge University Press.

Legislative Council of Fiji. (1891). *Council Paper No. 31 "Native Markets," approved by the Legislative Council, 30 November 1891.* Suva, Fiji: National Archives of Fiji.

McGregor, A. (2006). *Solomons Islands smallholder study: Volume 3, markets and marketing issues.* Canberra, AU: AusAID.

MacGaffey, J., & Bazenguissa-Ganga, R. (2000). *Congo-Paris: Transnational traders on the margins of the law.* Bloomington, IN: Indiana University Press.

MacKenzie, M. (1991). *Androgynous objects: String bags and gender in Central New Guinea.* New York: Routledge.

Mauss, M. (2000 [1872]). *The gift: The form and reason for exchange in archaic societies.* New York: W. W. Norton & Company.

Meagher, K. (2010). *Identity economics: Social networks and the informal economy in Nigeria.* Oxford, UK: James Currey.

Milgram, B. L., & Brown (eds.) (2009). *Economics and morality: Anthropological approaches.* AltaMira.

Mintz, S. (1985). *Sweetness and power.* New York: Random House.

Mintz, S. (1974). *The worker in the cane.* New York: Norton.

Mishra, M. (2008). The emergence of feminism in Fiji. *Women's History Review, 17*(1), 39–55.

Mosko, M. (1999). Magical money: Commodity and the linkage of maketsi ("market") and kangakanga ("custom") in contemporary North Mekeo. In D. Akin & J. Robbins (Eds.), *Money and modernity: State and local currencies in Melanesia* (41–61). Pittsburgh, PA: University of Pittsburgh Press.

Obukhova, E., & Guyer J. (2002). Transcending the formal/informal distinction: Commercial relations in Africa and Russia in the post-1989 world. In J. Ensminger (Ed.), *Theory in economic anthropology* (pp. 199–220). Lanham, MD: Altamira Press.

Overton, J. (1999). Vakavanua, vakamatanitū: Discourses of development in Fiji. *Asia Pacific Viewpoint, 40*(2), 173–186.

Parreñas, R. (2011). *Illicit flirtations: Labor, migration, and sex trafficking in Tokyo.* Palo Alto, CA: Stanford University Press.

Parreñas, R. (2008). *The force of domesticity: Filipina migrants and globalization.* New York: New York University Press.

Pollard, C. (1987). Domestic service in Suva, Fiji: Social and occupational mobility of Fijian housegirls. *Journal of Pacific Studies, 13*, 36–46.

Rakaseta, V. (1995). Women's work and fertility in Fiji. *Pacific Health Dialog, 2*(1), 17–24.

Sahlins, M. (1972). *Stone age economics.* Chicago, IL: Aldine.

Salzinger, L. (2003). *Genders in production: Making workers in Mexico's global factories.* Berkeley: University of California Press.

Seligmann, L. (2004). *Peruvian street lives: Culture, power, and economy among market women of Cuzco.* Urbana: University of Illinois Press.

Serrano, K. (2007). Sweet like sugar: Does the EU's new sugar regime become Fiji's bitter reality or welcome opportunity? *Journal of South Pacific Law, 11*(2), 169–193.

Sofer, M. (2007). Yaqona and the Fijian periphery revisited. *Asia Pacific Viewpoint, 48*(2), 234–249.

Stoller, P. (2002). *Money has no smell: The Africanization of New York City.* Chicago, IL: University of Chicago Press.

Strathern, M. (1990). *The gender of the gift: Problems with women and problems with society in Melanesia.* Berkeley: University of California Press.

Sullivan, N., & Ram-Bidesi, B. (2008). *Gender issues in Pacific Island tuna fisheries: Case studies in Papua New Guinea, Fiji and Kiribati.* Suva, Fiji: Pacific Islands Forum Secretariat, Forum Fisheries Agency, and Secretariat of the Pacific Community.

Suva City Council. (2011). *Notice of Ordinary Meetings, 26 April.* Suva, Fiji: Suva City Council.

Suva City Council. (2010). *Notice of Ordinary Meetings, 17 December.* Suva, Fiji: Suva City Council.

Suva City Council. (2005). *Notice of Ordinary Meetings, 19 May.* Suva, Fiji: Suva City Council.

Suva City Council. (2008). *Notice of Ordinary Meetings, 24 January.* Suva, Fiji: Suva City Council.

Suva City Council. (2004). *Notice of Ordinary Meetings, 16 February.* Suva, Fiji: Suva City Council.

Suva City Council. (1998). *Notice of Ordinary Meetings, 20 March.* Suva, Fiji: Suva City Council.

Suva City Council. (1992). *Notice of Ordinary Meetings, 23 October.* Suva, Fiji: Suva City Council.

Suva City Council. (1990). *By-laws of the Suva Municipal Market.* Suva City Council, Notice of Ordinary Meetings, 24 August. Suva, Fiji: Suva City Council.

Suva City Council. (1988a). *Notice of Ordinary Meetings, 19 February.* Suva, Fiji: Suva City Council.

Suva City Council. (1988b). *Annual Report.* Suva, Fiji: Suva City Council.

Suva City Council. (1987a). *Notice of Ordinary Meetings, 23 October.* Suva, Fiji: Suva City Council.

Suva City Council. (1987b). *Notice of Ordinary Meetings, 20 November.* Suva, Fiji: Suva City Council.

Suva Times, The. (1885, February 6). Letter to the editor. *The Suva Times,* p. 2.

Sykes, K. (2007). The moral grounds of critique: Between possessive individuals, entrepreneurs, and big men in Papua New Guinea. *Anthropological Forum, 17*(3), 255–268.

Taulealea, S. (2005). A feasibility study for developing a marketing center at the Navuso Agricultural School in Fiji (MA thesis). International Studies, University of Wyoming.

Vosamana, S. (2011, July 1). $586m on Food Imports. *The Fiji Times.* Retrieved from: http://www.fijitimes.com/story.aspx?id=173947

Wardlow, H. (2006). *Wayward women: Sexuality and agency in a New Guinea Society*. Berkeley: University of California Press.

Weiner, A. (1976). *Women of value, men of renown: New perspectives on Trobriand exchange*. Austin: University of Texas Press.

CHAPTER SIXTEEN

China in Africa

Dislocating Cultures, Re-examining the Role of the Nation-State, and the China Model in the Process of Development

SETH N. ASUMAH

Introduction

In an ironic twist, China has done particularly well by taking advantage of the West's refusal to deal with "rogue states." In the Middle East and Africa, for example, China has openly refused to condition trade on compliance with international human rights treaties, have the European Union and the United States, giving China greater access to valuable resources in countries like Angola, Burma, Congo, and Libya. While many protest the U.S. government's inadequate peacekeeping and humanitarian response in Darfur, China has happily established itself as the largest investor in Sudan's massive oil fields.

—Amy Chua, *Day of Empire*

A Chinese official in Africa argued that "economic rights" are the main priority of developing nations and take precedence over personal, individual rights as conceptualized in the West. Indeed, the view among some senior Chinese officials is that "multi-party politics fuels social turmoil, ethnic conflicts and civil wars." China also sees human rights discourse as a tool of Western neo-imperialism. This is a particularly attractive philosophy for incumbent African political elites, and is helped by its plausibility.

—Padraig R. Carmody and Francis Y. Owusu,
Taking Sides, Clashing Views on African Issues

The tragedy is that the CCP's drive to survive has forged a
brutal mercantilist policy that seduces impoverished, resources-
rich regimes with low or no interest loans and the promise
of non-interference in internal affairs in return for long-term
lease of energy and mineral resources. Unlike the IMF and the
World Bank, China's financial package comes without requiring
government reforms, respect for human rights, transparency,
anti-corruption measures or environmental improvements.

—Stephan Halper, *The Beijing Consensus*

From Angola to Zimbabwe, and from bicycle factories in Accra to
soccer stadiums in Zanzibar, the Chinese presence in Africa is irrepressible, and China's investments on the continent are increasing at galloping rates. Recent economic downturns in the United
States, Europe, and China's trade relations and economic development projects in Africa have Sino-Optimists, Sino-Pessimists, and
Sino-Cautionists reassessing the "China Model" in Africa, and what
has become the role of the African nation-state in development. The
foreign policy elites of China have not by any means hidden China's
political agendas in Africa. They are proud to announce that China has a strategic partnership with Africa. This partnership places
emphasis on political equality, mutual trust, win-win development
projects, and exchanges based on cultural relativism.

Yet, the advent of the Chinese in Africa in the post-Colonial
era has called to question the place of African cultures and the role
of the nation-state in the process of development and modernization. China's development activities in Africa and the China Model
for development are raising new questions about China's neobenevolent cultural imperialism, disregard for African cultures, and the
relevance of the authority of African nation-states in dealing with
China's hegemony and development approaches. African cultural
studies and development research must, therefore, consider cross-
cultural dynamics, and structural and systemic variables that contribute to sustainable development. Furthermore, in the processes of
modernization and development, the convergence theory maintains
that once African traditional cultures and nation-states are exposed
to the forces of modernization, Chinanization and development, the
marginal propensity of abandoning African cultures in the interest
of Chinese ones is very high. In this chapter, I argue that the Chinese approach to development and the forces of modernization and
development are contributing to the bastardization of the role of the
nation-state in nation building, and Sino-Africanization is gradually

causing the extinction of African traditional cultures. Unless Africans are able to navigate the dynamics of cultural imperialism, Chinanization and the hegemonic development approaches from China to become true development partners with the People's Republic of China, African development problems will continue to be irrepressible and insurmountable.

It is not unusual that the United States Council on Foreign Relations (CFR) continues to accuse China of protecting "rogue states" and vampire regimes in Africa through economic and business partnerships. The interlocutors of Sino-Africa relations have even more complex issues to examine as African people in recent times have shown their desire to embrace their own cultures, improve human rights conditions, engage in democratic projects and concomitantly promote and support the Forum on China-Africa Cooperation (FOCAC); Beijing in 2000, Addis Ababa in 2003, Beijing, again, in 2006. Events surrounding the 10th anniversary of FOCAC are testimony to the fact that the dragon has secured a place in Africa.

Furthermore, one must not forget the fact that historically, the Chinese presence in Africa could be traced as far back the 15th century, when China's imperial fleet led by Admiral Zheng landed in East Africa. So, arguably, before Bartolommeo Dias, the Portuguese explorer became the first European to reach Africa, the Chinese have been on the continent 60 years prior to the European contact with Africa (TIA-MYSOA, 2009). Nevertheless, this author is not interested in the debate as to whether the Xhosas and the Khoi-San people of South Africa are indeed of Chinese origin. What is important to note is that the Chinese presence in Africa is not recent, but China experienced a period of dormancy in interacting with Africa, and now it has reached the apogee in engaging the continent. The dragon is now awake in Africa, and the Chinese socioeconomic involvement on the continent could easily be characterized as another "Asian Tsunami" because of the intensity and scope of these activities.

The decolonization discourse needs a deliberate inclusion of the "China Model" of development and the effects of Chinanization on Africa in order to assess the realities of the African self and the Chinese other. Africans must begin to interrogate the forces of Chinanization as imperative for redefining African cultures in recent times and should not just accept China's position as a benevolent neoimperialist as a given. This is not the time for Africans to surrender, again, after their experiences with colonialism; framing them as exotic "cultural objects" and a reservoir of natural resources to satisfy the insatiable desire of those outside the continent. In this chapter, Chinanization is defined as China's approach to neocolonialism and cultural imperialism based on the Chinese perception of South–South relations and nation-state hegemony. Chinanization includes the utilization of many instruments and program for China's self-interest and security. Chinanization comprises of foreign investments, infrastructural development, and dependence on soft power tools in exchange for noninterference in internal affairs of African countries and the exploitation of raw materials and resources from Africa. Even though Japan is not directly involve in Chinanization, part of the China model is based on the Japanese loan structure after World War II that required China to sign an agreement with Japan to repay the loans in raw material. China is using the same method in Africa today.

The interlocutors of the recent Chinese presence in Africa include Sino-Pessimists, Sino-Optimists and Sino-Cautionists. In the camp of Sino-Optimists are Deborah Brautigum, Dambisa Mayo among others, inter alia, who claim that the Western media hype, the West's failure in Africa, and the fact that the West has been hypocritical about its own historical contradictions in Africa, are igniting this debate. Sino-Optimist maintain that China's investment in Africa is a win-win form of cooperation, and that it provides real opportunity for Africa and a new look at African development without a foreign aid formula that is usually failure-prone for Africans.

Sino-Pessimists include Peter Brookes, Stefan Halper, and others, who argue that China's human rights abuses, child labor law violation, employment conditions in most China-African projects, environmental disasters, noninterference approach, nonpolitical conditionality, empowering "rogue states," use of Africa as inferior goods dumping grounds, disrespect for Africans, exploitation of resources, marginalization of Africans, and disregard for African cultures must be assessed before applauding China for its success in Africa. Sino-Cautionists are interested in forging coequal partnership with China through the effective participation of African nation-states and working with and not for China to sustain the glorious past of African culture. They believe both Sino-Optimists and Sino-Pessimists have legitimate reasons for taking their respective positions on China in Africa, but what is imperative is acknowledging the reality of Africa's condition and uniting as a force for developing new principles in dealing with the China Model without culture wars.

Culture Wars: The Chinese Dragon and the African Warriors

The rift between African cultures and the process of the "China Model" of development and Chinanization could be characterized as the new "culture wars." The recent culture wars between African and Chinese cultures, development models, and the Chinese mode of interaction with Africans are different from that of the European colonialists. Chinese processes of modernization and development are at "war" with African cultures and economic activity or inactivity by nation-states in Africa. "Culture wars," as a phrase is a neologism whose roots come from the German transliteration—*Kulturkampf*, which translates into a "struggle for the control of the culture." A reference to German Chancellor Otto von Bismark in 1871 is appropriate in this perspective, in that he waged a *Kulturkampf* against the Catholic Church's imposition of Roman-style education and politics on Germany. Nonetheless, Bismarck's culture wars were discarded in 1878 because the general populace stood against it (Williams, 2003, p. 10). The recent culture wars between African and Chinese cultures and development are subterranean and yet more lethal to the African human condition and sustainable development because they evade the discourse over both discursive consciousness and practical consciousness.

With reference to the disregard for discursive consciousness, most Africans are not taking the discussion of Chinese cultural imperialism seriously now and many have already succumbed to verbalizations from Chinese cultures that are more palatable to their worldviews, because the Chinese are assisting in places where the Europeans and Americans have failed Africans. Neglect for practical consciousness ensues because there are no structured institutional arrangements to reconcile the forces of African historical, traditional, and contemporary cultures and the effects of Chinanization or Sino-Africanization on Africa. There are no known historical arrangements or policies established by African nation-states to mitigate the adverse effects of Sino-Africanization and development on African cultures. Perhaps, because culture is about everything we do, say, use, and acquire individually and institutionally and it evolves slowly, it is so elusive to realize when it is affected by outside agents and processes, especially in a time when global cultures are establishing hegemonic relations with indigenous African cultures.

Even though the Chinese presence could be seen as a blessing to Africa by many Sino-Optimists, Africans must prepare themselves against a reoccurrence of the cultural imperialism by European colonialists who have stifled Africans efforts toward development. Among the critical processes and institutions that Africans must put in place to balance China's efforts are: (a) concerted efforts and structures that would deal with African traditional and contemporary cultures in the era of Chinanization; (b) reducing and demystifying the difficulty in defining what the "Chinese Model" and "Beijing Consensus"

are; (c) re-examining inherited cultural practices and traditions that
obscure modern societal realities as they come in contact with Sino-
Africanization; (d) finding solutions to the inability to utilize African
traditional forms of arrangements and institutions to negotiate the
China Model and Chinanization; and (e) developing agency to deal
with Africa's inability to adopt cultural categories that could enable
Africans to strengthen their moral compasses and behavior in order
to interrogate foreign intrusion, the China Model and Chinanization.

Social and cultural capitals are important for the sustainability of any civilization in the era of Chinanization, nonetheless, the
process of acquiring cultural capital has been distressing to many
Africans because of China's recent influence in Africa, global forces,
and the ease by which subordinate African cultures often dislocate
the meaning of their existence in order to participate in global enter-
prises and accept Chinese socioeconomic activities, most of the time
without questions because of Africa's vulnerable position in global
politics. Anglo-American cultural imperialism in Africa was one thing,
but it is another thing when Africans succumb to China's benevolent
neoimperialism on the continent without assessing its ramifications.
Ironically, where Anglo-American cultural imperialism in Africa may
have failed, Chinese benevolent neoimperialism is succeeding. As
Michael Elliot reports in *Time* magazine, January 22, 2007, a senior
member of the United States National Security Council under President Bill Clinton, Kenneth Lieberthal notes, "The Chinese wouldn't
put it this way themselves. But in their hearts I think they believe
that the 21st Century is China's century" (Elliot, 2007, pp. 33–34).

Even though China's benevolent neocultural imperialism is
unlike Anglo-American pomposity in cross-cultural interactions, Chinese traditional cultures and the history of the "Middle Kingdom" (in
the middle of the heavens), guided parts of the Chinese people's perception of themselves as a great civilization. However within China,
ethnic differences among Cantonese, Shanghainese, and Hunanese,
for instances, could count for internal cultural and historical intolerance. Consequently, this internalized attitudes are easily transformed into the benevolent neocultural imperialism when Chinese
of all ethnicities, regardless of "all their differences and mutual
snobberies . . . think of themselves first and foremost as Chinese—
as *Zhongguo ren*, literally, 'people of the Middle Kingdom'" (Chua,
2007, p. 292), when the dragon enters the "Dark Continent"—Africa.
Lucian Pye asserts, "China is not just another nation-state in the
family of nations," rather, China is "a civilization pretending to be a
state" (Pye, 1990, p. 58). A civilization of that unique Chinese persona
maintains a culture that sometimes interrogates African cultures in

the process of socioeconomic development. Recently, China has been signing cultural exchange agreements all over Africa. Malone reports:

> And it's not just China trying to use culture to secure access to a continent overflowing with mineral resources and a largely untapped consumer market of nearly 1 billion people . . . Addis Ababa is host to Chinese . . . schools where Ethiopian children must sing the national anthems of those countries every morning, where they learn their languages, their dances, their songs, their particular set of manners. Such schools and "cultural exchange programs" are mushrooming all over the continent as the war for influence over African countries heats up (Malone, 2010, p. 1).

Across the continent, Confucius Institutes are mushrooming faster than African cultural centers. China continues to develop these institutes in order to make contacts with the rest of world in general, and Africa in particular. The rate of "youthification" in Africa, combined with lack of access to learning centers and opportunity for self-development and advancement, have made learning Chinese languages and culture attractive for young Africans who want to better themselves at the expense of their own cultures.

During these difficult times of economic downturns, there is a prevailing notion that Africans who learn and speak Chinese could trump the competition in the global market. But as noted by Li Haiwan, "we have brought a cultural performance troupe to the University of Lagos. We also brought a youth group here. We will have other cultural activities and new courses—not only language [and] things like Kung Fu" (Posthumus, 2011, p. 1). Is China able to engage Africa culturally and economically with alacrity because of the apparent underdevelopment of the continent, misdirected policies, and inability of the nation-states in Africa to maintain their raison d'être? Are Africans permanently vulnerable to systemic forces such as slavery, colonialism, imperialism, and Chinanization that the Chinese invasion in Africa could just not be epiphenomenal or anachronistic? To answer these questions one has to critically examine Africa's development problems and the "China Model" of socioeconomic development in Africa.

African Development Lacuna and Chinese Opportunism?

The development of underdevelopment of Africa and the gradual dislocation of African indigenous cultures, some may argue, are attributable to traditional cultural values that tend to impede the process of modernization and development. China is easily filling the vacuum and development lacuna—Sino-Africanization. Yet, the lacuna created in Africa started as far back as the Trans-Atlantic Slave Trade, the first phase of globalization's effect on Africa, when Africa's human and material resources were taken by global traders and slavers, whose work only benefited Arabs, Europeans, Chinese, and North Americans (Henriot, 2001, p. 2).

The second phase of globalization was the period of colonialism, when the Portuguese, Italians, Belgians, British, French, and Germans divided and conquered the African continent for their self-interests in 1884–1885 at the Berlin Conference. Just as the present form of globalization indicates, the benefits for the West always outweighed what the African people acquired through the other processes. Now the benefit for the Chinese is outweighing that of Africans. The third phase of globalization was the period of neocolonialism, the postindependent era, where Africa's fate was still controlled by alien transnational companies and foreign nation-states. Trade patterns, debt arrangements, investment policies, and the general political economies of African nation-states were primarily controlled by former colonial powers in the neocolonial era. The fourth, the present phase of globalization, is a global village where interdependence has made Africa even more dependent on foreign powers and resources than the period of colonialism. This period is also concomitant with Chinanization and Sino-Africanization.

Financial flows, technology, information highways, byways, and thoroughfares, movement of people, and cultures have direct benefit to the Western countries and China that have very little in mind regarding Africa's condition. Moreover, the global village would be dysfunctional if the dominant actors failed to carefully implement the tenets of the catalytic agents of globalization—liberalization and Chinanization. Liberalization drives the free market of the global village to the desired destination of hegemonic, Chinanization, and benevolent neoimperialism. One would argue that Africa has suffered under slavery, colonialism, postcolonialism, and structural adjustment programs that were all forced on the continent. So, one would argue that it is hypocritical that Sino-Pessimists would disregard all the recent development projects, infrastructural developments, agricultural and land-tenure reorganization, construction of water systems, railroads, hospitals, soccer stadiums, and the fact that China has become the biggest investor in mining, natural resources, and ranks second in the world (after the United States) in bilateral investment treaties.

Cooke (2008) asserts, "China's voracious appetite for resources, especially energy resources, is widely viewed as the primary motive for its expanding outreach to Africa" (p. 106). This may be the highest stage of Chinese "capitalism," or as the Chinese used to call it a "responsibility system" that could be neobenevolent imperialism. On the one hand, China has to reach places of resources to support its continued economic growth. On the other hand, Africa needs development projects and investments in order to reach a takeoff stage in development. So, arguably, do Africa and China have symbiotic relations? Not quite the case. The rapid growth of the Chinese economy has outstripped its local supplies of essential minerals, petroleum, and other variables needed to nurture the rate of this economic growth and Africa is the answer to this dilemma. China's economy is growing rapidly and the Chinese Communist Party has to find ways of maintaining sustainable development and stability. Natural resource-rich Africa is China's solution. The economy of China is growing between 7% and 10% per annum since the 1980s, and has multiplied every decade. This continuing growth requires China's presence in foreign markets and access to foreign natural resources, since China's domestic resources have not kept up with this rapid growth. China's economy has exceeded its domestic supplies of crucial manufacturing resources and petroleum products. Africa is the prime candidate for fulfilling China's needs for this exponential growth.

Africa has large quantities of crucial, essential, and precious natural resources such as aluminum, alumina, bauxite, coal, coltan, copper, gold, diamonds, iron ore, lead, manganese, nickel, oil, platinum, uranium, and more. It would defy logic for China to look elsewhere for the resources that it needs to bring resource availability and the rate of economic growth into equilibrium. Africa is the most logical continent to feed China's hunger for developmental resources. It is one thing to seek resources for economic growth and another to secure strategic minerals for weaponry. It is indubitable that China is doing both in Africa. So, if China is in South Africa, Zambia, and the Democratic Republic of Congo, it is in these countries for chromium and cobalt, as these African countries lead the world in the supply of these strategic resources. China signed a long-term infrastructural development accord with the Democratic Republic of the Congo to a tune of $9 billion (Whewell, 2008). China is rebuilding pipelines and infrastructure to strengthen Angola's oil supplies, and it has provided over $135 million for developing Angola's electricity, road and highway systems, and water plants (Simoa, 2008).

The picture in Zambia is not any different from that of Angola. Zambia has one of the richest copper deposits in Africa and the world, so it's not epiphenomenal or a deviation for the Chinese to secure their position in that African country. China has invested over $800 million in improvement projects and another $200 million in building a new cooper smelter in Zambia (Behar, 2008). China is receiving its share of the Republic of South Africa's chromium resources, and it is not new information that out of the 54 African nation-states, at least 40 of them have received some Chinese foreign direct investments (FDI). Angola, South Africa, Sudan, Democratic Republic of Congo, Equatorial Guinea, Libya, Algeria, Gabon, Mauritania, and Nigeria top the chart for African nation-states with Chinese FDI. As one would assume, China's FDI in Africa is closely linked to trade and development assistance; consequently, FDI has increased over the past 10 years in tandem with increased Sino-African trade in the countries mentioned above. Although China's FDI to Africa remains marginal in terms of its total outward FDI flows, the total FDI received by Africa from the rest of the world is 3% in 2007. According to the Chinese Ministry of Commerce, China's FDI in Africa has increased by 46% per year over the last decade (Kaplinsky & Morris, 2009). The stock of foreign investment stood at $4.46 billion in 2007 compared to $56 million in 1996 and $7.8 billion at the end of 2008, but others estimate FDI to be at least $20.billion (Shinn, 2010).

For a region that tops the developing world because of the numerical preponderance of the nation-states, Africa continues to suffer from decayed or archaic infrastructures that were built during the colonial period and newer ones are needed at this point of development. Infrastructural development is key to economic growth. Mary-Francoise Renard notes, "the Africa Infrastructure Diagnostic (AICD) study estimated that Africa needs $93 billion per year to address the deficit in this sector. Historically, infrastructure was one of the first sectors in which China invested in Africa (Renard, 2011, p. 20). Owing to the development lacuna in Africa, the Chinese have made gains in their endeavors to build over 10 hydroelectric power plants, which cost about $3.3 billion, roads and railway networks, $4 billion; and information networks which is worth about $3 billion (Renard, ibid). Nevertheless, most of these infrastructural development are in African countries with resources that are beneficial to the Chinese; Nigeria, Gabon, South Africa, Democratic Republic; and Sudan, to name a few. What is the actual role of the African nation-states in the process of Chinanization?

The Role of the African Nation-States in the Process of Sino-Africanization

Defined succinctly, the nation-state is the largest, most sophisticated, self-reliant, self-sufficient political configuration in the modern world.

Nation-states have four basic characteristics: namely, territorial area, general populace, a government, and recognition from other nation-states. Territorial area is one of the most fundamental components of economic development. Size, location, and natural resources are concomitant with territory or, in simple terms, land. Land is also one major element that serves as a platform on which nation-states extend their boundaries at the expense of others, and it represents the frontier of an increasing conflict over legitimate rights between nation-states and society rights vis-à-vis state authority.

The respective inhabitants of nation-states are another great asset that these entities could have. As human resources, the general populace of nation-states may differ greatly in their history, precepts, norms, culture, and their socioeconomic and political acumen. People make decisions in the global village, not computers. Productivity in any nation-state is dependent on the type of human resources available in that particular entity. Education and training can provide skilled or semiskilled labor and leadership. Intangible variables, such as knowledge, skill, and leadership can lead to the production of tangible needs, such as general infrastructures. African governments would have little to worry about in the global village if the majority of the general populace could be productive and reach a level of optimal efficiency. Population explosion, unemployment, refugees, health issues, and the preservation of human dignity are some of the problems that come with people in the nation-states of Africa.

The third characteristic, good governance is essential to the survival and sustenance of any nation-state in the global village. Governance refers to the arrangements and management of regime relations, and the laws and rules that create the framework to conduct politics in the global village (Hyden & Brattan, 1992). Here, formal institutional structures, sociopolitical processes, and their interaction with the general populace within the global village are the areas of contention. Governance in Africa in the process of globalization has become the most elusive "art form." The frequency and scope of predatory regimes, praetorian governments, struggle with alien political philosophies, ideologies, and resource scarcity have all contributed to making governance in Africa within the global sphere a risky business. But the nation-states in Africa must survive the entrances and exits of governments and regimes in order to compete in the global village.

The fourth and final characteristic of the nation-state is recognition from other nation-states in the global village. Recognition relates to the "acknowledgment of the existence of a new state or of a new government in an existing state, coupled with an expression

of willingness on the part of the recognizing state to enter into relations with the recognized entity or government" (Von Glahn, 1981, p.
82). More recently, recognition has become a political act with legal
ramification. Recognition involves diplomatic exchange, concluding
of agreements respecting the existence of the nation-state in question, and perhaps, membership in the United Nations. Recent global forces have made some of the elements of recognition somewhat
meaningless, since liberalization makes the borders and territories
of especially weaker nation-states more vulnerable for entrance and
exit of parastatal agencies, transnational corporations, and powerful
nation-states.

     As the modern nation-states evolve in Africa and it acquires
all the aforementioned characteristics, it retires into a new type of
entity in order to respond to the demands and needs of the society in
the global village and in the process of Chinanization. Nonetheless,
the authoritative actions of the nation-state to shape and constrain
the expectations, demands, and pressure from the general populace,
global actors like China, and institutions are modified according to
paradigmatic reorientation of the nation-state itself. Two paradigms,
the state-centered nation-state and the society-centered nation-state
analysis could be utilized to describe how the nation-state responds
to the forces Chinanization.

State-Centered and Society-Centered Nation-States
in Sino-Africanization

In accordance with the state-centered nation-state model, the state
acts as an independent entity—an independent variable that turns
its preferences into authoritative actions. The nation-state's autonomous actions often result in policy decisions that have little reflective
value to the immediate society, because it is more concerned about
global interaction and engaging China. Culminating in autonomous
actions and reactions, the state's ability to tap into resources outside
its perimeters is diminished. From structural development within the
state to global dynamics beyond the state's apparatus, the nation-
state propounds and makes policy choices that have little meaning
to the general populace of its own. African private actors, businesses, political parties, as well as affiliation and affinity groups cannot
easily transform their demands via the nation-state into preferable
socioeconomic and political agendas because of global forces over
and above their means. Since the Chinese political system itself is

authoritarian, it is easier for China to engage in Africa, especially in countries with authoritarian governments; Libya before the demise of the Kaddafi regime, Sudan, and the Democratic Republic of Congo.

The society-centered nation-state approach postulates a condition in Chinanization, where the private sector, transnational corporations, intergovernmental organizations (IGOs), and nongovernmental organizations (NGOs) within and outside the polity have symbiotic relations with the nation-state and China. The nation-state in this paradigm serves as a viable platform on which different sociopolitical and global actors come together to iron out their differences and galvanize their interests. These characterizations of the nation-state presume that the state has already reached a "takeoff stage"—a stage of prematurity, where the nation-state can interact with global forces without being marginalized or exploited. In fact, very few African nation-states, if any, fit this analysis or are able to maintain themselves during China's engagement in Africa.

The nation-states in Africa have been unable to acquire the society-centered nation-state status because of structural heterogeneity, which is the transfer of advanced but inadequate technology and institutions from China to undeveloped areas in Africa. Chinanization enhances structural heterogeneity but stifles socioeconomic activities because of the inadequate capacity of African nation-states to deal with China's leverage within the global village. Moreover, the lack of a sustainable private sector in Africa places limitations on the type of support the general populace could provide to the nation-state. Absent viable support from the external sphere of the state, it tends to rely on its own resources, which are insufficient to deal with forces within the global village.

For obvious reasons, most African nation-states would prefer the society-centered nation-state paradigm to deal with China. However, the society is not sufficiently equipped to provide the needed structures to facilitate the operation of such a paradigm. Indubitably, there is no entity that is exclusively nation-state-centered or society-centered. However, most Western nation-states are closer to the society-centered nation-state paradigm. China itself has a combination of state-centered and society center model—the Chinese model? The fundamental questions to be posed in attempting to determine the status of the African nation-state in the era of Chinanization are as follows:

1. How does the nation-state maintain its raison d'être in the process Sino-Africanization?

2. How are the nation-states' authoritative actions and inactions understood in reference to internal and external constraints during the process of Sino-Africanization?

3. To what extent do African nation-states still maintain their sovereignty in dealing with socioeconomic and policy initiatives from China?

The Fate of African Nation-States and Cultures in the Era of Globalization and Chinanization

Earlier in the twentieth century, both Vladimir Lenin and many internationalists projected the gradual demise of the nation-state—the withering away of the state, and that the highest state of capitalism is imperialism. In the 1990s, observers started revisiting Lenin's position and management consultants, such as Naisbitt (1994), have suggested that the contemporary advancement of globalization, Chinanization, and the activities of transnational corporations are creating a world beyond nation-state, cultures, and nationalities (p. 14). The present effects of Chinanization on the African nation-state only beg for a revisitation of the Weberian conceptualization of the state in order to determine the fate of the African nation-state in the process of Chinanization. Max Weber's defining properties of the nation-state include the following:

1. Defined boundaries under the state's control and an unchallenged territorial area. This property has been almost meaningless in the process of globalization and Chinanization in Africa since globalization and Sino-Africanization supports economic, social, and political activities across frontiers, regions, and continents.

2. The nation-state's monopoly of legitimate use of force to control its borders and general populace within its territory. Here, African nation-states, because of the forces of interdependence and Chinanization, have little monopoly of legitimate use of force and influence even within their own borders. China, great powers, and transnational corporations' irrepressible activities in Africa have diluted the nation-state's authority and the use of legitimate force in conducting its affairs.

3. The reliance on rules and regulations in the governance of its citizens and nationals. Here again, in the global

village, the rules and regulations propounded by China and transnational corporations prevail in the global village. The boundaries between domestic matters and global affairs have become increasingly blurred to an extent that the movers and shakers of the global village carry the day.

In reviewing the Weberian properties of the nation-state and how Chinanization has made the function and authority of the African nation-state questionable, one cannot confide in the sustainability of the nation-states on the continent. Yet, it would be erroneous to perform a premature autopsy on the African nation-state, even though there is sufficient evidence that Chinanization has intensified the crippling effect and paralysis of the nation-states in Africa. In general, Chinanization and globalization have uneven effects on African nation-states. One has to understand the China model of engagement in Africa well to evaluate the impact of China's presence in Africa.

The Implications for the China Model of Engagement in Africa: The Dragon Rules

Once upon a time in East Asia around 1978, an emerging powerhouse accessed resources from poor countries because this nation-state did not have what it takes to embark on its socioeconomic projects. It requested $10 billion line of credit from another country to start its development projects. The borrowing country repaid this loan in oil and coal, but it paid it 70 times more. This was the birth of the diversification of the economy of that borrowing country. The lender country was Japan, the borrower, China. Is this the "China model" in Africa? If it is not a "development model" then what is it? Some say the "China model" is a myth. Others claim it is a combination of principles: Chinese culture, demography, geography, and governing philosophy (Halper, 2010). Resource-backed loans are the same approach China used to develop its economy. Africa is the source of one third of the world's productive resources. China needs these resources. In 2006, President Hu Jintao said, "The Three 50s" in Africa are: China has been in Africa for over 50 years, engaged in 50 countries, and has spent over $50 billion in improving Africa. Is China submerged in benevolent imperialism, altruistic benevolence, or it is just a rogue donor? Halper notes that "To maintain its growth at current rates, Beijing must sustain relations with regimes across the developing world, regardless of the implications of its policies for human rights, the environment, and basic freedoms for the affected local population. . . . Just in 2008, for example, autocracies were a vital source of energy for China's growing needs" (Halper, 2010, p. 44). This is one of the concerns of this author. Is this how one interprets the China model? If it is, then it should be a reason for one to be optimistically cautious about China in Africa

Even though the China Model is not a new thing, because China, as stated above has been engaging Africa for over 50 years, the intensity and scope of its recent activity on the continent is what make the China Model in recent times different. As far back as 1964, when Premier Zhou Enlai visited Ghana, China has maintained a principle of nonpolitical conditionality and noninterference with sovereign rights and domestic affairs of other countries. Therefore, in doing business in Africa, China cares very little about what happens to the general populace of a particular African nation-state. Zhansui Yu refers to Zhuang Zizhong's characterization of the China Model as "democratic one-Party dictatorship, rule of law with social stability as its top priority, an authoritarian government for the people, a state-controlled market economy, fair competition dominated by the central government-owned enterprise . . . and national rejuvenation of the incomparable Chinese civilization" (Yu, 2010, p. 2). The model has element of oppression and exploitation, monopoly of state power, abuse of power and a technocracy full of corruption. One may ask if this is the type of model African nation-states want to aspire to.

The China Model is about developing sophisticated investment schemes. China was able to merge the Industrial and Commercial Bank of China, which became the largest in the world by value in 2007. The scheme included the purchase of some African banks, including South Africa's Standard Bank Group Limited for $4.5 billion (Butts and Bankus, 2009). Standard Bank operates in over 18 African countries and it is a banking leader in loaning funds to Africans, with assets over $120 billion (Caggeso, 2007). China also purchased shares in Barclay's Bank, one of the leading banks for Africans. With all these purchases of financial institutions that most African countries are tied to, China has completely cornered Africa financially. Africa has nowhere to run to, except China. The China Model works effectively for China with these banking schemes and yet African countries have to be careful about taking these loans that are tied to massive resource exploitation and environmental degradation or what Chinese diplomats label as resource-backed financing agreements.

With regard to manufactured and processed good, many studies, including the works of Mary-Francoise Renard (2011) and Zhansui Yu (2010), conclude that there is a negative correlation between African economies and the intensity of Chinese trade. China does not encourage Africans to participate in building infant industries. Africans are reduced to hullers of firewood and diggers of natural resources. One will not argue that it takes a very long time to recover from the shocks of high vulnerability of commodity prices on the world market. Africans are therefore entrapped in the old thinking of gaining comparative advantage by remaining agrarians and continuing to depend on China and the West for finished goods. Even when Africans are allowed to participate in highly skilled manufactures projects or infrastructural developments, the China model requires that the Chinese use only 30% of African labor vis-à-vis 70% of Chinese (African Politics Portals, 2008).

The China model is submerged in a pool of bilateral, subterranean, secretive, government to government agreements. There is very little transparency in this process. The danger of engaging in deals that are not transparent is that a new genesis of bribery, corruption, cronyism, and nepotism will continue to engulf a continent that has suffered for a long time because of colonialism, imperialism, predatory regimes, and vampire states. Elite to elite collusion (China and Africa) and a new class formation are emerging because of the China model. Many African people who make it to China and receive Chinese training are remaining in that country, beginning a new process of brain drain. Over 14,600 Africans are sponsored by the Chinese government every year for personnel training and with China noninterference policy; these people can elect to remain in China, which is what most of them are doing at the moment (Zhongxiang, 2009).

Indubitably, the China model does not benefit all sectors of the country and all countries in Africa equally. The countries in Africa that have abundance of natural resources have some short-term benefits, but in the long run the negatives will outweigh the positive. The dragon's presence in Africa must be re-examined and it requires rethinking. *Mutatis mutandis*, African nation-states will continue to be victims in Sino-Africanization and Chinanization. Africa's primary drawing card in the global market is as a source of cheap labor and producer of raw materials, which are relatively low in value vis-à-vis finished but shoddy goods from China. Even though fiscal trade liberalization has increased financial mobility in recent years, African markets are vulnerable to external changes, yuanization, and external shocks. These facts will not dissipate; they are the realities of

Chinanization that African nation-states have to come to terms with before blindly embracing the dragon and Sino-Africanization.

The euphoric prognoses by African statesmen and -women, and political economists about the benefits of the China model and the engagement of China in Africa are beginning to be questioned because many developing nation-states and African nation-states in particular have realized the extent of exploitation, marginalization, and cultural imperialism associated with neobenevolent imperialism and Chinanization. European cultural globalization rose with technological advancement in transportation and communication systems, which helped the West expand into Africa and other areas with new ideas of liberalism, capitalism, socialism, and science. Now the Internet, satellite, and digital technology have enhanced the process of global culture. Through radio, television, movies, and the Internet, exposure to different cultures and values has been more rapid than ever. In a similar vein, Chinanization has contributed to the dissipation of indigenous languages and cultures of Africa. *McCulturalization, dollarization, Coca-Colarization,* and *Yuanization* all continue to pose a threat to indigenous cultures. The recent Chinanization of culture in Africa is spearheaded both by financial institutions and China. Cultural imperialism has been more rampant than ever, where the dominant corporations and superordinate cultures' practices, institutions, and processes have become the norm for the rest of Africa. What does this mean to personal national identities and the authority of the African nation-state in this process of Chinanization?

Conclusion

The process of Chinanization is unstoppable and yet inevitable. Chinanization is transforming the world, but the transformation is concomitant with prosperity and gains for mostly China while most African nation-states are entrapped in a pool of destitution and instability. Globalization and Chinanization have increased the gap between the wealthy nation-states and the poorest ones, who are predominantly African. As Held, Goldblatt, & Parraton (2001) correctly note, "globalization and [Chinanization] have disrupted the neat correspondence between national territory, sovereignty, political space, and the democratic political community" (p. 146).

Also, during Chinanization, when African culture becomes synonymous with Chinese culture, there is a need for subordinate cultures to go back to their source of the essence of being (*Sankofa*) to search for productive elements that will bring new meanings to their lives. Indubitably, this is not the time for pessimism. Nevertheless, the nostalgia and trauma of slavery, colonialism, neocolonialism, and now Chinanization, always remind Africans how non-Africans have exploited the continent in the past. Chinanization is not a panacea to most of Africa's problems, as those who claim that the Chinese presence in Africa is a win-win situation. If African nation-states want their relations with China to progress, they must without second thoughts define what China is, and the ramifications for totally surrendering to the China model. If this present process of Chinanization continues into the next 25 years, African nation-states are likely to permanently reinscribe in a position of subjugation, exploitation, marginalization, and life-threatening status that is mystified by China's rationalization of sovereign rights, equal benefits, disregard for environmental issues, and human rights violations. Africans must continue to rethink, re-examine, and reassess the position of the dragon in Africa.

References

Arsene, C. African Politics Portal. (2008). *Top ten misconceptions about Chinese investment in Africa*. Retrieved from: http://codrinarsene.com/2008/07/top-10-misconceptions-about-chinese-investment-in-africa/

Behar, R. (2008). Mining copper in Zambia. Retrieved from: http://www.fastcompany.com/magazine/126/zambia-chinas-mine-shaft.html?page=0%2C0

Butts, K. H., & Bankus, B. (2009). China's pursuit of Africa's natural resources. *Center for Strategic Leadership, 1*(9).

Caggeso, M. (2007). China drills into Africa with $5.4 billion investment. *Investment News: Money Morning*. Retrieved from: http://www.moneymorning.com/2007/12/04/china-drills-into-africa-with54-billion-investment/

Chua, A. (2007). *Day of empire: How hyperpowers rise to global dominance and why they fall*. New York: Doubleday.

Cook, N. (2008). China's foreign policy and "soft power" in South America, Asia, and Africa. Retrieved from: http://www.fas.org//irp/congress/2008 rpt/crs-china.pdf

Elliot, M. (2007, January 22). The China century *Time*.

Halper, S. (2010). *The Beijing consensus: How China's authoritarian model will dominate the twenty first century*. New York: Basic Books.

Held, D., McGrew, A., Goldblatt D., & Parraton, J. (2001). Managing the challenge of globalization and institutionalizing cooperation through global governance. In C. Kegley & E. Wittkoft (Eds.), *The global agenda: Issues and perspectives*. New York: McGraw Hill.

Henriot, P. (2001). Globalization: Implications for Africa. Retrieved from: http://www.sedos.org/english/global.html

Hyden, G., & Brattan, M. (eds). (1992). *Governance and politics in Africa,* Bolder, CO: Lynne Rienner Publishers.

Kaplinsky, R., & Morris, M. (2009). Chinese FDI in Sub-Saharan Africa: Engaging with large dragons. *The European Journal of Development Research, 21*(4), 551–569.

Malone, B. (2010, January 22). How will Chinese culture influence Africa? Thomson Reuters. Retrieved from: http://blogs.reuters.com/africanews/tag/cultural-exchange-programs/

TIA-MYSOA. (2009, November 1). Evidence of early Chinese influence in Africa. *This is Africa.* Retrieved from: http://tia-mysoa.blogspot.com/2009/11/evidence-of-early-chinese-influence-in.html

Naisbitt, J. (1994). *Global paradoxes: The bigger the World economy, the more powerful its smallest players.* London: Bealey.

Pye, L. (1990). Erratic state, frustrated society. *Foreign Affairs, 69.*

Posthumus, B. (2010, June 26). China's cultural diplomacy in Africa. *Radio Netherlands Worldwide Africa.* Retrieved from: http://www.rnw.nl/africa/article/china%E2%80%99s-cultural-diplomacy-africa

Renard, M. F. (2011). Working paper series: China's trade and FDI in Africa. Tunisia: African Development Bank.

Simao, P. (2008). China expands credit line to oil-rich Angola. *Reuters Foundation Alert Net.* Retrieved from http://www.alertnet.org/thenews/newsdesk/L0460226.htm

Shinn, D. (2010, May). The paradox of China's transformation. Washington, DC: Elliot School of International Affairs, Symposium.

Von Glahn, G. (1981). *Law among nations: An introduction to public international law,* 4th ed. New York: Macmillan Publishers.

Whewell, T. (2008). China to seal $9bn DR Congo deal. BBC News. Retrieved from: http://news.bbc.co.uk/2/hi/programmes/newsnight/7343060.stm

Williams, M. (2003). *Culture wars: Opposing viewpoints.* Farmington Hill, MI: Greenhaven Press.

Yu, Z. (2010, July 28). Questioning the Chinese model of development. *The China beat.* Retrieved from: http://www.thechinabeat.org/?=2423

Zhang, Z. (2008, March). China's model of aiding Africa and its implications. *International Review,* Shanghai Institute for International Studies, *5,* 41–54.

CHAPTER SEVENTEEN

Political Struggle of Rural Migrant Hostesses for First-Class Citizenship in Postsocialist China

TIANTIAN ZHENG

Within the 50-plus years of Communist rule, China's sex industry has gone from bust to boom. During the Maoist era, the Communist Party attempted to level previous class distinctions and promote its egalitarian ideology by eliminating all forms of conspicuous consumption and "reactionary" leisure activities, including the consumption of commercial sex (Wang, 1995). The time, form, and content of leisure activities fell under the scrutiny and supervision of the state, and leisure itself was conceptualized as a form of collective action. In political indoctrination classes, unsanctioned leisure activities were denounced as capitalist behavior, and state propaganda advocated the ethos of "hard work and simple living" (Wang, 1995, p. 156).

Since 1978, the state's pro-consumption stance has opened the way for the reemergence of nightclubs and other leisure sites. To avoid any residual negative connotations left over from the previous era, when nightclubs, dance halls, and bars were condemned as emblems of a nonproletarian and decadent bourgeois lifestyle nightclubs, in the current post-Mao period such places are referred to as karaoke bars, karaoke plazas, or *liange ting* (literally, "singing practice halls"). These new consumption sites are prominent in the more economically prosperous Special Economic Zones (SEZs) (Jian, 2001). Visitors are mainly middle-aged businessmen, government officials, police officers, and foreign investors. Clients can partake of the services offered by hostesses and at the same time engage in "social interactions" (*yingchou*) that help cement "relationships" (*guanxi*) with their business partners or their patrons in the government

(Wang, 1995). Hostesses play an indispensable role in the rituals of these male-centered worlds of business and politics (Zheng, 2003).

The hostesses or escorts who work at karaoke bars are referred to by the Chinese government as *sanpei xiaojie*, literally, "young women who accompany men in three ways." These "ways" are generally understood to include varying combinations of alcohol consumption, dancing, and singing. Sexual services are an additional, unstated part of the work these women are expected to perform. These women, mainly 17 to 23 years of age, form a steadily growing contingent of illegal sex workers. Hostesses first emerged in modest numbers at the end of the 1980s. Their numbers expanded rapidly in the mid-1990s, as karaoke bars became favored sites not just for male recreation but also for transactions between male businessmen and political elites. Paradoxically, the state agents responsible for policing karaoke bars comprise one of the main segments of the karaoke bar customer base.

The majority of these hostesses come from China's countryside. Of the 2 hundred hostesses with whom I worked, only 4 were from cities. They were extremely averse to exposing their rural origins. At the beginning of my field research, hostesses always told me that they were from large, metropolitan cities, such as Dalian, Shanghai, and Anshan. It was only after becoming close friends that they confided to me that they were actually from rural areas on the outskirts of these cities.

During 20 months of fieldwork in Dalian, I lived and worked with the hostesses as a hostess myself. I lived with the hostesses in a karaoke bar for a year, where I worked as a hostess serving drinks, carrying out conversations, singing songs, playing games, and dancing with customers, with the exception of sexual services. My research sample includes approximately 2 hundred bar hostesses in 10 karaoke bars. I was intensively involved in 3 karaoke bars categorized respectively as high, middle, and low class. In the first section of this article, I explicate how rural migrants obtain political identities as second-class citizens. In the second section, I discuss how rural migrant women's cultural and social identities are naturalized as derogatory second-class citizens in the media. Their bodies are a site where the imperatives of state politics become legible. In the third section, I demonstrate how such a derogatory cultural representation, while tying the hostesses to the constructed identities in a constraining way, paradoxically leaves some room for the hostesses to maneuver. Specifically, I argue that rural migrant hostesses perform this image as a means to accumulate the accoutrements for legitimate first-class citizenship, which is synonymous with elite status.

Migration and Political Second-Class Citizenship in Post-Mao Dalian

In 1958, the Chinese government initiated the household registration system, classifying the national population into mutually exclusive urban-rural categories possessing unequal political, economical, social, and legal access (Flemming, 1999). Rural residents found themselves on the losing end of a heavily lopsided distribution of social wealth. Concomitant with the broad-based restructuring of society, the "peasantry" as a derogatory cultural category but revolutionary mainstay, was further refined and concretized (Cohen, 1993). The Maoist government portrayal of the countryside in peasant administrative categories involving the household registration system and mobility restrictions reinforced the cultural stereotypes of rural identities and segregated and branded the peasants as the reservoir of backward feudalism and superstition and a major obstacle to national development and salvation (Brownell, 1995).

Relaxation of state mobility controls in recent years has allowed rural residents to migrate to urban regions, where they are now labeled the "floating population" (*liudong renkou*) (Solinger, 1995). In search of job opportunities and adventure, these migrants have become the "vanguard" in China's largest population movement since 1949 and harbingers of the market economy in the post-1978 era of economic reforms (Solinger, 1995). As China's engagement with the global economy and experiments with economic reform continue, cities highlight the deepening disparities between permanent urban "citizens" (those with urban residence permits) and migrant populations without residence permits.

Although the state today tolerates a higher degree of population mobility than under the Mao Zedong government, the urban-rural gap is still the main fault line between rich and poor in Chinese society. Inequalities are perpetuated and even aggravated by post-Mao state policies that transfer the brunt of the state and collectives' tax burden onto poor rural households. This situation has not gone unnoticed by peasants themselves. Since 1985, peasants have launched collective protests against taxes, fines, cadre corruption, and the drastic urban-rural income gap. This unrest points to their discontent with local authorities and constitutes one of the major threats to the Chinese Communist Party's power and stability (Li and O'Brien, 1996).

With 100 million rural migrants on the move, modern China's urban landscape is now faced with the management of individuals who by definition are "outsiders" (*waidiren, wailaigong*) (Honig, 1992; Zhang, 2001). Despite their contributions to local and overall economic growth, migrants encounter severe institutional and social discrimination. Blamed for blemishing the appearance of cities and contributing to overcrowding, migrants have become the scapegoats for a multitude of social problems, ranging from crime to urban pollution (Siu, 1990). As the "losers" in China's market reforms, migrant workers are denied civil, political, and residential rights.

Women account for over 30% of the total number of rural-urban migrant laborers (Sheng, 1996). Providers of labor power for the state, they are important social and political actors. Institutional (such as the household registration system) and social discrimination (such as the derogatory category of migrants) forces most female migrants onto the lowest rungs of the labor market, where they commonly work as garbage collectors, restaurant waitresses, domestic maids, factory workers, and bar hostesses.

Migration and Cultural Second-Class Citizenship in Popular Media

Defined and viewed as "the political economy of communication" (Bourdieu, 1991), discourse is the place where relations of power are exercised and enacted. In this section, I discuss the ways in which media discourse defines, constrains, and ties rural migrant women to their labeled identities in the coercive discursive regime that affects "their participation in employment, in development programs and in education in profound and immense ways" (Moore, 1994).

Concerned that an oversized population is a major impediment to economic growth and an indirect cause of a myriad of social ills that carry the potential for disrupting social stability (e.g., a tight labor market), the Chinese government has made population control a key item on its agenda of economic expansion and continued political dominance (Huang, 1988).

The state sees rural women's mobility as a serious threat to government population policy. Women migrants' "floating" lifestyle puts them out of reach of regular monitoring techniques administered through "grassroots" (*jiceng*) government organs—namely, the countryside's village committee and the city's street office (*jiedao banshichu*). Indeed, ruralists are sometimes even accused of purposefully using migration as a way to escape detection (Huang, 1988).

The government's anxieties are amplified by the perception that rural women are naturally prone to high fertility. Indeed, the media depict the entire countryside as a hotbed of sexual activity driven by raw, animalistic passions (Xu, 2001). Some scholars lend scientific credence to this view. Based on a nationwide survey of sexual behavior, prominent sex sociologist Liu Dalin claims that there is not only a higher rate of premarital and extramarital sex but also a greater overall frequency of sexual intercourse in the countryside than in the city (Liu, 1995). Rural women's sexuality is implicated as the critical variable for explaining urban-rural differences in sexual behavior:

> Many rural women have precocious sexual biology but late-maturing sexual psychology. For many, the period of sexual hunger is too long, but they cannot get married in time [to satisfy this hunger]. Lovers have frequent contact with each other, but their sexual control is weak. If by chance a male shows interest, the female lover, also in the grasp of "an unbearable hunger," will give herself to the man (Tong, 1995).

In this passage, rural women's sexual promiscuity is portrayed as a product of their carnal urges. Other scholars emphasize rural women's lack of culture to explain their behavior (Wen & Zhong, 1991). These two angles—biological and cultural—are not mutually exclusive but rather complementary: Rural women's bodies intensify their sexual urges at the same time that their lack of culture reduces their ability to resist these impulses. This dual-level explanation reflects larger patterns in the discriminatory representations of peasants and national minorities.

Regardless of the approach, however, rural women's sexuality is always implicated as the critical variable that explains the differences in sexual behavior between rural and urban areas. Studies rarely draw attention to men's sexuality, implicitly taking the level of men's sexual desires as a constant across the urban-rural divide. By assuming that all men are equally likely to engage in sexual conduct, responsibility for the countryside's alleged sexual promiscuity is pinned on the rural woman for failing to fulfill the traditional female duty of policing the body and thereby maintaining the community's moral order. The culpability of those women is extenuated only because they are acting under the influence of passions, against which they are culturally defenseless.

Even before migration skyrocketed in the earlier 1990s, the *People's Daily* began featuring articles on the dangers of the unchecked fertility of migrant women. The earliest example—a 1988 article titled, "Concerns About Over-Reproduction" (*chaosheng de danyou*)—helped introduce the issue to the general public: "They [migrant women] bear children above the one-child quota, disturbing the implementation of the family planning policy" (Huang, 1990). Urbanites suddenly awoke to find that their homes and neighborhoods had become a haven for rural fugitives from state reproductive policies.

These twin characteristics of mobility and fertility are condensed in the epithet, "over-quota guerrilla force" (*chaosheng youjidui*)—also the title of a comedy skit featured in the 1990 Spring Festival broadcast (Huang, 1988). In this performance, a rural husband and wife—performed by Huang Hong and Song Dandan, respectively—engage in a humorous dialogue about their reproductive travails. The husband is frustrated by the fact that, among the six children to whom his wife has given birth, not a single one is a boy. He vows to continue to enlarge his family until his wife successfully produces a son. To create such a large family, the couple has had to evade family-planning officials by wandering nonstop throughout the country. The names of their daughters testify to the breadth of their travels; each child is named after the place in which she was born, including some of China's most exotic and out-of-the-way locations like Hainandao (on China's southernmost tip) and Tulufan (on the eastern border of Xinjiang). Thus, by the early 1990s, the Chinese public was well acquainted with the "problem" of migrant women and the increased rate of their fertility.

In the popular media, violence and sexuality are intertwined in the portrayal of rural women in pornographic magazines sold at train stations. These pornographic magazines are meant to satisfy the sexual desires of travelers and city men and to provide economic profits. Because of the state censorship of pornography, these magazines combine violence (rape, abuse, and crime) and sexual descriptions under the camouflage of "legal education." As McClintock argues, "There is every evidence that where sexual reciprocity is censored, sexual violence prevails" (McClintock, 1992, p. 114).

These magazines contain stories of promiscuous, sexually available, and fallen rural women. One article says that the goal of all rural women in a village is to "make love to every male worker in the adjacent village." The women are said to invite the male workers to sleep with them. One rural woman allegedly sleeps with six men per night; some seduce the workers into a one-night stand just for a meal; others have 60 workers waiting in a line to make love to them (Li, 2000). Articles also recount stories of rural women who exchange male rural partners every day or make love to men in public parks. They not only engage in the "mad" process, but also cruelly murder the men's wives. The magazines record stories of rural women murdering other women for a male lover, or seducing every driver who comes to the village. They even wait on the roads, targeting drivers to satisfy their primitive sexual desires (Dong, 1995).

Whereas pornographic magazines depict rural women as promiscuous to stimulate and satisfy male readers' sexual desires, the state media tries to control and manage rural women's alleged unbridled sexuality. A 40-episode TV drama called *Red Spider* provides a lively media education (Zhang and Xiao, 1998). This TV series relates the stories of the short lives of 10 female criminals. These women "used to have their own dreams and ideals, but chose a road to their ruin, for which they were severely punished." This TV drama is designed to "warn women to respect high morals, family responsibilities and social consciences and to lead healthy lives." Female criminals are compared to "red spiders," with "red" signifying "female," and "spider" signifying "poisonous," "dangerous," and "vicious." These women's criminal experiences are dramatized in the play by focusing on their locked handcuffs and tearful confessions before execution.

One of the episodes describes a vicious rural woman named Lan Hua. Lan is bought into her husband's village with 5 thousand yuan, and later gives birth to a son. She is involved with a married man, Zhu, from the same village. Because of her extramarital affairs, Lan's husband severely abuses her at home. Unable to bear the physical abuse, she deliberately irritates her husband every day by recounting her sexual escapades with her lover. Infuriated, her husband eventually succumbs to a fatal disease and passes away. After his death, Lan murders both her own seven-year-old son and her husband's brother because of their attempts to meddle with her affairs with her lover, Zhu. Irrational and dependent, Lan asks Zhu to take her away. In the end, Lan is arrested and executed because, as a police officer observes, "immoral love leads to death."

In this TV play, Lan is portrayed as a slave to her sexuality and emotions. In reality, this image has become so influential that Chinese police officer arrested and nearly executed one innocent peasant woman. Before any investigation or interviews were conducted, this peasant woman was presumed to have conspired with her "extramarital lover" to murder her own husband (Liu, 1998). After several years of petitioning the Supreme Court, her case was finally cleared. Other recorded cases involve rural women being brutally beaten up and mistakenly arrested by police on charges of prostitution (He, 2001; Yang, 2001). In these cases, a demonstration of their virginity is necessary for their release. A loss of virginity signifies moral failing and prostitution (Liu, 2000). Lan's case in this play not only reinforces the stereotype of rural women, but also warns other rural women to protect their sexuality and morality.

This othering process is accomplished by the marginalization and degradation of the dangerous social group of rural migrant women. In particular, their "threatening" and "contaminating" sexuality and their desire to "occupy" and "transgress" the urban space constitute the state's biggest concern. The state's call for migrants' return to their rural hometowns becomes the central message. When this message fails to work and migrant women choose to stay rather than leave the city, the state has to reintensify the boundary between the moral, demure, and modest urban woman and the sexually unbridled, rural migrant women.

Performing Constructed Images

Media discourse powerfully locks in rural migrant women as static political and cultural second-class citizens. Do they have any way out? Moore argues that the resistance does not need to be "discursive, coherent or conscious" (Moore, 1994). In fact, if one cannot resist outside the dominant discourse or structure, one can at least displace oneself within it. Women can refuse the construction of gender by approaching it "deviously and ironically," or "refer to it endlessly," or, a shift in meaning can result from a "reordering of practical activities" (Moore, 1994). One of the major ways to contest the discourse is to interpret and reinterpret. In this section, I argue that hostesses' resistance takes place within this hegemonic structure, epitomized by their performance of the represented images.

Based on Foucault's work, Butler contends that there is no inner essential self; it is only through performance that identities are made in a hierarchical relationship (1993). As such, performance is both a constitutive and political act. More specifically, Butler theorizes gender as a performance or an enactment of cultural norms. In other words, female and male opposition become naturalized and reified as people repeatedly act out, perform, or cite the conventions of maleness and femaleness. Thus, Butler pinpoints the theatrical agency of the drags who, through performing a hyperbolic version of "female," parody the naturalized gender dichotomy and ultimately call it into question. Similarly, hostesses perform the constructed negative images imposed on them as a survival strategy and a means of resistance within a hierarchical relationship. Their performance is a self-conscious negotiation with the hegemonic imperative and a vehicle or space in which to imagine a sense of belonging and a first-class citizenship.

The job of the bar hostess is to serve her clients. In exchange, the client compensates the hostess with money. Within this seemingly simple exchange relationship, however, hostesses are in constant negotiation with male customers. Hostesses attempt to extract from their clients additional benefits that go beyond the basic, flat-rate fee for their services. These perquisites include tips and gifts and, most important, access to the customers' social networks. One of my informants, a twenty-year-old rural woman from Hunan, explained to me that the key to being a successful hostess is the ability to establish a stable relationship with the customer and then to exploit him. To reach this goal, as she and many other hostesses emphasized, the hostess needs to play on customer's *expectations* and *stereotypes* of how a hostess should act.

Consider this scene I witnessed in a karaoke room during my fieldwork: Around 20 women, sent in by *Mami*, lined up before several male clients in a karaoke suite. The male customers, casually sitting on a sofa, inspected the women from left to right, with critical expressions on their faces. Eager to be chosen, the women struck provocative poses to gain the men's attention. They played with hair and winked at the clients. In the middle of this examination process, *Mami* pulled one hostess over to the front and said, "What about this one? She's got big eyes!" A customer pointed at the woman and said, "Big eyes mean big vagina!" followed by fits of laughter from the other customers. At these words, the woman quietly retreated into the group. This embarrassing remark did not stop *Mami*. "We also have one with tight buttocks. She will surely serve you well!" She called out, "Come over here, Tight Buttocks! Come to the front, Tight Buttocks!" At these words, I saw a pretty woman in a tight cheongsam move to the front. A male customer raised one finger at her, motioning her to come over. At this gesture, the woman almost leaped to the man's side and hung on to his arm. Another customer pointed at a plump woman in the group and shouted at her, "Hey, are those breasts fake or real?" The hostess responded by gently shaking her full figure. The customer, apparently unsatisfied, turned to all the women and cried out, "Whose breasts are the largest? Who wants her breast to be fondled? Come and sit beside me!"

In this scene, the hostesses perform in hypersexual manner with provocative poses and salacious winking in response to clients' licentious remarks. Such a hypersexual image projects the rural women's cultural portrait as sexually promiscuous and available. As shown in this scene, one hostess, despite the customer's insulting comments about her breasts, continued her erotic performance to gain the customer's favor. The woman with "tight buttocks" demonstrated her willingness to be sexually dominated by jumping to the embrace of the customer.

To lure clients, hostesses present a hypersexual and lustful image by winking at the clients, wearing revealing clothes, and assuming seductive postures. They purr, laugh, scream, or moan when clients prey on their bodies, and they sing songs to seduce clients and convey their "devotion." For instance, a hostess chose a song titled "Why Do You Love Other Women Behind My Back? (*weishenmo ni beizhe wo ai bieren?*)" As she was singing the song, she fondled her client, leaned her whole body over him, and coquettishly asked him, "My husband [*laogong*], why do you make love to other women behind my back?" Outside of karaoke bars, hostesses send tantalizing phone messages to their clients, such as "Making love is fun. A woman with large breasts is like a tiger or a wolf. A woman with flat breasts has unfathomably superior techniques. Let's make love. . . ." Hostesses commonly boast to each other about the "whore-like sexuality" (*sao*) that their clients love most.

By allowing their bodies to be sexually fragmented and erotically staged for marketing, hostesses refuse the state's attempt to regulate rural women's promiscuous and transgressive sexuality and to control their sexuality for purely reproductive purposes. Hostesses perform media images of their hypersexuality in order to extract profit from male clients.

Cultural Legitimacy and Flexible Citizenship

In *Flexible Citizenship*, Aihwa Ong (1999) delineates the cultural strategy of flexible citizenship of the overseas Chinese business elite. Some purchase houses and send their children to prestigious universities in the United States. Others rely on *guanxi*—personal and kinship networks—to earn rights of residence in Australia, Canada, and the United States. As such, their economic power is converted into social and cultural capital. At times when it meets the obstacle of symbolic racial hierarchies already established in the American places of residence, some use philanthropy, particularly to the arts and to universities, as a strategy to gain social prestige and acceptance and offset White resistance to Asian mobility.

Similarly, hostesses convert their economic power and *guanxi* with clients to cultural legitimacy and first-class citizenship. Considering their job to be both a sacrifice and a stepping-stone to their goals, almost every hostess derives some degree of social and cultural advantage from her relationships with clients. Such cultural legitimacy includes travel, marriage to clients, further education, and business investment opportunities.

My hostess friend Hong learned English, typing, and computer science from her client boyfriend Chen. Chen even offered her a computer to practice with. She told me that having Chen as a free instructor instead of paying for classes saved her a great deal of money. Ever since she learned to type and send e-mails, we have been updating each other about changes in our lives through the Internet. During my research in Dalian, I also witnessed quite a few hostesses who paid for classes to learn occupational skills such as tailoring, hairdressing, and beautification.

Hostesses also enjoy increasing physical mobility. Clients often drive hostesses around the city or take them along on sightseeing trips. Hostess Zhang used to show me piles of photographs taken in Shanghai, Beijing, Shenyang, and other major cities. Hostesses not only traveled with clients, but also traveled in groups or at times, alone. During my research in the karaoke bars, four hostesses traveled to Beijing to meet an internet friend who studied at the China University of Political Science and Law. My friends Huang and Li traveled to Shanghai alone for different purposes. Huang went to temples at Shanghai to pray for good fortune in the new year; Li went to Shanghai to meet with her hostess friends who were working in Shanghai. While physical mobility is hard to achieve for most in China today, hostesses' economic power and their relationships with clients give them easy access to travel.

Some hostesses managed to procure first-class political citizenship. It is by no means rare for their clients who are officials to issue them free temporary resident cards or urban household registration cards (*hukou*). This transforms them into legitimate first-class citizens. For instance, my friend Yu went out with a client who was an official. He arranged for her temporary resident card to be stamped for a whole year free of charge. Another hostess, Han, had an urban household registration card issued to her for free. She was then holding two registration cards, one rural and one urban. She was very proud and deemed herself "a very successful woman."

Wealthy clients kept a great number of hostesses. As a result, some hostesses became not only "legitimate urbanites with urban residency cards," but also entrepreneurial owners of businesses such as sauna bars, gift shops, karaoke bars, and restaurants. Of the 2 hundred hostesses I studied, 6 were able to move beyond their profession through marriage to their clients. For instance, hostess Han was married to the treasury director of a prestigious hotel in Dalian. Before marriage, Han earned enough money to buy two houses, one for her family in her rural hometown in Heilongjiang, the other in Dalian. She told me that nine people in her family were supported by her income alone: her parents and seven other brothers and sisters. Han gave her brother 25,000 yuan as a wedding present and similar amounts to her sisters on the birth of their children. She has now been married for more than two years and runs a hair salon bought by her husband in Shenzhen.

Clients commonly introduce hostesses to new job opportunities, including work in other industries such as beauty parlors. While in Dalian, I helped out during the day at a small clothing boutique run by a former hostess, Zhang. At the time we were introduced, Zhang had already been retired from hostessing for a few months. Her ability to open the store and keep it afloat, however, crucially depended on the financial backing of her lover, whom she had met while still working at the karaoke bar. Money from her lover also made it possible for her to maintain her former fashion habits. Clothing remained a central preoccupation for Zhang, even though she was no longer subject to the occupational demands of hostessing. Her particular clothing practices, however, had been altered to fit in with her new environment. Zhang was now surrounded not by other hostesses but by city women who worked in the surrounding stores in the same shopping plaza. Her old wardrobe from her days at the bar would have scandalized these women and instantly revealed her former identity as a sex worker, exposing Zhang to discrimination, harassment, and most likely eviction. The threat of exposure was intensified by the talk of other vendors who claimed to be able to detect hostesses by their unseemly garb.

By looking for those elements that remain constant across these changes, we can tell which aspects of hostesses' clothing are nonnegotiable and therefore most likely tied up with their sense of identity and self. Zhang toned down her look but tellingly without discarding the hostesses' characteristic penchant for foreign fashion. In particular, Zhang switched from the sexy fashions of Korean clothes to cute and more modest Japanese fashion.

Zhang would sometimes take advantage of my presence at her boutique to slip out during lulls in business and do some shopping of her own. After one such shopping excursion, Zhang returned dressed head to toe in a cute, Japanese-style outfit. The centerpiece of the outfit was a form-fitting, pink T-shirt with the global Americanized girl-chic Hello-Kitty cartoon emblazoned across the chest. Zhang introduced the outfit to the other vendors, emphasizing above all that she was wearing genuine imported Japanese clothes. Her strategy worked. Zhang was awash with accolades from the other vendors. "It's so cute!" (*Zhen keai!*), they chorused.

Zhang's case illustrates how some retired hostesses are transformed into legitimate first-class citizens through the acquisition of a legitimate economic identity. In this case, her body became a site where appropriate fashion could legitimate her first-class citizenship. As another hostess, Sun, proudly boasted to me, "My boyfriend always says that I do not look like a rural woman at all. When I walk on the street, police cannot tell that I am from the countryside, so they don't ask me for my temporary resident card anymore." Like other migrants in the city, Sun had previously been required to show her temporary resident card on the street, and this caused her to live in constant fear and anxiety. By not being harassed by the police, Sun had passed the most important test of the legitimacy of her first-class citizenship.

Hostesses' resistance and performance of their constructed image during sex work helps them redistribute urban men's political, economic, and social resources and obtain legitimate first-class citizenship. Hostesses fake, ridicule, and rebel against their representation in the media. Indeed, media representations become tools for hostesses' political, cultural, and economic gain. The expressive freedom enjoyed by hostesses in their offstage lives allows them to construct a "true" and "ideal" self. If the onstage hostess is a weak and vulnerable victim, the offstage hostess is a strong and aggressive manipulator. Boundary-maintenance performance in sexual transaction helps hostesses subvert gender and rural-urban political and cultural hierarchy by gleaning first-class citizenship from urban men. The high status that hostesses achieve, however, is always at risk because of the entrenched stigma attached to their rural origins and sex work.

References

Bourdieu, P. (1991). *Language and symbolic power*. Cambridge: Polity Press.

Brownell, S. (1995). *Training the body for China: Sports in the moral order of the People's Republic*. Chicago, IL: University of Chicago Press.

Butler, J. (1993). *Bodies that matter: On the discursive limits of "sex."* New York: Routledge.

Chapkis, W. (1997). *Live sex acts: Women performing erotic labor*. New York: Routledge.

Chen, H. (2001, May 11). Jiemei "zhengfu" yinfa shaqin canju. [Two sisters attempt to murder each other for a man.] *Bandao Morning Post*, p. 20.

Chen, M. (2001). Nuzhuchi ren diyici shiyu taizhang zuojiaoyi. [A migrant woman's sexual transaction with her employer]. *Gaobie Chunu [Fairwell to Virginity]*, *43*, 49–56.

Chen, M. (2001). Beiqiangjian juran shuotinghao. [The woman likes to be raped]. *Gaobie Chunu [Fairwell to Virginity]*, *43*, 57–59.

Christiansen, C. (1990). Hu kou in China: Issues and studies. In D. Solinger (Ed.), *Contesting citizenship* (pp. 23–42). Berkeley: University of California Press.

Cohen, M. (1993). Cultural and political inventions in modern China: The case of the Chinese "peasant." *Daedalus* (Spring), 151–170.

Dong, M. (1995). Fengkuang zuoai zai sharenhou. [Make love crazily in Sharenhou]. *Se Cai Qi An [Surprising Cases of Beauty and Money]*, (June), 65–67.

Honig, E. (1992). *Creating Chinese ethnicity: Subei people in Shanghai, 1850–1980*. New Haven: Yale University Press.

Huang, H. (1990). *Chaosheng Youjidui*. [The over-quota rural family]. Beijing: CCTV Spring Festival Evening.

Huang, J. (1999, September 5). Anmonu fuwu shangmen, dapaisong zhufu huyu qudi [Sauna hostess offer services at the door, wives appeal for a crackdown]. *Guangzhou Daily*, p. 3.

Huang, H. (1988. January 14). Chao sheng de dan you. [Worry of over-quota]. *People's Daily*, p. 3.

Jian, P. (2001). *Caifang shouji: Jingyan Dalian*. [Interview memoirs in Dalian]. *New Weekly*, pp. 10, 44.

Khan, A. R., & Riskin, C. (1998). Income and inequality in China: Composition, distribution and growth of household income, 1988–1995, *China Quarterly*, *154*, 221–253.

Li, L., & O'Brien, K. (1996). Villagers and popular resistance in contemporary China. *Modern China*, *22*(1), 28–61.

Li, M. (2000). Meikuangli gongren paiduigan nuren. [Mine workers line up to do it with the women]. *The Red Light District in China*, *83*, 42–44.

Li, Y. (1999, August 12). Kaojin mingpai daxue liangcaizi bei xiaojie yinyou ranshang linbing, *chengdu shangbao*. [An outstanding student in a key university is seduced by a hostess and contracted an STD]. *Chengdu Commerce Newspaper*, p. 2.

Liu, D. (1995). *Zhongguo dangdai xingwenhua—Zhongguo wanli "xingwenming" diaochabaogao.*[Sex culture in Chinese contemporary society—The survey of sex culture in China]. Shanghai, China: Sanlian Publisher.

Liu, J. (1998, August 20). Sanpeinu chengwei fanzui gaofa qunti, *zhongguo qingnianbao*. [The highest crime rate is found in the group of bar hostesses], *Chinese Youth Newspaper*, p. 3.

Lu, L. (1998, January 24). Xiandai ren, hechu shi jiaxiang? Liudong zhong de xiangqing he qinqing, *renmin ribao*. [Modern people, where is the hometown? The Sentiment to Family and Hometown]. *People's Daily*, p. 11.

Lu, X. (2000). Zouchu "chengxiang fenzhi, yiguo liangce" de kunjing. [Out of the city-countryside dichotomy in a nation]. *Du Shu Reading, 5,* 3–10.

Ma, Z. and Qu. (2001, July 11). "Yuantao, 'da'nai' fanghuo shao "ernai" [The first wife sets fire to burn the second wife]. *Dalian Evening Newspaper,* p. 14.

McClintock, M. (1992). Gonad the barbarian and the Venus flytrap. In L. Segal & M. McIntosh (Eds.), *Sex exposed: Sexuality and the pornography debate* (pp. 111–131, esp. p. 114). London: Virago Press.

Moore, H. (1994). *A passion for difference.* Bloomington: Indiana University Press.

Ong, A. (1999). *Flexible citizenship: The cultural logics of transnationality.* Durham, NC; London: Duke University Press.

Siu, H. (1989). *Agents and victim.* New Haven, CT: Yale University Press.

Solinger, S. (1995). The floating population in the cities: Chances for assimilation. In D. S. Davis, R. Kraus, B. Naughton, & E. J. Perry (Eds.), *Urban spaces in contemporary China.* Cambridge, UK; New York: Cambridge University Press.

Tan, T. (1996). Gender difference in the migration of rural labor force. Paper read at the Conference on Migrant Labor in China, Hong Kong.

Wang, J. & Sisun, X. (1997). Xinsheng maiyinnu xinggoucheng, shenxin tezheng yu xingwei zhiyuanqi. [The psychological and physical characteristics of sex workers, equality and development]. In X. Li, H. Zhu, & X. Dong (Eds.), *Pingdeng Yu Fazhan* [Equality and Development] (pp. 276–297). Beijing, China: Sanlian Publisher.

Wang, W. (1995). The politics of private time: Changing leisure patterns in urban China. In D. S. Davis, R. Kraus, B. Naughton, & E. J. Perry (Eds.), *Urban spaces in contemporary China* (pp. 149–173). Cambridge, UK; New York: Cambridge University Press.

Wang, X. (1999). *Youmin wenhua yu Zhongguo shehui.* [Drifters' culture and Chinese society]. Beijing, China: Xueyuan Chubanshe.

Xu, T. (2001, November 15). Wanbei nongcun "zuo chuang nu' zou cun cuan hu." ["Bed-sitting women" in Wanbei countryside]. *Bandao Morning Post,* p. 20.

Zhang, J., & Xiao, G. (1998). *Hong zhi zhu* [Red spider]. Guangzhou, China: Guangzhou Yinxiang Chubanshe.

Zhang, L. (2001). *Strangers in the City: Reconfigurations of space, power, and social networks within China's floating population.* Palo Alto, CA: Stanford University Press.

Zheng, T. (2003). Consumption, body image, and rural-urban apartheid in contemporary China. *City and society, xv*(2), 143–163.

CHAPTER EIGHTEEN

Understanding Disability Rights in a Global Context

JANET M. DUNCAN

This article discusses the historical and present-day situations of people with disabilities in the United States and internationally. Subjected to routine abuse, living in poverty, and denied basic rights and freedoms, more attention needs to be paid to equal protections for people with disabilities. By drawing parallels with other groups with minority status, critical disability studies theorists have indicated a way forward that demonstrates the capabilities and aspirations of citizens with disabilities, and with protections and rights guaranteed through the United Nations Convention on the Rights of Persons with Disabilities (2007), perhaps equality is in sight.

The field of disability studies is a relatively new area of critical inquiry that promotes a social model of understanding people with disabilities[1] in the context of their families, communities, and societies (Gabel & Danforth, 2008; Valle & Connor, 2011). By examining the intersection between and among race, class, gender, poverty, and disability, we can strengthen, and possibly revise, our culturally and socially constructed understanding of the issues for people with disabilities on a local (North American) and international level. This is important in terms of inclusive international development and assistance, human rights, health and welfare, and civil society (Berman Bieler, 2009). It is equally crucial to understand the varying conditions for persons with disabilities since there is a history of primarily Western nations offering technical and monetary assistance to developing nations, which are then obligated to demonstrate "tangible results and products" (i.e., building institutions and congregate care facilities[2]), thereby reifying the social problems we have tried to remedy in North American society (Peters, 2008).

Consider Some Statistics About People With Disabilities

Persons with disabilities account for 10% of the world's population, with 80% of those living in developing countries (Disabled World, 2011). According to statistics provided by the World Bank, as reported by Disabled World (2011), 20% of citizens living in the poorest countries are considered to have a disability. Today there are an estimated 700 million people worldwide who have some form of a disability (Disabled World, 2011).

The United Nations' definition of a disability includes "those who have long term physical, mental, intellectual, or sensory impairments which in interaction with the various barriers may hinder their full and effective participation in society on an equal basis with others" (UN, 2011). The definition of "daily life functioning" as described by the World Health Organization (WHO) is a condition whereby a person cannot complete activities that would ordinarily be considered part of daily life activities (Mont, 2007).

Seven hundred million people may seem like an extraordinary, perhaps exaggerated number of people. However, when we consider all the people living in poverty, with food insecurity or malnutrition in many countries; war-torn regions with children being armed for conflicts; a lack of education and health care for many young girls and women; children living in dangerous toxic environments and forced to work at an early age, without an education; and, those born having a congenital disability or developmental delay, in totality there are a large number of people globally, who are affected by a disabling condition. In fact, people with disabilities constitute the largest minority in the world (Disabled World,[3] 2011). Learning and living in untenable situations creates a huge barrier to academic and social success as a citizen (Collier, 2010).

In contrast to the social model of disability, the medical model for disability, formerly promoted by the World Health Organization and other United Nations entities, relied on identifying individuals as having particular disorders, diseases, congenital abnormalities, acquired disfigurements, and psychological problems (Mont, 2007). Understanding disability from a medical model perspective required one to consider that the person is sick, broken, damaged, or diseased in some fashion (Gabel & Danforth, 2008). For the purposes of "counting" the number of people who might have a disability, neither the World Health Organization, nor the UN and the World Bank could agree on a comprehensive definition of disability. Further, if such a definition were to be determined, individuals were likely to underreport their circumstances and conditions due to social stigma (Mont, 2007).

From a Medical Model to a Social Model of Disability

In the eighteenth and nineteenth centuries, negative definitions of people with disabilities caused significant trauma and social stigma within North American society (Goffman, 1961; Wolfensberger, 1971, 2011; Trent, 1994). The long-held medical view was that people with disabilities needed to be: diagnosed (within the medical community); prescribed a treatment (in a clinical setting such as an institution); governed and permitted to get better (with a professional cure, again, in an institution); or languish and die, without care for the "incurables" (D'Antonio, 2004). The professional judgment of the medical system was deemed omniscient and final (Penney & Stastny, 2008).

In Wolf Wolfensberger's classic article, "Will There Always Be an Institution? I: The Impact of Epidemiological Trends" (Wolfensberger, 2011), institutions are characterized by efforts to separate people from the "outside" using a process of *deindividualization*. The following features of such places are:

1. An environment that aims at a low common denominator among its residents;

2. Congregation of persons into residential groups larger than those typically found in the community;

3. Reduced autonomy of residents, and increased regimentation;

4. Ordinary citizens sleep, study, work, and play in separate contexts and settings. . . . [T]hese settings tend to be physically fixed under one roof or on one contiguous campus (Wolfensberger, 2011, pp. 416–417).

In contrast to the limiting and dehumanizing medical model, the disability studies social model promotes the needs and interests of persons with disabilities within a social context, relying on individual perspectives and less on clinical professional judgment (Valle & Conner, 2011). Persons with disabilities can and do speak for themselves, educating others about their unique situation in society. Learning directly from a person with a particular disability is the best way to understand and accept the person's capabilities, rather than focus on the deficits of the person (Giangreco & Taylor, 2003; Lehr, 2009). This way of thinking has opened up a new way of appreciating the gifts, talents, and opportunities we have when we include persons with disabilities in our everyday lives, whether professionally, socially, or/ and personally.

Intersections Between Other Oppressed Groups

Scholars of disability studies often compare this emerging field to the civil rights movement involving African Americans in the 1950s, and as Longmore (2003) notes: ". . . social scientists studying the disability experience have increasingly turned to a minority group model, defining 'disability' not as fated and 'inevitable' condition, but as a socially constructed identity and role triggered by a stigmatized biological trait" (p. 37). Similar to the women's movement, a core issue for feminist disability studies scholars is to uphold the value of different ways of knowing and understanding borne of the lived experience of having a disability as a woman (Mairs, 1996; Garland-Thomson, 1997 & 2001). By making connections between race, class, gender, and disability, critical theorists have supported the intersectionality of all four groups (Conner, 2008). There is a shared history of oppression in North America among: people of color, with shifting definitions of "color" (Shapiro, 1993); those who are poor and living in poverty, including the "hidden" poverty of formerly middle-class citizens who are unemployed and now homeless;[4] women, and exclusionary practices in education, the workplace and in general society; and disability, a condition that tends to frighten most people and make the "disabled body" disgusting (Bogdan, 1988).

Similar to other oppressed groups, people with disabilities in North America have been subjected to: experimentation (D'Antonio, 2004); segregation (Wolfensberger, 1971, 2011); punishment, and control (Lovett, 1984; Kohn, 1996); abuse at the hand of caregivers (Sobsey, 1994); and, are often considered to be subhuman (Bogdan, 1988; Wen, 2011). Further, individuals with disabilities are often trapped in social roles that deny their sexuality, ability to parent, and the fundamental right to live with whom, and wherever they choose (Shapiro, 2004).

Internationally, people with disabilities, in particular women and children, do not fare well either. As reported by the UN, and the organizations Disabled World (2011) and Inclusion International (2011), persons with disabilities are more likely to be victims of violence or rape, with less access to police intervention, legal protections, or preventive care. A survey in Orissa, India, found that almost all of the women and girls with disabilities were beaten at home, 25% of women with intellectual disabilities had been raped and 6% of women with disabilities had been forcibly sterilized (Disabled World, 2011). Research indicates that violence against children with disabilities occurs at annual rates at least 1.7 times greater than for their peers without disabilities (Global Campaign for Education, 2011).

Still a Long Way to Go

Even though the social model of disability sounds reasonable and acceptable on face value, we know there is still a long way to go in terms of attitudes in North America and around the world. Western society still holds ableist views, which hold the person with a disability up to the same standard of performance and ability as those who are able-bodied, and fears the person with a disability (Gabel & Danforth, 2008). It is one of the last bastions of discrimination in the United States, and can be very subtle and unconscious on the part of the citizen, in spite of laws to protect against discrimination (The Americans with Disabilities Act, 1990) and guarantees to educate all citizens (Individuals With Disabilities Education Improvement Act, 2009).

In fact, persons with disabilities have an employment ratio of 18% compared to 63% of workers in the United States (Bureau of Labor Statistics, 2010). Students with disabilities have the highest drop-out rate in secondary education, approximately 70% in the United States (U.S. Dept. of Education, 2010). Women and children with disabilities are more than 2.5 times likely to be physically or sexually abused, often at the hand of a caregiver (Sobsey, 1994; Morton, 2009). Persons with disabilities are more than 2.5 times likely to have physician-assisted suicide suggested to them as a viable "way out," presumably to make things easier for the family caregivers (Not Dead Yet, 1996). Equally, there are examples of women choosing to terminate their pregnancy based on genetic counseling, after being advised that their child *might* have a disability such as Down syndrome. A recent court decision in Florida granted a family over $10 million in damages because their son was born without arms and one leg; had they known in advance of his birth, according to the mother, they would have elected termination (Heasley, 2011).

Ethicist and animal rights advocate Peter Singer (1993) proposes a quality of life algorithm with which we can determine how likely a newborn with a disability will perceive his or her quality of life, with an argument that some infants with disabilities are not worth extending life-saving treatments, in contrast to higher-level primates and mammals who *clearly* [emphasis added] have a higher potential than a newborn with a disability (Drake, 2009). Singer (1993) has also written about individuals with physical disabilities, including quadriplegia, cerebral palsy, and hydrocephaly, to name a few, claiming they are considered to be a burden on society. Animal rights notwithstanding, some suggest that adding a binary argument that pits people against animals is not helpful to anyone, be it human or nonhuman animals (Nocella, Bentley, & Duncan, 2012).

The same arguments about an inferior or reduced quality of life are considered within the court system, enabling acquittal for defendants who committed infanticide, homicide, or fratricide against a person with a disability (Drake, 2009). Most juries "sympathize" with the heroic caregiver who has certainly given up a fulfilling life in order to care for their disabled loved one. Medical procedures have also been devised to keep a child's body from growing into maturity, to "ease her comfort" (by not having to menstruate and having large breasts), to "keep her body small for lifting" (known as *attenuated growth* by a method using growth-stunting hormones), all with her "best interests at heart" (The Ashley Treatment, 2009). This technique could be considered as "boutique medicine," forever altering a person's body for the convenience of others and not for aesthetic value concerning the person (Gibbs, 2007). One could argue that the Ashley Treatment is not dissimilar to plastic and cosmetic surgery, however the main issue is that Ashley herself did not choose the procedure that fundamentally changed her life, keeping her in miniature.

The United Nations Convention on the Rights for Persons With Disabilities

In order to protect the rights of persons with disabilities, who obviously were not protected under the standard UN Declaration of Human Rights, the United Nations developed the Convention on the Rights of Persons with Disabilities (2007), which has 181 states parties as signatories to date, and 106 ratifications by states (UN Enable, 2011). This convention is necessary to ensure that the needs and interests of persons with disabilities are considered and provided in all aspects of life: community, education, health care, and citizenship.[5] The Convention on the Rights of Persons with Disabilities contains 35 articles that are intended to ensure rights in education, community living, employment, legal capacities, health and welfare, and equal opportunity. The guiding principles of the convention are as follows:

1. Respect for inherent dignity, individual autonomy including the freedom to make one's own choices, and independence of persons

2. Nondiscrimination

3. Full and effective participation and inclusion in society

4. Respect for difference and acceptance of persons with disabilities as part of human diversity and humanity

5. Equality of opportunity

6. Accessibility

7. Equality between men and women

8. Respect for the evolving capacities of children with disabilities and respect for the right of children with disabilities to preserve their identities (UN Enable, 2008, preamble)

To bolster the efforts to educate children, the United Nations has also adopted the "Education for All by 2015" policy, which includes children with disabilities (UNESCO, 2008). Specifically, inclusive education is promoted as the best way to educate all children, by including students in their neighborhood, home school, with peers, and by providing specific pedagogy that benefits all children (Inclusion International, 2011).

Continued Vigilance Is Necessary

People with disabilities have not always been considered within the international context for human rights. For example, it has taken the Washington, DC–based nongovernmental organization Mental Disability Rights International (MDRI) several years to be fully recognized within the same context as Amnesty International and Human Rights Watch. While the latter organizations have rightfully been publicizing the disappearance, torture and inhumane conditions of prisoners, MDRI has been documenting and reporting on the living conditions of persons with disabilities in institutions, which are abysmal, inhumane, and appalling to most citizens (MDRI reports, 2002, 2006, 2007, & 2011). Children are warehoused without clothing, proper nutrition, hygiene, and left to die in cribs, with their arms and legs bound in rags. *If* they survive, as adults with disabilities they now have permanent physical and emotional disabling conditions due to deprivation, abuse, malnutrition, disease, and have no hope for escape or release.

The work of MDRI has significantly affected the policy decisions made within the European Union, particularly as it relates to preconditions for state membership within the EU. For example, Romania was forced to examine its treatment of institutionalized children and adults with disabilities, as a precondition for accession to the EU, and subsequently, with advocacy from within the country, the group Pentru Voi has provided training, community living options, and support for families within a large area of Romania (Inclusion International, 2009). A report on the conditions on living conditions in Serbia was released (MDRI, 2007), indicating deplorable conditions for individuals with disabilities living in state care facilities. This report has been used as leverage to require Serbia to conform to better social conditions as a precondition for EU membership.

Another issue in international advocacy efforts is the use of electroshock (also known as electroconvulsive therapy, or ECT) against prisoners and people with disabilities as a punishment. For example, in Turkey (MDRI, 2008) and Argentina (MDRI, 2007), until recently it was a common psychiatric practice to use electroshock treatment, *without anesthesia,* to "teach adults [with a disability] a lesson." The international standards for care within the psychiatric mental health community were not being applied in certain countries, even though the primary psychiatrists knew this would violate current practices and would certainly cause significant pain (MDRI Turkey report, 2008; MDRI Argentina report, 2007).

Lest we remain smug in the United States, believing we do it better here with more modern facilities, there have been several recent cases of abuse and neglect for individuals with a disability. One prominent case involves a behavioral intervention school in Massachusetts that has used aversive behavioral techniques for decades (Wen, 2011). Students have died in residence and while under their care, as a result of electric shock cattle prods; wearing specially designed helmets that emit harsh auditory stimulation; noxious substances squirted into nostrils; being held in four-point restraints for days on end; and random shocks that exceed the industrial standards of care for animal livestock. It is reported that the cattle prods used at this school are designed to provide a shock that is twice the legal limit for cattle.

Mental Disability Rights International successfully petitioned the United Nations Special Rapporteur on behalf of the children and adults held at the "school" (known as the Judge Rotenberg Center), citing these violations as human rights abuses using the Geneva Convention Against Torture (MDRI, 2011). While the school is still operating, the Director, Dr. Matthew Israel, was forced to resign and serve five years probation in a plea deal (Wen, 2011). A court-appointed monitor is now in place at the school to keep an eye on the situation. The irony is that the school, originally called the Behavior Research Institute (BRI) was also under court supervision and renamed the Judge Rotenberg Center (JRC) when these recent charges were laid. Clearly government oversight in this situation was lacking and inconsequential.

While the previous examples of mistreatment of persons with disabilities in the United States are clearly harmful, more subtle forms of discrimination can be seen in our society. Here are a few to consider: the use of the word *retard* in everyday language in the media; a lack of physical accessibility, even though the Americans with Disabilities Act has been enforced since 1990; selective genetic counseling to terminate pregnancies for "suspected disabilities"; and neighborhood opposition to group homes continues. How can we turn the tide against abuse and discrimination of people with disabilities and support each other to become valued members in our society?

Given that this group is the largest minority in the world, we have an untapped sector in all societies that have been marginalized, ignored, and underappreciated. With a commitment to education, health care, nutrition, public safety, and security, these individuals and their families can be (and already are) contributing members of society. In the international development aid system, nongovernmental organizations (NGOs) tend to view their mission as a single set of outcomes, such as providing wells for a village, better nutrition, immunizations, education, and organizational structures for civil society, all of which are laudable and necessary. A new framework of *inclusive development* considers all aspects of human growth and well-being within a society, with a particular emphasis on persons with disabilities as contributors with capabilities, and not as a burden on society (Nussbaum, 1997, 2006).

A Way Forward

There are positive examples to study and inform our understanding, using Nussbaum's Capabilities Approach (2006), which offers 10 factors to promote the needs of people with disabilities, in order for them to live a fulfilling life. Nussbaum's work is an *aspirational* set of ideals, listed below in Table 18.1. If we combine these ideals with the guaranteed rights under the UN Convention, we have a newer, positive way of thinking about supports for our most vulnerable citizens. If we choose to support people with disabilities in our personal lives, in our communities, and in society, here are some ways we can use the Capabilities Approach as set of "golden rules" to live by.

Table 18.1. The Capabilities Approach Framework (Nussbaum, 2006) and Comparative Articles from UN Convention on the Rights of Persons With Disabilities (2007)

Capabilities Framework and Corresponding Articles From the UN Convention on Rights of Persons With Disabilities	Examples of Aspirations and Expectations
1. Life Lived to the fullest Articles 10, 15, 25	• Life spans of WHO expectations for all countries • Quality of life and end of life decision-making
2. & 3. Bodily health and bodily integrity Freedom to pursue a healthy life without restraint Articles 10, 11, 14–17, 19, 25, 26, 28	**Freedom from:** • Attenuated Growth Treatment, "Ashley Treatment" to artificially keep someone small, "easier" to care for • Forced sterilization • Do not resuscitate orders • Experimental drug and surgical treatments • Abuse & aversive behavioral therapy
4. Senses, imagination, and thought Freedom to experience nature within natural ecosystem Articles 8, 10, 14–21, 24, 28–30	• Inclusive community living • Education for all 2015 • Opportunities for exploration of environment • Sensory stimulation • Guaranteed a form of communication with assistive technology

continued on next page

Table 18.1. *Continued*

Capabilities Framework and Corresponding Articles From the UN Convention on Rights of Persons With Disabilities	Examples of Aspirations and Expectations
5. Emotions Freedom to express natural emotional life and intelligence Articles 8, 12, 14, 18, 19, 21, 23, 24, 28–30	• Emotional lives interpreted as "appropriate behavior"; not dangerous • Permitted to marry and have families, or adopt • Seen as emotionally mature
6. Practical Reason Viewed as capable, competent, sentient beings Articles 5, 12–14, 17, 18, 21, 22, 28	• Legally competent (i.e., rule of law, legal court system, witnesses) • Capable of decision making for self, have guardians who assist • Personal futures planning • Realistic to dream beyond present
7. Affiliation Freedom to associate with all species of choice Articles 5–7, 12–14, 17, 21–23	• Living with family and chosen friends • Inclusive communities • Inclusive recreation and leisure
8. Other Species Respect for all species, not just own Articles 5, 10–18, 22, 23	• Given inclusive opportunities to investigate or explore nature • Animals viewed as companions or loved ones not just in servitude (i.e., guide dogs)
9. Play Inclusive opportunities for play and recreation Articles 5, 8, 9, 18–21, 24, 30	• Inclusive creation in communities • Accessible play spaces or adapted equipment
10. Control over one's environment Dignity of space, place in community and society Articles 5, 8, 9, 12–18, 30	• Living wage and opportunities for employment • Viewed as competent to own property • Permitted to speak or use technology to communicate • Valued roles in society • Freedom to live with whom you choose

In summary, people with disabilities, locally in the United States, and globally continue to face enormous obstacles for full participation in society. Constituting the largest minority in the world, cutting across all ethnic, cultural, economic, and social ties, there should be a stronger emphasis placed on public education, health, and inclusive community living in order to incorporate all citizens. With protections and rights afforded by the United Nations Convention on the Rights of Persons with Disabilities, it is within our reach to attain these goals in our society. By assuming that people are more capable, everyone can benefit with equal participation and inclusion.

Notes

1. The author uses "person-first" language to discuss people with disabilities. This terminology places the individual ahead of the disabling label. This is a legal requirement in New York State for all government offices and state-funded public institutions, and is a preferred term by self-advocates who have disabilities, according to Inclusion International that represents 200 member organizations from 115 countries.

2. In 2011 the organization Mental Disability Rights International reported that the EU was pressured to not grant funds to Serbia to build a congregate care facility.

3. For a more detailed, global account of the status of persons living with a disability see "World Facts and Statistics on Disabilities and Disability Issues," from Disabled World, 2011.

4. For a detailed and thorough account of employment statistics for persons with disabilities see the 2010 Labor Force Statistics, U.S. Bureau of Labor Statistics at www.bls.gov/news.release/disabl.nr0.htm.

5. For example, in China, newborns with disabilities are often abandoned at the hospital, without receiving their family name on official documents. This leaves the infant in a state of not being able to be legally adopted, thereby denying him or her the ordinary rights of a citizen. Similarly, other countries deny citizens the right to vote based on the perceived disability.

References

Ashley Treatment. (2011). Retrieved from: http://en.wikipedia.org/wiki/Ashley_Treatment

Americans with Disabilities Act. (1990). United States Department of Labor Retrieved from http://www.dol.gov/dol/topic/disability/ada.htm.

Berman Bieler, R. (2009). Breaking the poverty cycle and promoting inclusion for people with disabilities. Paper presented at Shafallah Center's International Forum 2009. Doha, Qatar.

Bogdan, R. (1988). *Freak show. Presenting human oddities for amusement and profit.* Chicago, IL: University of Chicago Press.

Collier, P. (2010). *The bottom billion.* UK: Oxford University Press.

Conner, D. J. (2008). *Not so strange bedfellows: The promise of disability studies and critical race theory.* In S. L. Gabel & S. Danforth (Eds.), *Disability and the politics of education: An international reader.* New York: Peter Lang Press.

D'Antonio, M. (2004). *The state boys rebellion.* New York: Simon and Schuster.

Drake, S. (2009). *Not Dead Yet.* http://notdeadyetnewscommentary.blogspot.com/

Gabel, S. L. & Danforth, S. (eds.). (2008). *Disability and the politics of education: An international reader.* New York: Peter Lang Press.

Garland-Thomson, R. (1997). *Extraordinary bodies.* New York: Columbia University Press.

Garland-Thomson, R. (2001). Toward a feminist disability theory. Paper presented at the Gender and Disability Conference, March 2–3, Rutgers University, NJ.

Giangreco, M., & Taylor, S. J. (2003). "Scientifically based research" and qualitative inquiry. *Research and Practice for Persons with Severe Disabilities, 28*(3), 133–137.

Gibbs, N. (2007, January 7). Pillow angel ethics. Retrieved from: http://www.time.com/time/nation/article/0,8599,1574851,00.html#ixzz1YOy6zRLD

Goffman, E. (1961). *Asylums.* Garden City, NY: Anchor.

Heasley, S. (2011). Mom awarded $4.5 million after son born with disabilities. *Disability scoop.* Retrieved from: http://disabilityscoop.com

Inclusion International (2011). http://www.inclusion-international.org/

Kohn, A. (1996). *Beyond discipline: From compliance to community.* Alexandria, VA: ASCD.

Lehr, S. (2009). *Beautiful Ben: My son with autism.* Tully, NY: Ariminta Press.

Longmore, P. (2003). *Why I burned my book and other essays on disability.* PA: Temple University Press.

Lovett, H. (1984). *Cognitive counseling for persons with severe handicaps.* Boston, MA: Paul Brookes Publishing.

Mairs, N. (1996). *Waist-high in the world: A life among the nondisabled.* Boston, MA: Beacon.

Mental Disability Rights International Report. (1995). *Human rights & mental health: Uruguay.* Washington, DC: MDRI.

Mental Disability Rights International Report. (2000). *Human rights & mental health: Mexico.* Washington, DC: MDRI.

Mental Disability Rights International Report. (2002). *Not on the agenda: Human rights of people with mental disabilities in Kosovo.* Washington, DC: MDRI.

Mental Disability Rights International Report. (2005). *Behind closed doors: Human rights abuses in the psychiatric facilities, orphanages and rehabilitation centers of Turkey.* Washington, DC: MDRI.

Mental Disability Rights International Report. (2006). *Hidden suffering: Romania's segregation and abuse of infants and children with disabilities*. Washington, DC: MDRI.

Mental Disability Rights International Report. (2007). *Ruined lives: Segregation from society in Argentina's psychiatric asylums*. Washington, DC: MDRI.

Mental Disability Rights International. (2007). *Torment not treatment: Serbia's segregation and abuse of children and adults with disabilities*. Washington, DC: MDRI.

Mental Disability Rights International. (2010). *Abandoned and disappeared: Mexico's segregation and abuse of children and adults with disabilities*. Washington, DC: MDRI.

Mental Disability Rights International. (2010). *Torture not treatment: Electric shock and long-term restraint in the United States on children and adults with disabilities at the Judge Rotenberg Center*. Washington, DC: MDRI.

Mont, D. (2007). Measuring disability prevalence. Social Protection Discussion Paper #0706. World Bank.

Morton, M. (2009). Silenced in the court: Meanings of research and difference in the U.S. legal system. *Disability & Society, 24*(7), 883–895.

Nocella, A. J., III, Bentley, J. K., & Duncan, J. M (eds.). (2012). *Eco-ability: Nature, animals and disability*. New York: Peter Lang Publishing.

Nussbaum, M. (1997). *Sex and social justice*. UK: Oxford University Press.

Nussbaum, M. (2006). *Frontiers of justice: Disability, nationality, and species membership*. UK: Oxford University Press.

Penney, D., & Stastny, P. (2008). *The lives they left behind: Suitcases from a state hospital*. New York: Bellevue Literary Press.

Perlin, M. L. (2007). International human rights law and comparative mental disability law: The universal factors. *Syracuse Journal of International Law and Commerce, 34*(2), 333–358.

Peters, S., Wolbers, K., & Dimling, L. (2008). Reframing disability rights within an international context. In S. L. Gabel & S. Danforth (Eds.), *Disability and the politics of education: An international reader*. New York: Peter Lang Press.

Sen, A. (1999). *Development as freedom*. New York: Alfred A. Knopf.

Shapiro, J. P. (1993). *No pity: People with disabilities forging a new civil rights movement*. New York: Times Books.

Singer, P. (1993). *Taking life: Humans*. Practical ethics, 2nd ed. Cambridge, UK: Cambridge Uniersity Press, pp. 175–217.

Sobsey, D. (1994). *Violence and abuse in the lives of people with disabilities: The end of silent acceptance*. Baltimore, MD: Paul Brookes Publishing.

The Individuals with Disabilities Education Improvement Act. (2007). U.S. Department of Education. Retrieved from: http://www.nj.gov/education/specialed/idea/reauth/

Trent, J. W. (1994). *Inventing the feeble mind: A history of mental retardation in the United States*. Berkeley, CA: University of California Press.

UN Enable. (2008). Preamble. http://www.un.org/disabilities/default.asp?id=260

UNESCO. (2008). Education for All. Retrieved from: http://www.unes-co.org/new/en/education/themes/leading-the-international-agenda/education-for-all/

UN Convention on the Rights of Persons with Disabilities (2007). Retrieved from: http://www.un.org/disabilities/convention/conventionfull.shtml

U.S. Bureau of Labor Statistics. (2011). Retrieved from: http://www.bls.gov/news.release/disabl.nr0.htmU.S. Department of Labor. http://www.dol.gov/dol/topic/disability/ada.htm

Valle, J. W., & Conner, D. J. (2011). *Rethinking disability: A disability studies approach to inclusive practices.* New York, NY: McGraw Hill.

Wen, P. (2011, May 25). Head of Rotenberg Center agrees to leave post in deal with prosecutors. *The Boston Globe.*

Wolfensberger, W. (2011). Will there always be an institution? I: The impact of epidemiological trends. *Intellectual and Developmental Disabilities, 49*(6), 416–424. (Original work published 1971).

World Facts on Disability Statistics. (2011). Disabled World. Retrieved from: http://www.disabledworld.com/disability/statistics/#ixzz1f6jWrNvM

CHAPTER NINETEEN

Islam, Rentier States, and the Quest for Democracy in the Middle East and Africa

SETH N. ASUMAH

Introduction: Islam Today

The believers, men and women, are guardians of one another; they enjoin good and prohibit evil, perform the prayer, give alms, and obey God and His Prophet.

—Koran 9:71

Religion is among the strongest central categories of diversity in many nation-states, and Islam remains the fastest-growing religion among Africans of the continent and in the African Diaspora. In communities around the world, religion serves as a platform for cohesive organization of the general populace. However, religious diversity makes religious conflict inevitable. In contemplating the bloodshed that was concomitant with nation-building and nationalism, it would be difficult to ignore religion as a culprit. Nonetheless, religion also remains a dominant force in bringing about peace in many communities.

Of the major monotheistic religions in the world, Christianity, Judaism, and Islam, people who pursue the Islamic faith are ridiculed and stereotyped by many non-Muslims more than any other groups in the United States and Africa. In my course on the Middle East and North Africa (MENA), when I ask my students in the United States to participate in an exercise called "first thoughts" (what one thinks first of when, for instance, Islam is mentioned), I get a long list of stereotypes: "warmongers," "towel heads," "religious fanatics," "terrorists," "militaristic," "hijackers," "kidnappers," "polygamists," and "undemocratic." My students represent a cross-section of the opinion of not just the American populace but also Africans.

Some of these stereotypes may have validity, but most of them are the products of ignorance and xenophobia. Many people, especially Westerners, erroneously equate Islam and Islamization with Arab and Arabization. Certainly, they are related. The Prophet Muhammad, after all, was an Arab and received some of his Arabic cultural training from the Bedouins, the ancient desert dwellers in Arabia. Similarly, Muslims all over the world turn toward Mecca to say their prayers in Arabic. Yet not all Islamic adherents are Arabs, nor are all Arabs Muslims. Non-Arab Islamic people include Africans, African Americans, Persians, Indians, Chinese, Indonesians, and even Europeans.

Despite this diversity, in the balance of this essay, I will argue that Islam is not always compatible with Western democracy. Nonetheless, in the process of nation-building, African leaders in predominantly Islamic nation states have utilized rentier politics as a tool for securing acquiescence and quiescence from the general populace in order to sustain their hegemony through liberalization to legitimize their raison d'être until the recent Arab Spring. These rentier approaches and rentier shifts by regimes are concomitant with restructuring of power relations between the nation-states/power holders and different Islamic organizations and institutions within the African polity. Islam and rentierism in Africa present a challenge to the process of democratization. Concomitant with religion, Islamist movements, terrorism, conflicts over petrodollars, and the anthropomorphic nature of these nation-states are issues and questions involving the combined effects of Islam and rentier politics on the efficacy of state-citizen interaction. Contrary to the position of some political observers, for an example, Bernard Lewis (1993, 2011), that Islam and rentierism tend to distort the democratization process because they enhance hegemony maintenance of those in power, I argue that Islam supported by rentierism could reduce religious oppression and produce reasonable stability for political liberalization. Case studies from Algeria, Egypt, Nigeria, and Libya are used to analyze the effects of Islam and rentier politics on these nation-states.

The Arabic word *Islam*, derived from the root *salama*, meaning peace, is a neologism. The word's meaning is therefore currently open to several interpretations, and it has been translated to connote "submission," "resignation," and "obedience" to the will of Allah—the Islamic term for the only omnipresent, omnipotent, and merciful God, who has no feminine or plural attributes (Husain, 1995, p. 5). With over 1 billion adherents in the world today, it remains the second-largest religion spreading throughout Europe, Asia, North America, and Africa.

Nevertheless, the discourse over Islamic fundamentalism and the challenge to the authority of the modern nation-state, television images of a Muslim, events such as terrorism, the September 11, 2001 bombing of the World Trade Center in New York by Muslims, the challenge to the authority of the state by Islamic revivalists in Algeria, Egypt, Nigeria, and Libya and the renewed War on Terrorism by the West have all called for a re-examination of Islamic theosophy and its relationship to democracy. Furthermore, the dynamics of the world's political economy and the West's dependence on petroleum resources have posed a new challenge to the nation, the Islamic community—the *umma*. In the *umma*, Shiite-Sunni divergence, the nature of rentier politics in Africa, and the seeming incompatibility of Islam and democracy are complex issues that raise new questions about the authority of the nation-state.

In most Islamic nation states in Africa, politics and religion are inseparable, and rentier politics supported by primary resources such as petroleum can facilitate the process of legitimacy of the rulers in maintaining their hegemony. Islamic Middle Eastern nation-states around the Arabian Peninsula have been more successful in engaging in rentier politics than African countries with oil and large populations of Muslims. Yet Islamization, supported by rentier philosophies in some countries, has facilitated the process of nation building with a modicum of democracy in predominantly Muslim countries in Africa. As Calabresi, Crumley, Ghosh, MaCleod, McGirk, Hasnain, and Taseer note,

> Even Muslim critics of the Bush Administration's style say that its post-9/11 push for political liberalization has helped rekindle debates that have long simmered across the Muslim world. . . . how Islam can accommodate the influence of democratic ideals and Western culture. In this, Ayatollah Ruhol-lah Khomeini had it right when he declared that Islam is inseparable from politics (2004, p. 60).

Even though Islam advocates peace and harmony in the community, the process of attaining and maintaining power is somewhat different from that of Christian democratic entities. In traditional Islamic communities, the principle of election has no practical significance, nor were there mechanisms whereby the general populace could request accountability from the rulers. So far as the governors promised to abide by the Sharia—the Divine Law, legitimacy by deference ensues. I will return to this discussion later in this article.

Many non-Muslim Africans, Americans, and Europeans are appalled by the infusion of mosque and state in Islamic countries. The fact is that the principle of separation of mosque and state does not technically exist in Islamic countries. Does this lead to prejudice and, at times, discrimination against people from different political cultures? Is Islam a threat to Western democracy? Is the rising tide of Islamic fundamentalism aimed at purging the Muslim world of Western corruption, a "new" dynamic for challenging the state's authority and instituting the Holy Koran as the state's highest authority? Does the failure or the inability for the three monotheistic traditions—Judaism, Christianity, and Islam—to work out their problem of identification of divine exclusivity with ethnic-religious exclusivity serve as harbinger of ethno-religious prejudice? Will Islamic ethnonationalism continue to haunt predominantly Muslim countries in Africa where Islam is also a political force? To address these questions, I am inclined to argue that Islamic revivalism in the twenty-first century presents a new challenge to the power structure of the state and to Western democratic thinking, resulting in a misunderstanding of Islamic political culture and attitude in Africa.

Fundamentalism or Revivalism: Which Is More Oppressive and Threatening to the Nation-State?

Islamic Fundamentalism

Fundamentalism is one of the favorite terms used by the Western mass media in reporting about Muslims. The term was originally used and continues to be applied to a conservative Protestant movement of nineteenth-century America. It (fundamentalism) fell into disuse and was recoined to signify and symbolize conservative movements among the major religions in Africa and the world. Islamic fundamentalists are rather aggressive in political action. They spearhead the revolutionary spirit of Islam. Islamic fundamentalists become even more aggressive when modernizing institutions of the nation-state threaten their existence. They advocate anti-Western cultures and are against lifestyles that include such things as rock music, pornography, dancing, gambling, the use of drugs, and the sale of alcohol. Fundamentalists strictly observe and abide by the teachings of the Koran—God's holy book, and the Sharia—Islamic laws governing the individual and societal arrangements of Muslims.

The founding father of Wahhabism, Muhammad ibn Abd al Wahhab (1703–1792), engaged in total iconoclasm of "refined" Islam by returning to purity, simplicity, austerity, and the piety of Islam's classical period (Husain, 1995). Wahhabism has spread and sustained quite well in Egypt, Nigeria, Libya, and Algeria, and it is catching on quickly in the United States of America among African Americans. In Egypt, for instance, the founder of Egypt's Dchwan Al-Muslimun, a fundamentalist leader named Hassan Al-Banna (1906–1949), outlined ambitious plans for the establishment of an Islamic state.

Islamic reform movements such as the Muslim Brotherhood have concentrated their efforts on eradicating secular Islamic governments. Fundamentalism in Islam irritates Westerners because of its "antimodemist" position and tendencies. Most Western democratic nations associate Islamic fundamentalists with groups such as Hezbullah, and movements that have followed Khomeini's theosophy in Iran. Such groups advocate the expulsion of foreign influences and ideas, then work toward the achievement of social justice within the nation-state. Khomeini clearly painted the fundamentalist position on religion and politics and rejection of foreign conceptions of the politics/religion dichotomy. He asserts:

> Do not heed those who imagine that Islam is like present-day Christianity, that the mosque is no different than the church or that Islam is merely a relationship between individual and God. Imperialist institutions instilled evil in the hearts of men, saying that religion does not mix with politics. . . . [M]ost unfortunately, some of us have given credence to those lies (Khomeini, 1979, p. 7).

Islamic fundamentalists have a passionate and sincere desire to establish an Islamic nation state based on strict interpretation of the Sharia and antimodemist positions. Denunciation of Western ideas, including the challenge to Western democracy, becomes part of the revolutionary spirit of most fundamentalists. What then is Islamic revivalism? What is the connection between Islamic fundamentalists and revivalists? Is Islamic revivalism a threat to the West and democracy?

Islamic Revivalism

Islamic revivalism invokes the insurgence, reawakening and reinterpretation of the Islamic interests, symbols, precepts, norms, and ideals, especially after a long period of relative dormancy. Ali Hillal Dessonki reiterates this position:

Islamic Revivalism refers to an increasing political activism
in the name of Islam by governments and opposition groups
alike. . . . Islamic groups have assumed a more assertive
posture . . . as contenders for public loyalty. . . . Thus,
Islamic resurgence refers to the increasing prominence
and politicization of Islamic ideologies and symbols. Muslim societies and in the public life of Muslim individuals
(Dessouki, 1982, p. 4).

Islamic revivalism is thus a broader concept than Islamic fundamentalism. Fundamentalism is therefore a recent embodiment of
revivalism. Husain carefully notes that the manifestation of Islamic
revival can include a broad spectrum of the Muslim society: populists,
grassroots movements, schools, fundamentalists, government officials,
and academicians, including religious approaches in solving sociopolitical problems (Husain, 1995). For this matter, it is important to
emphasize that Islamic revivalism is not a monolithic force spearheaded by a single person or a group of Muslims. Islamic revivalism,
as a generic term, refers to anyone, a group of people, or process that
has contributed significantly to the revival of Islam.

The present form of Islamic revivalism is more globalized than
localized in predominantly Islamic countries. Its presence is evident in
Africa, Asia, the United States, as well as Europe. This globalization
of the faith makes Islamic revivalism polycentric and anthropomorphic. Islamic revivalists are generally preoccupied with the discourse
over theology, culture, economic disparity, justice, and the politics of
modern-day Islamic nation-states. Foreign affairs and international
relations for the good of the *umma* are a recent serious concern of
revivalists. The Organization of the Islamic Conference (OIC), established in 1969 by Islamic revivalists is charged with the promotion
of Islamic solidarity through socioeconomic and religio-political activities. The OIC encourages cooperation among 56 Muslim countries
including over 20 African countries and adherents of the Islamic faith
in other countries. Libya, Egypt, Algeria, and Nigeria are member
nation states of the OIC (Wright, 1993). The OIC practices "linkage
politics," a conception propounded by James Rosenau (1969), which
stresses the interconnectedness between domestic and international
dimensions of organizational functions. Domestic and international
politics of Islamic nations are inextricably connected and "linked." The
extraordinary turbulence that has defined Islamic fundamentalism
and that of revivalism, especially in between the 1980s and 2000s, continues unabated in Algeria, Egypt, Libya, Nigeria, and even in some
European countries such Spain and the United Kingdom. The demise

of communism and the reemergence of political Islam in both fundamentalism and revivalism have made the Western democracies and
emerging nation-states of Africa more conscious and cautiously per-
turbed about Islamization. In Western democracies and Africa today,
the preoccupation with political Islam is probably at the same level
as it once was with communism at its apogee. Similarly, Western fear
of the re-emergence of political Islam is rooted less in reality than in
misperceptions and misunderstanding of Islamic theosophy, culture,
and politics during the process of development and nation-building.
Included in development crises are identity, legitimacy, penetration,
participation, and distribution (Roskin, 1995).

First, identity crisis probes the issue of how the general Islamic
populace identifies with each other, accommodate Jews, Christians, and
other religious groups, and identify with the total "nation" of Islam
worldwide. Second, legitimacy is a nation-building crisis that questions the authority and leadership within the nation-state. Legitimacy is how the governed perceive that the governors are rightful.
Legitimacy is not only seen in the leadership of the community,
it is sought through the authority of the Koran and other religious
teachings. The basis of legitimacy is the Sharia, which is a body of
regulations drawn from the Koran and tradition. Third, political penetration relates to how community leaders gain legitimacy, formulate,
and implement community policy or goals without force or the threat
of force. There is no need to use force to gain obedience from the general populace or convert to Islam. Fourth, political participation, the
process whereby individuals within the community engage in activity
that impinges on the community structure and leadership capabilities,
brings the populace into the decision-making process. Elie Kedourie
(1992) acknowledges that:

> The duty to obey the caliph was not simply the outcome or
> concomitant of a civil contract between rulers and the ruled: it
> was grounded in religion. The Koran declares; "O believers!
> Obey God and Obey the Prophet and those who are in author-
> ity over you" (p. 4).

Finally, the crisis that the community would have to transcend
in order for it to maintain sustenance is distribution. This involves
equitable distribution of resources and political power. The problem
with political power is that it is the one thing in any community that is
never equally distributed, and the Islamic community is no exception.
Yet, Islam as a religion opposes all ethnic and racial differential that
would justify the superiority of one group over others (Enayat, 1993).

Several questions arise at this juncture. First, to what extent do Islamic revivalism and rentier politics come into conflict with the nation-building process and democracy? Second, owing to Islam's specific quality as a religion that advocates submission and obedience to the will of Allah and the nation-state, there remains a theoretical and doctrinal irreconcilability between Islam and democracy. So, what then are the chances for democracy to succeed in Islamic African countries? Third, do rentier states succeed in nation building by providing the basic needs for the people and buying the silence of the general populace so that there is very little opposition to the hegemony of the state? Fourth, what is unique about Islam that complements political rentierism in the process of liberalization or democratization? In order to address these questions, I will provide a synopsis of rentier politics and with specific references to Algeria, Egypt, Nigeria, and Libya, I will assess the relative propensity for democracy to succeed or fail in these nation-states.

Rentier Nation-States: Social Programs, Acquiescence, Quiescence, and Democracy

The crises of nation-building discussed above apply to all nation-states and not only Islamic ones. The modern nation state is the largest, self-sustaining, self-reliant, self-sufficient political configuration in the modern world. What political scientists call the modern nation-state is only about half a millennium old and could be traced back to the demise of older European monarchies and the emergence of strong states (Roskin, 2004). Strong modern nation-states have characteristics such as defined territorial areas, general populace, governments, and recognition from other nation-states. Nonetheless, because of global interaction and interdependence, the principles of self-sufficiency and self-reliance are all relative terms.

Rentier nation states obtain most or a substantial portion of their national revenues from the rent and profit attained from local primary resources such as oil sold to foreign clients and investors. These states therefore live off rent or income of oil or other natural resources and purchase support from their populaces by buying legitimacy through distribution of goods and services via the process of depoliticization and cooptation. Furthermore, rentier authorities practice *politics of emanation*, where the leaders treat themselves as an extension of the omnipresent and the people. If the superordinate regards him- or herself as an extension of an omnipotent being, then the subordinate denies him- or herself of independence due to mysticism surrounding the power holder.

A rentier state is anthropomorphic and it acts as a father figure for the citizens. The state indulges in placatory politics, subsidizing foodstuff, housing, and social benefits to the society. For placatory politics to be effective, in Islamic rentier states, the leaders play on Islamic philosophies, balancing the opposition and dividing resistance in order to remain hegemonic.

In Leonard Seabrooke's work on social source of financial power of Western states, he argues that "a rentier shift . . . leads to a propagation of economic social norms from the state on how the economy should work" (Seabrooke, 2006, p. 14). Furthermore, he contends that a "rentier shift is therefore a period in which the state has negatively intervened according to the above social mechanism" (Seabrooke, 2006, p. 15). In his observation of rentier politics in democratic capitalist states of England, Germany, United States, and Japan, Seabrooke conceptualizes rentier shift as negative intervention in the free market by the state when it provides assistantship to low-income groups (Seabrooke, 2006). Nonetheless, in Islamic nation-states of the Middle East and North Africa (MENA), as well as other Muslim countries in Africa, the phenomenon of states providing assistance to the general populace out of profits from exports and investments in primary resources may be seen by the objector as negative, but the process has produced, arguably, positive results. One may argue that the negative aspect of this practice (rentier politics) is the state's interference with the free market in addition to buying off resistance from the opposition.

Yet it is important to note that even the champion of democracy and the free market, the United States, under the Obama administration in 2009, engaged in a sort of rentier shift by bailing out Wall Street, the automobile industry, and major financial institutions to the tune of over 700 billion dollars. The Obama administration stimulus economic package of another 850 billion dollars in 2011, to assist middle income America is another rentier shift. Is this a rentier behavior? Why is rentier politics in Islamic African nation-states and the Middle East criticized, especially by Western observers?

Sorenson's work attempts to address the questions above by noting that in rentier wealth creation in Africa and the Middle East, only a few people are involved. These rentier states count on foreign investors and revenue for most of their income (Sorenson, 2006). Furthermore, in rentier politics, the states perform most of the economic activity on behalf of the general populace. The *Arab Human Development Report* of 2003 indicates that, "Economic returns do not necessarily accrue from hard work and high productivity, particularly in political systems that constrain freedom and do not encourage people to be industrious" (p. 134). In 2009, *The Arab Human Development*

Report characterized human security in the Arab world as "pervasive, often intense with consequences affecting large numbers of people—inhibits human development" (p. 2). Critics of rentier politics in the Arab world and Islamic nation-states have used the above arguments against states that lack democratic institutions and processes, and attempt to purchase the silence of the opposition in order to maintain state authority. Nonetheless, proponents of rentier politics have a concrete argument for state stability and the effective distribution of social programs and wealth of the nation-state, absent democratic processes. To tackle the issues of lack of democratic engagement in African Islamic countries, the following questions should be raised: Do all nation states need democracy to survive? Is the Western-style democracy the only process of governance for Islamic African nation-states?

Some Perspectives on Democracy

In order to appreciate the process and meaning of democracy in the Islamic countries of Africa, it is essential to have a clear understanding of democracy itself. According to Stephenson, democracy from a Western perspective requires a system of government based on the following four objectives:

1. majority rule expressed in free, periodic elections

2. full protection of minority rights against an irrational or tyrannical majority

3. protection of individual rights to freedom of speech, press, religion, petition, and assembly

4. equality before the law for all citizens, regardless of race, creed, color, gender, or national origin (Stephenson, 1992, p. 15).

Stephenson maintains that the four objectives for democracy are "to a degree, in conflict with one another" (p. 29). For democracy to work, therefore, there must be compromise in little bits, persuasion, and a deliberation until a specific goal is attained. Yet Stephenson's characterization of democracy affirms procedural more than relational democracy. While procedural democracy is more concerned with the process of governing fairly, relational democracy emphasizes freedom and justice where "the individual and society are inextricably linked in a range of possibilities and limitations . . . An aspirational idea—the dignity and equality of all human beings and their rights to freedom, justice, opportunity and self-determination" (AAC&U, 1995, p. 17).

Dahl (2000) argues that "Democracy cannot guarantee that its citizens will be happy, prosperous, healthy, wise, peaceful or just" (p. 60). This means that both the general populace and the nation-state make concerted efforts to secure the success of democracy. Yet, in countries where democracy has been successful, there is sufficient evidence that it evolved rather than being forced on or juxtaposed with indigenous structures or other forms of governmental systems. Regardless of the inadequacies and flaws of democracy though, most Western observers believe that the benefits outweigh the costs of establishing it.

If many of the benefits for democracy are true, then why have most Islamic African countries not been subscribing fully to the ideals of democracy? One can argue that the implications of the Western perspective of democracy to Islam are immense. In Islam, as noted earlier in this essay, the Sharia or Koranic holy law is the law of the land. This is critical when one speaks of human rights in Islamic African countries. The Sharia is what gives rulers their legitimacy and mandate to rule. This is a divine right to rule. Also, legislation passed by government may not contradict the doctrine laid out by the Sharia. Despite the legal authority of the Sharia, leaders in rentier nation-states circumvent the laws of the state in order to pacify the general populace in their efforts to establish their hegemonic powers. Under these circumstances, how could governments in Islamic nation-states carefully balance their democratic civic duties and rentier politics vis-à-vis the sacred obligations of their religion, Islam?

Islam, Rentier Politics, and Democratic Challenges in Algeria Before the Arab Spring

The case of Algeria is a clear example of the perceived incompatibility between Islam and the fundamental nature of democracy. Events before the Arab Spring of 2011, and, in particular, in Algeria, demonstrate this assertion. Since 1962, Algeria has been ruled by a one-party government. In 1988, there were a number of insurgencies, and a six-day civilian food riot in which 400 people were killed (Brumberg, 1991). This riot was indicative of the people's disenchantment with the incumbent government at that time. The government responded by amending the constitution on November 3, 1988, to enable more parties to participate in an electoral process. The socialist system in Algeria met its demise after the constitutional amendment, forcing the National Liberation Front (FLN), the party that has ruled the nation since independence, to entertain opposition for the very first time.

In June 1990, the Islamic Salvation Front (FIS) won 55% of the popular vote compared to 31% for the FLN (Brumberg, 1991). After the FIS stressed its desire to establish an Islamic state, the FLN engineered a coup d'état. The coup makers installed Muhammad Boudiaf, an Islamic modernist, to head a five-member "collegial presidency." Boudiaf was assassinated by Islamic fundamentalists in July of 1992. Algeria continues to sit on a time bomb of the development crisis of legitimacy, participation, and distribution discussed earlier in this article. An important question that arises after one study the Algerian case is, Can Islamic political fundamentalist movements coexist with secular parties in a "democratic system?" Also, if the party of Islamic fundamentalists believes it alone speaks for God, what are the chances of it handing over power graciously to another party after losing an election?

These questions are profound but need to be examined in the context of modern Islamic revivalism and its concomitant activities. In the wake of the Islamic Salvation Front's (FIS) victory, for instance, statements made by its leadership reiterated the seeming incompatibility between Islam and democracy. Entelis and Arone report that Sheikh Abdelcader Moghni of the FIS proclaimed: The Algerian people have given victory to Islam and have defeated democracy, which is nothing but apostasy (pp. 23–27).

The irony of this statement is that the FIS utilized the democratic process quite well to its advantage during the electoral campaign, but once it attained the votes, it planned against the very process that earned it victory. Had the FIS victory been recognized by the state's secular authorities, it would have marked the first time in Algeria's history for the fundamentalists to gain power through direct and legitimate elections.

The quest to establish an Islamic government and a nation-state based on Koranic law has not subsided. In the 1990s, militant Islamic laws continued to frustrate the hard-line military-backed government by attacking and killing innocent Algerians. Many of these murders have occurred during the Ramadan, the ninth month of the Islamic calendar, when most Muslims indulge in a rigorous, monthlong fast. Absent health problems, all adult Muslims during this holy month must abstain completely from drink, food, and sexual intercourse from dawn to dusk. Human endurance and resilience are at their lowest point and it is rather "unholy" or an act of cowardice that the militants elected the month of the Ramadan to make a religio-political statement to the government.

In January of 1998, *Liberte*, the Algerian independent paper, reported that 412 people were killed near the city of Relizane at sunset, just as they were breaking their fasts on the first day of the Ramadan. The insurgents killed indiscriminately. Men, women, and children died by swords and daggers. Throat slitting and beheading were not uncommon with the insurgents. Violence between government security forces and Muslim insurgents had claimed the lives of 75,000 since the Islamic Salvation Front was denied the right to change Algeria into a theocracy (Dunn, 1992, p. 16).

Relative peace returned to Algeria under President Boutiflika in the early 2000s, because of a peaceful negotiation by the president for the FIS Islamists to lay down their weapons in exchange for amnesty. During this negotiation, though, the struggle against other Islamists did not end. Currently, Algeria could be termed a multiparty state, but party politics is filled with antagonism. The government refuses to allow religious parties to send candidates to run for elections. This could be termed the politics of antipolitics, if some groups are deprived of the avenues for contesting in an election. In April 2004, President Boutiflika convincingly won 83% of the vote and propounded a Charter for Peace and National Reconciliation, offering an olive branch to the Islamists (Sorenson, 2008). In the 2012 elections, the National Liberation Front won 220 seats with only 66 seats going to the moderate Islamists. The Islamists challenged without success (Nossiter, NYT, 2012). The Algerian leaders made substantial efforts to publicize the elections to prevent the Arab Spring of 2011 that caused the toppling of governments in Egypt and Libya from reaching Algeria. Nonetheless, Algerian leaders have not been successful with rentierism.

Algeria's national oil company, Sonatrach and many foreign investors have not developed sufficient profit to pacify the Islamist opposition. There are signs of Algeria's transition to democracy, but as one observer succinctly notes, "Algeria's future includes the possibility that its petroleum resources may one day provide the springboard for sustained economic development and political stability" (Sorenson, 2008, p. 411). The observation above alludes to the fact that rentier politics could facilitate the process of democratization in resources-rich developing countries. With France's refusal to interfere in Algeria's domestic affairs and the oil industry's inability to pacify opponents of the regime, it would take a well planned strategy by the current Algerian government that would include the pacification of the opposition through the provision of social programs from oil revenue to achieve a lasting stability.

The Egyptian Example: Islamist Opposition and Weak Rentier Politics Under Mubarak

In Egypt, Islamic extremists and fundamentalists are challenging the state's authority and questioning the secular power of that nation-state. Historically, the fundamentalists group, Ikhwan ab-Musli-mun, had supported state power under Gamal Abdel Nasser, who attained power by overthrowing the monarchy of King Farouk in 1952. Nasser's rise to power was based on anti-imperialistic, revolutionary, Arab-nationalist inclination. The fundamentalists' support for the secular pan-Arabist position of Nassar lasted only up to 1954, when Nassar refused to accommodate their Islamic fundamentalist/revivalist position. This was hardly the end of the fundamentalists' politics in Egypt. They re-emerged in 1967, especially after the state relaxed its restriction against them.

Egyptian government's strategy to defuse fundamentalist violence against the state has been to reintegrate the latter into Egyptian political sphere, thus separating violent revivalists from nonviolent ones. Divide and conquer? Sadat not only did this in the 1970s, but also appropriated the title the "Believer President" and had the mass media cover his activities as a Muslim, including praying at the mosque, increasing the number of mosques in the country, and giving support to Islamic student's organizations. Paradoxically, Anwar Sadat's support for Islamic activities enhanced the legitimacy and revivalism of militant Islamic groups who later on condemned Sadat for being a hypocrite, un-Islamic, politically corrupt, and controlled by infidels of Western democracies (Esposito, 1991).

Sadat's pro-Western political and economic ties, the Camp David accords, and his condemnation of the Ayatollah Khomeini reconfirmed the fundamentalists' accusation against him and the Egyptian society as being "unbelievers." Even worse, was Sadat's vehement denunciation of his religious critics in February 1979, by calling for the separation of religion and politics in Egypt. This was clearly against Islam and the notion of an Islamic state. On October 6, 1981, he was assassinated by members of the Islamic fundamentalist group, *Tanzim al-Jihad* (Esposito, 1991).

In the 1990s and 2000s, President Hosni Mubarak, successor to Sadat, has been tested both by Islamic revivalists and fundamentalists. Still, while Islamic revivalism and extremism are on the rise and have become a significant irritant to government and society, it seems unlikely that the Algerian situation could replay in Egypt. The Mubarak administration was faced with a tough choice of fighting internecine warfare with Islamic militant groups like Al-Gamaa al-Islamiyya and the Muslim Brotherhood. It was projected that the only group that could undermine the government is the Muslim Brotherhood, because of the composition of its membership. Egypt's bourgeoisie, including scholars, lawyers, engineers, doctors, and businesspeople strongly support for the Muslim Brotherhood. The organization has seats in parliament, but would like to establish an Islamic state through nonviolent means. Hala Mustapha, a specialist in Islamic extremism, who operated in a Cairo-based think tank organization, relates the government's fear:

> When the government saw the growing presence of this group in associations and political and social organizations, it wanted to put a stop to it. The new law . . . indicates the government's concern (Grauh, 1993, p. 9).

The government's crackdown continued to be severe. It included widespread arrests and mop-ups of entire villages (Dunn, 1994). The Mubarak regime had engaged in state violence, mass arrest, and sometimes tortures to crack down on Islamist groups such as Jamaat al-Islamiyya (Fletcher, 2008). One complex aspect of the Egyptian case is that it has a profound international dimension because of extremists' attacks on foreigners. Violent activity by Islamic fundamentalists and extremists echoed not only along the Nile but in other nation-states. In 1993, Sheikh Umar Abd al-Rahman, the blind spiritual leader of *Al Gamaa* al Islamiyya, an extremist group that has continued to irritate the Egyptian government, was accused of complicity in the bombing of the World Trade Center in New York, and in an attempted coup to bomb the United Nations and traffic tunnels in New York. Abd al Rahman's connection to El-Sayyid Nosair, an Egyptian serving time in the United States for his involvement in the killing of the Jewish fundamentalist Rabbi Meir Kahane has heightened the awareness of violent activities by Muslims in the diaspora. These cases make the Egyptian Islamic revivalists even more threatening on a global level.

In 2005, to balance the efforts of dismantling Islamic groups and their leadership such as al-Jamaal and al-Jihad from politics with allowing more room for civil society to participate, President Mubarak was faced with a new challenge by the intelligentsia (Sorenson, 2008). This group, the Egyptian Movement for Change, also known as Kifaya, continued to denounce the Mubarak regime for being a puppet of the United States and an instrument of Zionism.

The Mubarak regime did not have adequate natural resources to be a good player in rentier politics. It has not been successful in silencing the opposition by providing them with socioeconomic benefits. The Egyptian economy, once dominated by the agriculture sector and infant industries, has shifted to the service sector with small industries. The unemployment rate of 10.1% is better than most African countries, yet the population explosion of 79 million people is creating a nation of unemployable youths that tend to depend on government for support (*CIA Factbook*, 2008). Furthermore, the tourism industry has suffered since the attacks by terrorist against tourists occurred in 2005. This sector generates about $9 billion annually for the Egyptian economy (Sorenson, 2008, p. 250). Aside from revenue (about $3 billion) from vessels using the Suez Canal, the United States' foreign aid to Egypt is the third-largest source of revenue for that nation-state.

The Arab Spring resulted in the demise of the Mubarak regime and the re-emergence of the Islamic Brotherhood and President Mohamed Morsi, the fifth president of Egypt. President Morsi, the first Islamist to be elected leader of an Arab state in 2012 made attempts to increase his power by sidelining the military, secular activists, and judges. Yet, without oil and the needed foreign assistance, he and the Muslim Brotherhood have a long road to travel in rentier politics. In 2013, Morsi's Freedom and Justice Party (FJP), backed by the Islamic Brotherhood, continued to face resistance from the people after he granted himself unlimited powers to "protect" the nation-state without judicial review and the ability to use executive instruments in policy making without checks from the judiciary. Morsi had gradually disassociated himself from the Islamic Brotherhood, claiming that he was a president for the entire Egyptian populace. Nonetheless, with the Egyptian bureaucracy filled with Mubarak's sympathizers, Morsi and the Islamic Brotherhood had the herculean job of convincing the Egyptian populace that an Islamist government is more effective than the secular one under Mubarak. The military did not give the Morsi regime time to mature and regime change through a bloodless coup d'état occurred in July 2013

Egypt has indulged in periodic rentier shifts by using United States' aid to thwart the efforts of the Muslim Brotherhood, Islamists, Jihadists, Tarfir wal-Hijna, and the new intelligentsia, but the previous government and the Morsi regime did not have the means or investment profits from primary resources to buy acquiescence and quiescence from the close to 94% Muslim population (Podeh, 1996, pp. 45–46; *The Washington Post*, 2004). The rentier shifts by the previous regime had supported the commercial and military elites in order for the government to maintain hegemonic power for qualified democracy to ensue. It was certain that Morsi's regime was too young in 2013 to stand the test of time, rentier politics and democracy.

Nigeria: Islam, Democratic Experiments and Failed Rentier Shift

Oil, petroleum products, foreign aid, and other resources are the major assets for Islamic African nation-states in this essay to sustain political power. Nigeria, the most populous Black nation-state (population of 146,255,312) has about 50% Muslims, and the country belongs to many Islamic organizations such as the Organization of Islamic Conference, nonetheless, the state is more secular than theocratic (*CIA Factbook*, 2008). Many of Nigeria political leaders have been Muslim, yet that nation has resisted the pressures of becoming a purely Islamic state. Nigeria is a megastate in the African context, and with over 250 ethnic groups and two major religions—Islam and Christianity, there is always an avenue for tribalism, nepotism, and religio-ethnonationalism.

Precolonial Nigeria was not a nation-state. Nonetheless, there were several city states and kingdoms such as the Hausa, Benin, Oyo, and Ife. The Hausa state is relevant to this work in that Islam reached Northern Nigeria around the fifteenth century (Aborisade & Mundt, 2001). Madrasahs and Koranic schools, concomitant with Islamic cultures, emerged in Northern Nigeria. The Hausa and the Fulani people sustained their Islamic culture from that time. The Fulani have their origin in Western Sudan. Even though the Hausa and Fulani developed trade routes and established a commercial capital in Sokoto, now Northern Nigeria, the Fulani, under the leadership of Usman dan Fodio revolted against the Hausa kings, and Usman dan Fodio's son became the sultan of Sokoto until the sultanate was defeated by the British in 1903 (Aborisade & Mundt, 2001).

British colonial policy galvanized Nigeria by bringing the north and south together as one nation-state in 1914. In most African states, the scars of colonialism and imperialism can never be totally erased in Nigeria. Exploitation of indigenous resources, missionary activity, Eurocentric political institutions, Western education, duality of cultures, dual economy, and interference in traditional institutions are some of the colonial legacies in Nigeria today. After gaining independence in 1960, Nigeria was submerged in praetorian politics (soldier in governance and coups d'état) for many years. From 1966 to the present, that nation-state has experienced over 10 major military coups. One interesting phenomenon in these military juntas is North/ Islamic and South/Christian rivalry. For instance, the 1990 failed coup against the Babangida regime was seen by most Nigerians as a "Christian coup against the Northern Muslim leadership" (Chazan & LeVine, 1991, p. 207). Furthermore, Northern Nigeria's Grand Kadi once stated, "a Muslim could not accept a non-Muslim to lead the nation and that if a Muslim leader is not acceptable to Christians, the country would have to be divided into two parts" (Forest, 1995, p. 117). Arguably, in Nigeria, Muslims, and Christians alike have maintained opposing viewpoints so far as leadership religious affiliation and autochthony are concerned.

Nigeria's membership in the Organization of Islamic Conference is a perplexing matter to the Christian population in that country, especially if one puts in perspective the objectives of the OIC. The charter has provisions, which include: (a) to preserve and promote the lofty Islamic values of peace, compassion, tolerance, equality, justice, and human dignity; (b) to endeavor to work for revitalizing Islam's pioneering role in the world while ensuring sustainable development, progress, and prosperity for the peoples of member states; (c) to enhance and strengthen the bond of unity and solidarity among the Muslim peoples and member states; and (d) to respect, safeguard, and defend the national sovereignty, independence, and territorial integrity of all Member States (OIC Charter, 2008). It is noteworthy that there are 20 objectives and over 20 other items in the charter that emphasize cooperation, solidarity, education, economics, science, and religion. The major issue at this point is whether it is prudent for a country that is slightly over 50% Muslim to become a member of the OIC, and if it is, where does that place the rest of the population?

Nigeria continues to toy with the Islamic question, but the issue of rentier politics or lack thereof and the struggle over oil and petroleum products are serious enough to create commotion and civil war in that country. Oil exploration started in the 1930s, but the production of petroleum products reached marketable levels in Nigeria in the 1970s and has since changed the nature of the political economy of that nation-state. One would think that Nigeria, with an Islamic population and oil resources, could easily engage in rentier politics to establish stability in that country. Nonetheless, oil has brought both a blessing and a curse to Nigeria. In 1995, after the Nigerian government executed an environmental activist, Ken Saro-Wiwa, against the plea of many observers in the world, the conflict between foreign-owned companies (Chevron-Texaco, Royal Dutch Shell, Total Fina Elf) and the Nigerian government, on one side, and the residents of the Niger River Delta, on the other side, has reached the apogee.

Nigeria's oil industry is the largest in Africa and the fifth-largest source of United States oil import, yet the residents of the Niger River Delta, especially the Ogoni people, dwell in poverty. Despite former President Olusegun Obasanjo's election in 1999, which was the beginning of a democratic transition in Nigeria, conflict over oil resources has ensued. Even though the conflict is more ethnic in nature, there have been "several communal clashes in recent years which led to death of hundreds of people in Plateau State . . . in clashes between Christian militias and Hausa Muslims" (*Afrol News*, 2008). Former president of Nigeria, Mr. Umaru Yar' Adua, worked to bring peace to Ogoniland, where the indigenous people where exploited and abandoned by Shell Oil Company 15 years ago. He promised to replace Shell Oil with another company that would develop a positive relationship with the Ogoni people (Clottey, 2008, p. l). In 2010, President Goodluck Jonathan came into power, and the problems over oil and religion have not subsided.

Nigeria has ample petroleum resources to enable the state to engage in rentier politics, yet there are endless conflicts between the government, oil companies, and the Niger River delta resident. These residents are both Christians and Muslims, so the issue is not about Islam, but an ethnonationalism and autochthony. It is only on Christmas Day 2009 that the failed attempt to blow up a Northwest Airline flight 254 from Amsterdam to Detroit by a young Nigerian Muslim, Umar Farouk Abdulmutallab, has called the world to question the Islamic revivalists motives against democracy in Nigeria. In recent times, Boko Haram, a Jihadist militant organization based in Northern Nigeria is engaged in iconoclasm of modern Islamic structures in order to establish the "true" laws of the Sharia in Nigeria. This Islamic extremist organization has killed between 5 thousand and 10 thousand people in the name of Islam and the organization's campaign against Western cultures (Shwayder, 2012). The transition to democracy, one would argue, could have been smoother if the government could "buy" peace with some of the oil revenue, but communal conflicts, Christian/Muslim rivalry for leadership, and mismanagement of the rentier resources have all reduced Nigeria to a failed rentier nation-state.

Libya: An Emerging Rentier State and Qualified Stability
Before the Arab Spring

Libya, for most of its history, has suffered from foreign invasions and control. These conquerors included the Phoenicians, Greeks, Romans, and the Turks. The name *Libya* was crafted by the Italians, referring to its coinage by the Greeks to describe North Africa, except Egypt. Consequently, after independence was attained in 1951, and King Idris was overthrown in a military junta, there was a restructuring of Libya from a kingdom to a republic. The Great Socialist People's Libyan Arab Jamahiriya remains the official name of Libya today. *Jamahiriya* was a term coined by former Libyan President Colonel Muammar al-Gaddafi, which was symbolic of the deliverance of state ownership to the rightful people, not the aristocracy, after his successful coup d'état in 1969. This North African country is a quintessential case for an Islamic rentier nation-state that is recently flirting with qualified democracy.

The 1959 discovery of petroleum in Cyrenaica, Libya, was the birth of petrodollars and wealth to Libya. As it is in most cases in the developing world, and Africa in particular, oil brought both a blessing and a curse to Libya. Colonial powers, and oil companies from both Great Britain and the United States exploited the country, and this exploitation was associated with resentment from the indigenous people, giving birth to autochthony, nationalism, and ethnonationalism (Sorenson, 2008, p. 384).

After the demise of the Libyan monarchy, Colonel Muammar al-Gaddafi, a praetorian leader, not only promoted a political theory of Afro-Arab socialism but initiated a new people's revolution. This revolution started with the politics of antipolitics, dismantling the King Idris's power base, developing a Revolutionary Command Council (RCC), later called the General People's Congress (GPC), and propounded the "third universal theory," which de-emphasized the tenets of Islam, but did not abandon it. The "four pillars" of Quadhafi's Afro-Arab socialism include: socialism, Arab unity, popular democracy, and progressive Islam (Sorenson, 2008, p. 385).

Quadhafi's challenge at the beginning of the revolution was to dismantle the Islamic base of the monarchy, which was a strict theosophy structured on the thinking of an Algerian Islamist, Sayid Muhammad bin Ali al-Sanusi—hence the Sanusi order. Al-Sanusi's theosophy is an aspect of Islamic revivalism. Al-Sanusi settled in Libya in the nineteenth century after being deported from Egypt and could not return to Algeria because of the French occupation (Ziadeh, 1958). Even though the monarchy's legitimacy was derived from

Islam, its illegitimacy was revealed by its lack of result-legitimacy. Before oil was found, it was only Islam that galvanized the tribal society of Libya as a nation state. Why then did Qadhafi dismantle Sanusi Islam?

Indubitably, it would be lethal for any leader with over 98% Sunni Muslim population to attempt to dismantle the very base of his or her legitimacy. With that in mind, Qadhafi forged alliances with the *ulama* (Islamic clerics), used Islamic institutions such as the mosques for political events, injected the Sharia (Islamic law) into the legal system, and Islamic educational institutions flourished. Nevertheless, by 1973, the colonel had sustained hegemonic power by redefining his position and vision on Islam and by effectively engaging in rentier politics. The ideological base for the consolidation of Qadhafi's power was the Third Universal Theory and three volumes of his *Green Book*. Egalitarianism, socialism, Arabism, and anti-imperialism will shape the "new" Libya (Al-Qadhafi, 1980). One could easily deduce from Qadhafi's philosophy that if he was not equating Islamization with Arabization, then, he almost circumvented Islam. Not too fast.

The "new" Libya did not totally eradicate the old form of Islam. Traditional Islam reemerged, and the only way President Muammar al-Gaddafi could curtail another Islamists revolution against the government was to consistently engage in rentier politics and using oil revenue to purchase the acquiescence and quiescence of the general populace. Sorenson asserts:

> Libya is a classic rentier state . . . Even before Qadhafi came to power, Libya derived considerable revenue from selling oil to other countries. The massive oil revenue allowed Libyan authorities to bypass the normal state economic regulatory institutions that guide economic development. Instead, Qadhafi and his small circle of close political allies could decide on economic distribution without the accountability that state agencies might provide (Sorenson, 2008, p. 390).

Rentier politics in Libya became even more meaningful to the regime's observers when Colonel Qadhafi coined the Jamahiriyya concept of giving governance to the people. This means that the Libyan government would become anthropomorphic, a father figure that provides for the people and in turn buys their silence in politics. Yet in the 1990s, the opposition to the regime increased. Many of Libya's middle class, revolutionaries who have lost faith in the socio-economic programs of the regime, Islamists, praetorians, and the new generation of Libyans, were questioning Qadhafi's policies (Takeyh,

2000). Furthermore, the sanctions imposed on Libya by the United States and the United Nations for the Pam Am flight 103 bombing in Lockerbie, Scotland interfered with the ability of the rentier state of Libya to provide adequate support for the general populace until the sanctions were lifted in 2004. Since then, the United States has re-established relations with Libya and a full American Embassy was re-established in 2006.

Libyan authorities in the previous regime and the security establishment had utilized rentierism quite successfully in that the opposition to Qadhafi's regime did not do serious damage, even when the government was confronted with external restrictions and economic sanctions. To soften the external opposition to Qadhadi's rule, he invited some 200 African kings in 2008, and convinced them sufficiently to crown him as "King of Kings" of Africa. Yet with all the wealth and rentier politics, Qadhafi was unable to buy the silence of those who rose against him (with Western assistance) during the Arab Spring of 2011. Forty-two years of rentier politics and hegemonic power submerged Qadhafi in a pool of arrogance and complacency until his demise. The post-Qadhafi Libya is very volatile, with terrorists attacking United States interest and the attack on the U.S. diplomatic mission in Benghazi on September 11, 2012. The lingering question is: Do rentier nation-states such as Libya thwart progress in democratic reforms? While some Western observers, including Seabrooke, would suggest that rentierism is sheer interference with the democratic process, Mufti nevertheless affirms that rentierism harms the prospects for democracy less than Islamic resistance and other factors such as economic downturns (Mufti, 1999). It is my observation that in the developing world, and in these cases in particular, rentierism serves as a catalyst for nation-building and limited democracy. In Islamic African nation-states and in Middle Eastern countries with petroleum products, rentierism could nurture the prospects for democracy.

Conclusion

Islam is not a violent religion. A very simple faith, Islam has over 2 billion adherents with diverging viewpoints and interpretation of the Koran. In this essay, I have attempted to draw on Islamic beliefs and conceptions that impact the process of nation-building both negatively and positively. The "new" concept of revivalism, which advocates Islamic autonomy within and without the nation, has been misassigned by many Westerners as undemocratic and backward. The West runs the risk of neglecting to see the possibility that Islamic states in Africa may have many qualified democratic elements and a large number of supporters universally, if Westerners only consider isolated negative events as the only criterion for measuring Islamization in the society.

Islam may not be compatible with democracy because the Sharia, which is a body of regulations from the Koran, and tradition facilitate the governing of the nation-state and not the people. Islam, for this matter, fails the test of popular participation and legitimacy of governance in a democracy. Nonetheless, the emergence of rentier politics and the dynamics of international political economy depending on petroleum resources, the nation-state and political reality have placed certain limitations on many of the old belief systems. As can be readily seen, Islam is a complete system providing spiritual, sociopolitical, and moral guidelines for its adherents, but as an international religio-political force, ideological conflicts, power struggles, questions concerning equality, social justice, political participation, and autonomy will continue to threaten the nature of Islamic nation-states, as dialectical forces of Islamic revivalism and rentier politics continue to challenge the process of democracy in Islamic nation-states in Africa.

What is new in this study is that perhaps the political culture of Islam as a peaceful religion, and one that advocates submission, tend to create a nurturing ground for African nation-states with ample petroleum resources to engage in rentier politics. The deeper the Islamic affinity with the state and the more the petroleum products the state has, the greater the marginal propensity to engage in rentier politics with limited democracy. Yet, I do not intend to perform a premature autopsy on democracy in Islamic African countries that practice rentier politics, nor do I believe that all countries and groups need democracy to survive. In the end, I believe the pressures of the twenty-first century and the global political economy that depends on petrodollars will inevitably push both Islam and democracy to recognize the utility of a symbiotic relationship.

References

Association of American Colleges and Universities. (1995). *The Drama of Diversity and Democracy*. Washington, DC: AAC&U.

Aborisade, O., & Mundt, R. (2001). *Politics in Nigeria*. New York: Longman.

Afrol News. (2008, July 16). Niger Delta residents flee militants. Retrieved from: wwwAfrol.com/aiticles/29854

Ali, Y. A. (1946). *The Koran: Text translation and commentary*, Washington, DC: American International Printing Company, 3:95.

Al-Quadhafi, M. (1980). *The Green Book*. Tripoli, Libya: The Green Book World Center.

Arab Fund for Social Development. (2003). *Building a knowledge society: Arab human development report*. New York: United Nations Development Program.

Bill, J. A., & Springborg, R. (1994). *Politics in the Middle East*. New York: Harper Collins.

Brumberg, D. (1991, winter). Islam, elections and reform in Algeria. *Journal of Democracy, 2*(1), 59–71.

Calabresi, M., Crumley, B., Ghosh, A., MaCleod, S., McGirk, T., Hasnain, G., & Taseer, A. (2004, September 13). Struggle for the Soul of Islam. *Time, 164*(11).

CIA. (2008). *CIA Factbook*. Washington DC: U.S. Government Publication.

Clotty, P. (2008, June 6). Residents in Nigeria restive Niger Delta hail president's decision about Shell Oil. *News VOA*.

Chazan, N., & Levine, V. (1991). Africa and the Middle East patterns of convergence and divergence. In J. W. Harbeson & D. Rothchild (Eds.), *Africa in world politics*. Boulder, CO: Westview Press.

Dahl, R. A. (2000). *On democracy*. New Haven, CT: Yale University Press.

Daniszewski, J. (1998, January). 412 reportedly killed in latest Algeria massacre. *Los Angeles Times*. Retrieved from: http://articles.latimes.com/1998/jan/03/news/mn-4566

Dawood, I. (1961). *The Koran*. Baltimore, MD: Penguin Books, 4:3.

Dermenghan, E. (1930). *The life of Mahomet*. London: Routledge and Sons.

Dessouki, A. H. (1982). *Islamic resurgence in the Arab world*. New York: Praeger.

Dunn, M. C. (1992). Revivalist Islam and democracy: Thinking about the Algerian quandary. *Middle East Policy, 1*(2), 16.

Dunn, M. C. (1994). Fundamentalism in Egypt. *Middle East Policy, 1*(8), 69.

Emuys, P. (1966). Consequences of the segregation of the sexes among the Arabs. Paper delivered at the Mediterranean Social Sciences Conference, Athens, Greece, p. 15.

Enayat, H. (1993). *Modern Islamic political thought*. Austin: University of Texas Press.

Entelis, P., & Arone, L. (1992). Algeria in turmoil: Islam, democracy and the state. *Middle East Policy* (Spring), 3–27.

Esposito, J. (1991). *Islam: The straight path*. New York: Oxford University Press.

Fletcher, H. (2008, May 30). Jamaat al-Islamiyya also known as: Gama'at al-Islamiyya, Al-Gama'at; Egyptian al-Gama'atal-Islamiyya; Islamic Gama'at; Islamic Group, Jama'a Islamia. Washington, DC: Council on Foreign Relations.

Forrest, T. (1995). *Politics and economic development in Nigeria*. Boulder, CO: Westview Press.

Frankel, G. (2004, January 6). "Egypt muzzles call for democracy." *The Washington Post*.

Grauh, S. (1993, May/June). "Terror on the Nile." *Africa Report*.

Guillaine, A. (1955). *The life of Muhammad*. London: Oxford University Press.

Husain, M. Z. (1995). *Global Islamic politics*. New York: Harper Collins.

Kedourie, E. (1992). *Politics in the Middle East*. New York: Oxford University Press.

Khomeini, A. (1979). *Islamic government*. New York: Manor Books.

Lewis, B. (2011, May; 1993, February). Islam and liberal democracy. *The Atlantic*. Retrieved from: http://www.theatlantic.com/past/docs/issues/93feb/lewis.htm

Mufti, M. (1999, February). Elites bargains and the onset of political liberalization in Jordan. *Comparative Political Studies*, 100–130.

Nossiter, A. (2012, May 11). Algerian election results draw disbelief. *The New York Times*.

Organization of Islamic Conference. (2008). *Charter*. Retrieved from: www.oic-oci.org/oicnew/home.asp

Podeh, E. (1996). Egypt struggle against the Militant Islamic Groups in *Terrorism and political violence*, *8*(2), 45–46.

Rosenau, J. (ed.). (1969), *Linkage Politics*. New York: Free Press.

Roskin, M. (1995). *Countries and concepts: An introduction to comparative politics*. Englewood Cliff, NJ: Prentice Hall.

Roskin, M. (2004). *Countries and concepts: An introduction to comparative politics*. Englewood Cliff, NJ: Prentice Hall.

Seabrooke, L. (2006). *The social sources of financial power: Domestic legitimacy and international financial order*. Ithaca, New York: Cornell University Press.

Shah, S. (1991, Summer). Allahu Akbar! *The Nuclear Times*.

Shwayder, S. (2012, August 27). Stirrings of hope: Nigeria stars 'back channel' talks with Boko Haram insurgents. *International Business Times*. Retrieved from: http://www.ibtimes.com

Sorenson, D. S. (2008). *An introduction to the modern Middle East*. Boulder, CO: Westview Press.

Spencer, W. (1994). *The Middle East*. Guilford, CT: Dushkin Publications.

Stephenson, G. (ed.). (1992). *American Government*. New York: Harper Collins.

The Arab Human Development Report. (2003). United Nations Development Programme. New York: United Nations Publications.

The Arab Human Development Report. (2009). United Nations Development Programme. New York: United Nations Publications.

Takeyh, R. (2000). Qadhafi's Libya and the prospect of Islamic succession. *Journal of Middle East Policy Council*, *VII*(2).

Wright, W. (ed.). (1993). *The universal almanac*. Kansas City, MO: Universal Press.

Ziadeh, N. (1958). *Sanusiyah: A study of a revivalist movement in Islam*. Leiden, Holland: E. J. Brill.

Zubaida, S. (1991). *Islam, the people and the state*. New York: Tauris.

CHAPTER TWENTY

African Relational Democracy

Reframing Diversity, Economic Development, and Society-Centered Governance for the Twenty-First Century *

SETH N. ASUMAH

Introduction

Major sociopolitical changes have taken place in Africa in the aftermath of slavery, colonialism, imperialism, and the new emergence of globalization. The decolonization period and the postcolonial discourse are submerged in the politics of uncertainty. Forces from within and without have remained inevitable in shaping the nation-states of Africa and their relationships with the people of the continent. Decolonization, quasi-colonialism, coups d'état, praetorianism, transnational agencies, international terrorism, poverty, environmental issues, predatory regimes, and vampire governments have all brought demanding questions and challenges to the assumed authority of the nation-state, the nature of African diversity, and the process of democratization. The euphoric prognosis about the benefit of self-governance, African socialism and democracy subsided during the immediate decolonization period in the 1960s and 1970s. The postindependence period has witnessed the pendulum of a political power swing back and forth from civilians to soldiers in politics, and from authoritarians to totalitarians, who sometime refuse to leave power even after they have been voted out by the general populace. What are the meanings of these forces to the essence of democracy in Africa?

Procedural and Relational Democracy

In the balance of this chapter, I argue that the democracy project in Africa is confronted with irrepressible challenges because Western procedural democracy, as a measure, is socioculturally different from African indigenous political cultures; unless the African people are willing to reframe new relational democratic models that will combine diversity and indigenous political cultures of Africans with the best democratic values and practices from the West to promote and sustain democracy, develop new economic measures in order to improve the human condition, and promote the efficacy of their own polities, the democracy project in Africa will succumb to failure-prone policies and actions of predatory regimes to the detriment of democracy itself—which could be lethal for the continent in the twenty-first century.

To understand the process of democratization and the institutions that sustain democratic entities, one has to know what democracy is and what it is not. The term *democracy* is a neologism, which is derived from the Greek word *demokratia*. Its roots are *demos*—for people, and *kratos*—for the rule of. So, literary democracy means rule of the people and by the people. Direct democracy would therefore require participation from the totality of the general populace. Such an idea is workable in small organizations, villages, and small group settings, but it is nearly impossible to exercise direct participatory democracy in modern complex societies. Why? The size of the modern nation-state and the population that should have full participation in elections and decision making that affect the lives of the people would not function properly in participatory democracy. Most nation-states are therefore left with representative democracy, which is quite a deviation from the ancient Greek-style democracy.

It is neither epiphenomenal nor anachronistic to discuss multicultural democracy in Africa in the twenty-first century. The colonial period did not prepare Africans sufficiently for democracy, and it emasculated and bastardized the indigenous political institutions of Africans. Decolonization itself left Africans with new powerless nation-states that were disorganized by cultures, ethnicities, traditions, precepts, and norms. Political communities with weak democratic foundations were the results of the Berlin Conference of 1884–1885 that carved out artificial entities to satisfy the greed of European colonial powers (Davidson, 1983, p. 3). It is ironic, one may argue, that a byproduct of European cultural imperialism—representative democracy—has gained universal coinage in the postcolonial era, which is now indispensible to governing multicultural, multiethnic, and multiperspectival nation-states of Africa. For that matter, multicultural, multiethnic, or relational democracy is an idea whose time has come. Relational democracy transcends the levels of the "procedural" concept of democracy, which places emphasis on process. Relational democracy refers to the idea that all humans share equal value, deserve equality in opportunity, respect, and participation in the life and direction of the society in which they reside. In this perspective, representation is genuine and reflective of the diversity of the populace, their culture, and the institutions that are embedded within the culture. The people's engagement and connection with their representatives are primordial, constant, and continuing. The political arrangements in relational democracy are not limited to the process of elections and party politics; rather, it is premised on the notion that the people's representatives are an extension of the people in a servant-leadership position. This idea encompasses a new politics of emanation, where leaders and followers are connected by the common good.

Nonetheless, these ideas are not on the lips of many African leaders. However, the same could be said of Black rule in South Africa, when the White minority Afrikaners held the seats of power for many years or even during the formation and sustenance of the United Nations. We need not be reminded that the coming into being of nation-states, organizations, and sociopolitical concepts, processes, and ideas are mostly dictated by history. In the past, the creation of organizations and ideas has been considered desirable when it originated from Europe and spearheaded by cerebral exercises of European philosophers. In the twenty-first century, such ideas and organizations may succumb to an ennobling and logical vestige in the sociopolitical evolution of the totality of the populace in a defined territorial area and other entities outside the boundaries of the nation-state. Multiethnic and relational democracy will therefore continue to be a sine qua non in sustaining the body politic in Africa and the world. The recent revolutions in Egypt, Algeria, Libya, and other parts of the Middle East and North Africa (MENA) are wake-up calls that the people are demanding participation in the affairs of their own countries and that they cannot leave the governance of these nation-states to the hands and pleasures of a few elites and predatory regimes.

Diversity and multicultural democracy are compatible in that diversity refers to the variety created in the society by the presence of different points of view and ways of making meaning by different participants in the polity because of differences in race, ethnicity, culture, religion, and the differences in the socialization of men and women. These differences also emerge from socioeconomic status, age, and developed ability (Asumah and Johnston-Anumonwo, 2002, p. 5). Multicultural democracy, in its relations with diversity, espouses the idea that all humans have equal natural rights, sociopolitical rights, equal values, deserve equal respect, must be treated with equal deference before the law, and should be given equal opportunity to participate fully in the life and direction of society (Asumah and Johnston-Anumonwo, 2002). Nevertheless, despite the continent's diversity, the differences in culture, ethnicity, race, gender, class, and learned ability have not been used as a viable platform for the institutions and processes of democracy. Rather, differences have been regarded as deficiencies. When differences are equated with deficiencies, they become counterproductive in remaking democratic institutions and processes. At this juncture, it is important to ask if Africa's diversity undermines democracy. Is it a truism that the more diverse an entity is, the more difficult for it to acquire democracy? Do affinity groups with linguistic, cultural, ethnic, and religious differences make the process of compromise and consensus-building difficult in Africa, therefore making democracy unattainable? Do poor nation-states in Africa have a chance to build democracy if the process involves reasonable resource acquisition and institutional development? These questions would help structure the balance of the discussion in this essay.

Rethinking the Democratic Project in Africa

Africans have continued to toy with both the concept of diversity and multicultural democracy since the decolonization period without any tangible results. The strongest argument against a relational multicultural democracy in Africa is a bleak one: without it, Africans and their cultures will continue to be submerged in the dynamics of irrepressible forces of oppression, dysfunctional governments, kleptocracies, and vampire regimes. Internecine warfare, terrorism, ethnonationalism, religio-ethnic conflicts, and disregard for human dignity will top the chart for diabolical human interaction. Ayittey asserts, "The inviolate ethic of the vampire elites is self-perpetuation in power. To achieve those objectives, they subvert every key institution of government: the civil service, judiciary, military, media, and banking. As a result, these institutions become paralyzed (Ayittey, 1999, p. 153). The cry for relational multicultural democracy is evident in recent affairs of many African nation-states, as the people begin to gather courage to tell their rulers that oppression is unacceptable.

African multicultural and relational democracy should be designed with the idea that all Africans and their allies have equal value, deserve equal respect, and should be given equal opportunity to fully participate in the life and direction of the society in which they belong. In this perspective, democracy should be considered an important element and a condition to attain social justice. Furthermore, a "just society" is one that makes democracy indispensible. African relational democracy provides a real challenge to Western traditional forms of democracy based on procedures and formal institutions of government. Traditional democratic entities, such as the United States, have experiences laden with unresolved social and political problems whose histories travel as far back as the inception of the nation-state itself. These traditional democracies, for instance, share an unfortunate legacy of slavery, racism, classism, elitism, sexism, homophobia, Afrophobia, Islamophobia, and androphobia.

Ronald Takaki cautions that nation-states that have these unfortunate legacies—and yet are regarded by many as champions of democracy—must overcome internal squabbles, and the people must be made aware of historical contradictions. Inner changes and such awareness "must come from re-visioned history" (Takaki, 1993, p. 426). The history of participatory and procedural democracy bears witness to the nature of a society that is racialized and filled with oppression and domination. Iris Young echoes Takaki's characterization of traditional democracies in her observation that, "critical theory and participatory democratic theory share with the liberal theory they challenge a tendency to suppress differences by conceiving the polity as universal and unified. This . . . has operated to effectively exclude from citizenship persons identified with the body and feeling—women, Jews, Blacks, American Indians, and so on" (Young, 1990, p. 10). This is the case in America, and in order for Africans to learn lessons from the ills of democratic exclusivities, they must make deliberate efforts to correct the inadequacy of traditional participatory democracy by ensuring that representation is genuine and reflective of the diversity of the general populace through devising a system that would reorganize the disenfranchised and the oppressed.

At this juncture the democratic experiment in Africa has created a pyramid of countries in four different levels. At the top of this pyramid are a few nation-states with elements of political economy and governments that are strong in the process of democratic experimentation. Benin, Botswana, Namibia, Mauritius, Ghana, Burkina Faso, Cape Verde, Sao Tomé, and Principe and South Africa could be counted for their efforts at the top, but they have not yet transcended the "take-off" stage to be considered consolidated democracies. The "take-off" phase is a state of prematurity for all the democratic and development pieces to be put in place. The second group of countries, according to Yohannes Woldemariam, are "those that have shown modest promise by reforming their economies and have carried out multiparty elections" (Woldemariam, 2008, p. 144). Malawi, Mozambique, Nigeria, Tanzania, and Uganda are in this second tier. The third category of nation-states in this experimentation are those that are following the perestroika of the economy but have asked democracy to wait while they work on bringing the economic sector into repair. Burundi, the Gambia, Ethiopia, and Rwanda are in this camp. The last group of African countries is struggling with its political economies and has a modicum of democratic reforms. Within that group, some have vampire regimes and others are on the verge of becoming failed states. Many African countries fit this category: Democratic Republic of the Congo, Eritrea, Equatorial Guinea, Sierra Leone, Sudan, and Somalia (Freedom House, 2010).

The democracy project has become the dominant theme in African politics and society since the demise of the Soviet Union at the end of the 1980s. The popularity of the democracy project is a result not just outside agents making such a demand, but of the general populace as we have observed recently in North Africa, demanding that vampire regimes and predatory governments vacate the seats of power. Yet, the bizarre case of the presidential elections in Côte D'Ivoire and the standoff in April 2011 left a sour taste in the mouths of those who have been advocating the remaking of democracy in Africa. It was an unusual case because both contestants declared themselves winners, even though there was only one election and one winner. Through procedural democracy, elections are designed to produce winners and losers; yet, even without a tie in this presidential race and electoral runoff, both candidates, former Prime Minister Alassane Quattara and incumbent President Laurent Gbagbo, declared themselves winners. Such a political behavior is not new to Ivoirians because it happened before in the 2000 presidential election, and it was settled by force or the threat of force. In recent times, the people are beginning to redefine public space and power and are gathering the courage to challenge totalitarians, authoritarians, and depots of Africa. Democratic elections seem to be working in Mali, Ghana, Benin, and South Africa. Yet, according to Freedom House, only 9 out of the 48 sub-Saharan African nation-states in 2010 could be called free consolidated democracies (Freedom House, 2011). Since the voice of the people is the voice of reason or the voice of God—Vox populi, vox Dei (Latin)—the people in the countries in Figure 20.1 have spoken about their experiences with democracy.

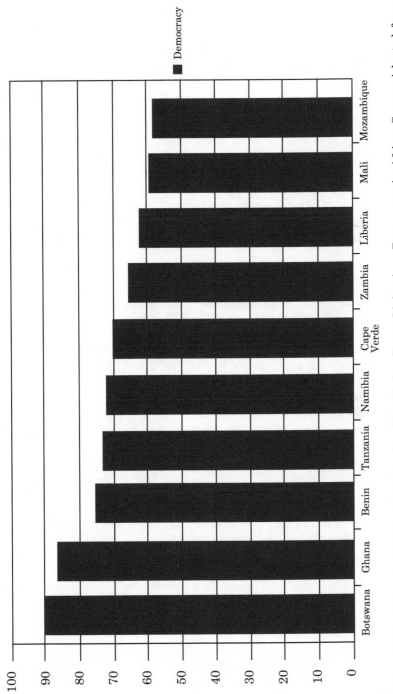

Figure 20.1. Percentage of People in the Top Ten Nation-States Living in a Democracy in Africa. *Source:* Adapted from Afrobarometer, 2009, "Neither Consolidating Nor Fully Democratic: The Evolution of African Political Regimes, 1999–2008." Briefng paper, number 67.

To tackle the issues of lack of democratic engagement in African countries, the following questions should be raised. Do all nation-states need democracy to survive? Is the Western-style democracy indispensible for governance in African?

Some Perspectives on Western Democracy and Its Implications for the Democracy Project of Africa

In order to appreciate the process and meaning of democracy in the countries of Africa, it is essential to have a clear understanding of democracy itself. According to Stephenson, democracy from a Western perspective requires a system of government based on four objectives:

1. majority rule expressed in free, periodic elections

2. full protection of minority rights against an irrational or tyrannical majority

3. protection of individual rights to freedom of speech, press, religion, petition, and assembly

4. equality before the law for all citizens, regardless of race, creed, color, gender, or national origin (Stephenson, 1992, p. 15).

Stephenson maintains that the four objectives for democracy are "to a degree, in conflict with one another" (p. 29). For democracy to work, therefore, there must be compromise in little bits, persuasion, and deliberation until a specific goal is attained. Yet Stephenson's characterization of democracy affirms procedural more than relational democracy. While procedural democracy is more concerned with the process of governing fairly, relational democracy emphasizes freedom and justice where "the individual and society are inextricably linked in a range of possibilities and limitations . . . An aspirational idea—dignity and equality of all human beings and their rights to freedom, justice, opportunity and self determination" (AAC&U, 1995, p. 17).

The African democracy project is more complex when one considers the essence of economic development as an inevitable element in restructuring a strong democratic system. It is believed that democracy and development have symbiotic relationships. However, this position is derived from the work of advocates of the modernization school, mostly from the United States, who believe that economic growth and development could lead the way to democracy. Larry

Diamond, an Africologist, argues that social pluralism and economics are the key ingredients for planting democracy in Africa. Diamond asserts, "the most widespread diffusion of democratic forms of governance since the inception of the nation state" is when "a society [is] energized and transformed by liberal economic growth demands and requires liberal politics as well" (Diamond, 1993, pp. 31–36). Again, most modernization theorists believe there is a strong connection between economic development and democracy. Nevertheless, one cannot be certain about an unambiguous causative relationship between the two. Cornel West cautions democracy observers and proponents of the modernization theory about the dogmatic effects of free market fundamentalism and corporatism that dominate the political economy of many nation-states, including the emerging democracies in Africa. Free-market fundamentalism, militarism, authoritarianism and unaccountable corporate tycoons, according to West, "bastardize and pulverize the precious word democracy" (West, 2004, p. 3), as power holders in many countries and predatory governments in Africa succumb to dynamics that belittle the ideals of democracy.

So, it is not epiphenomenal that in recent times it is the Chinese that are leading the way to African development and not the West and the modernization school. The Chinese model has little to say about democracy, it has more to say about using "soft power" in penetrating Africa—democracy must wait. Stefan Halper correctly notes that the Chinese model "stands as the world's largest billboard for market authoritarianism" (Halper, 2010, p. 2). Since the Chinese influence in Africa now surpasses that of the West, how would this Chinese authoritarianism shape African relational democracy? Some Sino-African observers may argue that the Chinese model is very similar to that of the modernization theory without canvassing for democracy at the end. The people in both China and Africa may demand change during the process of development, but the nature of change may not be similar to democratic change. It is rather a form of liberalization and an end to oppressive governments in China and Africa.

From this perspective, Philippe Schmitter and Terry Lynn Karl recognize that democracy may take different forms and processes in different regions and entities. So, African relational democracies may not resemble Western European–style democracies. Schmitter and Karl note that in emerging countries, "A bewildering array of parties, interests, and movements will simultaneously seek political influence in them, creating challenges to the polity that did not exist in the earlier processes of democratization" (Schmitter and Karl, 1991, p. 6). These two scholars agree with Dahl about procedural democracy, but they add two other elements: popularly elected officials must not succumb to praetorian politics so that coups are not tools for change of government, and the polity must maintain the ability to govern itself (Karl, 1991, p. 6). All the same, African governments have irrepressible conditions and circumstances for the above-mentioned elements in their democratic endeavors, and reaching a "take-off" stage for democracy has become a challenge.

Dahl (2000) argues that "Democracy cannot guarantee that its citizens will be happy, prosperous, healthy, wise, peaceful or just" (p. 60). This means that both the general populace and the nation-state (the largest, self-sustaining, political configuration) make concerted efforts to secure the success of democracy. Needless to mention, in countries where democracy has been successful, there is sufficient evidence that it evolved rather than being forced on or juxtaposed with indigenous structures or other forms of governmental systems. Regardless of the inadequacies and flaws of democracy though, most Western observers believe that the benefits outweigh the costs of establishing it. If many of the benefits for democracy are true, then why are most African countries not subscribing fully to the ideals of democracy? To tackle this question, one can make reference to Dahl (2002) in his assessment of the knowledge base of the Framers of the American Constitution and their ideas about democracy by stating that, "Wise as the framers were, they were necessarily limited by their profound ignorance" (Dahl, 2002, p. 8). His assertion is based on the account that the Framers did not foresee the future, "nor could they draw on the knowledge that might be gained from later experiences with democracy in America and elsewhere" (Dahl, 2002, p. 8). Are African leaders in recent times suffering the same setback as their American counterparts? Is ignorance inevitable in institutionalizing democracy?

According to Dahl, among several elements that the American Framers failed to confront in detail were the question of slavery, the right of suffrage, the process of electing the president and senators, the effects of the Connecticut Compromise, which awarded each state equal number of senators without regard to the size of the population, the limitation of Congress in controlling the economy, and the unlimited power of the judiciary (Dahl, 2002, pp. 16–20). Even though the amendments that came after the creation of the Constitution attempted to rectify most of these inadequacies, they do not provide an unshakable scaffold for the people to continue to build democracy as intended by the Framers. With this complication in mind, and noting that democracy evolves with programmatic endeavors and cannot be dictated, forced on, or transplanted very easily, one can argue that the implications for the Western perspective of democracy on Africa are immense.

Looking for Reasons to Fill Up the Democracy Lacuna in Africa: Economics, Oil, and Rentier Politics

Democracy observers and the interlocutors of liberal democracy have argued that the necessary prerequisites of democratic structures for a sustainable polity are absent in most African countries to enable the leaders to implement initiatives that would lead to democratic societies on the continent. These prerequisites are not limited to a solid constitutional framework with checks and balances, majority rule and minority rights, the protection of individual rights to freedom, and equality before the law, but the reduction of abject poverty, economic growth, equity, and development cannot be left out of the equation. Accepting the premise of modernization theory that economic variables are indispensable in creating a sustainable democratic society for the moment, it is indubitable that Africa is the poorest continent on the planet, with more than half of the population residing in poverty according to the World Bank. The employment structures for countries are one of the best predictors of economic development. Africa has about 40% of its labor force in the agriculture sector and over three quarters of the continent has between a 15.1% and over 20% proportion of the labor force unemployed (Allen and Sutton, 2011, pp. 110–111). The low levels of purchasing power, percentage of the populace living on less than a dollar a day, the nature of economic output per country, and the general rate of poverty in Africa create a discrepancy between the marginal propensity to convert economic resources into democratic realities and the actual established democratic institutions. Arguably, there is no direct and concrete corelationship between abundance of economic resources and successful consolidated democracies. Yet, the debate by the modernization school that since the 1950s, there is evidence that an educated middle-class and increases in wealth in most countries cause corresponding increases in political freedoms and better chances to remove oppressive regimes from power has not subsided. Similarly, the Chinese case of rapid economic development stands the modernization theory on its head.

Oil and rentier politics, Asumah argues, could improve liberalization and may lead to limited democratic reforms (see Asumah, 2010). Yet, African countries with resources have not been successful in rentier politics. "Rentier nation states obtain most or a substantial portion of their national revenue from the rent and profit acquired from local primary resources such as oil sold to foreign clients and investors. These states therefore live off rent or income of oil . . . and purchase support from their populace by buying legitimacy through distribution of goods and services via the process of de-politicization and cooptation" (Asumah, 2010, p. 403). A number of African countries—Libya, Algeria, Angola, Chad, and Equatorial Guinea—have toyed with the idea of rentier politics, but their efforts toward liberalization and democratization have not come to fruition. As noted by Freedom House, seven out of the eight countries that produce large quantities of oil in Africa are not free. The one country that comes anything near to "free" is Nigeria, but then again, it is only "partly free" (Freedom House, 2011). Steven Kretzmann, a director of a Washington-based organization that monitors the activities of the oil industry, globally sums the oil/democracy argument this way: "Unfortunately, you can't just drill your way to democracy and prosperity" (Kretzmann, 2005, p. 2).

In nation-states where the foundations for democracy and development are weak, oil can be both a blessing and a curse. As noted above in rentier politics, leaders in oil-rich nation-states have used revenue from petroleum trade to provide some social programs for the general populace in return for their acquiescence and quiescence in the political process. Other leaders have used oil revenue to buffer their security forces by purchasing expensive ammunition and rewarding the elite military officer corps in return for protection. Either way, it is still rentier politics. Ironically, the champion of democracy, the United States, continues to do business with oil-rich countries like Nigeria and Equatorial Guinea, where democracy has failed or is failing. It is unpardonable that the Obama administration's ambassador to Equatorial Guinea would characterize the Teodoro Obiang Ngume's regime as an "ally" to the United States; neither is it acceptable for the African Union (AU) to elect Obiang Ngume president of the AU after Amnesty International has found evidence of torture, execution, and detention of the president's opponents (McLure, 2012). Yet, without a legal proceeding or a trial one cannot determine if President Obieng Nguma is guilty of any the charges brought forth by Amnesty International. Nigeria is partially free according to Freedom House; however, one must not forget how the Nigerian government has been using force against the Oguni people in the Niger Delta, who are "sitting" on oil and petroleum resources but are submerged in pollution and poverty in Nigeria. Nigeria and Angola are prime examples of nation-states where oil has become a curse and a fuel for ethnic conflict.

Currently, Ghana is a test case for the oil/democracy and blessing/curse discourse. Ghanaians have been quite successful in the past 20 years with the democracy project in Africa. The 2008 Ghanaian presidential election and the race between Nana Akufo Addo of the ruling party and John Atta Mills, the opposition's candidate, was tight. In a runoff election three weeks later, John Atta Mill was elected president by 50.2% to 49.8%. This result was sufficient to fuel ethnic conflicts in most African countries since the contestants were from different ethnic groups in Ghana. John Atta Mills, the would-be president, is a Fanti from Ekumfi Otuam in the Central Region of Ghana, and his opponent is an Akan, born in the Greater Accra Region. Furthermore, the Ghanaian presidential election is praise-worthy for the democratic process in Africa. Mali, Benin, and Ghana appear to be gathering strength in the democratic process in one election after the other. Yet, elections are only one part of procedural democracy, and Ghana presents another test case with the discovery and drilling of oil from the Jubilee Fields. Would the oil wealth destroy the process of democracy in Ghana or create ethnic conflicts like other oil-rich African countries? Oil wealth contributes to economic growth, but does economic growth necessarily help the process of democratization? It is sound to tackle this question by noting that economic growth and development will facilitate the process of democracy only if they strongly support structural and socioeconomic status changes in the general populace. This phenomenon means that the nation-state must undergo changes in class structure. In Africa though, a middle class that would serve as a conceptual bridge between the rich and the poor is almost nonexistent. Absent this influential middle-class, the process of democratization is stifled and ethnic and kinship groups have to engage in the participatory process for some semblance of liberalization to ensue.

Ethnic Fragmentation, Diversity, and Civil Society

The human diversity in Africa is unrivaled in any continent on earth. This diversity is a blessing in several ways, including heterogeneous cultures, biological and sociological differences, adorned by the politics of difference, but this same diversity can also serve to undermine the process of democratization. There are many ethnic groups in Africa, with over 2 thousand languages, cultures, and norms. The 54 African nation-states (Southern Sudan seceded from the Arab/Muslim-controlled north and became an independent nation-state on July 9, 2011) are multilingual, except Somalia, Swaziland, Lesotho, and Botswana. Nigeria, the most populous nation-state in Africa (population 148.1 million) for instance, has over 3 hundred different linguistic groups. Different languages are concomitant with different cultures. Khapoya carefully reminds students and scholars of Africa that: "'Language' and 'culture' are virtually the same. It is helpful when studying the similarities and differences between African people, to adopt such a perspective. . . . a group's common elements of language and culture are seen as being most significant in identifying different 'people' or ethnic groups sharing common language and culture" (Khapoya, 2010, p. 12). Khapoya's observation strengthens the case for diversity and kinship in Africa. Africans should therefore celebrate the diversity of their cultures to create strong democratic institutions. Nevertheless, one can be puzzled by this question: How can the diverse cultures and languages survive (ethnic) conflict when the freedoms associated with self and cultural expressions can also be divisive?

Africans and Americans were witnesses of the ethnic conflict between Hutus and Tutsis in Rwanda and the genocide that ended the lives of 800,000 Tutsis and Hutus who opposed the massacre (Glazer, 2004, pp. 685–700). Sudan's 20-year-long civil war between the northern Arab/Muslims and the southern Black African Christians in western region of Darfur just ended with the creation of a newest nation-state in the world, the Republic of South Sudan, on July 9, 2011. Somalia, Kenya, and Nigeria, all have ethnic tensions. As McLure informs his readers:

> In fact, many Africans—even in the continent's most stable and democratic countries—consider their ethnic identity as equally or more important than their national identity. . . . Strong ethnic attachments can hamper the development of democracy if elections become mere ethnic headcounts, with winners dividing the spoils (McLure, 2012, pp. 7–8).

The ethnic conflicts are fueled by old colonial artificial boundaries that were drawn between brothers and sisters and kinship groups since the 1800s. Europeans created some of that obstacle to democracy that Africans are facing today. The Europeans created boundaries that bastardized ethnic identities for the benefit of natural resources, which has continued to render powerless national identity in the process of democratization. In addition to boundary problems, tribalism, nepotism, cronyism, and ethno-nationalism are culprits of ethnic conflicts. With these ethnic conflicts on the continent, and the fact that the people have not yet transcended affinity politics, the road to democracy in Africa will continue to be undulating.

It behooves this writer to muddy the discourse over ethnic diversity and democracy in Africa by making reference to Fish and Brooks's 2004 study that debunked Freedom House president Adrian Karantnycky's position (and the prevailing position) that multiethnic and diverse societies have less of a chance of building democracy and that "democracy has been significantly more successful in monoethnic societies than in ethnically divided and multiethnic societies" (Karantnycky, 2002, p. 107). In their quantitative analysis, using a number of multiethnic and "fractionalized" societies, including Benin, Botswana, Cape Verde, Mali, and Rwanda in Africa, Fish and Brooks (2004) conclude that contrary to conventional wisdom and empirical evidence about how linguistic, cultural, religious and ethnic difference could sabotage the process of democratization, "Our findings, which are based on analysis of some high-quality, highly differentiated new data, provide grounds for doubt about the idea that monoethnic societies have an edge when it comes to founding and preserving democratic rule" (Fish and Brooks, 2004, p. 164).

This is not to rehash the debate about how compatible or not diversity is to democracy. Nevertheless, the Fish and Brooks finding informs our observation of how Africologists can capitalize on Africa's diversity to improve democracy. It also enables us to remove predatory regimes that hide behind the facade of the difficulty for multiethnic societies in Africa to pursue democracy from their authoritarian domains. However, affinity politics is still very strong in Africa, and unless African countries transcend the "take-off" stage, a phase of strong prematurity, where all the structures of development are in position, civil society is strengthened, and linguistic/ethnic identity is transformed into national identity politics, the place of diversity in building democracy will remain questionable at best and lethal at worst.

Most African nation-states have maintained a state-centered state model in which the nation-states are independent actors that deal with diversity and turn their own preferences into public policy and programs in order to avoid multiethnic conflict. The state at this stage is anthropomorphic; it acts as a father figure without input from civil society. The quest for African nation-states for the twenty-first century is to utilize a society-centered state model that postulates a condition in which civil society within the polity has a symbiotic relationship with the nation-state. It is indubitable that there is a strong relationship between democracy and autonomous community associations and institutions, where individuals make the state accountable. In a society-centered state model, the state serves as a viable platform on which different sociopolitical actors come together to iron out their difference and galvanize their interest to assist the state to remain above a "take-off" stage. Even though there is no nation-state that is exclusively state-centered or society-centered, these generalizations are helpful in examining state-civil society integration and interaction. Society-centeredness, as a deliberate socioeconomic arrangement, strengthens the society-state relationship, the autonomy of the state, and the productivity of civil society.

All the same, in Africa civil society is mostly locally based. These local groups have limited penetration into national politics. Ethnic associations, kinship groups, market women's organizations, religious groups, age groups and farmers associations are examples of these locally based groups. More recently, student organizations and labor unions are beginning to form coalitions at the national levels, but their effect on politics is limited because they do not have the economic and organizational power to balance the hegemony of the state. Civil society itself derives from Western democratic theory so there is some difficulty in precisely adopting the concept in African politics and culture. Where does one place African primordial groups? Does the idea of civil society provide a clear dichotomy between affinity groups and affiliation groups or the communal vis-à-vis the societal? In attempting to answer similar questions about restructuring democracy in the African context, Woldemarian (2008) notes that:

> Nowhere in Africa is there a clear line of demarcation between state and society. The notion of civil society providing instruments of countervailing power that would force the African state to become accountable to the governed is either poorly developed or nonexistent in Africa. In such circumstances it makes little sense to look for definitions of civil society grounded in social, economic, and ethical arrangements considered as separate from the state (Woldemarian, 2008, p. 149).

In order for sociopolitical transformation to take place in Africa, civil society and the intelligentsia must galvanize their force to tame the current turbulent voyage of the premature nation-states of Africa to effectively engage the democracy project.

Reframing African Relational Democracy

Many components, institutions, processes, and procedural standards can assist political scientists and observers of democracy to identify whether a polity is democratic or not. One cannot overemphasize that these measures and processes are predominantly that of the global north or Western. Nonetheless, institutions and procedures alone are not sufficient or adequate variables in determining the nature of democracy in a particular state. The most effective approach in determining the state of democracy in a nation-state is by the approval of the ruled and not the rulers per se. Yet, the people's consent may vary from one country to another because of cultural differences and the nature of "civic culture" present in a polity. What becomes of an entity that lacks civil society, civic culture, or something different from what Western democracies identify as democracy? The African project on democracy is vulnerable to the question above. But Schmitter and Karl (1991) suggest a model that "rest(s) on the rule of prudence, not deeply ingrained habits of tolerance, moderation, mutual respect, fair play, readiness to compromise, or trust in public authorities. Waiting for such habits to sink deep and lasting roots implies a very slow process of regime consolidation—one that takes generations . . ." (Schmitter & Karl, 1991, p. 7). This statement encapsulates the nature and challenges confronted by the African democracy project. Africans have not reached a stage where the Western forms and elements of democracy are deeply ingrained in the people and the nation-states. At best, the countries that are advanced in the democratic project are those that are engaged in a democratic transition—a stage of movement from authoritarianism to democracy. If the aim for African countries is to reach democratic consolidation, then there should be a sense of urgency about reaching a stage of democratic development where the general populace and the key political actors, groups, and institutions accept the pre-eminence of democratic institutions and practice as their modus operandi and modus vivendi—way of doing business and way of life.

Democratic consolidation could be relatively easy if African countries could develop a hybrid of African sociocultural practices, such as traditional institutions and social norms and what had been borrowed from Western democracies, and then shape them into African relational democracy. This type of democracy transcends procedural democracy, which places emphasis on the *process* of elections and the protection of individual rights. A system of government in a nonconsolidated democratic entity that is process oriented tends to dislocate its function when those who benefit from the process of, say, elections, can get into positions of power and forget about the electorate or exploit the very people who elected them—hence, the magnitude and scope of bloodsucking, vampire and predatory regimes. African relational democracy will combine effective indigenous institutions, cultural practices, workable Western practices and institutions, and social freedoms as foundation of democracy to a point where society-state relationships are inextricably connected in what is attainable or unattainable. Relational democracy would encompass a condition that facilitates the politics of emanation, where the governors and the governed are connected by similar faith, purpose, and vision. The leaders, in this perspective, are an extension of the led and they (leaders) are not in power for self-aggrandizement but they assume their position to genuinely "relate" to the people in all aspects of their sociopolitical endeavors.

At this juncture, it is not unthinkable to revisit African indigenous political institutions and practices and examine how they could be merged with the uncompleted European models and processes that were left in the aftermath of colonialism. Even though some of the decolonization discourses have argued for a synthesis between African and European norms and conceptual decolonization, the debate is only seen in philosophical terms and has not been translated into effective democracy in Africa. Some African countries experimented with the juxtaposition of traditional institutions with Anglo-American ones, only to abandon them later for Western models. What this writer is proposing is a deliberate integration of African cultures and practices into the exclusively European colonial models that have proven to be ineffective in Africa. This integrative approach may enable African leaders to produce political systems built on the amalgamation of the African "self" and the European "other" for good governance and the preservation of African dignity because democracy tends to evolve by restructuring indigenous forms and norms into universal standards. Why? The European project in Africa during colonialism included denying Africans their culture through the process of assimilation and cultural imperialism. In order for democracy to flourish, however, its development must include indigenous systems and at the same time have sufficient room to challenge aspects of the system that are not democratic. After trial and error with the Western systems of democracy, the time has come to retrieve some of what was denied to Africans during colonialism in terms of precepts, norms, and culture—*sankofa*, the Akan term for retrieving the historical and cultural past. Nonetheless, some casual observers of African cultures and political systems are quick to invoke the nondemocratic qualities of indigenous African institutions and processes. Kwame Gyekye, an African philosopher, challenging such a position notes,

> V. G. Simiyu, a Kenyan historian, argues that the tradi-
> tional African political system was undemocratic. Simiyu's
> denial that the traditional African political practices was
> democratic is premised, as I understand it, on some basic
> assumptions. First, he assumes that the African society
> was hierarchical and stratified, allowing the political and
> economic domination of the lower classes by the royal and
> aristocratic groups: "The first general principle which seemed
> to lie at the base of nearly all African political systems was
> the concept of hierarchy." Furthermore, he adds, "In some
> societies, the class structure prevented the development of
> democratic tendencies . . . Simiyu's denial of democracy to
> traditional African political practice is not unqualified; it is
> sometimes even inconsistent (Gyekye, 1997, pp. 118–119).

Gyekye's objection to Simiyu's observation is not unusual because scholars such as Marina Ottaway, continue to hold a similar position (Ottaway, 2005, pp. 30–33). One can argue that the traditional African practices as far as politics and democracy were concerned were not about popular sovereignty, they were somewhat hierarchical, class-based and sexist. Ultimately, such qualities are present in Euro-American democracies, but they do not preclude them from becoming consolidated democratic nation-states. It is one thing to debate about democratic prerequisites and another to discuss consolidated democracy.

The sustenance of consolidated democracy in Africa may begin with reassessing the institutions of chieftaincy, the council of chiefs, paramount chiefs and how they can revive their roles in the postcolonial African nation-state. Chiefs serve as linchpins between their people and the polity, and once their roles are institutionalized, their political authority may not be questionable. If we understand the position of a chief as one that is hereditary, but the chief is enstooled (attain chieftaincy through the symbolic stool of the people, such as the Ashanti nation of Ghana) by the people and he or she serves at the will and consent of the people, then the level of legitimacy could be high. The root of relational democracy begins with the people and their chiefs who can represent them without questions. Two prominent British anthropologists, Fortes and Evans-Pritchards, once affirmed this observation by remarking that, "The structure of the African state implies that kings and chiefs rule by consent. A ruler's

subjects are fully aware of the duties they owe to him, and are able
to exert pressure to make him discharge these duties" (Fortes and
Evans-Pritchards, 1940, p. 12). It is not only the aspect of authority
that is so important but the process of consultation with the people
and elders and consensus building cannot be overemphasized. In
fact, human rights abuses, the establishment of authoritarianism,
and vampire regimes in Africa are not precolonial ideas; they are
practices that were absent in African indigenous politics. Jack Donnelly asserts, "authentic traditional cultural practices and values can
be an important check on the abuse of arbitrary power. Traditional
African cultures . . . usually were strongly constitutional, with major
customary limits on rulers" (Donnelly, 1984, pp. 413–414).

Sociopolitical leadership in indigenous African societies thus
contains some democratic qualities. However, these qualities are not
ingrained in the total structures of the nation-states in Africa. Aside
from chieftaincy, autonomous sociopolitical participation by affinity
groups has played a role in patterns of political interaction in Africa.
Like most sociocentric societies, the collective ethos is ubiquitous in
Africa. The society is not egocentric, but neither is it individualistic.
The survival of the group and the people is very important. John
Mbiti articulates this concept best, "I am because we are, and since
we are, therefore I am" (Mbiti, 1969, p. 141). Affinity and kinship
groups do well in the participatory process. Here, again, the structures are limited to the local ethnic and linguistic group level. These
groups do not penetrate the national political apparatus sufficiently
to affect the body politic. A case can be made that the democratic
institutions and qualities in indigenous African societies that have
not been tried in the postcolonial era should be tried and tested,
rather than performing a premature autopsy on indigenous African
institutions and their ability to inform the development of consolidated democracy in Africa.

Conclusion

In sum, the development of consolidated relational democracy in
Africa must transcend the take-off stage on socioeconomic development, petro-politics, ethnic restructuring, reframing of diversity,
revisiting indigenous African institutions to search for workable elements for democratic governance, and rethinking the utilization of
Western democratic value systems that are productive for African
cultures. Since more than 60% of Africans reside in the rural areas,
the work to engage the farming and fishing communities in political

participation must be deliberate. Traditional institutions that were downgraded during the process of decolonization must be resuscitated to augment their capacity for political participation. Patron-client relationships that were pronounced in the immediate decolonization period need restructuring to empower clients to be able to galvanize forces to remove patrons who are not providing adequate services to their clientele. National-local patronage has survived many Western failed structures. What is needed at this point in clientelist politics in Africa is the expansion of national-local clientele relationships so that the intricate networks of communication can enhance political participation.

In reframing African relational democracy, referencing the premise that some indigenous political systems have qualities of democracy, culturally effective Western democratic institutions and processes could be juxtaposed or redesigned to work with the indigenous systems. As Schmitter and Karl note, "since no single set of actual institutions, practices, or values embodies democracy, the politics of moving away from authoritarian rule can mix different components to produce different democracies" (Schmitter and Karl, 1991, pp. 7–8). Among the Western institutions and values that have a better chance in working well with African traditional political institutions to sustain democracy, a developed political-economy, majority rule, transparency, accountability, parliamentary sovereignty, party government, consensus, checks and balances, autonomous participation, and pluralism will serve Africa well for what they are worth.

A developed political economy will support the people and provide revenue for building democratic institutions. Majority rule puts the power of governance in the hands of the people, protects their freedoms of assembly and exercise of universal adult suffrage, and provides the people with the moral authority to protect minority groups. Majority rule also legitimizes party governance as both affinity and affiliation groups can galvanize their interests for aggregation and articulation purposes. Autonomous political participation and pluralism will ensure that hierarchical associations and monopolistic tycoons do not dominate the political process. Transparency invokes openness in conducting government business. Political transparency would be ensured through a new vision and practice that the nation-state is society centered and relational democracy seeks responsibility not just for one's self but for the sustenance of the state. This transformational process would require changes in cognitive structures, as well as behavioral and institutional modification. Transparency will expedite the eradication of the entitlement behavioral syndrome of many Africans. It will counteract the forces of bribery and corruption, cronyism and nepotism for government to function effectively. Accountability and transparency have symbiotic relationships. They involve responsibility and ethics in governance. Checks and balances provide a framework for maintaining accountability to the citizenry and keeping the indigenous and Western systems in harmony. The essence of parliamentary sovereignty enables law-governing nations to thrive. It includes both institutions and practices that put the supremacy of the law and rule of law in a centripetal arena of the nation-state. It is not only the legislature that is taken to task in this endeavor, it is the active involvement of the executive and judiciary branches of government that uphold the supremacy of the law. African nation-states are beginning to accept the concept of law-governance as an irrefutable quality of democracy, but the road to making this concept part of the fabric of society still remains undulating.

The genesis of true African relational democracies that are able to modify their institutions, processes, and rules despite the diversity and cultural difference of the continent will bear witness to the time of redefining the African "self" and the European "other" in terms of the democracy project. At that time, such a dichotomy will not be quite necessary because Africans will be able to utilize the best qualities of both worlds to make consolidated relational democracy a continental project for the twenty-first century.

Note

*Another version of this chapter was published in *The Social Contract in Africa*, 2014, African Institute of South Africa.

References

Afrobarometer. (2009). Neither consolidating nor fully democratic: The evolution of African political regimes: 1999–2008. A briefing paper, number 67. Retrieved from: http://www.afrobarometer.org/

Allen, J. L., & Sutton, C. J. (2011). *Student atlas of world politics*, 9th ed. New York: McGraw-Hill.

Asumah, S. N., & Johnston-Anumonwo, I. (2002). *Diversity, multiculturalism and social justice*. Binghamton, NY: Binghamton University Press.

Asumah, S. N. (2010). Islam, rentier states and the quest for democracy in Africa. *Western Journal of Black Studies, 34*(4), 399–411.

Ayittey, G. B. (1999). *Africa in chaos*. New York: St. Martin's Griffin.

Davidson, B. (1983). *Modern Africa*. New York: Longman.

Dahl, R. (2002). *How democratic is the American Constitution?* New Haven, CT: Yale University Press.

Diamond, L. (1992b). The globalization of democracy: Trends, types, causes and prospects. In R. Slater, B. Schutz, & S. Dorr (Eds.), *Global transformations in the third world.* Boulder, CO: Lynn Rienner Publishers.

Donnelly, J. (1984). Cultural relativism and universal human rights. *Human Rights Quarterly 6*(4).

Fish, S., & Brooks, R. (2004). Does diversity hurt democracy? *Journal of Democracy, 15*(1).

Fortes, M., & Evans-Pritchards, E. E. (1940). *African political systems.* Oxford, UK: Oxford University Press.

Freedom House. (2011). Freedom in the world 2011 survey release. Retrieved from: www.freedomhouse.org/template.cfm?page=594

Glazer, S. (2004). Stopping the genocide. *Congressional Quarterly Global Researcher.* Washington, DC: CQ Press.

Gyekye, K. (1997). *Tradition and modernity: Philosophical reflections on the African experience.* Oxford, UK: Oxford University Press.

Halper, S. (2010). *The Beijing consensus: How China's authoritarian model will dominate the twenty-first century.* New York: Basic Books.

Karantnycky, A. The 2001 Freedom House survey: Muslim countries and the democracy gap. *Journal of Democracy, 13.*

Khapoya, V. (2010). *The African experience: An introduction.* New York: Longman.

Kretzmann, S. (2005). Drilling into debt. Oil Change International. Retrieved from: http://priceofoil.org/educate/resources/drillinh-into-debt/

Mbiti, J. (1969). *African religions and philosophy.* Oxford, UK: Heinemann Educational Publishers.

McLure, J. (2012). Sub-Saharan democracy. *Global Issues.* Washington, DC: Congressional Quarterly Press, SAGE.

Ottaway, M. (2005). Africa is not ready for democracy. In L. Egendorf (Ed.), *Africa: Opposing viewpoints.* New York: Greenhaven Press.

Schmitter, P. C., & Karl, T. L. (1991). What democracy is . . . and is not. *Journal of Democracy* (Summer).

Takaki, R. (1993). *A different mirror: A history of multicultural America.* New York: Little, Brown and Company.

West, C. (2004). *Democracy matters: Winning the fight against imperialism.* New York: Penguin Press.

Woldemariam, Y. (2008). Democracy in Africa: Does it have a chance. In H. J. Wiarda (Ed.), *Comparative democracy and democratization.* Mason, OH: Cengage Learning.

Young, I. M. (1990). *Justice and the politics of difference.* Princeton, NJ: Princeton University Press.

About the Editors

Seth N. Asumah is State University of New York Distinguished Teaching Professor, professor of political science and Chair of the Africana Studies Department at SUNY Cortland. Asumah also is codirector of the Summer Institute for Infusing Diversity into the Curriculum at the State University of New York College at Cortland. The author, coauthor, and coeditor of eight books and numerous essays, articles, and book chapters, his publications include *Postethnophilosophy* (2011); *Prisons and Punishment: Reconsidering Global Penality* (2007); *Diversity, Multiculturalism and Social Justice* (2002); *The Africana Human Condition and Global Dimensions* (2002); *Issues in Africa and the African Diaspora* (2001); *Educating the Black Child* (2001); and *Issues in Multiculturalism: Cross National Perspectives* (1998, 1995). Asumah has won five excellence in teaching awards, including the SUNY Distinguished Teaching Professor Award (2007), the American Political Science Association Outstanding Teaching Award (2008), and the Rozanne Brooks Dedicated and Teaching Excellence Award (1999). He is an International Adviser to the International Conference on African Culture and Development (ICACD), Accra, Ghana; International Adviser to the Intercultural Migration Integration Center (IMIC), Hamburg, Germany; and a Visiting Scholar at the University of Ghana-Carnegie Diaspora Linkage Programme, University of Ghana, Lagon, Ghana.

Mechthild Nagel is professor of philosophy at the State University of New York College at Cortland, director of the Center for Gender and Intercultural Studies (CGIS), a Senior Visiting Fellow at the Institute for African Development at Cornell University, and a DAAD Visiting Professor at Fulda University of Applied Sciences, Germany (2012–2013). She is the author of a number of books including *Masking the Abject: A Genealogy of Play* (Lexington, 2002), and coeditor of *Race, Class, and Community Identity* (Humanities, 2000);

The Hydropolitics of Africa: A Contemporary Challenge (Cambridge Scholars Press, 2007); *Prisons and Punishment: Reconsidering Global Penality* (Africa World Press, 2007); *Dancing With Iris: The Philosophy of Iris Marion Young* (Oxford University Press, 2010); and *The End of Prisons: Reflections from the Decarceration Movement* (Rodopi Press, 2013). Her next book project is titled *An Ubuntu Ethic of Punishment*. Nagel is editor-in-chief of the online journal *Wagadu: A Journal of Transnational Women's and Gender Studies* (wagadu.org).

About the Contributors

The contributors of this volume include scholars from different disciplines, veteran and emerging scholars, diversity practitioners and administrators, men and women, all of whom provided inimitable and thought-provoking perspectives on some of the most pressing issues facing humankind in the areas of diversity, social justice, and inclusive excellence.

Tosha A. Asumah is a Psychology Associate II/Psychology Resident with the Forensic Unit at Southern Virginia Mental Health Institute (SVMHI) in Danville, Virginia. She is a recent graduate from Alliant International University, California School of Forensic Studies (CSFS). In addition to having earned a PsyD in forensic psychology, Asumah also has two master's degrees—an MA in forensic psychology from Alliant International University and an MA in counseling psychology from Fairleigh Dickinson University. Asumah completed her doctoral internship at Palomar Hospital, Intensive Outpatient Program, San Marcos, California. Her externships included Gateways Hospital Satellite Conditional Release Program in Los Angeles, and Shields for Families, Inc. in Long Beach, California. Asumah's introduction to the mental health field began with a behavioral health counselor position at Community Hope in Parsippany, New Jersey.

Cema Bolabola is a Fijian rural sociologist and gender equality advocate. She is an independent consultant, former secondary school teacher, who worked for the extension services and distance education at the University of the South Pacific. She has published a number of papers about Pacific women on community development, education, appropriate technology, and resource ownership. Two of her prominent publications include "Land Rights of Fijian Women: Cultural Constraints and Legal Progress" in *Land Rights of Pacific Women* (Suva, Fiji: IPS USP, 1986) and "Changes in Fijian Leader-

ship" in *Journal of Sociology in Australia and New Zealand* (1978).
Bolabola is involved with many women's organization in Fiji and the
Pacific region, longtime Trustee of the Fiji Women's Crisis Centre,
and known member and former vice president of the Fiji YWCA
movement. She recently worked as consultant for UN Women Pacific
Regional Office and UNDP Pacific Centre, working on projects to
improve the socioeconomic and political status of women market vendors in Fiji and the region.

Matthew Todd Bradley, PhD, is an associate professor of political
science at Indiana University Kokomo. He received his PhD from
Binghamton University. His research areas involve civil society
actors like nongovernmental organizations (NGOs) and the roles they
play in democratization efforts in "developing" countries. Bradley's
other area of research focuses on the impact of ethnicity/religion and
immigration issues. Among Bradley's peer-reviewed, scholarly publications are: "African Perceptions of Democracy," *African Journal of
Political Science and International Relations* (2011), "Chinese-Built
Dams, Africa and Economic Growth: Is There a Role for African
NGOs?" *Journal of the Indiana Academy of the Social Sciences* (2011).

William Taylor Laimaka Cox is a PhD candidate at University
of Wisconsin-Madison. His research takes a theory-driven approach
to stereotyping, across many contexts, including stereotypes about
others that can lead to prejudice, stereotypes that people use in categorization, and self-stereotypes that can lead to depression. These
scientific endeavors pull him into many areas of psychology, including
social, cognitive, clinical, and developmental.

Elizabeth Davis-Russell is the president of William Tubman University in Harper, Liberia, West Africa. Before her current position,
Davis-Russell was provost and vice president for Academic Affairs
at the State University of New York College at Cortland. She was a
professor and director of Cross Cultural Psychology Proficiency, dean
for Academic and Professional Affairs, and presidential associate of
the California School of Professional Psychology. She was responsible
for the development and implementation of the School of Education
and a founding member—later to become director—of Multicultural
Education, Research, Intervention, and Training (MERIT) and the
undergraduate school. She has also been a professor at the Chicago
School of Professional Psychology, where she developed the Center
for Intercultural Clinical Psychology.

Susan Dewey is an assistant professor of gender and women's studies (and an adjunct in international studies) at the University of Wyoming. She is the author or coeditor of six books, including *Neon Wasteland: On Love, Motherhood, and Sex Work in a Rust Belt Town* (University of California Press, 2011), *Policing Pleasure: Sex Work, Policy, and the State in Global Perspective* (New York University Press, 2011, with Patty Kelly), and *Conflict-Related Sexual Violence: International Law, Local Responses* (Kumarian Press, 2012, with Tonia St. Germain), and two dozen book chapters and journal articles. Her research focuses on feminized labor, with two ongoing funded projects with women market traders in Fiji and sex workers in Denver and New Orleans.

Janet M. Duncan is an associate professor in the Foundations and Social Advocacy Department, School of Education, State University of New York at Cortland. Her research interests focus on the international human and communications rights of individuals with disabilities. The chief goal of her work is to promote the competence of those with disabilities, through the efforts of the UN Convention on the Rights of Persons With Disabilities. She received her PhD from Syracuse University in special education.

Diane Carol Gooding is professor of psychology and psychiatry at University of Wisconsin–Madison. Her scholarly work integrates the study of the biological basis of severe and persistent mental illness along with psychometric, biobehavioral, and genetic risk for schizophrenia-spectrum disorders. Gooding has published extensively in the areas of individual differences and risk for psychopathology, psychophysiology, developmental psychopathology, neurocognition, emotion, and social cognition. Her writing for the general public has looked at the interpersonal, intrapersonal, and societal sequelae of severe mental illness. For several years, she served on the Board of Directors for the local and state chapters of National Alliance on Mental Illness (NAMI).

Debra F. Glaser, PhD, ABPP, is assistant professor at Alliant International University in the California School of Forensic Studies (CSFS). Glaser teaches the police psychology courses on the Los Angeles campus including stalking, police psychology, and crisis negotiation, as well general psychology courses. She is Board Certified in Police and Public Safety Psychology. She comes to Alliant after 26 years working for the Behavioral Science Services Section of the Los

Angeles Police Department (LAPD) and 9 years as their Chief Police Psychologist. At LAPD, Glaser worked with SWAT, the Threat Management Unit, Scientific Investigation Division, Internal Affairs, the Police Academy, and myriad other specialized units. She provided and supervised direct services and management consultation to the men and women, sworn and civilian, of the LAPD. In addition to teaching at Alliant, she has a private practice and continues to provide direct services and consultation to various law enforcement agencies.

Lori Gruen is professor of philosophy; feminist, gender, and sexuality studies; and environmental studies at Wesleyan University. Her work lies at the intersection of ethical theory and practice, with a particular focus on issues that impact those often overlooked in traditional ethical investigations, for example, women, people of color, and nonhuman animals. She has published extensively on topics in feminist ethics, animal ethics, and environmental philosophy. She recently authored *Ethics and Animals: An Introduction* (Cambridge, 2011) and coedited the second edition of *Reflecting on Nature* (Oxford, 2012).

Nancy J. Hirschmann is professor of political science at the University of Pennsylvania. She is the author of many articles and books, including *Gender, Class, and Freedom in Modern Political Theory* (2008); *The Subject of Liberty: Toward a Feminist Theory of Freedom* (2003), which won the Victoria Schuck Award; and coeditor of *Civil Disabilities: Citizenship, Membership, and Belonging* (2014). She has held fellowships from the American Council of Learned Societies, the Bunting Institute, the Institute for Advanced Study at Princeton, the National Endowment for the Humanities, and the Princeton University Center for Human Values.

Ibipo Johnston-Anumonwo is professor of geography at State University of New York at Cortland. She teaches general education courses such as Human Geography and Global Development. Her scholarly work integrates gender and ethnicity into geographic research and curriculum. A recipient of a Chancellor's Excellence in Scholarship Award, her extensively cited research on women's journey to work has attained authoritative levels in the discipline. Among her publications are two coedited books and two coauthored books, including *Diversity, Multiculturalism and Social Justice* published by Binghamton University Global Publications. She has served on the editorial board of *Gender, Place and Culture* and *Wagadu: Journal of Transnational Women's and Gender Studies*.

Christopher Latimer is an assistant dean of social sciences and associate professor of political science at Endicott College. He received his MA and PhD degrees in political science from State University of New York at Albany and his JD from American University's Washington College of Law. Latimer has published a number of articles related to same-sex marriage, political communication, new media, and civic engagement. His book, *Civil Liberties and the State*, about the relationship between individual rights and government intrusion, was published in 2010.

Gowri Parameswaran is professor and Chair of the Education Studies Department at State University of New York at New Paltz. She has published extensively in the areas of multiculturalism, diversity, and educational studies. She is the coeditor of *Women, Images, and Realities: A Multicultural Anthology,* 5th ed. (McGraw-Hill, 2013) and *Educational Access and Social Justice: A Global Perspective* (University Press of America, 2009).

Elizabeth Purcell is the Research and Grant Coordinator for the McDevitt Center for Creativity and Innovation and Lecturer in the Department of Philosophy at Le Moyne College. Her research specializes in ethics, the philosophy of disability, and feminism. Her dissertation, titled *Flourishing Bodies: Disability, Virtues, and Happiness*, focuses on the intersection of disability studies and virtue ethics. She has published on various topics in professional journals, including articles in *Radical Philosophy Review* and *Religion and the Arts*. She has also received national attention, appearing in *Glamour* magazine, and has been interviewed by the Pulitzer Prize–winning journalist Laura Sessions-Stepp, for her work in feminism and innovative teaching pedagogy.

Gale Young is professor of communications at California State University, East Bay. Young serves as Chair of the Western Association of Schools and Colleges (WASC) Accreditation Process, and has held a variety of positions including associate dean, affirmative action officer, and interim Chair of the Art Department. She was corecipient of the CSU Woman of the Year Award for contributing to diversity, an ACE Fellow (1998–1999) and the codirector for the Center of the Study Intercultural Relations. Young is the coauthor of two books, numerous articles, and the executive producer of the video, *Difficult Dialogues* (PBS, 1998).

Marion Iris Young, January 2, 1949–August 1, 2006, was professor of political science at the University of Chicago, and was affiliated with the Center for Gender Studies and the Human Rights program at that institution. Young was an internationally acknowledged feminist and a political philosopher. Her research covered contemporary political theory, feminist social theory, and normative analysis of public policy. Young's books include *Justice and the Politics of Difference* (1990); *Throwing Like a Girl and Other Essays in Feminist Philosophy and Social Theory* (1990); *Intersecting Voices: Dilemmas of Gender, Political Philosophy, and Policy* (1997); *Inclusion and Democracy* (2000); *On Female Body Experience: "Throwing Like a Girl" and Other Essays* (2005); and *Responsibility for Justice* (2010). Her writings have been translated into several languages, including Coatia, German, Italian, Portuguese, Spanish, and Swedish, and she lectured widely in North America, Europe, Australia, and South Africa.

Tiantian Zheng holds a PhD in anthropology from Yale University. She is professor of anthropology in the Department of Sociology/Anthropology at State University of New York at Cortland. Her book *Red Lights* is the Winner of the 2010 Sara A. Whaley Book Prize from the National Women's Studies Association for the significant contribution to the topic of women and labor. Her book *Ethnographies of Prostitution in Contemporary China* is the Winner of the 2011 Research Publication Book Award from the Association of Chinese Professors of Social Sciences in the United States. She is the author of four books on sex, gender, migration, HIV/AIDS, and the state.

Index